Engaging the Public
with Climate Change

Engaging the Public with Climate Change

Behaviour Change and Communication

Edited by

Lorraine Whitmarsh, Saffron O'Neill
and
Irene Lorenzoni

earthscan
from Routledge

First published by Earthscan in the UK and USA in 2011

For a full list of publications please contact:
Earthscan
2 Park Square, Milton Park, Abingdon, Oxfordshire OX14 4RN
711 Third Avenue, New York, NY 10017

First issued in paperback 2015

Earthscan is an imprint of the Taylor & Francis Group, an informa business

Notices
Practitioners and researchers must always rely on their own experience
and knowledge in evaluating and using any information, methods, compounds,
or experiments described herein. In using such information or methods they should be
mindful of their own safety and the safety of others, including parties for whom they
have a professional responsibility.

Product or corporate names may be trademarks or registered trademarks, and are
used only for identification and explanation without intent to infringe.

ISBN 13: 978-1-138-86690-4 (pbk)
ISBN 13: 978-1-8440-7928-5 (hbk)

Typeset by 4word Ltd, Bristol
Cover design by Adam Bohannon

A catalogue record for this book is available from the British Library

Library of Congress Cataloging-in-Publication Data

Engaging the public with climate change : behaviour change and communication / edited by
Lorraine Whitmarsh, Saffron O'Neill and Irene Lorenzoni.
    p. cm.
 Includes bibliographical references and index.
 ISBN 978-1-84407-928-5 (hbk.)
 1. Climatic changes—Psychological aspects. 2. Environmental psychology.
3. Environmentalism—Psychological aspects. 4. Environmental policy—Citizen participation.
I. Whitmarsh, Lorraine. II. O'Neill, Saffron. III. Lorenzoni, Irene.
 BF353.5.C55E54 2010
 304.2—dc22   2010014004

Contents

List of Figures, Tables and Boxes

Figures

Tables

Boxes

List of Contributors

Editors

Dr Lorraine Whitmarsh is a lecturer in environmental psychology at Cardiff University (UK), Visiting Fellow at the Tyndall Centre for Climate Change Research, and Research Associate of the Centre for Business Relationships, Accountability, Sustainability and Society (BRASS). She researches public and stakeholder engagement with climate change and other sustainability issues, using both qualitative and quantitative research methods.

Dr Saffron O'Neill is a Research Fellow in the Department of Resource Management and Geography at the University of Melbourne, and a Visiting Fellow at the Tyndall Centre for Climate Change Research. Saffron's research is interdisciplinary, investigating the emotional, cognitive and behavioural components of risk perception, risk communication and public engagement with environmental issues.

Dr Irene Lorenzoni is a lecturer at the School of Environmental Sciences at the University of East Anglia, Norwich (UK). She is particularly interested in understandings of, and engagement with, climate change and energy, at individual and policy levels within the contexts of adaptation and mitigation. She has published over 30 peer-reviewed papers and chapters; contributed to the Fourth Assessment Report of the IPCC, on barriers to adaptation, which was co-awarded the Nobel Peace Prize in 2007; and recently co-edited *Adapting to Climate Change* (2009, Cambridge University Press).

Authors

Dr Maxwell Boykoff is an environmental studies faculty member at the Centre for Science and Technology Policy Research, at the University of Colorado at Boulder. Max has ongoing interests in environmental governance, science and policy interactions, as well as political economy and the environment.

Fiona Brannigan currently works for Groundwork, a UK charity that engages with communities and organizations to bring about more sustainable patterns of behaviour. Fiona's research interests lie in the psychology of climate change and the way in which unconscious drivers influence our behaviour.

Savita Custead is Chief Executive of the Bristol Natural History Consortium, a charity and collaboration between Avon Wildlife Trust, BBC, Bristol City Council, Bristol Zoo Gardens, Defra, the Environment Agency, Natural England University of Bristol, University of the West of England, Wildscreen and Wildfowl & Wetlands Trust. Through the BNHC, Savita directs the annual Bristol Festival of Nature and the annual Communicate conference for environmental communicators. Savita is also a trustee of the participation and engagement charity ICA:UK and the Bristol Junior Chamber of Commerce.

Dr Sarah Darby researches social and behavioural aspects of energy use with the Lower Carbon Futures programme at the Environmental Change Institute, University of Oxford. She holds an interdisciplinary fellowship from the Research Council's UK Energy Programme, to work on domestic energy feedback in relation to smart metering, in-home displays and billing. Her DPhil on 'Awareness, action and feedback in domestic energy use' used learning theory to analyse how householders learn about their energy use and possibilities for change.

Scott Davidson is a behaviour change specialist with Global Action Plan (GAP). He ensures GAP stay up to date with the most effective methods of behaviour change available, and is passionate about the wider field's effectiveness. Scott regularly comments on pro-environmental behaviour change issues through speaking at conferences alongside book, magazine and radio interviews.

Ken Double is Head of Evaluation at the Energy Saving Trust. Ken has over 30 years' experience in the UK energy industry working in the energy supply industry and the Energy Saving Trust. He has been Head of Evaluation at EST for over eight years, responsible for the development and management of effective monitoring and evaluation systems, to assess the environmental and market impact of sustainable energy programmes.

Christopher C. Duke is a PhD student in psychology at the University of Exeter, where he studies the relationship between social groups, identity and pro-environmental behaviour. He is interested in how social influences affect how people perceive global issues and how social psychological theory can be applied to real-world problems.

Dr Nick Eyre is Jackson Senior Research Fellow in energy policy at the Environmental Change Institute, University of Oxford, and a Co-Director of the UK Energy Research Centre. He was previously Head of Policy Research and Director of Strategy at the Energy Saving Trust. He has been a researcher and policy analyst on energy demand, energy efficiency and environmental impacts of energy use for 25 years.

Brooke Flanagan is Head of Policy at the Energy Saving Trust. She has been working in climate change policy and research in the UK for the past four years, holding various roles at both the Energy Saving Trust and the Institute for Public Policy Research. Prior to arriving in the UK, Brooke was Executive Director of the Nature Conservation Council in Australia, a membership-based, campaigning environment non-governmental organization (NGO). Brooke has held a range of roles in industry and local government, working on a variety of issues including waste and recycling, water efficiency, public transport, local government reform and finance.

Jo Hamilton has coordinated the Oxfordshire ClimateXchange, an Oxfordshire climate change engagement project based at the University of Oxford's Environmental Change Institute, since 2006. During this time she has worked with over 50 local community groups active on climate change and energy in Oxfordshire, particularly regarding eco-renovation, peer to peer support and dissemination of best practice.

Dr Corina Höppner is a Research Fellow at the Swiss Federal Research Institute WSL within the Economics and Social Sciences Unit; previously she worked as a Visiting Research Fellow at the Environmental Change Institute, University of Oxford. She holds a PhD in geography and works on the social and political dimensions of climate change and natural hazards. A second strand of her research is on the psychological effects of citizen participation in natural resource planning.

Dr Peat Leith is a Research Fellow with the Adaptation Research Network for Marine Biodiversity and Resources at the University of Tasmania, Australia. Peat's research draws on diverse disciplinary traditions, but he is particularly interested in theoretical and empirical work from Science and Technology Studies, and its application in developing collaborative approaches to climate adaptation and natural resource governance.

Dr Thomas A. Morton (PhD, University of Queensland, Australia) is a senior lecturer in social psychology at the University of Exeter, United Kingdom. His research interests include group processes and intergroup relations, prejudice and stereotyping, stigma and minority identity, language and communication.

Dr Susanne Moser is Director of Susanne Moser Research & Consulting and a Research Associate at the University of California, Santa Cruz. Her work focuses on adaptation to climate change in the coastal, forest and conservation sectors, and urban and rural environments, resilience, decision support and effective climate change communication in support of social change. She is co-editor with Lisa Dilling (University of Colorado, Boulder) on a major anthology on climate change communication, called *Creating a Climate for Change: Communicating Climate Change and Facilitating Social Change*, published in 2007 by Cambridge University Press.

Dr Michael Nye is a Principal Research Scientist for Communities and Flooding at the Environment Agency, UK. He is also a research fellow in

Environmental Sociology at the School of Environmental Sciences at the University of East Anglia, Norwich (UK). He is interested in the spaces where environmental risk, personal responsibility and surrounding socio-technical systems meet.

Dr Anna Rabinovich (PhD, University of Exeter, UK) is a GWR research fellow in the School of Psychology, University of Exeter. Her research interests include behaviour change, attitude–behaviour consistency, time perspective, group processes, communicating risk and uncertainty.

Gemma Regniez has worked as a marketer in government communications for just over ten years, covering numerous behaviour change campaigns including anti-smoking, THINK! road safety and ACT ON CO_2. More recently she has joined the ranks of the Department for International Development, heading up strategic communications for their South Asia Division. She is a fellow of the Royal Society for the encouragement of Arts, Manufactures and Commerce (RSA).

Dr Gill Seyfang is an expert in low-carbon lifestyles, with a strong track record of researching community-based organizations working towards sustainable consumption. Her model of 'grassroots innovations' offers a new way of examining the potential of local initiatives such as local food systems, complementary currencies and low-impact eco-housing, and, in particular, the scope for such demonstration projects to scale up and influence mainstream consumption patterns. She is the author of *The New Economics of Sustainable Consumption: Seeds of Change* (2009, Palgrave Macmillan).

Tracey Todhunter is a freelance writer with over 15 years' experience of working with voluntary organizations on communications and engagement projects, particularly in the fields of environmental justice and community-led responses to climate change. She co-founded the Low Carbon Communities Network in 2007 to support communities and individuals who see the benefit of communicating their low-carbon behaviours to a wider audience, and ensuring their voice is heard by key decision makers when developing climate change policies at regional and national level. Her recent work includes collaborations with DEFRA and the Green Alliance. She is currently a freelance Strategy Advisor to the 10:10 Campaign.

Professor Bas Verplanken is professor of social psychology at the University of Bath. His research areas are in social health and environmental psychology. His recent research focuses on habitual behaviour and habitual thinking.

Dr Johanna Wolf is Postdoctoral Fellow at the Labrador Institute and the Faculty of Arts at Memorial University of Newfoundland. Her research examines the individual, social and institutional dimensions of responding to climate change. She was previously Senior Research Associate at the Tyndall Centre for Climate Change Research, UK, where she remains a Visiting

Fellow, and has acted as Senior Science Coordinator of the Global Environmental Change and Human Security (GECHS) project. She holds a PhD and MSc from the School of International Development at the University of East Anglia and a BSc in environmental science from Royal Roads University in Victoria, BC, Canada.

Foreword

Forward!

If we don't want to change,
we're going to have to change.

It must have been someone wiser than I who first said that, and I don't know in which context, but I deeply agree with that astute observation. To me, climate change has always seemed like Exhibit A for this truism.

We can deny the reality of climate change or its human causes, or simply not pay attention to it; there may be good explanations for why we're ignorant of the machinations of the climate and societal systems with all their inbuilt feedbacks and time lags; we (at least we in the mid-latitudinal, more affluent countries) still have the luxury to be indifferent to its implications; and yes, we can prioritize – for ever-so-legitimate reasons – everything else over climate change, and resist the need to change our behaviours, lifestyles, policies, market signals and the infrastructure that enable and constrain our actions. We can choose not to take actions to mitigate the problem or even to begin planning for adaptation. That is one possible choice indeed.

As a broadly trained scientist in both the physical and social sciences, I know of no law in physics, no reaction in chemistry, no interaction in ecology, however, that could 'save' us from the reality we are creating for ourselves and the rest of the life world on this planet. At least not in any way that would allow us to continue trundling along in the exact same way that we have. That means to me, if we don't rise to meet the challenge before us and change our ways, change will come to us. It's that simple.

Well, of course, it's never that simple. In fact, one could argue, we have too many choices currently over how to meet the climate challenge – some that involve undesirable trade-offs, others that are decent, or good, or even better choices, though probably none that are cost-free. Maybe that's too many choices. Maybe it will be a lot simpler later when we have fewer choices, when we have no other choice than to cope with climate change impacts as they unfold, when we have to make radical – and likely much more expensive – shifts in our economy, our energy supply and consumption, in our transportation system and travel behaviour, in the way we feed seven, eight or more billion people. Choice gets simpler when you don't have much of one.

In the largest sense then, communicating about climate change and find-ing effective ways to engage lay publics and public policy makers on this issue is motivated by the desire to involve people in making conscious and informed choices about 'spaceship Earth', and doing so at a time when we still have hope of steering our journey in a desirable direction.

The collection of chapters you hold in your hands is a welcome and timely contribution to a rapidly growing canon of social science research that could help inform such public communication and engagement efforts on climate change. Collectively, the chapters make the case for *why* we should communi-cate with and engage the public – cognitively, emotionally and behaviourally, in their private and public decisions. Some of the authors argue that in a dem-ocratic society, citizens should be actively engaged in public affairs so that they can better understand, help shape, support and implement public policy choices. The active debate around this normative argument in Great Britain (strongly reflected in this collection) is mirrored elsewhere in Europe, North America and beyond (e.g. Moser, 2009, 2010a). Other chapters, echoing recent high-profile papers in the same vein (e.g. Dietz et al, 2009; Allcott and Mullainathan, 2010), argue for engaging the public because individuals and households control many climate-relevant behaviours, and therefore are the most appropriate target for outreach campaigns. And indeed, however one chooses to slice the greenhouse gas emissions pie (by region, sector and type of actor), *someone* is making the decisions, enacting the behaviours, pushing for changes and implementing policies that ultimately lead to emissions or reductions in them. That someone is us.

The chapters in this volume also push forward our understanding of *how* to engage the public by offering synthetic, interdisciplinary insights, and crit-ical but constructive assessments of empirical cases and practices. Most of the empirical cases are from the UK (though not all) and confirm the broad-brush insights gained from an earlier collection with similar goals as this one, but largely focused on the US experience (Moser and Dilling, 2007). This is reas-suring from a scientific point of view, and maybe disquieting from a practical perspective.

In a relatively new field of inquiry such as climate change communication and engagement (for a review, see Moser, 2010b), it is indeed heartening to learn similar insights about human behaviour in different cultural contexts. In the UK, as in the USA, Canada, Australia and elsewhere, it will take a con-certed, lasting and far more creative effort than we've seen to date to engage the public on a challenging, complex, long-term, scientifically and morally uncertain problem like climate change. Now that we've raised basic awareness about global warming here and there, we can document that awareness-rais-ing is not nearly enough to foster change. On both sides of the Atlantic (and elsewhere), we find that public understanding of climate change is superficial at best, and needs to be improved and more strongly anchored so that it becomes less vulnerable to contrarian attacks on the science of climate change. We also find confirmed that information and understanding are not the most important drivers of behaviour change, and in many instances – for example, in much of our habitual behaviour – hardly relevant at all. Several chapters in this volume highlight again the strong social influences on our behaviour and how many outreach efforts do not sufficiently make use of this important reality. To do so, dialogic, two-way forms of communication are more conducive to fostering change than one-way information delivery. The book also confirms that change, hard as it is, is more easily achieved by facing the challenges and approaching the solutions together. And in trying to foster change, we should not focus only on consumption behaviour, but broaden our view to include civic and political engagement.

The comfort and importance of scientific consolidation aside, the chapters included here – together with much work in the wider field to date – also confirm how difficult it actually is to change. It is almost astonishing how resistant to certain types of change we modern humans really are (or, maybe, have become). Perhaps more appropriately, we should call it paradoxical that we are at once so willing and capable of adopting bewildering new technologies, or shift to completely new ways of communicating with each other in less than a generation, while at the same time defending a particular status quo with such vehemence; that is, with the might of solidified power positions, stabilizing institutions, monstrous infrastructures, ingrained social divisions and stubborn habits. Many of the ways in which we are technologically, institutionally, economically, demographically and socially apparently locked in seem to propel us to ever increasing emissions (e.g. Raupach et al, 2007; Solomon et al, 2009), pointing society increasingly to one of the more pessimistic climate futures (Pachauri and Reisinger, 2007; Moss et al, 2010).

Maybe the most encouraging aspects of this collection then, and the ones we should pay most attention to, are therefore those chapters that speak of people actually changing. They remind me of Paul Hawken's 2009 commencement speech at Portland State University, where he said:

> When asked if I am pessimistic or optimistic about the future, my answer is always the same: If you look at the science about what is happening on earth and aren't pessimistic, you don't understand data. But if you meet the people who are working to restore this earth and the lives of the poor, and you aren't optimistic, you haven't got a pulse.

The burning question arising from 'the science of what is happening on earth' is: how do we break out of our hardened habits of mind and practice – and do so soon? This book is an important contribution to help answer this question, but it does not answer it in one unified voice. Instead, the contributors suggest that there are many and encouraging, but no quick and easy, answers. Some favour bottom-up, grassroots initiatives and show promising examples; others seem to be accepting, maybe even supportive, of top-down mandates and give good rationales for those. Between the lines and chapters, I read that we probably need a messy mix of both.

Important and innovative contributions to this book also point us towards what remains to be answered. How do we rapidly scale up the promising grassroots initiatives? How do we get to top-down legislation in a highly polarized political environment that is generally reluctant to overtly direct individual behaviour? How and for what purposes do we most effectively use and combine different communication channels in a rapidly changing media landscape? How do we broaden the conversation and engagement to be about mitigation *and* adaptation? With the help of this book, we can point now to converging insights on how to engage publics on mitigation, and despite emerging insights here, we don't know yet whether or which of these insights also hold for adaptation. So how do we communicate and engage people on adaptation, on deeper societal transformation, or on increasingly discussed interventions such as geo-engineering? How do we redefine for ourselves how we humans fit into this interconnected planetary system, while most of us spend our days inside buildings and have lost almost all unmediated connection to the environment? How do we actually begin the difficult dialogues – albeit civil ones – about the grand values we all cherish yet find so difficult to live (such as responsibility, justice, a meaningful life), much less about the taboos (e.g. economic and population growth, power, broken political systems) we would rather avoid?

The important insights by the nearly two dozen authors collected here solidify the foundation from which we can begin to answer these questions; truly big questions. We don't have to answer them. We can choose to avoid working towards answers on how to bring about the depth and breadth of change that living safely and prosperously in the face of profound environmental change would demand. And working hard it would be. Yet without a doubt, the answers we might find, which we must bring to an increasingly impatient world, which must be applied and tested in practice, and which must be evaluated, refined and applied again, those answers would be worthy ones.

Alas: forward!

Susanne Moser
Independent Scholar
Susanne Moser Research & Consulting
June 2010

References

Allcott, H. and Mullainathan, S. (2010) 'Behavior and energy policy', *Science*, vol 327, no 5970, pp1204–1205

Dietz, T., Gardner, G. T., Gilligan, J., Stern, P. C. and Vandenbergh, M. P. (2009) 'Household actions can provide a behavioral wedge to rapidly reduce U.S. carbon emissions', *Proceedings of the National Academy of Sciences*, vol 106, pp18452–18456

Moser, S. C. (2009) 'Communicating climate change and motivating civic action: Renewing, activating, and building democracies', in H. Selin and S. D. VanDeveer (eds) *Changing Climates in North American Politics: Institutions, Policymaking and Multilevel Governance*, MIT Press, Cambridge, MA, pp283–302

Moser, S. C. (2010a) 'Costly knowledge – unaffordable denial: The politics of public understanding and engagement on climate change', in M. T. Boykoff (ed) *The Politics of Climate Change*, Routledge, Oxford, pp161–187

Moser, S. C. (2010b) 'Communicating climate change: History, challenges, process and future directions', *Wiley Interdisciplinary Reviews: Climate Change*, vol 1, no 1, pp31–53

Moser, S. C. and Dilling, L. (eds) (2007) *Creating a Climate for Change: Communicating Climate Change and Facilitating Social Change*, Cambridge University Press, Cambridge

Moss, R. H., Edmonds, J. A., Hibbard, K. A., Manning, M. R., Rose, S. K., van Vuuren, D. P., Carter, T. R., Emori, S., Kainuma, M., Kram, T., Meehl, G. A., Mitchell, J. F. B., Nakicenovic, N., Riahi, K., Smith, S. J., Stouffer, R. J., Thomson, A. M., Weyant, J. P. and Wilbanks, T. J. (2010) 'The next generation of scenarios for climate change research and assessment', *Nature*, vol 463, no 7282, pp747–756

Pachauri, R. and Reisinger, A. (eds) (2007) *Climate Change 2007: Synthesis Report of the Fourth Assessment of the Intergovernmental Panel on Climate Change*, Cambridge University Press, Cambridge

Raupach, M. R., Marland, G., Ciais, P., Le Quere, C., Canadell, J. G., Klepper, G. and Field, C. B. (2007) 'Global and regional drivers of accelerating CO_2 emissions', *Proceedings of the National Academy of Sciences*, vol 104, no 24, pp10288–10293

Solomon, S., Plattner, G-K., Knutti, R. and Friedlingstein, P. (2009) 'Irreversible climate change due to carbon dioxide emissions', *Proceedings of the National Academy of Sciences*, vol 106, no 6, pp1704–1709

List of Acronyms and Abbreviations

ABS   Australian Bureau of Statistics
AFP   Americans for Prosperity
AMI   advanced metering infrastructure
BERR   Department for Business, Enterprise and Regulatory Reform
BNHC   Bristol Natural History Consortium
BRASS   Centre for Business Relationships, Accountability, Sustainability and Society
BRC   British Retail Consortium
BRE   Building Research Establishment
C&C   contraction and convergence
CASE   Centre for Analysis of Social Exclusion
CAT   Centre for Alternative Technology
CC   complementary currency
CCC   Committee on Climate Change
CERT   Carbon Emissions Reduction Target
CFL   compact fluorescent lightbulb
CIBER   Centre for Information Behaviour and Evaluation of Research
COI   Central Office of Information
COIN   Climate Outreach Information Network
CPRE   Campaign to Protect Rural England
CRAG   carbon rationing action group
DAB   digital audio broadcasting
DCLG   Department of Communities and Local Government
DECC   Department of Energy and Climate Change
DEFRA   Department for the Environment, Food and Rural Affairs
DIYHEC   Do It Yourself Home Energy Check
DPRTF   Drought Policy Review Taskforce
DSS   decision support system
DTI   Department of Trade and Industry
DTQ   domestic tradable quota
DWP   Department for Work and Pensions
EAC   Environmental Audit Committee
ECI   Environmental Change Institute
EEAC   Energy Efficiency Advice Centre

EEIR	Energy Efficiency Innovation Review
EEPfH	Energy Efficiency Partnership for Homes
EESoP	Energy Efficiency Standards of Performance
ENSO	El Niño Southern Oscillation
EPC	Energy Performance Certificate
ESRC	Economic and Social Research Council
EST	Energy Saving Trust
ESTAC	EST Advice Centre
EU ESD	European Union Energy Services Directive
EU ETS	European Union Emissions Trading Scheme
GAP	Global Action Plan
GECHS	Global Environmental Change and Human Security
HESP	Home Energy Saving Programme
IPCC	Intergovernmental Panel on Climate Change
IPPR	Institute for Public Policy Research
ISM	Institute for Social Marketing
ITU	International Telecommunications Union
LCBP	Low Carbon Buildings Programme
LCCN	Low Carbon Communities Network
LCWO	Low Carbon West Oxford
LETS	local exchange trading scheme
MiCBT	mindfulness-integrated cognitive behaviour therapy
MoJ	Ministry of Justice
NAO	National Audit Office
NCC	National Consumer Council
NEA	National Energy Action
NESTA	National Endowment for Science, Technology and the Arts
NFER	National Foundation for Educational Research
NGO	non-governmental organization
NHER	National Home Energy Rating
PCA	personal carbon allowance
PCT	personal carbon trading
PIRC	Public Interest Research Centre
PSA	public service announcement
RCEP	Royal Commission on Environmental Pollution
RSA	Royal Society for the encouragement of Arts, Manufactures & Commerce
RSS	really simple syndication
SBU	Sustainable Behaviours Unit
SDC	Sustainable Development Commission
SIT	social identity theory
SSO	Student Switch Off
STS	science and technology studies
TEQ	tradable energy quota
TPB	Theory of planned behaviour
TRA	Theory of reasoned action

TrACE	Tracking Action on Carbon Emissions
UKERC	United Kingdom Energy Research Centre
UK ETS	United Kingdom Emissions Trading Scheme
VBN	value-belief-norm
WWF	World Wide Fund for Nature

Acknowledgements

The idea for this book arose from a workshop *'Engaging the public in climate change and energy demand reduction'*, held in October 2008 at St Hugh's College, Oxford. We acknowledge funding from the UK Energy Research Centre and the Tyndall Centre for Climate Change Research to hold the workshop. The editors would particularly like to thank Jennifer Otoadese, Sarah Keay-Bright and Karyn John from UKERC for their input to the organization and facilitation of the workshop; and to the workshop core team (including Nick Eyre, Yacob Mulugetta and Bas Verplanken) for their insights in guiding its content. We also acknowledge the participants themselves for many challenging and interesting interactions over the course of the workshop.

Thanks to all of the authors herein for their varied and insightful contributions. Mike Hulme provided the editors with feedback on several draft chapters, while Alison Kuznets and Claire Lamont at Earthscan guided the book through its commissioning and production stages.

Final thanks from the editors to the 'three James' (James Wookey, James Screen and James Goodwin) for their constant support and encouragement of the workshop and book, despite their imposition into family life and across time zones.

Introduction: Opportunities for and Barriers to Engaging Individuals with Climate Change

Lorraine Whitmarsh and Saffron O'Neill

1. Background and rationale for public engagement with climate change

In recent years, there has been growing international acceptance that climate change (both human-induced and natural) poses a serious threat to human well-being and ecological stability. The urgent need for a societal response to climate change has been reinforced by the Intergovernmental Panel on Climate Change's (IPCC) assessment of the most up-to-date science on climate change, stating that climate warming is 'unequivocal' (IPCC, 2007b). Governments, businesses and other organizations are beginning to respond to the dual challenge of mitigating climate change – through reduction of greenhouse gas emissions – and adapting to the inevitable impacts of climate change to which we are already committed.

Internationally, the policy response to climate change has been embodied in the Kyoto Protocol, the commitment period of which is due to end in 2012. The difficulties of achieving consensus on climate policy post-Kyoto were well demonstrated at the Copenhagen Conference of the Parties, in December 2009, as nation states sought to reconcile their political, cultural and economic differences towards the goal of an overarching climate agreement. Yet even in the absence of a global climate deal, several nations are starting to develop policies to address climate change. The UK was the first nation to develop a policy response to climate change, through the implementation of the Climate Change Act. The Act sets an ambitious target of (at least) an 80 per cent reduction in greenhouse gas emissions by 2050 with respect to a 1990 baseline, and aims to enhance the UK's ability to adapt to the impact of climate change. The USA have debated the merits of the 2009 American Clean Energy and Security Act (or Waxman–Markey Bill), which proposes a target of 83 per cent reduction in greenhouse gas emissions by 2050, compared to 2005 levels. Similarly to the USA, Australian national climate change policy remains a contentious issue, as debate continues over such targets as a 5–15 per cent reduction by 2020 (or 25 per cent if international agreement on a global deal is reached) with respect to 2000 levels.

These responses to climate change have profound implications for individual choices and behaviour, as well as for the social contexts and governance structures within which these take place. Timescales of technological innovation and implementation, or large-scale shifts in energy supply, also indicate that reliance on technology alone is insufficient (e.g. Bows et al, 2006). Significant reductions in carbon-intensive energy demand amongst developed countries are required, along with redistribution of energy consumption to address global inequity and injustice, both deeply embedded in the issue of climate change. With over one-third of many developed nations' carbon emissions[1] coming from private travel and domestic energy use (Defra, 2008), individuals and communities clearly have a key role to play in any potential shift towards a low-carbon society. An individual can act in several roles towards promoting a low-carbon society, including as a low-carbon citizen (e.g. voting for a 'green' policy), as a low-carbon consumer (e.g. buying energy-efficient appliances), as a member of a campaigning group to promote a low-carbon society (e.g. Friends of the Earth) and as a low-carbon employee (through the knock-on effects of individual engagement with climate change on businesses and government).

Policy attention has primarily focused on mitigation, while adaptation to climate change is a more embryonic policy issue. Nevertheless, it is clear that even with a strong mitigation agenda, impacts from climate change will be unavoidable. For example, it is estimated that there were around 35,000 excess deaths from the European heatwave in 2003 (IPCC, 2007a), an extreme weather event of the type likely to increase with climate change (IPCC, 2007b). The risk of flooding in the UK is expected to increase by up to 30 times in the next 75 years, costing tens of billions of pounds every year from damage to property (King, 2004). Again, there are major implications for individuals. Understanding and evaluating the risks associated with climate change are prerequisites for informed decisions about where and how to live.

The rationale, then, for public engagement with climate change is multifaceted. From the perspective of policy, effective and democratic climate change governance involves societal engagement. Public support for, and enactment of, climate change policy is a key concern of political organizations and world leaders. Such policies may directly call for public action – such as information campaigns and economic policies designed to encourage individual behaviour change (e.g. conserving energy in the home); but even policies which focus on developing technologies and adapting infrastructures require public support. Meaningful engagement over issues of technology choice and use is crucial in developing low-carbon technologies and resilient infrastructures. More fundamentally, most Western governments have an interest in engaging the public in debate about the type of society they want to live in and empowering communities to bring about change to that effect. Here, the focus is on public participation in policy making, community decision making and grassroots innovation. Climate change offers new ways and new vocabularies for challenging assumptions about quality of life, economic development and consumption, and can be approached as much a cultural issue as a scientific one (Hulme, 2009). Contestation – which often reflects divergent beliefs, values and interests – over climate change and attendant social, economic and technological responses implies a role for deliberative as well as analytic input to policy.

For other groups there may be different reasons for being interested in the public's understanding of and responses to climate change. Businesses may be involved with formal climate change communication as part of a corporate social responsibility or a product marketing agenda (and often both); and non-governmental organizations (NGOs) may do so because climate change intersects with their existing environmental and social concerns and interests (e.g. biodiversity loss, social justice, development, health). However, communication is not restricted to formal communication campaigns aimed to achieve some predefined end. Climate change has become common parlance within print, broadcast and new media and in everyday conversation. A range of interests, discourses, frames and languages influence how climate change is communicated and understood, and whether (and how) it is responded to; and the methods and media used to communicate the issue are no less diverse than the range of communicators or audiences (e.g. Nerlich et al, 2010). The heterogeneity of audiences – or 'publics'[2] – and of messages, media and contexts of communication undermine any presumption that communicating climate change is a simple task, or indeed that communication will lead to any (or predictable) outcomes in terms of understandings or behaviours.

2. Challenges for engaging the public with climate change

Despite the clear implications of climate change mitigation and adaptation for individual values, choices and behaviours, public engagement with climate change is currently limited. On the mitigation side, energy demand for both domestic uses and transport is rising in most developed countries (Defra, 2008). Although a large majority of the public now recognizes terms such as 'climate change', understanding and emotional buy-in are far lower (Defra, 2007; Lorenzoni et al, 2007). Pro-environmental behavioural responses to climate change are even more limited; few people are prepared to take actions beyond recycling or domestic energy conservation (Bord et al, 2000; Maibach et al, 2009; O'Neill and Hulme, 2009; Whitmarsh, 2009b). At the same time, few are taking actions to adapt to climate change; indeed, awareness of the need for adaptation is very low (Whitmarsh, 2009b). Even flood victims rarely associate flooding with climate change, and are no more concerned about or likely to take action to tackle climate change than other people (Whitmarsh, 2008). In respect of both mitigation and adaptation, then, there is a lack of meaningful engagement with the issue of climate change.

We define 'engagement' here in broad terms as the personal connection with climate change, comprising cognitive, emotional and behavioural aspects (see Lorenzoni et al, 2007). In other words, engagement encompasses what people know, feel and do in relation to climate change. The three facets of engagement are not related in a linear fashion; rather, they comprise complex behavioural ecologies. For instance, behaviour change can precede cognitive or affective change; and cognitive, affective and behavioural aspects of engagement are in large part a product of social and institutional contexts. Different engagement strategies – as outlined in this volume – may aim to address one or more of these dimensions. As suggested, these three dimensions map onto both mitigation and adaptation such that individuals understand, assess and may respond to both the causes and consequences of climate change. In relation to the behavioural dimension of engagement, we emphasize the multiple roles and activities which individuals can perform in relation to climate change. As mentioned, these include buying and using products (i.e. consumption), but also political, workplace and community activities. These two categories of action – private-sphere and public-sphere (Stern, 2000) – are reflected in the range of engagement approaches discussed in this book.

In part, the lack of engagement around climate change is one of understanding: there is a general lack among the public of knowledge about the emissions impacts of different actions, including which activities produce the most emissions (Whitmarsh et al, 2009). However, research and practice in science communication clearly demonstrates the inadequacy of assuming that information can either change behaviour or produce public support for policy. The so-called 'information deficit model', which assumes that the public are 'empty vessels' waiting to be filled with information which will propel them into rational action, has implicitly underpinned much public policy, but is widely criticized as inappropriate and ineffective (e.g. Irwin and Wynne, 1996). Not least, this model ignores the heterogeneous nature of the public, as there are multiple publics with diverse resources and values rather than one monolithic public; and these diverse publics interpret and use (or ignore) information in diverse ways.

This is not to say that education is not part of an effective public engagement and social change agenda, but rather that it should be based on an understanding of individuals' existing knowledge, their concerns and abilities, and broader institutional relationships, and should be accompanied by efforts to provide greater opportunities for public participation in democratic policy making (Whitmarsh et al, 2009). (We note here that public participation in policy making does not necessarily lead to more environmentally sustainable outcomes; but that it can lead to better quality and more acceptable decisions, and can improve institutional relationships and trust; e.g. Dietz and Stern, 2008.) Further, given the complexity and uncertainty (both informational and moral) associated with climate change (Hulme, 2009), carbon literacy implies an ability to evaluate the reliability (bias, agenda, uncertainty, etc.) of different information sources about how to achieve a low-carbon lifestyle. For example, media representation of climate change as controversial and uncertain may be more reflective of journalistic norms (of balance, dramatization, politicization, etc.) than of schism within mainstream scientific opinion (Boykoff and Boykoff, 2004). Currently, however, much of the public is poorly equipped to deal with scientific uncertainty and tend to be confused by expert disagreement; for example, most people in the UK agree that 'there is so much conflicting information about science that it is difficult to know what to believe' (Poortinga and Pidgeon, 2003, p16).

There is also a lack of personal connection with an issue which is global, long term and complex: most individuals see climate change as distant both spatially (caused by and impacting other regions or countries) and temporally (impacting future generations) (Poortinga and Pidgeon, 2003; Norton and Leaman, 2004; Lorenzoni et al, 2007; O'Neill and Hulme, 2009). Many are also sceptical about the human influence on climate or uncertain about the implications for individuals (Lorenzoni and Pidgeon, 2006; Whitmarsh, 2009a). Concern about the issue also fluctuates in relation to other, more immediate, problems, recent events or media coverage (e.g. Upham et al, 2009). Denial about the reality or severity of climate change may be a psychological reaction to the uncomfortable dissonance individuals experience when confronted with the impact of their (carbon-intensive) lifestyles and their reluctance (or inability) to change their behaviour (Stoll-Kleeman et al, 2001).

However, there are clearly broader structural constraints and disincentives to adopting a low-carbon lifestyle, which reduces individuals' motivation and ability to change their behaviour. These include perceived social inaction and the 'free rider effect', inadequate or unattractive alternatives to energy intensive activities such as driving (Lorenzoni et al, 2007), as well as the broader 'systems of provision' which feed and respond to consumption and ultimately shape lifestyles (Spaargaren, 2003). Individuals differ in respect of their perceived ability to influence these systems, but there are also cultural differences in norms and opportunities for individuals to influence the structural context in which they live.

These barriers to public engagement with climate change are addressed only very partially through current climate and energy policies. The limited attention given to behavioural change in most developed nation's climate change policies focuses primarily on voluntary reduction of energy use by individuals, encouraged through provision of information and economic measures – an approach which has had little impact on the behaviour of individuals, as evidenced by continued growth in energy demand. Although mass media information campaigns may have contributed to the rise in public awareness of climate change in recent years, they have done little to address psychological or structural barriers to engagement. Furthermore, there has been little attempt to incorporate adaptation messages into public communication initiatives on climate change or to consider more fundamental, moral dimensions of climate change, such as intra- and intergenerational injustice and inequity, within these initiatives.

Frustrated by a perceived lack of political action to adequately tackle climate change, grassroots movements, such as Transition Towns and Carbon Reduction Action Groups, are emerging to pioneer social innovations for addressing climate change and demonstrate real-world experiments in low-carbon living at the community level (e.g. Ockwell et al, 2009). Many political leaders support this grassroots change, perhaps because it provides a mandate for more concerted and ambitious policy response to meet the climate challenge. Most recently, the then UK Secretary of State for Energy and Climate Change, Ed Miliband, called for the creation of a global 'popular mobilization' campaign to pressure world leaders into tackling climate change (cited in

Adam and Jowit, 2008); and the UN Secretary-General, Ban Ki-moon, announced the formation of a global Climate Change Communication Initiative to 'explain, educate and ask for engagement' on climate change (Ban, 2009).

3. Aims, structure and features of this book

This book directly answers these calls for the mobilization of society to help address climate change, and examines the interaction between climate change and diverse publics. In particular, it presents a timely analysis of how to engage diverse publics through both theoretical insights and innovative practical initiatives. The volume is interdisciplinary, drawing on diverse disciplinary expertise from across the social and behavioural sciences. Chapters draw on both academic and practitioner perspectives, and apply lessons from across different issue contexts, such as health and finance, to inform understanding and practice on communicating and stimulating behaviour change in relation to climate change. Finally, the book brings together learning from a range of geographical contexts (including studies from Europe, North America and Australia), to provide an international perspective on public engagement.

The book originated from a number of research projects, led by the Editors at the Tyndall Centre for Climate Change Research, on public engagement with climate change. The Editors convened an international workshop (co-funded by the Tyndall Centre and the UK Energy Research Centre) in Oxford in October 2008 on this topic, and the resulting papers, selected through a peer review process, form the basis of this volume.

The book is divided into two themes, which address two broad questions:

- *Part 1: Theories and models.* How can different theoretical perspectives help us develop effective communication and behaviour change strategies, and understand the limits to public engagement?
- *Part 2: Methods, media and tools.* How can we more effectively communicate with the public about climate change, and foster cognitive, affective and behavioural engagement with the issue?

The chapters draw on theoretical and empirical studies, with lessons from practical examples, to elaborate the themes. Together, the chapters illustrate that engaging the public with these complex issues is necessary, but also fraught with difficulties and challenges. Often, multiple theoretical perspectives and a combination of practical initiatives or policies are required to overcome the various barriers to engagement (some even calling for systemic change). These range from informational approaches, through social and community-based schemes, to top-down structural adjustments to encourage and enable change at both individual and social levels. These approaches are mapped out in Table I.1, below. Some chapters focus specifically on energy behaviour, or on adaptation to climate change, while others consider climate change as a whole (and even reframing the issue as part of a broader perspective on sustainability). Similarly, some focus on individuals, some on

Table I.1 *Overview of chapters*

Chapter	Author (location)	Summary of engagement approach	Disciplinary influences
		Part 1 Theories and Models	
1	Verplanken (UK)	Breaking and creating habits for low-carbon lifestyles	social psychology, sociology
2	Lorenzoni, Seyfang and Nye (UK)	Finance management as an analogue for managing carbon budgets	economic and social psychology, political science
3	Höppner (Switzerland) and Whitmarsh (UK)	New forms of participatory democracy	political science, psychology
4	Rabinovich, Morton and Duke (UK)	Social comparisons, identities and norms in promoting engagement with climate change	social psychology
5	Brannigan (UK)	Engaging individuals through emotions and values	neuroscience
6	Leith (Australia)	Co-production of knowledge for climate adaptation	science and technology studies
7	Wolf (Canada)	Ecological citizenship in climate engagement	psychology, political science
		Part 2 Methods, Media and Tools	
8	Eyre, Flanagan and Double (UK)	Nationwide advice centres and website providing information and advice on domestic energy conservation	communication, marketing
9	Hamilton (UK)	Eco-home open days providing demonstration and observational learning on domestic energy conservation and provision	sociology, education, marketing
10	Davidson (UK)	'Eco-teams' household behaviour change scheme, providing information and advice on sustainable lifestyles	social psychology, sociology
11	Regniez and Custead (UK)	Business marketing and governmental/non-governmental information campaigns, providing information on decarbonized lifestyles	communication, marketing
12	Darby (UK)	Smart-metering and related technologies to foster energy conservation in the home	semiotics, communication, sociology
13	O'Neill (Australia) and Boykoff (USA)	New media approaches providing information on climate change and decarbonized lifestyles	communication, sociology, political science
14	Todhunter (UK)	Participatory community engagement with low-carbon lifestyles and sustainability	social psychology, marketing

social groups, others on broader structural structures, with several chapters combining multiple approaches. Fundamentally, successful public engagement requires acknowledgement of the diversity of knowledge, abilities and values reflected within society, which imply a need for tailored and context-sensitive approaches for dealing with these heterogeneous 'publics'.

Part 1 of the book provides a conceptual foundation for public engagement, drawing on political, social and psychological theories to elucidate the role of the public in responding to climate change, and to develop effective communication and behaviour change strategies.

Psychological models of behaviour are outlined and critiqued in Chapter 1. Bas Verplanken argues that most behaviours that have ecological consequences are repetitive and habitual. However, prevalent models of behaviour, such as the theory of planned behaviour, do not well accommodate this aspect. Similarly, interventions to change everyday behaviours often attempt to change people's beliefs and intentions. These interventions are unlikely to be an effective means to change behaviours which have become established habits. Successful habit-change interventions involve disrupting the contextual factors that automatically cue habit performance. The chapter discusses how old (carbon-intensive) habits can be broken and new (low-carbon) habits embedded, drawing on examples from a range of behavioural contexts (including health, transport and consumption) and from studies undertaken in a number of European countries. Some of the most promising avenues for creating new sustainable behaviours involve providing informational input at points when habits are vulnerable to change, such as when people are undergoing naturally occurring changes in lifestyle or environment (e.g. moving home, changing jobs, having a baby). Verplanken thus argues that the formation of greener habits should become the focus of targeted behaviour change interventions.

In Chapter 2, individual and societal perspectives are brought together through the concept of 'carbon capability'. According to Irene Lorenzoni, Gill Seyfang and Mike Nye, 'carbon capability' captures the contextual meanings associated with carbon, whilst also referring to an individual's ability and motivation to reduce emissions within the broader institutional and social context. Lorenzoni and colleagues argue that carbon capable actors will understand the impacts of daily activities on climate, while also being aware of, and seeking to influence, through collective and political mechanisms, societal structures (policies, systems of provision, infrastructure, etc.) in order to overcome the system-level barriers to low-carbon lifestyles and societies. Carbon capability is an analogue to financial capability applied to human-caused climate change, and involves managing budgets, planning ahead, staying informed and making choices. Indeed, these are the same driving forces, and comparable consumer issues with both types of capability, which require a holistic approach to learning about sustainable consumption in ,both financial and resource terms. The chapter focuses on the importance of carbon capability for the effective implementation of a personal carbon trading scheme, in which individuals need to manage carbon budgets and trade carbon credits.

A comparative analysis of political and public perceptions of individuals' role in addressing climate change is provided in Chapter 3. Here, Corina Höppner and Lorraine Whitmarsh examine commonalities and divergences in how the roles and responsibilities of the public have been constructed within recent climate change and related policy documents in the UK, and how the public themselves see their role in addressing climate change. The official preference for individual action in the form of enlightened consumer choice fails to acknowledge that public engagement has many facets that influence each other. Engagement can take place in the private sphere (e.g. individual action through green consumerism, conservation behaviour) and in the public sphere (i.e. sociopolitical participation). The latter is a vital element of democracies that ideally shortens the distance between government and the public, fosters people's willingness to address challenges such as climate change collectively, develops democratic virtues, and most importantly stimulates people's belief that they can make a difference. The authors argue that the emergence and popularity of new grassroots movements (e.g. Transition Towns, CRAGs) and the overwhelming number of citizens responding to the draft Climate Change Bill consultation, for instance, show that there is an urgent need to broaden official thinking about spaces and scopes for public engagement to accommodate the divergent roles ascribed to, and by, the public in addressing climate change.

Chapter 4 demonstrates the powerful influence of social factors and individuals' need to belong to social groups on perceptions and behaviour in relation to climate change and other sustainability issues. Anna Rabinovich, Thomas Morton and Christopher Duke focus on social comparison theory, and how information can be adapted to present pro-environmental actions as 'normal' and thereby motivate behaviour change. Analysis from a series of psychological experiments shows that positive intergroup comparisons (e.g. the UK versus Sweden or the USA) that encourage people to see green values as defining of their own group, and by virtue of this, themselves, may be more effective in stimulating public engagement than negative comparisons that bring to the fore underperformance in comparison to other, more environmentally friendly groups.

Fiona Brannigan also criticizes the emphasis of traditional information provision approaches for ignoring important psychological drivers of behaviour. In Chapter 5, Brannigan argues that by relying on traditional marketing paradigms there is a danger of being seduced by short-term easy wins which focus on extrinsic values (such as saving money), but which may in the long run prove detrimental to significantly altering the way we live our lives. She argues that if we are to really create a sustainable future we must transform the 'myths' by which we live, addressing fundamental questions about happiness and how we achieve it. To change these intrinsic values (such as the way we think and feel about energy), we need to challenge the mechanisms which lock us into the Consumerism–Happiness myth (primarily marketing and the quest for economic growth fuelled by an ever increasing consumption of products). Brannigan suggests there has never been a better time for this to happen: we are currently experiencing a breakdown of economic structures which have for so long been accepted as the model for 'the way the world works'.

Engagement with adaptation is considered in Chapter 6 by Peat Leith. The author analyses the recent history of scientific management of climate risk and uncertainty in Australian agriculture, finding that the approaches pragmatically developed by scientists to engage farmers and graziers with climate variability can inform engagement for intentional adaptation to climate change, especially because they are oriented by forms of social learning and action research. Leith describes how vulnerability to climate extremes highlights the need to address individual and institutional dimensions of resilience and adaptation, helping to shed light on how to better engage the public in climate change adaptation. Leith argues that the public have a role to play in knowledge *production* as well as application (e.g. in terms of behaviour change), thus providing a different framing for what 'engagement' might entail.

Ecological citizenship is the focus of Chapter 7. Like Brannigan, Johanna Wolf argues that people who perceive a responsibility for climate change enact the normative concept of ecological citizenship, which reframes pro-environmental behaviour in terms of individuals' rights and responsibilities in relation to the environment. Wolf's work with the Canadian public examines how ecological citizens distinguish themselves by feeling responsible and acting on climate change. Their engagement, however, goes beyond changing behaviour as a result of knowing and being concerned about the problem, and includes civic engagement that aims to enhance their agency as individuals. In this respect, ecological citizens exhibit a commitment to changing the structures and institutions that govern their engagement. Despite this engagement, the obstacles and barriers highlighted here suggest that even ecological citizens may not reduce their emissions effectively. A lack of knowledge about how to achieve effective emission reductions, accompanied by structural impediments and lack of incentives for low-carbon lifestyles, are critical obstacles in making engagement meaningful. Here we see some convergence with the model presented by Lorenzoni and colleagues in Chapter 2: both carbon capability and ecological citizenship highlight the importance of individual engagement with societal and political structures in order to create opportunities for more equitable and low-carbon global societies. In both cases, though, there is recognition of the importance of cultural and institutional context in fostering political engagement amongst the public; while trust and efficacy may be a common currency in some communities, others have long suffered from public disillusionment and disenfranchisement, which acts to limit individuals' engagement with political systems.

Part 2 then applies many of the conceptual and theoretical insights from Part 1, in a range of real-world examples and case studies on public engagement with climate change.

Firstly, Chapter 8 focuses on tailored information provision through long-running nationwide energy savings programmes. Here, Nick Eyre, Brooke Flanagan, Nick Double discuss lessons learnt from the UK Energy Saving Trust, which (since 1992) has aimed to encourage and enable energy saving amongst the public, primarily through a network of advice centres and a website. Costing over £300 million, the programmes are the largest engagement programme on energy demand ever attempted in the UK and have resulted in over 120Mt of lifetime carbon dioxide savings. The chapter presents evaluation findings which indicate differences between approaches, trends and potential improvements in the context of an increasingly complex environment of policy intervention.

In contrast to the national-level approach discussed in Chapter 8, Chapters 9 and 10 describe more individually or community tailored communication and behaviour change approaches. In Chapter 9, Jo Hamilton considers the impacts and lessons learnt from the Eco-homes Open Days. Between September 2007 and September 2008, communities and organizations across the UK organized eight area-wide open day events focusing on home eco-renovation and eco-new build, plus a host of single event open days at eco-renovated homes. These have proved extremely popular, with an average of 500 visitors per event, and have provided novel opportunities for social learning (observation, demonstration) about greenhouse gas reductions from eco-renovated and environmental new-build houses. They have translated the 'one size fits all' approach of national energy savings agencies into individually appropriate and socially aspirational renovations according to the house type. The chapter evaluates the open days and their achievements against the crucial need for step change to the UK's approach to eco-renovation. Hamilton addresses crucial questions such as: What barriers and opportunities need to be addressed to ensure interest on the open days translates into action and reduction in carbon dioxide at home?

A fundamentally social approach to fostering low-carbon lifestyles is described by Scott Davidson from Global Action Plan (GAP) in Chapter 10. GAP's *EcoTeams* model has been developed on the basis of well-researched behaviour change principles, including the importance of fun, positive and tailored engagement; and embedding individuals' behaviour change within social groups. Davidson also emphasizes the importance of measurement and evaluation for improving and up-scaling behaviour change programmes. Chapters 10 and 11 have in common an emphasis on the need for collaboration and partnering by policy makers and community organizations to share learning on how to up-scale and develop effective public engagement methods.

A comparative analysis of information and marketing approaches is provided in Chapter 11, in which Gemma Regniez and Savita Custead attempt to bring together examples of governmental, grassroots and business-led communication campaigns, and assess their effectiveness in engaging the public with climate change. Their analysis of government and business-led campaigns, and community projects and networks, includes a selection of many well-known UK examples such as 'Act on CO_2', '10:10' and 'Plan A'. Success criteria for these campaigns are defined as: levels of engagement, ability to feed into policy, sustainability and relations to national indicators, as well as indicators of success identified by communicators themselves (ministers, communications professionals and leaders of community groups).

Measurement, technology and feedback are themes which feature in Chapter 12. Here, Sarah Darby tackles the problem of the intangibility of energy for changing energy behaviours. Drawing on her work on domestic energy consumption and conservation, she presents a novel perspective on communicating energy demand which draws on theories of semiotics and social practices. She questions the extent to which energy users might be expected to know about their energy use, drawing attention to some of the things that we notice, do not notice and cannot notice when we use different fuels or energy sources, and connects these with the infrastructures of things and practices that make up energy systems. This forms the background to a discussion of the changes in metering gas and electricity that are under way around the world, and of how 'smart meters' relate to government, utility and customer objectives. Darby asks how new meters take their place in energy systems, as 'things', as communicators and as symbols; what potential do they hold for better public engagement with energy issues; and what may be the possible pitfalls.

A central focus of Chapter 13 is also technology, and the interaction between individuals and new information and communication technologies. Specifically, Saffron O'Neill and Maxwell Boykoff discuss the potential and limitations of new media, including the internet, to engage the public with climate change. New media have been described by some as one of the greatest tools for achieving a true democracy – a claim others state requires a much more critical reading. O'Neill and Boykoff argue that new media actors play multiple roles – providing information, facilitating engagement, widening participation. Equally, new media actors can increase fragmentation or reach only already-engaged audiences. With these conflicting positions in mind, this chapter reviews and critically evaluates the current role, and potential future roles, new media could play in engaging the public with climate change. This chapter also contains a more detailed examination of two climate engagement approaches (one a community-based emissions reduction programme, the other a climate contrarian engagement approach) that have successfully utilized new media to engage audiences with climate change.

Social models of action and innovation theory underpin the analysis in Chapter 14 of grassroots projects across the UK – ranging from community-owned renewable projects to refurbishment courses – to develop low-carbon communities. Tracey Todhunter reviews these diverse initiatives that have achieved significant reductions in household carbon emissions, and highlights the role played by inspiring individuals and exemplar communities to motivate wider change. Many of these initiatives aim to show that, not only are low-carbon lifestyles achievable, they may be aspirational. These locally developed activities meet local needs, creating a system of structured support where neighbours share experiences, and build cohesion and trust. Like Davidson, Todhunter highlights the barriers to up-scaling, including lack of funding and policy support.

Finally, in the concluding chapter, we draw out implications for both practice and theory from the preceding chapters. In particular, we present summary guidance for communicating climate change and fostering behaviour change for use by policy makers, grassroots NGOs and other practitioners. This guidance will refer to both examples of successful implementation of communication and behaviour change lessons, and, where relevant, to theoretical underpinnings. Finally, this chapter identifies areas for further research and practical experiments to advance understanding about, and test new approaches to, public engagement with climate change and energy.

Notes

1   We use the term 'carbon emissions' as a conventional shorthand for greenhouse gas emissions.
2   We acknowledge the more realistic description of multiple *publics*, but tend to refer to 'the public' by way of convention.

References

Adam, D. and Jowit, J. (2008) 'People power vital to climate deal – minister', *Guardian*, 8 December, www.guardian.co.uk/environment/2008/dec/08/ed-miliband-climate-politics-environment, accessed 18 December 2009

Ban, K.-M. (2009) Remarks at event entitled 'Shaping the Climate Change Message' at the World Economic Forum, David, Switzerland, 29 January 2009

Bows, A., Mander, S., Starkey, R., Bleda, M. and Anderson, K. (2006) *Living Within a Carbon Budget*, Tyndall Centre for Climate Change Research, Manchester

Boykoff, M. T. and Boykoff, J. M. (2004) 'Balance as bias: Global warming and the US prestige press', *Global Environmental Change*, vol 14, pp125–136

Claeson, B., Martin, E., Richardson, W., Schoch-Spana, M. and Taussig, K. (1996) 'Scientific literacy, what it is, why it's important, and why scientists think we don't have it', in L. Nader (ed) *Naked Science*, University of Chicago Press, Chicago, IL, pp101–116

Defra (2007) *Survey of Public Attitudes and Behaviors towards the Environment: 2007*, Defra, London

Defra (2008) 'UK climate change sustainable development indicator: 2006 greenhouse gas emissions', http://www.whitehallpages.net/news/archive/20970, accessed 20 August 2010

Dietz, T. and Stern, P. C. (eds) (2008) *Public Participation in Environmental Assessment and Decision Making*, National Academies Press, Washington, DC

Hulme, M. (2009) *Why We Disagree About Climate Change*, Cambridge University Press, Cambridge, UK

IPCC (2007a) *Climate Change 2007: Impacts, Adaptation and Vulnerability. Contribution of Working Group II to the Fourth Assessment Report of the Intergovernmental Panel on Climate Change*, M. L. Parry, O. F. Canziani, J. P. Palutikof, P. J. van der Linden and C. E. Hanson (eds) Cambridge University Press, Cambridge, UK

IPCC (2007b) *Climate Change 2007: Synthesis Report. Contribution of Working Groups I, II and III to the Fourth Assessment Report of the Intergovernmental Panel on Climate Change*, R. K. Pachauri and A. Reisinger (eds) IPCC, Geneva, Switzerland

Irwin, A. and Wynne, B. (eds) (1996) *Misunderstanding Science? The Public Reconstruction of Science and Technology*, Cambridge University Press, Cambridge

King, D. (2004) 'Climate change science: Adapt, mitigate, or ignore?', *Science*, vol 303, pp176–177

Lorenzoni, I. and Pidgeon, N. (2006) 'Public views on climate change: European and USA perspectives', *Climatic Change*, vol 77, pp73–95

Lorenzoni, I., Nicholson-Cole, S. and Whitmarsh, L. (2007) 'Barriers perceived to engaging with climate change among the UK public and their policy implications', *Global Environmental Change*, vol 17, pp445–459

Maibach, E., Roser-Renouf, C. and Leiserowitz, A. (2009) Global Warming's Six Americas 2009: An Audience Segmentation Analysis. Available at: http://www.climatechangecommunication.org/images/files/GlobalWarmingsSi xAmericas2009c.pdf

Nerlich, B., Koteyko, N. and Brown, B. (2010) 'Theory and language of climate change communication', *WIREs Climate Change*, vol 1, no 1, pp97–110

New, M., Liverman, D. and Anderson, K. (2009) 'Mind the gap', *Nature Reports Climate Change*, vol 3, pp143–144

Norton, A. and Leaman, J. (2004) *The Day After Tomorrow: Public Opinion on Climate Change*, MORI Social Research Institute, London

Ockwell, D., Whitmarsh, L. and O'Neill, S. (2009) 'Reorienting climate change communication for effective mitigation – forcing people to be green or fostering grass-roots engagement?', *Science Communication*, vol 30, no 3, pp305–327

O'Neill, S. J. and Hulme, M. (2009) 'An iconic approach for representing climate change', *Global Environmental Change*, vol 19, pp402–410

Poortinga, W. and Pidgeon, N. (2003) *Public Perceptions of Risk, Science and Governance*, University of East Anglia/MORI, Norwich

Spaargaren, G. (2003) 'Sustainable consumption: A theoretical and environmental policy perspective', *Society and Natural Resources*, vol 16, pp687–701

Stern, P. (2000) 'Toward a coherent theory of environmentally significant behavior', *Journal of Social Issues*, vol 56, no 3, pp407–424

Stoll-Kleemann, S., O'Riordan, T. and Jaeger, C. C. (2001) 'The psychology of denial concerning climate mitigation measures: evidence from Swiss focus groups', *Global environmental change*, vol 11, no 2, pp107–118

Upham, P., Whitmarsh, L., Poortinga, W., Purdam, K., Darnton, A., McLachlan, C. and Devine-Wright, P. (2009) *Public Attitudes to Environmental Change: a selective review of theory and practice. A research synthesis for the Living with Environmental Change Programme*, Research Councils UK, www.lwec.org.uk/ sites/default/files/Public%20attitudes%20to%20environmental%20change_final% 20report_301009.pdf, accessed 1 December 2009

Whitmarsh, L. (2008) 'Are flood victims more concerned about climate change than other people? The role of direct experience in risk perception and behavioural response', *Journal of Risk Research*, vol 11, no 3, pp351–374

Whitmarsh, L. (2009a) 'What's in a name? Commonalities and differences in public understanding of "climate change" and "global warming"', *Public Understanding of Science*, vol 18, pp401–420

Whitmarsh, L. (2009b) 'Behavioural responses to climate change: Asymmetry of intentions and impacts', *Journal of Environmental Psychology*, vol 29, pp13–23

Whitmarsh, L., O'Neill, S., Seyfang, G. and Lorenzoni, I. (2009) *Carbon Capability: what does it mean, how prevalent is it, and how can we promote it?* Tyndall Working Paper, No. 132, www.tyndall.ac.uk/sites/default/files/twp132.pdf, accessed 18 December 2009

PART 1

THEORIES AND MODELS

How can different theoretical perspectives help us develop effective communication and behaviour change strategies and understand the limits to public engagement?

1
Old Habits and New Routes to Sustainable Behaviour

Bas Verplanken

1. Introduction

Although people are sensitive to what they think are beneficial or detrimental choices, most behaviours seem to be driven by mere repetition and habit rather than by conscious deliberation of costs and benefits. This also holds for behaviours that have a potential impact on our natural environment. In this chapter, I first discuss models of environmental behaviour. I then focus on the repetitive nature of behaviour. I will outline why old, unsustainable habits form barriers to change, but I will stress also that there exist opportunities to turn new, sustainable behaviours into habits. Finally, I argue that as climate change requires drastic changes in behaviour amongst large sections of our societies, time is running out to wait for people to change their values and attitudes, and measures are necessary that directly regulate behaviour. Psychologists may have much to offer in making this happen in socially acceptable ways.

2. Antecedents of environmental behaviour

Models of expected utility and planned behaviour

Why do we behave as we do? Common sense perhaps tells us that our behaviour is guided by the balance of perceived costs and benefits; that is, overall value. When we shop, we choose products that we think provide value for money. When we travel, we consider attributes such as travel time, monetary costs and comfort. In our homes we use the appliances and gadgets that we consider useful or pleasurable. The assumption underlying this view is that people are driven by maximizing the expected value of a particular behaviour. This indeed is the prevalent view of behaviour amongst economists, and forms the basis for influential models of behaviour in psychology. Whereas economists interpret 'value' in monetary terms, psychologists use the concept of 'utility', or more precisely 'subjective expected utility', to designate the expectation of the perceived value of a behavioural outcome (Edwards, 1954). The principle of subjective expected utility became the key building stone of preva-lent models of behaviour, most notably the theory of reasoned action (TRA; Ajzen and Fishbein, 1980) and the theory of planned behaviour (TPB; Ajzen, 1988). According to these models, the specific perceptions of expected costs and benefits associated with a behavioural choice (e.g. price, comfort, useful-ness) lead to the formation of an attitude. An attitude is a summary evaluation; that is, how favourable or unfavourable one feels towards engag-ing in that behaviour. TRA and TPB suggest that attitudes guide behaviour through the operation of behavioural intentions. An intention thus represents a person's motivation to engage in a particular behaviour. The models pro-pose that in addition to an attitude, intentions are also determined by the felt pressure from the social environment, such as expectations of friends or fam-ily, which is represented as a subjective norm. In addition, the TPB, which is an extension of TRA, includes the perceptions of control over behaviour (e.g. perceived difficulties) as a third determinant of intentions. Perceived behav-ioural control is assumed to determine intentions or, if the perception of control reflects actual control, behaviour directly. The TPB is represented in Figure 1.1.

Research over almost four decades has provided a strong evidence base for the validity and utility of the TRA and TPB in a wide variety of behavioural domains, including ecology-related behaviours. A series of meta-analyses demonstrated that intentions are reasonably good predictors of behaviour (Armitage and Conner, 2001; Ajzen and Fishbein, 2005), and typ-ically explain some 25 per cent of the variation in behaviour (Sheeran, 2002). Also, the prediction of intentions by attitudes, subjective norms and perceived behavioural control has received firm empirical support (e.g. Armitage and Conner, 2001).

Some important caveats should be noted. The first is that the arrows in the TPB model suggest causal relations. Behaviour is thus assumed to be *caused* by an intention, while intentions are considered to be *caused* by some combined influence of attitudes, subjective norms and perceived behavioural control. There is some but not a great quantity of empirical evidence to

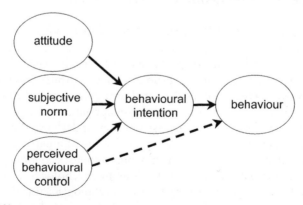

Source: Ajzen, 1999

Figure 1.1 *The theory of planned behaviour*

support this claim, while there are demonstrations of reverse causal flows as well, such as self-perception processes whereby individuals 'infer' their attitudes from their behaviour (Olsen and Stone, 2005; see later). Secondly, the model suggests that all influences on behaviour, whether these are internal (e.g. personality) or external (e.g. external information), are routed from left to right in the model. In other words, these factors are assumed to influence attitude, subjective norm or perceived behavioural control, and thus intentions and behaviour. In one sense, this is a strong aspect of the model; it maps alternative routes to behavioural change. For instance, information campaigns may be tailored to the leg of the model that drives a particular behaviour. Information may thus be provided that either changes the balance of perceived costs and benefits (the attitude route), beliefs about norms (the normative route) or ways to overcome particular barriers to behaviour (the perceived control route). On the other hand, there is some evidence that behaviour may be influenced by factors that are *not* mediated by the model variables, such as impulsive or non-conscious processes. I will return to this issue when discussing the role of past behaviour and habit.

The TPB model reveals potential problems for attempts to change behaviour through the provision of information: even if information changes attitudes, subjective norms or perceptions of behavioural control, this does not guarantee changes in intentions and certainly not changes in behaviour. The links between attitudes and intentions and behaviour are particularly fragile when attitudes are weak in the first place; for instance, when individuals are uninvolved in, or ambivalent about, a particular issue (Petty and Krosnick, 1995). Also, if information affects one of the antecedents of intention (e.g. an attitude), there may remain a reverse influence of other antecedents (subjective norm or perceived behavioural control), which thus may maintain the original intention and behaviour. Finally, although intentions predict behaviours reasonably well, there remains a gap. Intentions may not be enacted for a host of reasons. For instance, intentions may not be well formed or may be temporally unstable (e.g. Sheeran et al, 1999; Ajzen, 2002). There may also be problems in the execution phase, such as not knowing how or when to start, getting derailed, or simply forgetting one's intentions (e.g. Gollwitzer and Sheeran, 2006).

Other models of pro-environmental behaviour

Although the TRA and TPB as general models of behaviour have been successfully applied to document and predict pro-environmental behaviours, other models have been developed specifically for this behavioural domain. Some are extensions of the TRA/TPB, such as the addition of personal norms (Harland et al, 1999) or self-identity (e.g. Terry et al, 1999). Other models have their roots in the norm-activation theory of altruistic behaviour (e.g. Schwartz, 1977). This theory asserts that altruistic behaviour is driven by 'personal norms' (i.e. a sense of personal obligation), which are associated with fundamental values. This theory proposes a causal chain of variables that leads to pro-environmental behaviour. The chain starts with relatively stable altruistic personal values and beliefs about the relation between humans and the environment. These beliefs are activated when individuals are confronted with environmental conditions that violate them. This in turn activates beliefs that valued objects are threatened, beliefs about the individual's ability to act and the felt responsibility to act, which may then lead to a choice of pro-environmental action. A suite of models based on the norm-activation theory have recently been integrated into the value–belief–norm (VBN) theory of environmentalism (Stern, 2000). This model is depicted in Figure 1.2.

The VBN theory stipulates the importance of altruistic personal values and an ecologically friendly worldview for pro-environmental behaviour. The model thus suggests ways to promote pro-environmental behaviours among segments of the population who hold pro-environmental norms and values, but do not translate these into action. The model also points towards the difficulty of changing ecologically unfriendly behaviour; the most problematic segments of the population may not endorse the pro-environmental norms and values in the first place, which the VBN theory specifies as being conditional to change. In general, values do not easily translate into behaviour. In an experimental programme, Verplanken and Holland (2002) demonstrated that values are enacted only if they are central to a person's self-concept and are cognitively activated. Two important observations were thus made. The first is that cherishing pro-environmental values per se does not necessarily lead to pro-environmental action, even when the opportunity to act in an environmentally friendly way arises. The second observation is that drawing people's attention to pro-environmental issues leads to action only if pro-environmental values are part of a person's self-identity (i.e. their sense of who they are). This may indeed be quite rare. The VBN model therefore seems to apply only to individuals who prioritize pro-environmental values and to actions that are clearly earmarked as serving pro-environmental goals. For some, pro-environmental values may drive energy conservation behaviour (e.g. Black et al, 1985), but often low-carbon choices are motivated by non-environmental considerations such as saving money, convenience or health benefits (Brandon and Lewis, 1999; Whitmarsh, 2009). One study (Bamberg and Schmidt, 2003) sought to compare the efficacy of different behavioural models, including the TPB and a norm-based model (a predecessor of the VBN), in predicting students' transport choices, and found that energy use is primarily determined by perceived personal costs and benefits and by habit (see next section), while moral concerns are less influential. Even people with high pro-environmental values will tend to conserve energy only if the threat to self-interest (e.g. cost) is not considered too great (Black et al, 1985; Clark et al, 2003; Poortinga et al, 2004). In sum, it is clear that energy use and energy conservation actions are typically a product of a complex ecology of motivations and external influences, and that consequently there is little consistency in apparently 'low-carbon' behaviours across different contexts such as home, work, travel and leisure (e.g. Darnton, 2008).

3. The role of past behaviour and habit

Although the models discussed so far have proven useful (at least in certain contexts), they do not do justice to the dynamic nature of behaviour. In

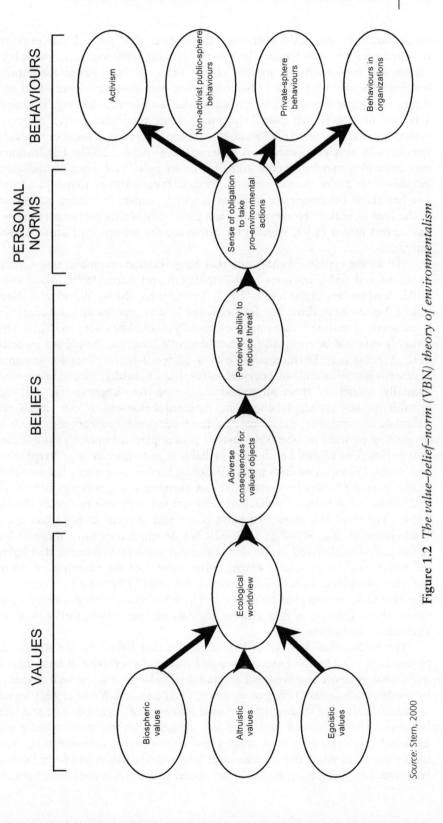

Figure 1.2 *The value–belief–norm (VBN) theory of environmentalism*

Source: Stern, 2000

particular, they do not incorporate the notion that most behaviours are repeated over and over again. The role of previous behaviour has always been elusive and problematic in models of behaviour. In spite of the assumption contained in the TRA and TPB models that previous experiences feed into future behaviour through their impact on the model variables (e.g. attitudes), a robust finding is that past behaviour retains predictive power of future behaviour over and above all model variables. There are a number of explanations why this phenomenon is observed (e.g. Ajzen, 2002). For instance, past behaviour may be a better guide for future behaviour when attitudes and intentions are ambivalent or not well formed. It may also be that expectations one has about behaviour are inaccurate, which renders intentions inadequate in the face of reality. However, another possibility is that previous behaviour has turned into a *habit*, which may attenuate the influence of attitudes and intentions.

Habits are repeated behaviours that have become automatic responses in recurrent and stable contexts (e.g. Verplanken and Aarts, 1999; Wood et al, 2002; Verplanken and Orbell, 2003; Verplanken, 2006; Wood and Neal, 2007). Habits have three key features. The first is repetition; habits form by successfully repeating behaviour. 'Successfully' should be interpreted in a wide sense. It may not be confined to what objective observers would see as desirable. A habit may be successful from a personal perspective; for instance, because it is comfortable or provides status, but unhealthy, asocial or environmentally unfriendly from an outsider's perspective. Importantly, although a habit implies repeated behaviour, repeated behaviour is not necessarily habitual. For instance, decisions that have pervasive consequences, such as diagnosing patients or operating nuclear power plants, hopefully do not turn into habits. The second key feature of habit is automaticity (e.g. Verplanken and Aarts, 1999). 'Automaticity' itself can be broken down into features such as the absence of conscious intent, lack of awareness, the difficulty to control, and the fact that habitual behaviour does not tax cognitive resources (Bargh, 1994). The third key feature of habit is the fact that habits are executed in stable contexts (e.g. Wood et al, 2002). We do our habits often more or less at the same location and at the same time. An important caveat is that habitual behaviours are to a large extent under control of the environment where the acts take place. That is, one executes a habit not because of a conscious intention or willpower, but because it is 8 a.m. or because one passes by a particular shop. Those cues thus seem to regulate our behaviour, rather than our attitudes or intentions.

The mechanism that drives habits implies that habits do not follow the processes implied by the models discussed earlier. As a matter of fact, there is quite some evidence that frequent and habitual behaviour is less well described by models such as the TPB. For instance, Ouellette and Wood (1998) found, in a meta-analysis of studies that included measures of intention, past and later behaviour, that behaviour correlated less strongly with intentions when it was frequently performed. Primary studies also demonstrated that intentions were less or not at all predictive of behaviour when strong habits had been formed. For instance, Verplanken et al (1998) found near-zero correlations between intentions to travel by car versus public transport and actual travel mode choices among participants with strong car use habits, whereas intentions of those with weak habits predicted behaviour very well. Other evidence for the absence of deliberation and intention when habits have formed comes from research on information processing (Aarts et al, 1997; Verplanken et al, 1997). Using a variety of different paradigms, these authors demonstrated how habits lead to 'tunnel vision'; that is, the fact that habitual judgements and choices are based on little information and simple choice rules. In conclusion, while socio-cognitive models such as the TRA and TPB, which suggest that behaviour is motivation-driven and guided by intentions, have proven useful and valid in many contexts, habits form boundary conditions to their validity. This has wider ramifications, which especially are relevant for the question why old habits are difficult to change, to which I will turn next.

Why information campaigns do not change habits

There is a general sense of optimism about the power of providing information to change behaviour (e.g. Maibach et al, 2008). Many resources are being spent on information campaigns aimed at behaviour change (see Chapter 11). However, there is little evidence that such campaigns lead to significant or sustainable effects. This is a more serious problem when the target behaviour is strongly habitual (Verplanken and Wood, 2006). The reasons for this are two-fold, and relate to two phases in the persuasion process. First, in order for informational campaigns to be effective, recipients should pay attention to the campaign and process the information that is offered. This is a difficult process in general. For instance, Weenig and Midden (1997) investigated the effects of three mass-media informational campaigns on environment-related behaviours in the Netherlands. Even the most relaxed effect measure, which was whether respondents were aware of the campaigns, showed that only 37–40 per cent of the respondents had heard of the campaigns, in spite of the fact that these had been running for approximately five months. In other words, the information campaigns had already lost more than two-thirds of their targeted audiences before any information processing or changes could occur. In the case of strong habits, the tunnel vision that accompanies habits poses an additional setback to an already serious problem. Put simply, habits make people less interested in information than they already are by default. In addition, Verplanken et al (1997) found that if habit-driven individuals were interested in information in the first place, their interest concerned primarily information about the options they already used rather than alternative options. The second reason for pessimism about the effects of information provision is that *if* campaigns succeed in changing people's attitudes and even intentions, the weak links with behaviour among strong habit individuals do not bode well for the effectiveness of information campaigns. In other words, even people who do pay attention to messages about saving energy will have to overcome the strong contextual drivers and automatic processes underpinning habits. While the links between attitudes or intentions and behaviour are stronger for non-habitual individuals, these are usually not the prime targets of behaviour change campaigns.

Bright sides of habit

There are at least three reasons why an analysis of behaviour in terms of its habitual quality may lead to some optimism. The first is the notion that not all behaviour is habitual. For instance, most people do not habitually purchase electric appliances such as washing machines or freezers. Such purchases are usually well considered. Information about environmental aspects may thus be one of the attributes in the decision process. The way such information is presented – for instance, electricity use in the form of easy-to-read information labels may enhance its salience and thus the likelihood it is used in the decision-making process (e.g. Verplanken and Weenig, 1993). Pro-environmental interventions may thus aim at giving the environmental argument more weight in purchase decisions.

A second reason for optimism is that interventions may target unsustainable behaviours *before* these become habitual. For instance, new drivers may be taught to drive economically ('eco-driving'), and thus promote the formation of driving styles that are environmentally less taxing. Two important issues must be addressed in this respect. The first is to identify the optimal moment of intervention. In the driving example, driving schools might thus be appropriate intermediates in delivering such interventions; for instance, by incorporating eco-driving in their curriculum. The second issue is that it is one thing to prevent undesirable habits; another thing is the formation of new, sustainable, habits. Interventions often stop at the phase where new behaviour is supposed to be in place. However, intervention planning might incorporate habit formation as an explicit goal and monitor the habit formation process; for instance, by assessing habit strength over time. The use of implementation intentions has been suggested as a promising technique to kick-start habits. Implementation intentions are detailed plans of action, which incorporate the specific formulation of the cues in the behavioural environment and the required responses to those cues (e.g. Gollwitzer and Sheeran, 2006). When people practise these plans (i.e. behaving in an environmentally friendly fashion in response to the cues that were identified in the implementation plans), these may become future habits in due time (e.g. Holland et al, 2006). However, in order to test such hypotheses more rigorously, adequate assessments of habit should be obtained over longer periods of time, in particular measures that distinguish habit from behavioural frequency per se. The Self-Report Habit Index (Verplanken and Orbell, 2003) is an instrument that provides such assessments. It consists of 12 items that tap various facets of habit, in particular the experience of repetition and automaticity. Lally et al (2009) monitored the formation of new habits over a three-month period using this index, and were able to estimate a number of parameters of habit formation curves, such as the speed of habituation and the degree to which a behaviour became automatic. This work may reveal important factors that promote habit formation.

A third route to optimism is related to the third key feature of habit; given that habits are a function of stable contexts, opportunities for change arise when such contexts are broken or become unstable (Wood et al, 2005; Bamberg, 2006; Verplanken and Wood, 2006). This has been referred to as the *habit discontinuity hypothesis* (Verplanken et al, 2008). Notions such as these have been suggested in other areas, such as the concept of 'teachable moments' in the relationship between clinicians and patients (e.g. Lawson and Flocke, 2009), and the concept of 'policy windows' to describe key agenda-setting and policy change moments (Kingdon, 1984). The core of this approach is that when individuals undergo changes or when the environment in which they operate changes, they may be relatively susceptible to new information and advice in order to find satisfactory replacements of their old habits and routines. Such context changes may occur in a natural fashion; for instance, in the form of life course changes such as transitions from school to work, starting a family, moving house or retirement. Changes may also come from outside, such as companies that move or merge, or occur at a large scale, such as the 2008–9 economic downturn. Although the habit discontinuity idea may be appealing, there is no systematic empirical evidence in the environmental domain. A recent study by Verplanken et al (2008) at least provided circumstantial evidence for the habit discontinuity hypothesis. Participants in that study were employees of a university. In a survey they were asked how they commuted to the university, whether or not they had moved house in the last year, and about their environmental values. The pattern of results supported the habit discontinuity hypothesis; participants who recently had moved house and who had strong environmental values were the least likely to use the car as a primary mode of commuting to work. Interestingly, participants with strong environmental values and who had *not* moved house used their car relatively frequently, and in fact could not be distinguished from those who did not adhere to environmental values. While alternative interpretations cannot be excluded, a habit discontinuity interpretation is that moving house made individuals more likely to act upon important values (cf. Verplanken and Holland, 2002). Interventions may be developed that are aimed at finding habit discontinuities, and instigate and consolidate pro-environmental behaviour. Bamberg (2006), for example, delivered an intervention to promote the use of public transport immediately after participants had moved residence. The intervention combined a small material incentive (a one-day free ticket for public transport) with personally tailored information about public transport services and schedules. He found that the intervention was highly effective, although the design of his study did not allow us to infer whether moving residence itself was the key factor.

Other approaches for breaking habits do not necessarily rely on naturally occurring context changes. Rather, the source of the effective implementation plan is a deliberative process (an implementation intention, discussed earlier) and the result is an automatic process, whereby cues and responses are stored and automatically guide action once the stimulus cue is encountered. Implementation intentions have been found to be effective in the environmental behaviour domain; for example, using a new bus route and shopping in an organic shop (Bamberg, 2002), or recycling in the workplace (Holland et al, 2006). Holland et al's (2006) experiment to promote workplace recycling asked half the employees of a Dutch telecoms firm to form an implementation intention (i.e. to plan when, where and how to recycle old paper and used plastic cups, and to visualize and write down these plans). Measurements of the weight of paper and plastic cups in the bin two months later showed a reduction of over two-thirds of recyclable waste in the implementation intention condition.

4. Why not start with changing behaviour?

All the models I discussed earlier suggest that behaviour is the outcome of cognitive processes that involve our beliefs and cognitions; that is, beliefs about expected costs and benefits, other people's expectations and self-efficacy, or personal norms and responsibilities. According to this conception, behaviour change can be accomplished when new beliefs are formed or existing beliefs are changed. Interventions thus aim at bringing about cognitive and motivational changes in the hope that these will lead to behaviour change. This notion not only dominates the social scientific literature on behaviour change, it represents most laypersons' as well as policy-makers' theories about the causes of behaviour and ways to bring about behaviour change. However, as was discussed above, the reliance on cognitive changes and people's motivation to actually change their behaviour has often proved unwarranted, and is especially likely to fall short when this is aimed at changing strong habits. Given the seriousness of the environmental challenges we are currently facing, and thus the urgency and scale of the changes that are needed in order to make any noticeable difference, one might argue that there is simply no time to wait for large segments of the population to change their values, attitudes or beliefs, and trust them to use willpower to make significant changes. Instead, it may be worthwhile to consider more seriously the options of changing behaviour *first* (e.g. through legislation), and consolidate behaviour change with cognitive and motivational changes afterwards. Interventions may thus be geared initially towards accepting measures that directly regulate behaviour (e.g. legislation), and subsequently adapt attitudes and value priorities accordingly (e.g. via information approaches and education).

Anecdotal evidence of real-life examples such as the success of the smoking ban in many countries suggests that such pervasive legislation-driven changes may, perhaps unexpectedly for some, go down very well, and may in fact have led to more negative attitudes towards smoking. In social psychology there is a good body of evidence suggesting that behaviour change may indeed lead to changes in attitudes and belief systems (e.g. Olson and Stone, 2005). One such mechanism is self-perception (e.g. Bem, 1972). Self-perception theory asserts that people often infer their own internal states (e.g. an attitude) from external cues, which they would use to infer other people's internal states. People's own overt behaviour may fulfil such a role; the realization that one behaves in an environmentally friendly way may lead to more pro-environmental attitudes or to upgrading the priority of environmental values. One condition under which this may occur is that existing attitudes are weak or ambiguous. For instance, Holland et al (2002) measured attitudes towards Greenpeace, as well as the strength of those attitudes. A week later, participants were given the opportunity to donate money to Greenpeace, and their attitudes were reassessed. As would be predicted by self-perception theory, the reassessed attitudes of those with weak attitudes were influenced by whether or not they had donated. A second condition for self-perception to work is that the behaviour is voluntary. This condition may be more difficult to fulfil when the direct behaviour interventions have recently been implemented. However, over time the feeling of coercion may fade away. When this is the case, the conditions for self-perception become favourable, and self-perception may be made to work in consolidating attitudes and values.

Interventions that change behaviour directly may be of various kinds. Perhaps the most powerful one is legislation. Legislation may regulate specific behaviours through a variety of measures such as taxation (e.g. congestion and airport taxes), changes in infrastructure (e.g. designating car pool priority lanes, water metering for individual households), or regulating the availability of products (e.g. only allowing energy-saving lightbulbs). The advantages of such measures are obvious; once legislation is in place, behaviour change is relatively easily accomplished. The disadvantages are also obvious; our democratic systems, especially those that are based on locally elected MPs, often work against such measures, as most politicians have an innate fear of suggesting unpopular measures, even if these would be highly effective. Regulation of behaviour through legislation may also have to be accompanied by other initiatives, such as measures to protect low-income groups. There is a role for communication to facilitate public acceptance of climate change policies, but also to stimulate grassroots *demand* for such policies (Ockwell et al, 2009). In Chapter 3, such an active role for the public in climate change governance, deliberation and societal change is considered in more detail. Other measures that directly influence behaviour are technological developments, such as speed limiters or energy-efficient cars. These of course take time to take effect, and some may also have to be embedded in legislation. Other chapters (e.g. 9, 12) consider such technological and infrastructural changes, and the extent to which they are intrinsically linked to social and behavioural factors.

5. Conclusions

Changing people's behaviour towards an environmentally friendly direction is difficult for many reasons. One is that large portions of the population are either not interested in changing, or are not in the position to make changes due to personal, social or other circumstances. In addition, many behaviours are locked by being strongly habitual, and embedded in routines and social practices. Information-based interventions, and certainly the traditional mass media informational campaigns, are clearly not delivering the fundamental and substantial changes in behaviour that are required if we want to make a difference. New and unconventional interventions are needed to make these changes. Initiatives need to be taken at different levels. For instance, capitalizing on habit discontinuities, such as life-course changes, may form the basis of a new generation of interventions, which aim at specific target groups. Legislation and other large-scale measures which regulate behaviour directly should be considered whenever political support seems viable. Involving the public in decision-making about these broader changes will help improve the quality and acceptability of these decisions. Above all, if we acknowledge the urgency of the environmental problems that we and the next generations will be facing, it is clear that governments cannot afford to wait much longer, but have to act decisively and in concert with other social actors.

References

Aarts, H., Verplanken, B. and van Knippenberg, A. (1997) 'Habit and information use in travel mode choices', *Acta Psychologica*, vol 96, no 1, pp1–14

Aarts, H., Verplanken, B. and van Knippenberg, A. (1998) 'Predicting behavior from actions in the past: Repeated decision-making or a matter of habit?', *Journal of Applied Social Psychology*, vol 28, no 15, pp1355–1374

Ajzen, I. (1988) *Attitudes, Personality, and Behavior*, Open University Press, Milton Keynes

Ajzen, I. (2002) 'Residual effects of past on later behavior: Habituation and reasoned action perspectives', *Personality and Social Psychology Review*, vol 6, no 2, pp107–122

Ajzen, I. and Fishbein, M. (2005) 'The influence of attitudes on behavior', in D. Albarracín, B. T. Johnson and M. P. Zanna (eds) *The Handbook of Attitudes*, Erlbaum, Mahwah, NJ

Armitage, C. J. and Conner, M. (2001) 'Efficacy of the theory of planned behaviour: A meta-analytic review', *British Journal of Social Psychology*, vol 40, no 4, pp471–499

Bamberg, S. (2002) 'Implementation intention versus monetary incentive comparing the effects of interventions to promote the purchase of organically produced food', *Journal of Economic Psychology*, vol 23, no 5, pp573–587

Bamberg, S. (2006) 'Is a residential relocation a good opportunity to change people's travel behavior? Results from a theory-driven intervention study', *Environment and Behavior*, vol 38, no 6, pp820–840

Bamberg, S. and Schmidt, P. (2003) 'Incentives, morality, or habit? Predicting students' car use for university routes with the models of Ajzen, Schwartz, and Triandis', *Environment and Behavior*, vol 35, no 2, pp264–285

Bargh, J. A. (1994) 'The four horsemen of automaticity: Awareness, intention, efficiency, and control in social cognition', in R. S. Wyer and T. K. Srull (eds) *Handbook of Social Cognition*, Erlbaum, Mahwah, NJ

Bem, D. J. (1972) 'Self-perception theory', in L. Berkowitz (ed) *Advances in Experimental Social Psychology (vol 6)*, Academic Press, San Diego, CA

Black, J. S., Stern, P. C. and Elworth, J. T. (1985) 'Personal and contextual influences on household energy adaptations', *Journal of Applied Psychology*, vol 70, no 1, pp3–21

Brandon, G. and Lewis, A. (1999) 'Reducing household energy consumption: a qualitative and quantitative field study', *Journal of Environmental Psychology*, vol 19, no 1, pp75–85

Clark, C. F., Kotchen, M. J. and Moore, M. R. (2003) 'Internal and external influences on pro-environmental behavior: Participation in a green electricity program', *Journal of Environmental Psychology*, vol 23, no 3, pp237–246

Darnton, A. (2008) *GSR Behaviour change knowledge review. Practical guide: an overview of behaviour change models and their uses. Report for Government Social*

Research Unit, Centre for Sustainable Development, University of Westminster, London

Edwards, W. (1954) 'The theory of decision making', *Psychological Bulletin*, vol 51, no 4, pp380–417

Gollwitzer, P. M. and Sheeran, P. (2006) 'Implementation intentions and goal achievement: A meta-analysis of effects and processes', in M. P. Zanna (ed), *Advances in Experimental Social Psychology (vol 38)*, Elsevier Academic Press, San Diego, CA

Harland, P., Staats, H. and Wilke, H. A. M. (1999) 'Explaining proenvironmental intention and behavior by personal norms and the theory of planned behavior', *Journal of Applied Social Psychology*, vol 29, no 12, pp2505–2528

Holland, R. W., Aarts, H. and Langendam, D. (2006) 'Breaking and creating habits on the working floor: A field-experiment on the power of implementation intentions', *Journal of Experimental Social Psychology*, vol 42, no 6, pp776–783

Holland, R. W., Verplanken, B. and van Knippenberg, A. (2002) 'On the nature of attitude-behavior relations: The strong guide, the weak follow', *European Journal of Social Psychology*, vol 32, no 6, pp869–876

Kingdon, J. (1984) *Agendas, Alternatives, and Public Policies*, Little Brown, Boston

Lally, P., van Jaarsveld, C. H. M., Potts, H. W. W. and Wardle, J. (2009) 'How are habits formed: Modelling habit formation in the real world', *European Journal of Social Psychology*, in press

Lawson, P. J. and Flocke, S. A. (2009) 'Teachable moments for health behavior change: A concept analysis', *Patient Education and Counceling*, vol 76, no 1, pp25–30

Maibach, E. W., Roser-Renouf, C. and Leiserowitz, A. (2008) 'Communication and marketing as climate change intervention assets: A public health perspective', *American Journal of Preventive Medicine*, vol 35, no 5, pp488–500

Ockwell, D., Whitmarsh, L. and O'Neill, S. (2009) 'Reorienting climate change communication for effective mitigation – forcing people to be green or fostering grass-roots engagement?', *Science Communication*, vol 30, no 3, pp305–327

Olson, J. M. and Stone, J. (2005) 'The influence of behavior on attitudes', in D. Albarracín, B. T. Johnson and M. P. Zanna (eds) *The Handbook of Attitudes*, Erlbaum, Mahwah, NJ

Ouellette, J. A. and Wood, W. (1998) 'Habit and intention in everyday life: The multiple processes by which past behavior predicts future behavior', *Psychological Bulletin*, vol 124, no 1, pp54–74

Petty, R. E. and Krosnick, J. A. (eds) (1995) *Attitude Strength: Antecedents and Consequences*, Erlbaum, Hillsdale, NJ

Poortinga, W., Steg, L. and Vlek, C. (2004) 'Values, environmental concern, and environmental behavior: a study into household energy use', *Environment and Behavior*, vol 36, no 1, pp70–93

Schwartz, S. H. (1977) 'Normative influences on altruism', in L. Berkowitz (ed), *Advances in Experimental Social Psychology (vol 10)*, Academic Press, San Diego, CA

Sheeran, P. (2002) 'Intention-behavior relations: A conceptual and empirical review', in W. Stroebe and M. Hewstone (eds) *European Review of Social Psychology (vol 12)*, Psychology Press, New York

Sheeran, P., Orbell, S. and Trafimow, D. (1999) 'Does the temporal stability of behavioral intentions moderate intention-behavior and past behavior-future behavior relations?', *Personality and Social Psychology Bulletin*, vol 25, no 6, pp721–730

Stern, P. C. (2000) 'Toward a coherent theory of environmentally significant behavior', *Journal of Social Issues*, vol 56, no 3, pp407–424

Terry, D. J., Hogg, M. A. and White, K. M. (1999) 'The theory of planned behaviour: Self-identity, social identity and group norms', *British Journal of Social Psychology*, vol 38, no 3, pp225–244

Verplanken, B. (2006) 'Beyond frequency: Habit as mental construct', *British Journal of Social Psychology*, vol 45, no 3, pp639–656

Verplanken, B. and Weenig, M. W. H. (1993) 'Graphical energy labels and consumers' decisions on home appliances: A process tracing approach', *Journal of Economic Psychology*, vol 14, no 4, pp739–752

Verplanken, B. and Aarts, H. (1999) 'Habit, attitude, and planned behaviour: Is habit an empty construct or an interesting case of automaticity?', in W. Stroebe and M. Hewstone (eds) *European Review of Social Psychology (vol 10)*, Psychology Press, New York

Verplanken, B. and Holland, R. (2002) 'Motivated decision-making: Effects of activation and self-centrality of values on choices and behavior', *Journal of Personality and Social Psychology*, vol 82, no 3, pp434–447

Verplanken, B. and Orbell, S. (2003) 'Reflections on past behavior: A self-report index of habit strength', *Journal of Applied Social Psychology*, vol 33, no 6, pp1313–1330

Verplanken, B. and Wood, W. (2006) 'Interventions to break and create consumer habits', *Journal of Public Policy and Marketing*, vol 25, no 1, pp90–103

Verplanken, B., Aarts, H. and van Knippenberg, A. (1997) 'Habit, information acquisition, and the process of making travel mode choices', *European Journal of Social Psychology*, vol 27, no 5, pp539–560

Verplanken, B., Aarts, H., van Knippenberg, A. and Moonen, A. (1998) 'Habit versus planned behaviour: A field experiment', *British Journal of Social Psychology*, vol 37, no 1, pp111–128

Verplanken, B., Walker, I., Davis, A. and Jurasek, M. (2008) 'Context change and travel mode choice: Combing the habit discontinuity and self-activation hypotheses', *Journal of Environmental Psychology*, vol 28, no 2, pp121–127

Weenig, W. H. and Midden, C. J. H. (1997) 'Mass-media information campaigns and knowledge-gap effects', *Journal of Applied Social Psychology*, vol 27, no 11, pp945–959

Whitmarsh, L. (2009) 'Behavioural responses to climate change: Asymmetry of intentions and impacts', *Journal of Environmental Psychology*, vol 29, no 1, pp13–23

Wood, W. and Neal, D. T. (2007) 'A new look at habits and the habit-goal interface', *Psychological Review*, vol 114, no 4, pp843–863

Wood, W., Quinn, J. M. and Kashy, D. A. (2002) 'Habits in everyday life: Thought, emotion, and action', *Journal of Personality and Social Psychology*, vol 83, no 6, pp1281–1297

Wood, W., Tam, L. and Guerrero Witt, M. (2005) 'Changing circumstances, disrupting habits', *Journal of Personality and Social Psychology*, vol 88, no 6, pp918–933

2
Carbon Budgets and Carbon Capability: Lessons from Personal Carbon Trading

Irene Lorenzoni, Gill Seyfang and Michael Nye

1. Introduction

> *[Imagine] we carry bank cards that store both pounds and carbon points. When we buy electricity, gas and fuel, we use our carbon points, as well as pounds. To help reduce carbon emissions, the Government would set limits on the amount of carbon that could be used. (Miliband, 2006)*

Issuing tradable personal carbon dioxide (CO_2) emission rights (in the form of carbon credits) to citizens forms the basis of recent proposals to mitigate climate change at individual and societal levels. Proposals suggest that individuals would manage their emissions and could trade the emissions they have been allocated (hence 'personal carbon trading' – PCT). Capping emissions, it would enable year-on-year cuts in the national carbon budget. Although the technical and policy feasibility, legitimacy and acceptability (Starkey and Anderson, 2005; Roberts and Thumim, 2006; RSA, 2007a) of such proposals have been explored, there are few studies on the behavioural (both economic and psychological) aspects of PCT (Capstick and Lewis, 2008), as well as completed trials on the practicalities of implementing such proposals (Fawcett et al, 2007; Bird and Lockwood, 2009).

Thus public responses to PCT remain understudied. This chapter critically examines how psychological and financial aspects of individual and social decision making might affect the implementation of PCT. Conceptually it aims to provide an overview of knowledge in these areas, identifies the gaps in current thinking, and problematizes some of the implicit assumptions underlying the proposals. We first discuss the origins and development of PCT ideas, identifying key players and proponents, and the scientific, political and economic contexts of their development. We then draw lessons from related areas of experience (carbon markets, Carbon Rationing Action Groups and complementary currencies) to examine likely success factors, and inform future policy and implementation of PCT. From this discussion, critical issues emerge, which straddle political, social, economic, environmental, cultural and ethical domains, and which demand greater attention. We conclude with initial thoughts for a research agenda and critical implications for climate change policy.

2. Personal carbon trading: scientific and political origins

The origins of allocation of personal emission rights stem from discussions on progressively stricter national carbon budgets, as a plausible method of achieving large-scale cuts in global greenhouse gas emissions through a Contraction and Convergence (C&C) framework (Meyer, 2000). Under such a scheme, intended to redistribute responsibility for climate change mitigation equitably worldwide, emission rights assigned to countries on a per capita basis would converge over time ('contraction'), eventually resulting in globally equal per capita emissions ('convergence').

UK mitigation policy is partly based on C&C (RCEP, 2000). Exploring its implementation at the subnational level, models were developed proposing mandatory allocations and trading of emissions permits: personal carbon allowances – PCAs (Hillman, 2004; Hillman and Fawcett, 2005); fuel quotas, which evolved into domestic tradable quotas (DTQs) and more recently tradable energy quotas (Fleming 1996, 2005; see also Starkey and Anderson, 2005). All are aimed at reducing and stabilizing anthropogenic CO_2 emissions at some scientifically established policy target level. Although there are some striking differences between specific proposals (e.g. DTQs encompass all carbon emissions within the national economy covering all end-users purchasing fossil fuel energy; PCAs only deal with individual CO_2 emissions[1]), in this chapter we refer generically to 'personal carbon trading' (PCT), by which we mean both the allocation of DTQs to individuals and PCA schemes, and any variants of these which relate to compulsory issuing of carbon emission[2] rights to individuals.

Interest in PCT started permeating UK high-level politics following a Private Member's Bill on establishing a domestic trading system for carbon dioxide emissions (Challen, 2004). Subsequently, PCT was publicly discussed by the then Secretary of State for Environment, Food and Rural Affairs, David Miliband, in 2006, who called for a 'thought experiment' on the idea, effectively hoping to test the effectiveness of these concepts against other proposals, spurred by the need for effective public engagement in mitigation through behavioural change. In this context, PCT was seen as having 'great potential as a policy tool' (EAC, 2008a, p5). Interest waned with personality reshuffles (Hilary Benn took over from David Miliband in 2007); Defra's pre-feasibility study (2008) conclusions on PCT (high implementation costs, burden on the vulnerable, concerns about public acceptability) froze further governmental considerations of this option. An EAC inquiry into PCT (2008b) expressed disappointment in the government's lack of interest, and argued that political and public acceptability should be explored further.

Outside government, PCT attracts much attention. It is a feature of the UK Green Party's climate change policy. A radical strategy identified PCT as the sole option for eliminating Britain's carbon emissions by 2027 (CAT, 2007). Bottom-up interest prompted an e-petition urging the UK government to adopt PCT (PM, 2007). PCT increasingly features in business reports (e.g. AccountAbility and Consumers International, 2007), and there are several initiatives assessing the advantages and disadvantages of PCT in comparison to other mitigation options at the individual level (e.g. IPPR in Bird and Lockwood, 2009; see Seyfang et al, 2009 for more details).

3. Rationales and assumptions of personal carbon trading

PCT is based on three key elements: setting the national carbon budget, distributing individual allowances and surrendering allowances (Fleming, 1996). Both PCA and DTQ models propose that carbon credits might be spent alongside money when purchasing fuel or energy, either explicitly (surrendering carbon units when paying bills) or implicitly (carbon costs being incorporated into petrol pump prices). Allowances will be tradable, and high-energy users will need to purchase additional carbon credits, while low-energy users will be able to sell their surplus credits for profit; each year the overall budget will be reduced. Embodied carbon in goods and particularly imports are outside the scope of PCT, as this deals only with direct energy use within the UK. Proposals also vary in details such as the precise coverage of allocations (e.g. public transport) and how children are treated (e.g. no allowance for children, or a half-allowance).

The claimed benefits of PCT over traditional policy measures of information, regulation and taxation can be summarized as fourfold:

- it is an efficient market mechanism, allowing individuals to respond to the carbon price signals flexibly (unlike regulation);
- it is effective, offering the certainty of a predetermined emissions limit (unlike taxation);
- it is equitable, as low-income households tend to be low-energy users, and would benefit financially from selling their surplus credits, whereas high-income households are more able to afford the extra cost of purchasing additional carbon credits;
- it is empowering, generating 'common purpose' and active citizenship, encouraging individuals to actively engage with and contribute towards climate change mitigation (in contrast to taxation which can provoke resentment, as seen with fuel protests prompted by the UK fuel tax escalator) (Fleming, 2005; Starkey and Anderson, 2005).

The assumption is that long-run carbon budgets allow individuals to plan for future restrictions in carbon allowances, creating an incentive system encouraging adaptation towards a low-carbon economy, rewarding those who adapt early in switching to low-carbon energy sources, and reducing energy demand through conservation and efficiency measures.

Despite the claims for the behavioural outcomes underpinning the potential viability of PCT, these have been only marginally examined (see Capstick and Lewis, 2008), validating Roberts and Thumim's assertion (2006, p3): 'the differences between the schemes appear to be less important at this stage than the largely untested assumptions shared by them all about public response and political feasibility'. The aim of this chapter is therefore to highlight the lessons from economics and psychology that could be applied to PCT.

Our work indicates that fundamentally the principles of PCT draw on assumptions from neo-classical economic theory about markets and consumer rationality.[3] The basic premise is that market mechanisms and prices offer a more efficient and lower-cost alternative to emissions *regulation* or 'command and control' of quantities. Under a 'cap and trade' system, scarce allowances become valuable commodities, and a carbon market equalizes the maximum marginal abatement (emissions reduction) cost of meeting targets for all participants, whilst offering added options for compliance (Joskow et al, 1998). The cost effectiveness of PCT hinges on the *option* to use the market should the marginal cost of abatement prove higher than the cost of an allowance (a participant need never trade to benefit from the increased efficiency of an emissions market over mandated standards). Ideally, carbon abatement or purchasing decisions respond to the market price for carbon, and participants behave in a utility-maximizing manner, choosing the most cost-effective method of compliance. Although Fleming (2005) espouses a 'common purpose' as an intended *end* of PCT, the day-to-day *practice* of carbon trading necessarily represents an exercise in cost-minimization. He argues there is 'a shared incentive to reduce our dependence on oil, gas and coal ... because the price I have to pay for units is affected by your demand' (2005, p19), presupposing considerable faith in neo-classical economic rationality on the part of consumers. However, it may be imprudent to assume (at least so hastily) that a market-based *policy instrument* would function in the same efficient manner as a model 'free market', or that participants in the former would and could behave as *homo economicus*, with the knowledge and skills to maximize their utility in a carbon market (Nye, 2008). This is a key issue to which we return below.

4. Learning from related experiences: what do we already know?

Given that existing knowledge of PCT is based largely on theoretical models rather than empirical evidence, we argue that an examination of lived experience will highlight issues important to understanding of PCT. We consider three areas where key facets of PCT have already been implemented through different initiatives, and draw transferable theoretical and practical lessons for PCT.

Experience with existing emissions trading schemes
Research on carbon trading in other contexts provides important insights into how participants might behave in a carbon market, and how this market might practically operate. One of the most studied, the UK Emissions Trading

Scheme (the first ever economy-wide emissions trading scheme, which ran from 2002 to 2006), was heavily criticized because the voluntary, incentive-based scheme designed to reduce CO_2 emissions from key industries attracted fairly undemanding targets (NAO, 2004), which required little, if any, operational commitment from participants (Roeser and Jackson, 2003). Similarly, Phase 1 of the current cap-and-trade EU Emissions Trading Scheme (into which the UK ETS was subsumed), has delivered little emissions-reduction because the initial national allocations are too accommodating (Ecofys, 2004; Betz et al, 2006), largely due to a lack of good quality data for estimating emissions levels, and for creating accurate and robust national allocation plans (e.g. Ellerman and Buchner, 2007).

These findings raise two important considerations for the design and successful functioning of a PCT scheme. Firstly, an efficient emissions market relies on a fairly delicate chain of well-informed, neo-classically rational users making correct market decisions in a relatively liquid market, driven by sufficient demand for permits (dependent on a sufficiently tight cap and allocation). Ideally, this chain would be supported by a series of procedural conditions, including 'perfect competition ... absence of market power and perfect enforcement in the case of non-compliance' (Woerdman, 2001, p295). Secondly, markets take time to develop, and significant transaction costs can arise, particularly in early years, around establishing these effective administrative structures and procedural conditions. Participants may be 'irrationally' reluctant to utilize the trading mechanism for compliance, or may lack the skills and knowledge to use the market's price signals strategically when making emissions-reduction decisions (Nye, 2008). It is reasonable to assume that planning and organizing carbon budgets will take significant time, especially in the early years, which could decrease the cost effectiveness of the system compared to other, more familiar market instruments like taxation. Other transaction costs observed in emissions trading schemes include costs for the negotiation of trades, approval and regulatory costs, external risk monitoring charges, and 'ex-ante' costs associated with designing and implementing a controversial instrument amongst a political field of competing interests (see Woerdman, 2001).

Experience with voluntary carbon rationing action groups

Carbon Rationing Action Groups (CRAGs) are community-based organizations whose members ('Craggers') agree to reduce their carbon emissions using a simple measuring system, and by increasing personal knowledge in an encouraging and supportive social context. There are over 30 groups across the UK, and the idea has spread to the USA and Canada (CRAGs, 2007). The members of each CRAG decide on a CO_2 target per person at the beginning of a 'carbon year' and the price per kg of carbon (usually in excess of current EU ETS prices, as CRAGs aim to make climate change mitigation directly tangible for individuals).[4] Each Cragger records their personal carbon emissions from air and car travel, plus home energy use (electricity and heating), using the same metrics, aided sometimes by 'carbon accountants'. At regular intervals, members share their results with others in the group, and at year-end, members exceeding their personal target pay a financial penalty for non-compliance (i.e. price per kg of emissions above target). Generally, penalty monies are paid into a bank account and then redistributed to Craggers who saved carbon. No specific criteria exist to measure CRAG success, but key factors are: social support, simple joining instructions and easy carbon accountability (Shrubsole, 2007a).

CRAGs aim to make individuals more aware of their carbon emissions, and build community cohesion and support amongst like-minded individuals (CRAGs, 2007). The latter goal includes both encouraging others to remain committed to a low-carbon lifestyle and sharing knowledge about how to do so. Shrubsole (personal communication, 2007) explains: 'You feel encouraged that others are doing this too; individual actions are less isolated and seemingly pointless. You also feel a little pressurized to meet your target.' Social diffusion of both practical knowledge and commitment to action could prove to be particularly strong drivers for behaviour change and emissions-reduction. Studies of other environmentally significant practices (notably recycling) indicate that pro-environmental behaviour is encouraged by making public commitments and pledges (e.g. Oskamp et al, 1991), and where communities have strong pro-environmental norms (Hopper and Nielsen, 1991).

CRAGs can be considered the first experimental field trial of some aspects of PCT, albeit in a very confined and limited voluntary 'market', giving people the experience of working with others towards personal emissions-measuring, targets and reduction. Most Craggers support the idea of nationwide PCT. The CRAG system is essentially a pricing instrument: the financial penalty is set iteratively, and there is neither an absolute cap on overall emissions nor a market (potentially all Craggers could be in credit, having saved emissions) (Shrubsole, personal communication, 2007). The mechanisms of CRAGs are dissimilar to a cap-and-trade system like PCT. Nevertheless, there are important elements of overlap between the two schemes, particularly carbon awareness and capability for individuals and communities, and building a sense of 'common purpose' and mutual support. This element of support is significant: for domestic households, options for emissions reduction are often determined by surrounding infrastructure and systems of provision. Individuals can only do what local transport systems, living arrangements or energy infrastructures allow them to do (Van Vliet et al, 2005). Accordingly, locally relevant knowledge about how to achieve emissions reductions in specific places and spaces is necessary for the smooth operation of PCT (or any market-based instrument for carbon reduction). Without this, individuals face a severely reduced set of generalized and fairly unattractive emissions reduction options based on curtailment. This places greater responsibility on community leaders to disseminate practical and locally relevant knowledge for change in an accessible format and context.

Experience with complementary currencies

Complementary currencies (CCs) are new systems of exchange which operate alongside conventional money, and have been rapidly growing in number since the 1990s in developed and developing countries. They include mainstream commercial schemes (air miles, supermarket loyalty points), and community-based initiatives for economic development, social justice and environmental protection (Local Exchange Trading Schemes (LETS), Time Banks) (Seyfang, 2006; DeMeulenaere, 2007). The rationale for CCs is that 'money' is a socially constructed institution which promotes particular behaviours. Mainstream money (as a means of exchange within current market economies) is not a value-free, neutral technology: it has characteristics which incentivize unsustainability. It values some types of labour and not others; it values scarcity (encouraging exploitation of abundant goods such as ecosystem services), promotes competition and externalizes certain costs. In contrast, CCs are specifically designed to overcome these problems and incentivize sustainable development; for example, by internalizing environmental costs or valuing non-marketed labour (Lietaer, 2001; Boyle, 2002).

Economists traditionally define money according to its functions: as a means of exchange, a unit of account and a store of value (Lipsey and Chrystal, 2007), although money need not serve all these (potentially conflicting) functions in one form (Boyle, 2002). PCT, with its 'carbon budgets', 'carbon points' and 'carbon credit cards', is proposing a new carbon currency, to be budgeted and spent alongside money. It operates as a medium of exchange (permits are surrendered in exchange for the CO_2 emissions associated with purchased goods and services – petrol, electricity, heating oil, flights, etc.). It is a unit of account (representing permission to emit a standard unit of CO_2), but it is not a store of value (permits expire after a certain time). Although carbon credits can be exchanged for money, they are nevertheless spendable in their own right and can be considered a 'limited purpose' or 'special money', with particular distinguishing socio-technical meanings which will influence its use (Dodd, 1994; Zelizer, 1994). Indeed, internalizing carbon emissions into decision making, and making them tangible, requires that consumers begin to count the carbon cost of their actions. Carbon allowances would be conceptualized and used ('spent' and 'saved') much as other virtual currencies (e.g. air miles) are at present, and it is useful to see PCT in this light to consider how public experience with using CCs offers lessons for PCT, despite vastly different scope, scale and development. Capstick and Lewis (2008) have suggested that the promotion of carbon as a currency could engender positive perceptions of PCT as a mechanism imbued with social and environmental connotations, leading to the expression of such values, and even foster a carbon moral economy.

A comparative analysis of a diverse range of CCs with social, economic and environmental objectives by Seyfang (2007) reveals five critical success factors for CC development, which are likely to be of central importance to the successful adoption and effectiveness of PCT. First, a supportive policy context is essential for ensuring top-down support and resources, but lack of 'joined-up thinking' can result in policy barriers. For example, CCs tackling social exclusion are hampered by welfare benefit regulations preventing the most disadvantaged groups from participating. Second, CCs require supportive social contexts, either small groups with high personal contact (Time Banks) or larger city-wide systems with a conducive culture (Dutch green reward points). Third, CCs must use easily comprehensible, credible and convenient mechanisms to be widely adopted and successfully utilized; the Dutch system successfully utilizes familiar smart-card technology. Fourth, the skills and capabilities of participants are critical to CC success, particularly when dealing with new and unfamiliar units of value such as time. Finally, CCs succeed best when they harness collective 'active citizenship' energy and values, empowering users to co-create new social institutions.

5. Discussion: carbon capability

Building on our initial analysis of the assumptions underpinning PCT proposals, and drawing evidence from our three related areas of experience above, this section examines critical issues around the theory and potential practice of PCT (including its links to wider societal responses to climate change), which we argue have not previously been adequately researched.

The preceding section discussed how PCT is akin to introducing a new carbon currency; here we extend the analogy and consider how consumers need to be as skilled in managing carbon as they are with money. Indeed, there are the same driving forces and comparable consumer issues with both, requiring a holistic approach to learning about sustainable consumption in both financial and resource terms. Excessive material consumption in developed countries is widely acknowledged as a principal cause of unsustainable development: if the whole world consumed at the rate of North Americans, we would need five Earths to supply the resources (Simms, 2006). Yet beyond basic necessities, this growth in consumption is not matched by increases in well-being or happiness (Max-Neef, 1995) – what Jackson (2007) terms the 'well-being paradox'. Several explanations have been put forward for this, ranging from psychological and social theories about using consumption to meet non-material needs for status, display, distinction and the importance of relative rather than absolute wealth (Ropke, 1999; Jackson 2007; see also Chapter 5) to structural theories about the capitalist economy's need for continual expansion (Daly, 1992). In all cases, an outcome is rising consumption (threatening ecosystem viability) and increasing consumer spending (financed by borrowing) and over-indebtedness, representing in itself a profound cultural shift from 'thrift ethic' to 'consumption ethic' over the last couple of generations (Dixon, 2006, p1).

This 'credit culture', fuelled by social pressure to consume and enabled by deregulation and technological changes in financial institutions, is doubtless responsible for developed nations' recent period of economic growth (Cohen, 2007). The sheer intangibility of credit finance compared with cash has also contributed to its widespread acceptance (although recently cash has made a comeback as a visible way of controlling spending; BRC, 2008), bringing attendant social problems. In the UK, almost one in ten households finds its repayments a 'heavy burden', and during 2006–7 there was an increase in households with mortgage arrears, house repossessions, credit card arrears and personal insolvencies (BERR et al, 2007); and of course the global financial crisis has demonstrated the precariousness of this economic model for growth and the vulnerability with which it leaves individual consumers. Given the state's reliance upon this economic development model, government's response has been to emphasize individuals' responsibility to successfully navigate perilous financial markets, and to promote 'financial capability' (implying both actions and knowledge) as a basic skill required for financial inclusion. Binkley (2006) describes this as a 'governmentality' model, whereby a deregulated economy is governed not by government, but rather by individual producers and consumers' self-restraint and competencies. In the intensifying consumer realm, 'it is increasingly imperative that one knows how to expose oneself to seductions without surrendering to them entirely'; that is, deal with the pathology of shopaholism (Binkley, 2006, p345). Managing material consumption, and managing carbon emissions, raise some similar issues.

Carbon emissions persist as an abstracted concept, intangible and unfamiliar to the consumer. Consequently, new skills and capabilities are required to engage with this new commodity and understand its full ramifications. How is this need addressed in the PCT literature? While the major PCT writers acknowledge that awareness-raising campaigns will be needed to ensure public acceptance of PCT, they nevertheless claim that 'understanding [PCT] is not a prerequisite for using it' (Starkey and Anderson, 2005, p30). The presumption appears to be that introducing the carbon trading system will be sufficient to redirect (rational, utilitarian) consumer decision making towards low-carbon behaviour. Consumers could legitimately sell their allowances immediately and 'pay as they go', without directly engaging in carbon budgeting at all – albeit paying more for the privilege (Fleming, 2005). However, previous experience with both CCs and the ETS demonstrates that participants' skills, capabilities and confidence in the new carbon trading system are crucial to its success. Capstick and Lewis (2008) discuss the potential of combining PCT with other feedback mechanisms (such as smart metering) and psychological processes (such as goal setting) to increase the visibility of carbon in relation to behavioural responses, thus explicitly promoting an understanding at the individual level of the effects of particular behaviours, resulting in further positive action.

Using PCT may be a technically trivial matter, almost invisible in everyday transactions, but we argue that it will be *socially non-trivial* as the issue of genuinely understanding and managing carbon budgets is an unacknowledged and undeveloped competency. The challenge is therefore to identify the range of skills required for PCT to achieve its objectives of inducing behaviour change towards carbon reduction. We term this 'carbon capability' as an analogue of financial capability (see Whitmarsh et al, 2009).

Financial capability can be defined as 'the ability to make informed judgements and to take effective decisions regarding the use and management of money' (National Foundation for Educational Research; quoted in AdFLAG, 2000, para 4.2). A recent study established indicators of financial capability and conducted a UK baseline survey. It covered four key areas of attitudes and practice: managing money, planning ahead, choosing products and staying informed (Atkinson et al, 2007). It found that although most people in the UK are competent at 'making ends meet', almost half are unable or unwilling to plan for the future, and there is 'wide variation' in the degree to which people stay informed about things which are likely to affect their finances (Atkinson et al, 2007, p33). Translating these concepts and techniques into carbon management, 'carbon capability' therefore refers to technical, material and social aspects of knowledge, understanding and practice.

Carbon capability implies having a good grasp of the causes and consequences of carbon emissions, the role individuals play in producing them, the scope for adaptation and emissions reductions in one's personal life and what is possible through collective action, how to manage a carbon budget, where to get help and information, and so on (Roberts and Thumim, 2006, come to similar conclusions). Examination of the behavioural economic and psychological dimensions of managing carbon suggests that practices resulting from PCT could be contradictory (Capstick and Lewis, 2008, 2009). More specifically, if carbon allowances[5] are allocated initially at no cost (i.e. free) to individuals by government, people may consider them of lower value than other types of income (in accordance with mental accounting theories). This could result in some wastefulness of allowances; until, that is, the personal allowance limit is reached, and extra allowances have to be purchased at a cost. On the other hand, people tend to value more highly items they possess (endowment effect), which may spur individuals to retain their own carbon allowances; budgeting and committing to a certain outcome or action (as learnt from financial capability research; Dixon, 2006) have been shown to motivate people to actualize some of their intended behaviours, which could – in this context – translate into carbon reduction in the long term. These would, however, need to be balanced against existing (and often entrenched or habitualized) individual and social norms, usually difficult to supplant (see Chapter 1). It is also possible that new individual behaviours and social norms may arise as a consequence of carbon trading. As the psychology and financial literature reiterate, attitudes and motivations do not necessarily result in corresponding behaviours. PCT might generate a perverse social acceptability of carbon debt and borrowing, marginalizing the effect of individual mitigation, especially if procedural fairness is not inbuilt and the PCT model is perceived as imposed 'from above' (Capstick and Lewis, 2008; Bird and Lockwood, 2009).

Initiatives currently working to develop carbon capability include the RSA's Carbon DAQ voluntary online (virtual) carbon market (RSA, 2007b) and the CRAGs discussed above: 'like offsets and carbon labels, they are another way of improving popular "carbon literacy"' (Shrubsole, personal communication, 2007). Further evidence of this vital cultural shift is appearing as the concept of 'carbon footprints' has become widespread (Siegel, 2007). More broadly, a new vocabulary is developing in which carbon is made meaningful through linguistic links to concepts of lifestyle and morality (e.g. 'carbon diet', 'carbon indulgence'; Nerlich and Koteyko, 2009). In practical terms, using PCT will introduce new technologies, procedures and demands on people, but little research has been undertaken on how people may interact and respond to these. A preliminary computer simulation of PCA, based in part on carbon footprints (Capstick and Lewis, 2009), suggests that simplified communication and products (in line with findings on financial capability; Dixon,

2006) are attractive to people. It also indicates that declared carbon reducing behaviours are inversely related to the size of an individual's footprint (i.e. those with the largest carbon emissions are inclined to cut them the least), whereas pro-environmental outlooks seem to link with increased carbon conservation. This is consistent with the broader literature which shows environmental concern tends to be higher amongst more affluent groups, but that income also positively correlates with energy consumption (e.g. Poortinga et al, 2004). Invariably, more research is needed on the components of carbon capability and the further skills required to use PCT effectively.

Another little-researched social aspect of carbon capability relates to the redistribution of carbon allowances within the household. This raises a range of issues including gender relations, relative economic advantage and fuel poverty. Although mainstream economic theory tends to treat the household as a single unit or 'black box', there is evidence (particularly from work in development studies and feminist economics) that pooled resources are not necessarily shared or distributed equally or equitably amongst family members (Folbre, 1986). Household or family members rarely have fully aggregated or solidly altruistic preferences. For instance, men and women tend to prioritize the spending of earned income in very different ways, mentally earmarking men's income and women's income for different purposes, even to the point of them being almost separate currencies (Zelizer, 1994; Phipps and Burton, 1998; Pahl, 2000). Women tend to be more altruistic and egalitarian in their intra-household resource distribution (Folbre, 1986; Doss, 1996), but have less bargaining power over resources (Doss, 1996; Agarwal, 1997).

The internal redistribution of valuable carbon allowances within households, and differentiated prioritization of the surrender or purchase of allowances, could have a tremendous impact on the overall efficacy of a PCT scheme, by disrupting the efficient use of market signals to direct behaviour. It also impacts on a household's quality of life – for example, choosing to fuel a private car at the expense of a warm home – especially for lower-income householders who would struggle to purchase extra allowances at premium rates to compensate for the possible selfish behaviour of other household members. A number of key questions remain unanswered: How will individuals allocated carbon allowances negotiate with others? How will living with carbon quotas shape consumption, lifestyles and relationships?

Referring back to the more general analysis of consumption behaviour, carbon capability must retain a focus on helping people to resist – and create alternatives to – broad social pressures to increase consumption in order to effectively manage carbon budgets, taking into account the vagaries and differences between moral economies of households.

6. Conclusions

We have examined proposals for PCT, and sought to unravel some of their assumptions and rationales, in order to fully explore the potential usefulness of PCT as a climate change mitigation policy in the UK. We identified PCT as a market instrument emerging from a neo-classical economic perspective (although its proponents might not agree with the political implications of their economic model), albeit one which has yet to be implemented or fully trialled. Turning, therefore, to existing initiatives which offer related experience in partial aspects of PCT (other emissions trading schemes, voluntary carbon rationing groups and complementary currencies), we sought transferable lessons for PCT, and indications of the critical issues to be addressed before a fully functional PCT scheme could be rolled out in the UK.

Overall, we conclude that for PCT to be implemented, more research is needed into the wider set of factors which influence individual and societal choice, decision making and behaviour, and which would therefore impact on the functionality (efficiency, equity and effectiveness) of a PCT scheme and its public acceptability. Specifically we highlight issues of units of measurement, distributive justice within society and households, skills required to 'manage' carbon budgets, and the role, responsibilities and duties of individuals as citizens. We argue these critical areas are currently underdeveloped in PCT thinking, and we recommend they become priorities for future PCT research in order to more fully understand the potential of this policy proposal.

The flourishing of small-scale bottom-up initiatives based on environmentally balanced community living, including in some cases moving towards a decarbonized UK economy, indicates that there is interest in citizenly activities for sustainable development. Reflecting upon CRAGs, Shrubsole concludes: 'I think they have begun to demonstrate that a new form of environmental citizenship is needed to address climate change ... In order to take behaviour change to a new level ... we need new social inventions. CRAGs may point the way to this – or they may prove to be too demanding of members to be that popular.' Here he touches upon a key question for PCT: is it achievable?

The notion of a 'common purpose' might not suffice in today's society as a strong enough motivation for UK citizens to enact their personal responsibility towards current and future generations by supporting PCT. Our consumerist culture rewards individualism and personal spending as a means of gratification; climate change is near enough to cause concern, but far enough away to not warrant immediate individual action. Nevertheless, despite our reservations about the current willingness of either politicians or publics to implement more radical measures to reduce domestic CO_2 emissions, we do support the concept of PCT as a means of making our contributions to climate change tangible, and of exploring how to manage energy demand equitably and efficiently. We feel that the potential of PCT deserves further empirical and applied exploration, alongside other possibilities for individual and community carbon reduction, especially given the likely need for means other than policy, regulation and taxation, to implement the UK's ambitious mitigation targets.

Acknowledgements

The authors would like to thank Guy Shrubsole for his insightful comments on the CRAGs experience, and Jacquie Burgess and Lorraine Whitmarsh for helpful comments on an earlier version of this paper.

Notes

1   The PCT literature rather myopically focuses on CO_2, which raises practical considerations about meaningful mitigation considering the impact of a variety of other greenhouse gases.
2   Although scientifically incorrect, carbon dioxide emissions in the context of personal allowances and trading are often referred to in the literature as simply 'carbon emissions'.
3   We recognize that PCT advocates do not necessarily endorse a neo-classical economic perspective, but the PCT model is a market mechanism reliant upon utilitarian principles.
4   In multi-person households, CRAGs suggest that individuals bear proportional responsibility for the household's emissions, but have to solely account for all emissions from any mode of transport they own (CRAGs, 2007).
5   Although PCT is often accurately referred to as 'rationing' (e.g. Hillman and Fawcett, 2005; CRAGs, 2007), this framing is avoided for its negative connotations of wartime scarcity, curtailment of personal freedom and government control. Alternatives such as 'allowances', 'quota' or 'entitlement' are generally preferred (e.g. Capstick and Lewis, 2008; Bird and Lockwood, 2009).

References

AccountAbility and Consumers International (2007) *What Assures Consumers on Climate Change? Switching on Citizen Power*, Belmont Press, Northampton

AdFLAG (2000) Adult Financial Literacy Group Report to the Secretary of State for Education and Employment, Department for Education and Skills, London

Agarwal, B. (1997) 'Bargaining and gender relations: Within and beyond the household', *Feminist Economics*, vol 3, no 1, pp1–51

Atkinson, A., McKay, S., Collard, S. and Kempson, E. (2007) 'Levels of financial capability in the UK', *Public Money and Management*, vol 27, no 1, pp29–36

Betz, R., Rogge, K. and Schleich, J. (2006) 'EU emissions trading: an early analysis of national allocation plans for 2008–2012', *Climate Policy*, vol 6, pp361–394

Binkley, S. (2006) 'The perilous freedoms of consumption: Toward a theory of the conduct of consumer conduct', *Journal for Cultural Research*, vol 10, no 4, pp 343–362

Bird, J. and Lockwood, M. (2009) *Plan B? The Prospects for Personal Carbon Trading*, IPPR, London

Boyle, D. (ed) (2002) *The Money Changers: Currency Reform From Aristotle To E-Cash*, Earthscan, London

British Retail Consortium (BRC) (2008) 'Tough times prompt cash comeback', www.brc.org.uk/details04.asp?id=1360, accessed 20 November 2009

Capstick, S. and Lewis, A. (2008) *Personal Carbon Trading: Perspectives from Psychology and Behavioural Economics*, IPPR, London

Capstick, S. and Lewis, A. (2009) *Personal Carbon Allowances: A Pilot Simulation and Questionnaire*, UKERC, Oxford

Carbon Action Rationing Groups (CRAGs) (2007) 'Carbon Rationing Action Groups: A short guide', www.carbonrationing.org.uk/wiki/crags-a-short-guide?, accessed 20 November 2009

Centre for Alternative Technology (CAT) (2007) *Zero Carbon Britain. An Alternative Energy Strategy*, CAT, Wales

Challen, C. (2004) 'New bill on climate change introduced', www.colinchallen.org.uk/record.jsp?ID=18&type=article, accessed 20 November 2009 and also in Hansard (2004), vol 423, col 81 (7 July 2004).

Cohen, M. J. (2007) 'Consumer credit, household financial management, and sustainable consumption', *International Journal of Consumer Studies*, vol 31, pp57–65

Daly, H. (1992) *Steady State Economics*, Earthscan, London

DeMeulenaere, S. (2007) 2006 Annual Report of the Worldwide Database Of Complementary Currency Systems, *International Journal of Community Currency Research, 11*, www.uea.ac.uk/env/ijccr/, accessed 22 April 2008

Department for the Environment, Food and Rural Affairs (Defra) (2008) *Synthesis report on the findings from Defra's pre-feasibility study into personal carbon trading*, Defra, London

Department for Business, Enterprise and Regulatory Reform, Department for Work and Pensions, Ministry of Justice (BERR, DWP and MoJ) (2007) *Tackling Over-indebtedness*, BERR, London

Dixon, M. (2006) *Rethinking Financial Capability: Lessons from Economic Psychology and Behavioural Finance*, IPPR, London

Dodd, N. (1994) *The Sociology of Money: Economics, Reason and Contemporary Society*, Polity, Cambridge

Doss, C. (1996) 'Testing among models of intrahousehold resource allocation', *World Development*, vol 24, no 10, pp1597–1609

Ecofys (2004) *Analysis of the National Allocation Plans for the EU ETS*, Ecofys, London

Ellerman, D. and Buchner, B. (2007) 'The European Union Emissions Trading Scheme: Origins, allocation, and early results', *Review of Environmental Economics and Policy*, vol 1, no 1, pp66–87

Environmental Audit Committee (EAC) (2008a) *Personal Carbon Trading. Fifth Report of Session 2007-08*, The Stationery Office Ltd, London

Environmental Audit Committee (EAC) (2008b) *Personal Carbon Trading: Government Response to the Committee's Fifth Report of Session 2007–08. Seventh Special Report of Session 2007–08*, The Stationery Office Ltd, London

Fawcett, T. (2005) *Personal Carbon Allowances*, ECI, Oxford

Fawcett, T., Bottrill, C., Boardman, B. and Lye, G. (2007) *Trialling Personal Carbon Allowances*, UKERC, Oxford

Fleming, D. (1996) 'Stopping the Traffic', *Country Life*, vol 140, no 19, pp62–65

Fleming, D. (2005) *Energy and the Common Purpose: Descending the Energy Staircase with Tradable Energy Quotas (TEQs)*, The Lean Economy Connection, London

Folbre, N. (1986) 'Hearts and spades: Paradigms of household economics', *World Development*, vol 14, no 2, pp245–255

Hillman, M. (2004) *How we can Save the Planet*, Penguin, London

Hillman, M. and Fawcett, T. (eds) (2005) *Living in a low carbon world: the policy implications of rationing. Meeting report DR1*, UKERC and PSI, Oxford

Hopper, J. R. and Nielsen, J. M. (1991) 'Recycling as altruistic behavior: normative and behavioral strategies to expand participation in a community recycling program', *Environment and Behavior*, vol 23, no 2, pp195–220

Jackson, T. (2007) 'Consuming paradise? Towards a social and cultural psychology of sustainable consumption', in T. Jackson (ed) *The Earthscan Reader In Sustainable Consumption*, Earthscan, London

Joskow, P., Schmalensee, R. and Bailey, E. (1998) 'The market for sulfur dioxide emissions', *The American Economic Review*, vol 88, no 4, pp669–685

Lietaer, B. (2001) *The Future Of Money: Creating New Wealth, Work and a Wiser World*, Century, London

Lipsey, R. and Chrystal, K. (2007) *Economics*, Oxford University Press, Oxford

Max-Neef, M. (1995) 'Economic growth and quality of life: a threshold hypothesis', *Ecological Economics*, vol 15, no 2, pp115–118

Meyer, A. (2000) *Contraction & Convergence. The Global Solution to Climate Change*, Green Books, Totnes

Miliband, D. (2006) 'The great stink: towards an environmental contract'. Speech at the Audit Commission annual lecture, Wednesday 19 July 2006, www.defra. gov.uk/corporate/ministers/speeches/david-miliband/dm060719.htm, accessed 20 July 2007

National Audit Office (NAO) (2004) *The UK Emissions Trading Scheme – A New Way to Combat Global Climate Change*, NAO, London

Nerlich, B. and Koteyko, N. (2009) 'Compounds, creativity and complexity in climate change communication: The case of "carbon indulgences"', *Global Environmental Change*, vol 19, no 3, pp345–353

Nye, M. (2008) 'Understanding business participation in UK emissions trading: Dimensions of choice and influences on market development', in R. Antes, B. Hansjürgens and P. Letmathe (eds) *Emissions Trading: Institutional Design, Decision Making and Corporate Strategies*, Springer, New York

Oskamp, S., Harrington, M., Edwards, T., Sherwood, D., Okuda, S. and Swanson, D. (1991) 'Factors influencing household recycling behavior', *Environment and Behavior*, vol 23, no 4, pp494–519

Pahl, J. (2000) 'The gendering of spending within households', *Radical Statistics*, vol 75, pp38–48

Phipps, S. and Burton, P. (1998) 'What's mine is yours? The influence of male and female incomes on patterns of household expenditure', *Economica*, vol 65, no 260, pp599–613

Poortinga, W., Steg, L. and Vlek, C. (2004) 'Values, environmental concerns and environmental behaviour: A study into household energy use', *Environment and Behavior*, vol 36, pp70–93

Prime Minister's Office (PM) (2007) 'Carbon rationing. E-Petition reply', www.pm. gov.uk/output/Page13691.asp accessed 20 November 2009

Roberts, S. and Thumim, J. (2006) *A Rough Guide To Individual Carbon Trading: The Ideas, the Issues and the Next Steps*, Defra, London

Roeser, F. and Jackson, T. (2003) 'Early experience with emissions trading in the UK', *Greener Management International*, vol 39, pp43–54

Ropke, I. (1999) 'The dynamics of willingness to consume', *Ecological Economics*, vol 28, pp399–420

Royal Commission on Environmental Pollution (RCEP) (2000) *The Royal Commission on Environmental Pollution's 22nd Report: Energy – The Changing Climate*, RCEP, London

Royal Society for the encouragement of Arts, Manufactures & Commerce (RSA) (2007a) 'CarbonLimited and Energy 2020', http://www.thersa.org/projects/past-projects/carbon-limited, accessed 20 July 2010

Royal Society for the encouragement of Arts, Manufactures & Commerce (RSA) (2007b) *Technical Requirements for Personal Carbon Trading*, RSA Working Paper, RSA, London

Seyfang, G. (2006) 'Sustainable consumption, the new economics and community currencies: Developing new institutions for environmental governance', *Regional Studies*, vol 40, no 7, pp781–791

Seyfang, G. (2007) 'Personal Carbon Trading: Lessons from complementary currencies', CSERGE Working Paper ECM 2007-01, CSERGE, Norwich

Seyfang, G., Lorenzoni, I. and Nye, M. (2009) 'Personal Carbon Trading: a critical examination of proposals for the UK', Tyndall Working Paper, Tyndall Centre, Norwich

Shrubsole, G. (2007) 'This time it's personal', *The Guardian*, 8 August 2007, Society, p8

Siegel, L. (2007) 'The low-carbon diet', *Observer Magazine*, 21 January 2007, pp24–29

Simms, A. (2006) *The UK Interdependence Report: How the World Sustains the Nation's Lifestyles and the Price it Pays*, New Economics Foundation, London

Starkey, R. and Anderson, K. (2005) 'Investigating Domestic Tradable Quotas: a policy instrument for reducing greenhouse gas emissions from energy use', Tyndall Working Paper, Tyndall Centre, Norwich

Van Vliet, B., Chappells, H. and Shove, E. (2005) *Infrastructures of Consumption: Environmental Innovation In The Utility Industries*, Earthscan, London

Whitmarsh, L., O'Neill, S., Seyfang, G. and Lorenzoni, I. (2009) 'Carbon capability: what does it mean and how can we promote it?', in A. Stibbe (ed) *The Handbook Of Sustainability Literacy: Skills for a Changing World*, John Elford, Green Books, Totnes

Woerdman, E. (2001) 'Emissions trading and transaction costs: Analyzing the flaws in the discussion', *Ecological Economics*, vol 38, no 2, pp293–304

Zelizer, V. A. (1994) *The Social Meaning of Money*, Basic Books, New York

3
Public Engagement in Climate Action: Policy and Public Expectations

Corina Höppner and Lorraine Whitmarsh

1. Introduction

The UK government has released a number of major policy documents on climate change such as the UK Climate Change Programme (Defra, 2006) and the Climate Change Act (HM Government, 2008). The latter is the world's first legally binding framework to cut carbon emissions by 2020 and 2050 respectively. Similar bills are under consideration elsewhere too, such as the Waxman–Markey Bill in the USA. In the UK, these official documents have positioned the public as one actor that needs to be engaged to successfully mitigate climate change. Hence, it is good news that recent surveys show widespread public awareness and concern regarding climate change – although concern seems to wax and wane slightly over time (e.g. Defra, 2007a). When it comes to the public's knowledge of the issue and their willingness to change relevant behaviours, however, survey results usually suggest a more worrying picture. Gaps between reported concern on the one hand, and limited knowledge of the issue and a comparatively low willingness to substantially alter behaviours on the other, tend to nourish doubt as to the public as a body of responsible and competent citizens. Public education to facilitate behaviour change has thus become the baseline on which contemporary official approaches to public engagement in climate change appear to rest.

We argue that serious efforts to inform citizens about climate change and to facilitate behaviour change cannot come too soon. However, implicit understandings of citizen engagement and agency, as communicated in governmental documents, are problematically shorthanded compared with the reality and complexity of human engagement. This chapter provides an analysis of how the responsibilities and engagement of the public have been constructed within recent climate change and related policy documents in the UK, and how and why the public takes actions, or not. While UK environmental policy has traditionally framed the role of the public as 'consumers' typically exhorting voluntary behaviour change by individuals through information campaigns, this fails to acknowledge that public engagement can take many forms that influence each other. Engagement can take place in the private sphere (e.g. individual action through green consumerism, conservation behaviour) and in the form of socio-political participation. As we discuss here, the latter is a vital element of democracies and helps to stimulate people's belief that they can make a difference. We use evidence from documentary policy analysis, public attitude surveys, and public engagement in policy consultations and grassroots organizations, to infer how policy makers and the public themselves perceive the multiple roles and opportunities for the public to address climate change. We also outline the diverse motivations for public engagement with climate change, as well as the individual and social barriers and the limitations to engagement. We focus primarily in this chapter on public engagement with climate change mitigation, but many of the implications from our analysis may equally be applied to engagement with climate adaptation.

2. Engagement with climate change

Human engagement with climate change may be understood as a person's state of connection to climate change, and comprises different though interconnected aspects: cognitive, emotional and behavioural (Lorenzoni et al, 2007). In other words, it encompasses knowledge, concern, attitudes, risk perception and behaviour. Importantly, behavioural responses to climate change encompass a range of actions, and are driven by diverse (and often multiple) motivations and expectations – only one of which may be environmental concern. Research also highlights that there are individual and social barriers to translating cognitive and emotional concern into behaviour (Lorenzoni et al, 2007). Accordingly, one barrier is people's belief that they lack the knowledge, skills or capacities to act (a low sense of self-efficacy). Another barrier is people's perception that reciprocal political action and engagement by other actors is lacking, and that they cannot do anything about it (a low sense of political and collective efficacy). Both the diversity of motivations and individual–social barriers to engagement will be key issues to which we later return.

Based on extensive literature on environment–behaviour interactions, Stern (2000) distinguishes four types of environmentally significant individual behaviour:

1 environmental activism (e.g. taking part in a demonstration);
2 non-activist behaviours in the public sphere (e.g. signing a petition, joining an environmental organization);
3 private sphere environmentalism (i.e. the purchase, use and disposal of personal or household goods); and
4 professional or organizational decision making (e.g. a designer may use only sustainable materials in his or her products; a banker may invest only in ethical firms).

The first two types may both be considered 'public sphere' (or civic) actions, and are usually contrasted with the private sphere actions. Others have worked to subdivide these categories; for example, Pattie et al (2003) identify three types of 'public sphere' engagement: individualistic-based actions, contact with those in authority and collective action; and Defra (2008b), the UK Department for Environment, Food and Rural Affairs, has classified 'private sphere' behaviours into categories of low and high environmental impact actions, as well as one-off and regular decisions, relating to four behavioural domains: domestic energy and water use, waste behaviour, transport and eco-friendly shopping (for other groupings see Barr et al, 2005). In terms of primary behavioural categories, though, the Stern framework appears to be robust and (to our knowledge) unchallenged. In this paper, we are particularly interested in the first three categories, and in comparing public-sphere environmental behaviour (activism and non-activist civic actions) and private-sphere environmentalism.

Current theoretical and empirical literature seldom integrates the study of private-sphere and public-sphere behaviours. Thus far, climate change related engagement studies have largely focused on one type of behaviour, as researchers usually draw on their specific backgrounds in social movement studies, political participation or environmental psychology. Most work has examined private-sphere environmental behaviour as it is supposed to have the most direct effect on the environment, rather than also looking at 'invited' and 'claimed' engagement in the public sphere, which is deemed to yield more indirect effects (Stern, 2000; Gaventa, 2006). Latta (2007, p378) even claims that current academic debates generally focus on engagement as a tool for 'cultivating "green" attitudes and behaviours in individual citizens, leaving questions of democracy and collective action on the sidelines'. While 'only' yielding indirect effects on the environment, it is such engagement in the public sphere that is valued by political scientists for its potential merits for participating individuals as well as for society as a whole. Accordingly, it is crucial practice to foster democratic values, to develop the capacities for and enlarge the practice of active citizenship, to increase people's sense of efficacy, and to build trust and understanding between citizen and government (Holder, 1988; Warren, 1992; Latta, 2007).

This disciplinary separation has furthermore translated into an under-emphasis of the interrelationships between individual and collective engagement in the private and public sphere. Yet, studies on socio-political participation suggest that different types and forms of engagement are actually interconnected. Pattie et al (2003), for instance, identify individualistic, contact and collective engagement as three partly overlapping forms of civic engagement in modern Britain. It is furthermore important to consider that empowering one form of engagement might have an influence on the realization of other forms, either negatively by restricting resources or positively by stimulating more demand (MacGregor, 2006; Latta, 2007; Defra, 2008a; WWF-UK, 2009; Whitmarsh and O'Neill, in press). Understanding these links (or the lack of them) between types of environmentally significant behaviour may be better achieved by a more interdisciplinary perspective that draws on political science and environmental psychology perspectives.

3. Policy and public expectations regarding public engagement

In this section, we first take a closer look at the notion of public engagement in major policy documents on climate change in the UK and therewith at the role that has been officially allocated to the public. Specifically, we refer to the UK Strategy for Sustainable Development (Defra, 2005), the UK Climate Change Programme (Defra, 2006) and the Citizen's Agenda (Defra, 2007b), as these documents explicitly attempt to link climate change action with public engagement frameworks and are points of reference for sectoral policies and mitigation practice. After this, we examine how the public themselves see their role in tackling climate change, the actions they are prepared to take (and are taking) and the potential for expanding this role. The analysis methods we have used here include documentary policy analysis and a literature review of public attitude survey and interview data. In the following analysis of policy documents, we examine who should get engaged in climate mitigation, in what way, to what end and by which means.

Policy expectations

Climate change has a prominent place in the UK Strategy for Sustainable Development (Defra, 2005), though it is addressed largely as an energy saving issue. The UK, as an 'international frontrunner in the development of SD [Sustainable Development] strategies, has developed a vast array of mechanisms, processes and organizations to help implement SD' (Russel, 2007, p196), which are enshrined in the strategy paper. Indeed, the document makes a considerable effort to deliver a diversified strategy for public engagement at local community level, more than its precedents. One of the key tools endorsed therein is a new programme for community engagement (Community Action 2020 – Together We Can), which basically rests on the following assumption: 'We can learn and change our behaviour more effectively in groups: Community groups can help tackle climate change, develop community energy and transport projects, help minimize waste, improve the quality of the local environment, and promote fair trade and sustainable consumption and production' (DTI, 2007, p25). The document explicitly tries to couple a transition towards more sustainable behaviour in the private sphere with greater local democracy, and sets out the government's commitment to give local people more say in local decisions via tools such as participatory budgeting and citizens' juries. Through the 'Big Energy Shift', UK policy makers have also sought to engage with communities (Ipsos-MORI, 2009). Yet, despite these notable efforts to couple private-sphere with public-sphere engagement at community level, to date, the focus amongst policy makers appears to be on individual behaviour change and private sphere environmental behaviour. This focus on individual consumer behaviours is apparent in the UK government's 'Pro-Environmental Behaviour Framework' (Defra, 2008b), the latest public information campaign on climate change, *Act on CO$_2$* (for details see Chapter 11), and previous energy and sustainability information campaigns (e.g. *Energy Efficiency – It's Clever Stuff, Save Energy, Money, Environment* and *Are you doing your bit?*) exhorting individuals to conserve resources and to buy environmentally friendly products.

The pioneering UK Climate Change Programme 2006 (Defra, 2006) takes strong inspiration from the Strategy for Sustainable Development and puts a strong emphasis on the role of the public in tackling climate change:

> *this Climate Change Programme sets out the Government's commitments both at international and domestic levels to meet the challenge of climate change. It also sets out our approach to strengthening the role that individuals can play. We will encourage individuals, citizens, consumers, motorists and business people to take action needed to help meet our goals. (Defra, 2006, p4)*

The specific rationale for public engagement is probably best illustrated by the following excerpt:

> *Engaging with the public on climate change is a vital part of the UK climate change programme both to encourage specific behaviours to reduce carbon dioxide emissions directly and to gain acceptance for more ambitious Government policy. (Defra, 2006, p121)*

The section of the document that deals with mitigation of climate change initially addresses individuals as citizens. However, the document then switches to the exclusive use of the term 'consumer' and channels the scope of engagement towards individual behaviour change. Accordingly, climate friendly behaviours and lifestyles are promoted through specific awareness-raising funds, campaigns and information initiatives. The document concludes by emphasizing the leadership role of the government and business in editing consumers' choices, and in advising consumers about better lifestyle choices.

To stimulate individual behaviour change, the Climate Change Programme promotes a model consisting of four 'Es' to 'exemplify', 'enable', 'engage' and 'encourage' climate related attitudes and behaviours. This model originates from the UK Strategy for Sustainable Development (Defra, 2005). Under the label 'exemplify', the government recognizes the importance of reciprocal action and commits itself to setting a good example. 'Enabling' behavioural change is the next concern: 'We need to help people make responsible choices by providing them with accessible alternatives and suitable infrastructure, and supporting them with the necessary skills and information' (Defra, 2006, p119). Here, product labelling and voluntary agreements with industries and retailers are expected to facilitate alternative consumer behaviour. Additionally, a specific fund (Climate Change Challenge Fund) should support 'community groups in taking small simple actions on energy, waste and water which add up to make a big difference nationwide' (Defra, 2006, p119). In comparison, the component 'engage' appears rather weak and nebulous. What becomes clear, however, is that the document stresses the importance of proper communication materials and media channels for engaging people at the local level. Under 'Encourage – give the right signals', the document sets out how consumers will be supported by the work of the Energy Saving Trust (for more on the work of the EST, see Chapter 8). Consumers' demand for energy efficiency is again the focal point. In its next section the document jumps back from consumers' behaviour change to 'educating the public' and specifies the educational tools:

> *The public need clear and reliable advice about the environ-mental impact of different products and services and how they can make the most sustainable consumption choices. The Government believes the best way of making this available is through the internet, and is planning a new online information service ...This will aim to enhance consumers' image of sustain-able living so that it is perceived as attractive and desirable rather than about compromising quality of life. (Defra, 2006, p121)*

Another relevant policy document is the 'Citizen's agenda', which was launched by Defra in 2005 (Defra, 2007b). The agenda is exclusively dedi-cated to the question 'how the ordinary citizen can change his or her lifestyle to minimize the impact of climate change and to mitigate its effects' (Defra, 2007b, p5). The document adopts a general focus on awareness raising and behaviour change, and deals with the question of 'What are the barriers to uptake climate change mitigation strategies at the level of the individual, and how can they be overcome?' (Defra, 2007b, p6). Even more importantly, the document points at a further crucial question that still needs to be answered: 'What is the real scope for individual and local community action to con-tribute to tackling climate change?' (Defra, 2007b, p5). The agenda frames this scope around several areas: energy efficiency and energy consumption, the provision of low-carbon alternatives, microgeneration, 'smart metering', awareness raising and informing about the role of the individual in tackling climate change. Whilst the document raises questions vital for taking the con-ceptualization of citizen engagement with climate change beyond the private sphere, it fails to deliver a practical programme for creating and supporting climate related social–political engagement at community and other levels. Tensions between purely instrumental understandings of citizen engagement as a means to cut carbon emissions and normative democratic understandings of empowering citizens without prescribing the outcomes of their engagement remain unaddressed, although frequently compromising mitigation and adap-tation practice (Höppner, 2009).

Overall, the UK's official approach to public engagement in climate change relies on two main foci. On one hand, there is a focus on behaviour and the related lifestyle changes that individual consumers can make in the private sphere (by fostering awareness and responsibility). On the other hand, there is a focus on local communities (community in its geographical and social meaning) as places and spaces to achieve the desired changes. The conceptualization of collective engagement (activist and non-activist) that goes beyond the private sphere, though, appears to be vague or absent, particularly in the documents specifically dealing with climate change. While the UK Sustainability Strategy supports both individual behaviour change and citizens' socio-political empowerment in the public sphere of communities, the Climate Change Programme and Citizen's Agenda appear to have a narrower understanding of citizen engagement. Accordingly, community groups are primarily valued as a means to increase the numbers of individuals that voluntarily reduce their carbon footprint to 'make up a big difference nationwide' (Defra, 2006, p119).

Public expectations and engagement

In the UK, research which has explicitly asked the public what action they are taking 'out of concern for climate change' found that amongst the one-third of the public who are taking any action, this almost exclusively takes the form of private-sphere environmentalism (Whitmarsh, 2009). In fact, this action is restricted to a *subset* of possible private-sphere behaviours: most commonly, recycling, and, to a lesser extent, energy conservation. In general, few have changed (or are willing to change) their travel or eating behaviours (e.g. Whitmarsh et al, 2009). Where private-sphere environmental actions are taken, this is often not, or only partly, for environmental reasons. Energy conservation is most commonly undertaken for financial reasons (i.e. to save money) or for other personal benefits (e.g. walking for health); where environmental concern features at all, it is usually a secondary motive (Brandon and Lewis, 1999; Whitmarsh, 2009).

Public-sphere engagement is even less common: according to a recent survey of residents in two UK regions (Whitmarsh et al, 2009), fewer than 10 per cent have ever contacted their MP or taken part in a protest regarding an environmental issue, compared to 99 per cent who claim they recycle at least 'occasionally'. This is consistent with the broader political disengagement and apathy that is evident within the UK. Hansard's latest Audit of Political Engagement (Hansard, 2008) shows that interest in politics has fallen 3 per cent down to 51 per cent; more than half the UK public claim to know not very much or nothing at all about politics (55 per cent, an increase of 4 per cent since the previous year); and only around 12 per cent of people are politically active (defined as having done at least three of eight political activities in the last 2–3 years; 48 per cent haven't done any). The survey also highlights the lack of political efficacy amongst the UK public: less than one-third of people believe that 'when people like me get involved in politics, they can really change the way the country is run'. This profound political disenfranchisement, distrust and fatalism amongst the British public have been noted elsewhere (Grove-White, 1996; Poortinga and Pidgeon, 2003). There has been a decline in electoral participation in recent decades, and while there has also been a rise in non-electoral forms of social participation and protest, this has largely been the preserve of highly educated groups who also vote (Curtice and Seyd, 2003). In many countries, such as the UK, there is an increasing tendency for the public to question those in authority (House of

Lords Select Committee on Science and Technology, 2000) and to feel their opinions are irrelevant to policy makers (Macnaghten and Jacobs, 1997).

When it comes to climate change, the same picture of disenfranchisement and lack of self-efficacy and political efficacy emerges. Although most people in Britain say they 'would be prepared to change the way they live in order to lessen the possible impact of global warming', a little over half the population (54 per cent) believe that changing their own behaviour would not have any impact on climate change (BBC, 2004). This is unfortunate, as appeals to engage can trigger frustration and stimulate disengagement if people are concerned about an issue but doubt the efficacy of their actions (Höppner et al, 2008). Further, a minority believes the government shares their own views on the issue or listens to public concerns (Poortinga and Pidgeon, 2003). Although public and community involvement in decision making about climate change is something the public has explicitly stated should happen, when asked whether they would personally like to be consulted in policy-making decisions about climate change, agreement is much lower (Poortinga and Pidgeon, 2003). This suggests apathy and disengagement from political processes has become customary for many people, who perhaps are sceptical about the utility of contributing to political debates. While most look to government to take the lead (or 'exemplify' to use Defra's four 'Es' terminology) in tackling climate change (e.g. Lorenzoni et al, 2007), the majority also lack confidence in the government in tackling climate change, believing it to be unduly influenced by industry in responding to the issue (Poortinga and Pidgeon, 2003). This distrust and perceived governmental inaction in relation to climate change, which is evident across Europe (Querol et al, 2003), undoubtedly influences public beliefs about the need and efficacy of individual action.

Invited engagement

Spaces for public engagement are either invited by authorities and governments, or claimed and created autonomously by citizens and non-governmental organizations (Gaventa, 2006). In the following we present some recent examples of invited and claimed spaces to shed light on people's motivations and expectations regarding public engagement.

Public consultation to the UK Draft Climate Change Bill

The consultation on the UK Climate Change Bill in 2007 is an example of invited engagement in the public sphere. With a total of 16,919 responses, the consultation received the largest number of responses to a 'routine' consultation in Defra history (for a comprehensive analysis of the consultation and description of method,s see Maciejewski Scheer, 2008; Maciejewski Scheer and Höppner, 2010). According to the official report (Bomel Ltd, 2007), the consultation received 15,722 'campaign' responses and 1197 'unique' responses (campaign responses were identical, as the campaign organizers had provided individuals with standard wording to submit, whereas unique responses were different from each other). The high number of campaign responses shows that organizations, largely NGOs, played a central role in mediating and facilitating citizen participation in the consultation.

Interviews with Defra officials (full details of methods and findings reported in Maciejewski Scheer, 2008; Maciejewski Scheer and Höppner, 2010) showed that they rationalized citizen participation normatively as people's democratic right to have their say. The motive to give 'anyone interested' the opportunity to participate was entangled with the expectation that this would increase the legitimacy of the outcome. In comparison, interviews with people responding to the consultation revealed that they did not only feel that they had a right to have a say, but that they had a responsibility and duty to try to make a difference as they felt strongly about climate change (strong emotional engagement). Some, even if they disagreed with the format of the consultation or with the scope of questions, nevertheless participated to show government their concern. Furthermore, respondents wanted to make a substantive difference to the Bill, amend parts or introduce new points. They felt that this was one of the rare or only chances to give government feedback on their work and to influence the context in which their individual actions take place. Even if people were sceptical about the influence they could actually have on the Bill, they decided to respond out of a strong feeling of responsibility and duty to act. Furthermore, they felt that this was an opportunity to at least support organization campaigns to get the numbers of responses. In this case a feeling of collective efficacy (as people's shared belief in their collective power to produce desired results; see Bandura, 2000) arguably compensated for a low belief in individual influence on political decisions (political efficacy).

Maciejewski Scheer and Höppner (2010) furthermore show that there appears to be a lack of clarity by government over the substantive input of citizens in climate policy. The strong focus on the consultation as a means to provide people with the right to be involved and to legitimize the Bill appears to distract from other efforts, namely: to specify what sort of substantive input a consultation of this format can and should facilitate (to amend or to enrich options, or to select between proposed options); and to reflect on what sort of substantive input people might actually seek to contribute, but which the consultation format cannot accommodate (e.g. extending the debate to other questions, reframing issues, exploring cross-connections between single aspects). Furthermore, people's emotional and cognitive engagement and their wish to contribute to the Bill was arguably devalued by government as it did not respond to the public consultation (government responded jointly to pre-legislative scrutiny and public consultation without clarifying how the processes impacted on the Bill). This very likely undermined the potential of the engagement process to legitimize the outcome, and to build trust in government policy and people's political efficacy beliefs. Furthermore, the room for the public to meaningfully shape the legislation (or indeed to learn about alternative perspectives) was limited by the one-sided framing of the debate. Although Defra's public engagement activities (including citizens' summit) to inform development of the Climate Change Bill increased citizens' understanding about climate change and the need for action, and enabled them to express their views on climate change policy, deliberation was limited by the exclusion of opposing arguments (Warburton, 2008).

It becomes clear that in practice the consultation via written documents is necessary, and indeed appears to provide people who feel responsible and concerned with an opportunity to act in a way they feel is more efficacious in bringing about change than private-sphere environmental behaviour or engagement at the local level alone. Public-sphere engagement appears to be important to do justice to people's cognitive and emotional engagement with the issue, and can provide a sense of collective agency on the collective challenge of climate change. However, such consultations cannot accommodate all of the rationales people might have for engagement (e.g. reframe the issue and substantially alter policy). The unprecedented number of respondents to the consultation, the 1197 'unique responses', and the fact that 684 respondents commented on climate change related aspects that were not asked in the consultation, suggests that there is a demand for in-depth and formative political engagement (e.g. deliberative events to open-up debate alongside quantitative consultations).

Renewable energy planning

The field of wind energy planning is a good example for different concurrent approaches to (local) engagement. On one hand there is a growing empirical literature examining prescribed top-down engagement (consultations to proposed planning schemes); on the other hand there are claims for the development of decentralized, community-based renewable energy schemes (Rogers et al, 2008; Walker, 2008).

Rogers et al (2008) showed that residents have very diverse expectations regarding their engagement at local level which transcend the private- and public-sphere divide. Interestingly, it is particularly 'low level' participation which is imagined in diverse forms: attending fundraising events, contributing general labour or specialist skills, making changes in own homes/businesses, attending public meetings, choosing between renewable technologies for the community, helping raise awareness, running educational activities, producing newsletters, and so on. Rogers and colleagues conclude that although there is 'likely to be enthusiasm for community-based energy projects' among residents, there are serious structural barriers to such engagement. Institutional support and facilitation of 'possibilities for different types of projects and participation' appear to be needed (Rogers et al, 2008, p4225). Indeed, actual engagement depends much on individuals' knowledge of engagement opportunities, and it is often only by engaging in some form that people find out whether, and in what form, they want to engage henceforth (Höppner et al, 2007). Moreover, people's motivation to engage does not only evolve with their own engagement experiences, but also with what they hear about other people's experiences and what they perceive to be the social norm of engagement. Knowledge on ways to engage, however, is likely to be low after 'a long history of centralized control of energy policy and planning' (Rogers et al, 2008, p4225).

Interviewing locals, Rogers et al (2008) also found that people's expectations regarding their engagement are diverse and not limited to environmental concerns. Rather, people expected a community-owned wind energy scheme to strengthen locals' sense of community, and to produce economic benefits for themselves and the community as a whole. A further motivation to participate was to exercise their right to have a say in the community. These findings are consistent with those of Pattie et al (2003), who found multiple determinants of civic engagement. They furthermore attest to the idea that engagement motivations and expectations can be environmental, social, economic and political. People arguably use these diverse expectations to evaluate renewable energy schemes, whether they are community-planned or purely top-down proposed, rather than exclusively looking at emission reductions. This means that even if people agree to policy targets (reduce emissions) and are cognitively and emotionally engaged with climate change, they are likely to evaluate local projects and their engagement against a broader set of criteria.

Claimed engagement
There are also pockets of more radical grassroots innovation, which demonstrate not only that some groups are very willing to make significant changes to their lifestyles for the sake of the environment, but also that these groups are channelling their frustration about perceived political inaction into creative forms of social innovation (e.g. Seyfang and Smith, 2007). Groups, such as carbon reduction action groups (CRAGs) and Transition Towns, are claiming spaces for both public- and private-sphere engagement which appear to highlight viable alternative models of community life, while at the same time contributing to climate change mitigation. Importantly, the motivations for engagement in these groups are not restricted to environmental concern; consistent with the community engagement examples mentioned above, individuals get involved for various (e.g. social) reasons such as support from, and interaction with, like-minded people (see Seyfang et al, 2007; Howell, 2009).

There are some within the UK government who have welcomed such demonstrations of radical change; a climate change minister, Ed Miliband (cited in Adam and Jowit, 2008), called for the creation of a global 'popular mobilization' campaign to pressure world leaders into tackling climate change. Public demand for policy change can provide greater legitimacy for political leaders willing to introduce bolder policies (Ockwell et al, 2009). As discussed earlier, there also appears to be support for grassroots, community action within some policy documents, such as the Climate Change Programme. Yet, the extent to which these groups have influenced and connected with policy is debatable. While some argue they act as real-world experiments which demonstrate the viability of policy options like personal carbon trading (PCT) (Seyfang et al, 2007; see also Chapter 2), their influence is limited, while they remain small-scale grassroots activities which do not threaten dominant interests. Policy makers appear to be more swayed by the views of the 'motoring majority' (Bulkeley and Rayner, 2003), who tend vehemently and very publicly to oppose proposals (e.g. road charging) which might disrupt lifestyles and threaten cherished institutions (e.g. individual mobility, consumer freedom). Governments are reluctant to regulate in large part because of the fear of public backlash and loss of political support (Carter and Ockwell, 2007).

Consequently, across the political spectrum, there is a great interest in the latest methods to 'edit choices' or 'nudge' lifestyles in a desired direction through cost-effective and socially acceptable approaches (e.g. Cialdini, 2006; Thaler and Sunstein, 2008), 'without [recourse to] huge centralized bureaucracy' (Letwin; cited in Chakrabortty, 2008) or compromising consumer sovereignty (Hinchliffe, 1996). It would seem, then, that the degree of claimed engagement has so far not been sufficient to overcome politicians' innate risk aversion with respect to implementing bolder climate change policies, such as PCT or stringent legislation.

4. Towards a broader conception of public engagement with climate change

Emerging from the literature and examples provided in this chapter are substantial barriers to the public adopting an expanded role in tackling climate change. These exist partly at the level of individuals – in terms of their perceived self-efficacy, knowledge, interest and motivations – embedded within socio-cultural and physical (e.g. transport, built environment) structures (Lorenzoni et al, 2007). As we have particularly noted here, there are profound social and institutional barriers to political engagement (e.g. political and collective efficacy, distrust, apathy) which exist in the UK, but also in many other countries. These constraints limit the (perceived) possibilities for public engagement, and undermine individuals' willingness to participate in efforts both at individual and community levels to tackle climate change.

Yet, our analysis also highlights the diverse motivations for public engagement with climate change – both in relation to private-sphere and public-sphere actions (see Table 3.1). We point to some of the ways in which the barriers, described above, might be overcome. Promoting the various benefits of engagement might appeal to a wider group of citizens–consumers than the 'keen greens' involved in the most active examples of engagement (e.g. CRAGs). This suggestion is consistent with the findings of Pattie et al (2003), who conclude: 'people need to be persuaded of the existence of benefits emerging from involvement, and they need to see that their actions are having an effect, at least some of the time' (p465). Similarly, in the private environmentalism sphere, energy conservation actions can be promoted by highlighting the benefits to individuals (e.g. saving money, keeping fit) and to the community, as well as to the environment. Furthermore, the evidence from sociopolitical participation indicates that initial experiences with engagement might encourage people to engage through other forms of participation. For instance, attending information events or workshops on community development can stimulate further engagement in local groups by nurturing people's efficacy beliefs (Höppner et al, 2007). Similar catalyst effects may also exist within private environmentalism and across these broad categories of environmental behaviour (e.g. Whitmarsh and O'Neill, in press).

Future work should hence focus on understanding the links between private- and public-sphere climate change action. Of course, many of the individuals engaging in public-sphere action (e.g. Transition Towns members) also

Table 3.1 *Types of, and motivations for, public engagement action in relation to climate change*

Types of action	Example actions	Motivations
Private-sphere	Domestic energy conservation (turning off lights, using energy-saving lightbulbs)	To save money, to protect the environment
	Walking/cycling to work	For health, convenience, to protect the environment, to save money
	Using public transport	Convenience, affordability, to protect the environment
	Reducing waste, recycling, reusing	To protect the environment, social norms
	Food choices (e.g. avoiding meat, choosing local/seasonal produce)	To protect the environment, health benefits, animal welfare, support local business
	Buying environmentally friendly products	To protect the environment, environmental self-identity
Public-sphere	Voting	Political efficacy, exercise democratic/civil rights
	Taking part in an environmental campaign or protest	To protect the environment, social support/interaction
	Responding to a policy consultation	Sense of responsibility, exercise democratic/civil rights, to protect environment/society from environmental risks, substantially influence policies, perceived political efficacy
	Joining an environmental NGO	To protect the environment, perceived collective efficacy
	Grassroots community groups	Social interaction, learning new skills and (e.g. CRAGs, Transition Towns) gaining advice, environmental concern
	Community renewables projects	Build sense of community, economic benefits to self/community, ethical and environmental commitment, lower energy cost and reliable local supply

Sources: Brandon and Lewis, 1999; Howell, 2009; Maciejewski Scheer and Höppner, 2010; Pattie et al, 2003; Rogers et al, 2008; Walker, 2008; Whitmarsh, 2009; Whitmarsh and O'Neill, in press.

engage in private-sphere actions such as energy conservation (e.g. Whitmarsh et al, 2009). Yet, to date, little research has examined spillover across these broad domains of action; for example, does engaging in energy conservation inspire individuals to take part in a protest, or vice versa? Previous research on citizens' involvement in deliberative climate change workshops highlights that long-term behaviour change may sometimes be triggered by involvement in participatory environmental assessment (Bull et al, 2008), but that it typically requires more than discrete interventions of this kind because of the range of barriers (psychological, infrastructural, etc.) that exist to leading low-carbon lifestyles (Stoll-Kleemann et al, 2001). A related issue is whether strong policies to address climate change (e.g. legislation), perhaps instigated by public-sphere action by individuals and communities, would negate the need for private-sphere action (e.g. energy conservation). Clearly, under this scenario, private-sphere action would become a legal requirement rather than a voluntary lifestyle choice, but intrinsic motivations to make environmentally responsible choices could be eroded. These kinds of synergies across private- and public-sphere action should be the focus of future research.

An important implication of the diversity of forms of, and motivations for, engagement is that policy makers should not be too prescriptive in the actions they seek from the public in response to climate change. Clearly, targets to mitigate climate change are required, but within an equitable and transparent mitigation framework, flexibility should be sought which does not erode the intrinsic motivations of pro-environmental and innovative groups seeking to cut carbon, while also encouraging less environmentally conscious groups to participate (see Ockwell et al, 2009). Such a framework should not only be open to diverse forms of engagement, but also value and actively encourage them to the same extent. Activist and non-activist public-sphere engagement should be perceived as equally important as private-sphere behaviour, as they shape cultural norms of engagement, values (democratic, environmental, social) and people's feelings of self-efficacy, collective efficacy and political efficacy. Indeed, decades of research on the latter have established efficacy as one key foundation of human agency (Bandura, 2000). In the case of climate change as a collective long-term challenge, engagement fostering collective and political efficacy appears to be crucial, as such beliefs influence how much effort people put into actions, the persistence of their efforts even if they fail to produce quick results or meet opposition, and people's vulnerability to discouragement (Bandura, 2000). In this context it is unfortunate that people's actual engagement in processes such as the consultation to the UK Climate Change Bill usually receives little attention in the media, and can thus hardly reduce feelings of disenfranchisement and powerlessness in the wider public.

Indeed, with a more holistic approach that acknowledges different forms of engagement as interconnected and fluid in terms of motivations, expectations, spheres and scales, some of the barriers to engagement identified by Lorenzoni et al (2007) might be (partly) overcome in the long term. More specifically, by fostering private- and public-sphere engagement, increased perceived collective and political efficacy might reduce fatalism, 'drop in the ocean' feelings, a perceived lack of political action, and free-rider effects. Furthermore, the display of the diversity of engagement actually taking place might reduce the perception that climate change is a distant issue, while also establishing social norms for engagement.

Finally, we also acknowledge the limitations to public engagement with climate change. Crucially, as a collective and global problem, individuals acting alone – or even in communities or interest groups – can only do so much, without a coherent and equitable framework implemented by governments to mitigate climate change. Individuals may call for such a framework, but their options for leading low-carbon lifestyles will inevitably be constrained by the infrastructures in place (which currently promote carbon-intensive lifestyles). Public-sphere engagement may also be limited by issues of scale and cost (e.g. Dietz and Stern, 2008). Since climate change is a global and urgent problem (IPCC, 2007), the scope for in-depth, deliberative engagement with communities may be more limited than for local or less pressing issues. Clearly, the cost of intensive forms of engagement on this scale is also prohibitive. Yet, such concerns should not undermine efforts to transform governance systems over the long term so that they offer more opportunities for public involvement in decision making. Furthermore, there are methods – such as internet debates – which may allow for rapid, low-cost and mass public participation (Dietz and Stern, 2008; see also Chapter 13 on engagement via new media). Given that people's perceived efficacy and motivations to engage can be influenced by their perception of how other people behave and with what effects, actual invited and claimed engagement should be made more visible to a wider public. For instance, media could facilitate public engagement by highlighting what people are doing and what the benefits are of engagement, rather than merely emphasizing where groups oppose actions or public apathy and incapacities (Höppner, 2010).

5. Conclusions

Our analysis reiterates that when asked to engage in mitigating climate change, people are likely to evaluate their engagement against a set of environmental, social, economic and political criteria, rather than clinically just focusing on de-contextualized cuts in greenhouse gas emissions – which official guidelines to engagement currently exhort people to do. Although such private-sphere engagement measures may to some extent target non-environmental motivations (e.g. financial savings from energy conservation; see Defra, 2008b), other values and motivations (particularly for public-sphere engagement) are ignored (Crompton, 2008). Such a limited view of engagement bears the risk of mismatching with people's broader expectations regarding their engagement and of being unresponsive to forms of engagement that might yield indirect effects on the environment, and direct effects on people's efficacy feelings and guiding societal norms of engagement. Furthermore, focusing on a narrow set of motivations, such as economic self-interest or materialism, risks reinforcing these and eroding more fundamental intrinsic motivations (e.g. self-actualization, community belonging; Crompton, 2008), citizenship skills, and pro-social or pro-environmental values (Dobson, 2003).

Finally, climate change is a collective problem and a political issue. Thus, it will not be sufficient to increase awareness, individual knowledge on climate change and consumer capacities; it will also require societal debate about the type of future climate, societal structures, energy options and adaptation solutions we would like (Hulme, 2009), as well as a strengthening of people's perceived collective and political efficacy to engage in such debates through a continuous revitalization of public-sphere engagement. Official thinking about engagement should hence not only consider direct environmental impacts of specific behaviours (engagement). Rather, it should also take into account the indirect impact on people's efficacy beliefs (self-efficacy, collective efficacy, political efficacy), on people's motivations (which they might reinforce or erode), and reflect on the institutional and infrastructural support to foster them. In future, documents and initiatives should thus endeavour to elaborate a more integrative framework on how to enact private- and public-sphere engagement concurrently. While it is impossible to quantify the effects of such an approach on greenhouse gas emission cuts, in a democracy it appears to be the only discernible way to overcome the substantial social barriers to engagement, and to decrease levels of apathy and disenfranchisement. Finally, such a framework would be a vital step towards actively addressing and resolving current disjunctions and tensions (Höppner, 2009) between different understandings of public engagement in climate change-relevant policies.

References

Adam, D. and Jowit, J. (2008) 'People power vital to climate deal – minister', *The Guardian*, 8 December, www.guardian.co.uk/environment/2008/dec/08/ed-miliband-climate-politics-environment. accessed 18 December 2009

Bandura, A. (2000) 'Exercise of human agency through collective efficacy', *Current Directions in Psychological Science*, vol 9, pp75–78

Barr, S., Gilg, A. W. and Ford, N. (2005) 'The household energy gap: Examining the divide between habitual- and purchase-related conservation behaviours', *Energy Policy*, vol 33, pp1425–1444

BBC (2004) *Poll for climate change special*, http://news.bbc.co.uk/nol/shared/bsp/hi/pdfs/28_07_04_climatepoll.pdf, accessed 12 January 2005

Bomel Ltd. (2007) *Final report to the consultation on the draft Climate Change Bill from 13 March–12 June 2007, Prepared for Department of Environment, Rural Affairs and Food (Defra)*, www.defra.gov.uk/environment/climatechange/uk/legislation/docs.htm, accessed 20 May 2008

Brandon, G. and Lewis, A. (1999) 'Reducing household energy consumption: A qualitative and quantitative field study', *Journal of Environmental Psychology*, vol 19, pp75–85

Bulkeley, H. and Rayner, T. (2003) 'New realism and local realities: Local transport planning in Leicester and Cambridgeshire', *Urban Studies*, vol 40, no 1, pp35–55

Bull, R., Petts, J. and Evans, J. (2008) 'Social learning from public engagement: dreaming the impossible?', *Journal of Environmental Planning and Management*, vol 51, no 5, pp701–716

Carter, N. and Ockwell, D. G. (2007) *New Labour, new environment? An analysis of the Labour government's policy on climate change and biodiversity loss. Report prepared for Friends of the Earth*, www.york.ac.uk/res/celp/projects/foe/docs/fullreportfinal.pdf, Centre for Ecology Law and Policy (CELP), University of York

Chakrabortty, A. (2008) 'From Obama to Cameron, why do so many politicians want a piece of Richard Thaler?', *Guardian Online*, www.guardian.co.uk/politics/2008/jul/12/economy.conservatives, accessed 18 December 2009

Cialdini, R. B. (2006) *Influence: Psychology of Persuasion*, Collins Business Essentials Edition, HarperCollins, New York

Crompton, T. (2008) *Weathercocks and Signposts, The environment movement at a cross roads*, WWF, www.wwf.org.uk/filelibrary/pdf/weathercocks_report2.pdf, accessed 18 December 2009

Defra (2005) *Securing the future – The UK Government Sustainable Development Strategy*, Department for Environment, Food and Rural Affairs, London

Defra (2006) *Climate Change – The UK Programme 2006*, Department for Environment, Food and Rural Affairs, London

Defra (2007a) *Survey of Public Attitudes and Behaviours toward the Environment: 2007*, Department for Environment, Food and Rural Affairs, London

Defra (2007b) *Climate Change: The 'Citizen's Agenda'*, Volume 1, Department for Environment, Food and Rural Affairs, London

Defra (2008a) *Science and Research Projects: Exploring Catalyst Behaviour – EV0508*, http://randd.defra.gov.uk/Default.aspx?Menu=Menu&Module=More&Location=None&Completed=0&ProjectID=16324, accessed 18 December 2009

Defra (2008b) *A Framework For Pro-Environmental Behaviours*, Department for Environment, Food and Rural Affairs, London

Dietz, T. and Stern, P. C. (eds) (2008) *Public Participation in Environmental Assessment and Decision Making*, National Academies Press, Washington, DC

Dobson, A. (2003) *Environment and Citizenship*, Oxford University Press, Oxford

DTI (2007) *Meeting the Energy Challenge – A White Paper on Energy*, Department of Trade and Industry, London

Grove-White, R. (1996) 'Environmental knowledge and public policy needs: on humanising the research agenda', in S. Lash, B. Szerszynski and B. Wynne (eds) *Risk, Modernity and Environment: Towards a New Ecology*, Sage Publications, London

Hansard (2008) *Audit of Political Engagement – Parliament and Government*, www.hansardsociety.org.uk/blogs/parliament_and_government/archive/2008/03/27/audit5.aspx, accessed 18 December 2009

Hinchliffe, S. (1996) 'Helping the earth begins at home: the social construction of socio-environmental responsibilities', *Global Environmental Change*, vol 6, pp53–62

HM Government (2008) *Climate Change Bill; Commons amendments at 3rd reading*, www.publications.parliament.uk/pa/ld200708/ldbills/087/2008087.pdf, accessed 18 December 2009

Holden, B. (1988) *Understanding Liberal Democracy*, The Alden Press, Oxford

Höppner, C. (2009) 'Public engagement in climate change – Disjunctions, tensions and blind spots in the UK', *IOP Conference Series, Earth and Environmental Science*, vol 8, 012010, p13

Höppner, C. (2010) 'Rereading public opinion polls on climate change in the UK press', *International Journal of Communication*, vol 4, pp977–1005

Höppner, C., Frick, J. and Buchecker, M. (2007) 'Assessing psycho-social effects of participatory landscape planning', *Landscape and Urban Planning*, vol 83, pp197–207

Höppner, C., Frick, J. and Buchecker, M. (2008) 'What drives people's willingness to discuss local landscape development?', *Landscape Research*, vol 33, pp605–622

House of Lords Select Committee on Science and Technology (2000) *Science and Society: Third Report of the Session 1999–2000*, HMSO, London

Howell, R. (2009) *The Experience of Carbon Rationing Action Groups: Implications for a Personal Carbon Allowances Policy. Final report for UKERC Demand Reduction Theme*, www.eci.ox.ac.uk/publications/downloads/howell09crags.pdf, accessed 18 December 2009

Hulme, M. (2009) *Why we Disagree about Climate Change*, Cambridge University Press, Cambridge

IPCC (2007) *The Physical Science Basis. Summary for Policymakers. Contribution of Working Group I to the Fourth Assessment Report of the Intergovernmental Panel on Climate Change*, IPCC, Geneva

Ipsos-MORI (2009) *The Big Energy Shift. Report from citizens' forums*, Ipsos-MORI, London

Latta, A. (2007) 'Locating democratic politics in ecological citizenship', *Environmental Politics*, vol 16, pp377–393

Lorenzoni, I., Nicholson-Cole, S. and Whitmarsh, L. (2007) 'Barriers perceived to engaging with climate change among the UK public and their policy implications', *Global Environmental Change*, vol 17, pp445–459

MacGregor, S. (2006) 'No sustainability without justice: A feminist critique of environmental citizenship', in A. Dobson and D. Bell (eds) *Environmental Citizenship*, MIT Press, Cambridge MA, pp101–126

Maciejewski Scheer, A. (2008) Looking for 'Joe Public'. An exploration of the consultation to the UK's Draft Climate Change Bill, Dissertation, Master of Science in Environmental Change and Management at Oxford University

Maciejewski Scheer, A. and Höppner, C. (2010) 'The public consultation to the UK Climate Change Act 2008 – A critical analysis', *Climate Policy*, vol 10, pp261–276

Ockwell, D., Whitmarsh, L. and O'Neill, S. (2009) 'Reorienting climate change communication for effective mitigation – forcing people to be green or fostering grass-roots engagement?', *Science Communication*, vol 30, pp305–327

Pattie, C., Seyd, P. and Whiteley, P. (2003) 'Citizenship and civic engagement: Attitudes and behaviour in Britain', *Political Studies*, vol 51, pp443–468

Poortinga, W. and Pidgeon, N. (2003) *Public Perceptions of Risk, Science and Governance: Main Findings of a British survey of five risk cases*, University of East Anglia and MORI, Norwich

Querol, C., Swartling, A. G., Kasemir, B. and Tabara, D. (2003) 'Citizens' reports on climate strategies', in B. Kasemir, J. Jager, C. C. Jaeger and M. T. Gardner (eds) *Public Participation in Sustainability Science: A Handbook*, Cambridge, Cambridge University Press, pp126–152

Rogers, J. C., Simmons, E. A., Convery, I. and Weatherall, A. (2008) 'Public perceptions of opportunities for community-based renewable energy projects', *Energy Policy*, vol 36, pp4217–4226

Russel, D. (2007) 'The United Kingdom's sustainable development strategies: Leading the way or flattering to deceive?', *European Environment*, vol 17, pp189–200

Seyfang, G. and Smith, A. (2007) 'Grassroots innovations for sustainable development: towards a new research and policy agenda', *Environmental Politics*, vol 16, pp584–603

Seyfang, G., Lorenzoni, I. and Nye, M. (2007) *Personal Carbon Trading: notional concept or workable proposition? Exploring theoretical, ideological and practical underpinnings. CSERGE Working Paper EDM 07-03*, UEA, Norwich

Stern, P. (2000) 'Toward a coherent theory of environmentally significant behavior', *Journal of Social Issues*, vol 56, pp407–424

Stoll-Kleemann, S., O'Riordan, T. and Jaeger, C. C. (2001) 'The psychology of denial concerning climate mitigation measures: evidence from Swiss focus groups', *Global Environmental Change*, vol 11, no 2, pp107–118

Thaler, R. H. and Sunstein, C. R. (2008) *Nudge: Improving Decisions about Health, Wealth, and Happiness*, Yale University Press, New Haven, CT

Walker, G. (2008) 'What are the barriers and incentives for community-owned means of energy production and use?', *Energy Policy*, vol 36, pp4401–4405

Warburton, D. (2008) *Evaluation of Defra's Public Engagement Process On Climate Change. Final report*, Shared Practice, Brighton

Warren, M. (1992) 'Democracy theory and self-transformation', *The American Political Science Review*, vol 86, pp8–23

Whitmarsh, L. (2009) 'Behavioural responses to climate change: Asymmetry of intentions and impacts', *Journal of Environmental Psychology*, vol 29, pp13–23

Whitmarsh, L. and O'Neill, S. (in press) 'Green identity, green living? The role of pro-environmental self-identity in determining consistency across diverse pro-environmental behaviours', *Journal of Environmental Psychology*

Whitmarsh, L., O'Neill, S., Seyfang, G. and Lorenzoni, I. (2009) *Carbon Capability: what does it mean, how prevalent is it, and how can we promote it? Tyndall Working Paper, No. 132*, www.tyndall.ac.uk/sites/default/files/twp132.pdf, accessed 18 December 2009

WWF-UK (2009) *Simple and Painless? The limitations of spillover in environmental campaigning*, WWF-UK, Godalming, UK, http://assets.wwf.org.uk/downloads/simple_painless_report.pdf, accessed 18 December 2009

4
Collective Self and Individual Choice: The Role of Social Comparisons in Promoting Public Engagement with Climate Change

Anna Rabinovich, Thomas A. Morton and Christopher C. Duke

1. Introduction

> *Britain lags behind on bioenergy.*
>
> *The UK dumps more household waste into landfill sites than any other EU state.*
>
> *While Europe recycles 90% of recovered material the UK recycles just half.*
>
> *Britain has long been a laggard at recycling.[1]*

These statements are taken from a number of British newspapers that try to attract readers' attention to sustainability issues by highlighting negative comparisons between their audience's performance and that of other European countries. Proclaiming that the UK is performing worse than others on the environmental domains (e.g. recycling) reflects an implicit assumption that highlighting such poor performance will intensify individual efforts in this area. Is this an effective approach to increasing public engagement with green issues? Specifically, do negative comparisons with other groups encourage us to improve our own performance? Or would positive comparisons that highlight previous success work better? This chapter seeks to answer these questions, and to explore conditions under which positive and negative comparisons translate into increased engagement with climate change and broader sustainability issues.

In contrast to active use of intergroup comparisons in the mass media, in psychology the task of increasing public engagement with climate change issues and encouraging sustainable behaviour has been often approached from the individual-level perspective. In particular, researchers and practitioners have investigated the effects of individual attitudes, beliefs, opportunities and dispositions on environmental action (Barr, 2006). Recently, however, there has been a growing understanding that true and sustained behaviour change in the environmental domain involves more than targeting individual attitudes or knowledge (Stern et al, 1986; Stern, 1999; Kollmuss and Agyeman, 2002; Gardner and Stern, 2003). Instead, *social contexts* must also change because these frame and constrain individual behavioural choices. This understanding comes from both research (e.g. Hornik, 1997) and the practitioner community (e.g. grassroots programmes; see Ockwell et al 2009; see also Chapters 9 and 10). This social context is particularly critical for *collective* resource dilemmas such as climate change. Tying the above ideas together, in the present chapter we consider how activating comparisons with various social groups may be one way in which social contexts can be harnessed to produce behaviour change. To begin this exploration, we start with a discussion of the theoretical approach that informed our thinking on the role of the social context in behaviour change, namely self-categorization theory. We then provide an overview of research informed by this theoretical perspective on the role of social comparisons in stimulating engagement with climate change and broader sustainability issues.

2. Self-categorization perspective on behaviour change

From group norms to individual behaviour

Self-categorization theory (Turner et al, 1987) suggests that people tend to classify others and themselves into social groups: perception of the social world is structured into categories. This categorization process has an adaptive function – it renders the social world more predictable and manageable. The cost of this simplification, however, is that perception of individuals becomes depersonalized – we perceive and evaluate others in terms of their belonging to a particular group rather than their unique qualities.

Importantly, the same categorization process influences self-perception. When people think about themselves in terms of group membership, they tend to ascribe the same traits to themselves and their fellow group members (i.e. self-perception becomes depersonalized: Simon et al, 1991; Simon and Hamilton, 1994; Spears et al, 1997). This process is known as self-stereotyping. In this way, an important source of knowledge about who we are as individuals stems from our knowledge about the groups that we belong to and what these represent. For example, if an individual knows that his or her community does not see climate change as an important issue, they will be likely to see themselves as a person low on environmental concern.

In addition to affecting self-perception, self-categorization processes also serve as a basis for group-based action. Previous research has demonstrated that individuals tend to behave in line with what they perceive to be group norms and standards (Simon and Hamilton, 1994; Simon et al, 1995; Smith and Henry, 1996; Smith et al, 1999; Terry et al, 2000; Turner and Reynolds, 2001). Norm-based behaviour is particularly likely for those who strongly identify with the group (i.e. those who perceive group membership as highly important: Spears et al, 1997; Jetten et al, 2002; Pickett et al, 2002; McAuliffe et al, 2003) or when group membership becomes salient in a given context (e.g. when intergroup comparisons are made: Hogg and Turner, 1987; Simon et al, 1991). In the context of behaviour change, the above findings would suggest that in order to increase individual engagement with climate change issues and encourage sustainable behaviour, one would need to increase individuals' identification with groups that promote the principles of sustainable living as a group norm. Alternatively, behaviour change agents could work with groups that are already highly meaningful for individuals (e.g. national identities, local communities) and try to shift the norms of these groups towards higher sustainability. Although shifting group norms may seem as formidable a task as shifting individual attitudes, self-categorization theory argues that group norms are not fixed; rather they are flexible, dynamic and subject to contextual change (see Turner et al, 1994; Hogg and Abrams, 1998). This opens up a range of possibilities for intervening in behaviour via group norms. The specific possibility we focus on here is tied to the intergroup comparative context.

From intergroup context to group norms

According to self-categorization theory, group members derive information about their own group (the 'ingroup') from engaging in intergroup comparisons with relevant 'outgroups' (i.e. those in other social groups; Tajfel and Turner, 1986; Turner et al, 1987). Intergroup comparisons serve two primary purposes. First, comparisons are usually conducted in ways that help to maintain positive ingroup image. Group members tend to conclude that their group is better than other groups, which contributes to individual self-esteem. In other words, people engage in intergroup comparisons in order to feel better about themselves. Thus, such comparisons provide information not only about groups that we belong to, but also about ourselves as individuals and group members (Turner et al, 1994).

Second, intergroup comparisons are made in order to maintain ingroup distinctiveness – a sense that one's group is different from other groups in the social field (see Jetten et al, 1997). To maximize differences between ingroup and outgroups, in the process of intergroup comparisons individuals use the contrast principle: when group members learn that an outgroup is high on a particular quality, they tend to conclude that their own group is low on this quality and vice versa (Oakes et al, 1994). Thus, what we conclude about ourselves and our groups depends on the intergroup comparative context – which groups are being compared and the standard that this implies. In this way, the content of group norms depends on the norms of salient outgroups and perceptions of ingroup norms are readjusted according to current social contexts. Indeed, previous research has demonstrated that group norms shift away from the norms of an outgroup used as a comparison standard (Hogg et al, 1990; Hopkins et al, 1997).

Applying the contrast principle of intergroup comparison to the environmental domain, we could predict that individuals who compare their group to strongly pro-environmental outgroups will be likely to conclude that their ingroup is relatively low on environmentalism. To the extent that they categorize themselves as a member of this group they will align their self-perceptions to this newly acquired group norm, and accordingly will become less likely to behave sustainably. Conversely, when individuals compare themselves to an outgroup which is apparently un-environmental, they will be likely to differentiate from the comparison standard by highlighting green values of their ingroup, and incorporating these values in their self-perceptions and behaviour. In other words, individuals learn who they *are* and how they should behave by learning who they *are not*.

Testing the above predictions remains not only a theoretically interesting question (in terms of testing the validity of predictions derived on the basis of self-categorization theory), but is also important from an applied point of view. If the above predictions are correct, shifting group norms and self-stereotypes via intergroup comparisons has the potential to inform behaviour change in the environmental domain. This particular approach, focused on the broader social context, could supplement more individual approaches centred around targeting individual attitudes and awareness (e.g. via persuasion). Although many studies attest to the important role that values and personal norms (i.e. beliefs about how one should act) play for individual sustainable choices (e.g. Kaiser et al, 1999; Nordlund and Garvill, 2002; Nilsson et al, 2004; Barr, 2007), research that has explored the social context of these values and behaviours is relatively scarce (Fielding et al, 2008). At the same time, environmental information is frequently presented in an intergroup context (as in the quotes in our opening paragraph), and the applied field of environmental psychology would benefit from understanding how this social comparative information affects groups and individuals.

3. Empirically exploring self-categorization effects on intentions to act sustainably

With the above issues in mind, we have conducted a programme of research directed at better understanding the role of social contexts, and social comparisons in particular, in individual behaviour in the environmental domain. As a first step in this programme we tested the hypothesis that intergroup comparison context (salient outgroups) affects perceived group norms and individual environmental intentions. Following on from this, we have also considered a range of additional factors that may affect the role of social comparisons. In particular, our research has considered the relative normativeness of comparison groups (i.e. who is perceived to 'set the standard'), and whether comparisons are conducted *between* or *within* the groups. Below we review the main outcomes of this research programme.

Differentiating us from them: intergroup comparative context and individual environmental intentions

Since intergroup comparisons in the environmental domain are frequently invoked in an international context (i.e. comparing performance of different countries), our research began by focusing on big national groups as social categories and sources of comparison. Specifically, we explored how comparisons with different nations influenced British participants' perception of the British as a group, the perceived norms of their nation with respect to the environment, and the translation of these perceptions into individual sustainable values and intentions (see Rabinovich et al, 2009, for full details).

In two studies ($N = 189^2$) we surveyed British members of the public about their individual environmental values and intentions, while experimentally varying intergroup comparison context. Participants were randomly allocated to one of the three experimental groups. To manipulate intergroup comparison context, we asked participants in one group to write about differences between the British and a nation that was perceived to be doing worse on the environmental domain (i.e. the USA). Another group was asked to write about the differences between British people in general and a nation that was perceived to be doing better in terms of sustainability (i.e. Sweden). In theoretical terms, participants who compared their national group to the USA were involved in a positive intergroup comparison, whereas those who compared their national group to Sweden were involved in a negative intergroup comparison. A control group was not asked to compare their nation to any other group: participants in this group simply described British people in general. Importantly, the dimension of environmental behaviour was not explicitly mentioned in this comparison task, and very few participants spontaneously referred to environmental issues in their lists of differences. Thus outgroup environmental stereotypes (perceptions of an outgroup as either pro- or un-environmental) were activated implicitly.

After the comparison task, we asked participants how environmentally friendly they thought British people were in general (perceived ingroup norm), about the centrality (subjective importance) of environmental values to their individual selves, and their own intentions to perform a range of environmentally friendly behaviours (such as reducing electricity and gas consumption, buying mostly organic products, etc.). In line with self-categorization theory, the results of both studies demonstrated that participants shifted their ingroup perception away from the salient outgroup comparison standard. Those who compared their national group to Sweden, engaging in a negative comparison with the group that was performing better, perceived their own group as being *less* environmentally friendly than participants in the control group (who did not engage in intergroup comparisons). Conversely, participants who compared themselves to the USA, engaging in a positive comparison with the group that was performing worse, perceived their own national group as being *more* environmentally friendly than participants in the control group (see Figure 4.1). In other words, negative comparison reduced perceived green ingroup norm, while positive comparison encouraged thinking about one's own group as strongly environmental.

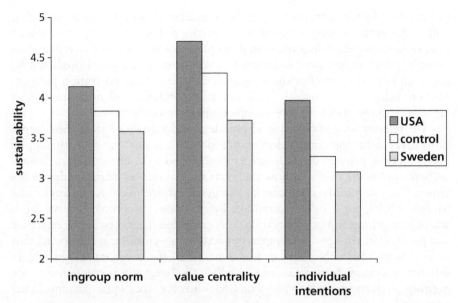

Figure 4.1 *The effect of intergroup comparisons on green ingroup norm, environmental values centrality and individual intentions to behave sustainably*

Moreover, these shifts in perceived ingroup norm translated into concordant shifts in the centrality of individual environmental values and intentions to behave in a sustainable way. Participants who engaged in negative comparison reported that green values were less central to their own lives than participants in the control group. Conversely, participants who engaged in positive comparisons reported that environmental values were more central to who they were as individuals. These effects on environmental values were paralleled by significant shifts in behavioural intentions: After comparing their national group to Sweden, British participants reported reduced environmental intentions, but after comparing their group to the USA, British participants increased their reported intentions (see Figure 4.1). Thus, overall participants were acting in line with the ingroup–outgroup differentiation principle ('we are different from them') by shifting their group evaluations and self-evaluations *away* from the comparison standard.

Boundaries of differentiation: the role of comparison focus

The results of the above two studies suggest that positive intergroup comparisons (where ingroup is compared to an outgroup that is doing comparatively worse) are encouraging, while negative comparisons (where ingroup is compared upwards to a better-performing outgroup) may be undermining. However, intuitively it is also easy to imagine situations where positive comparisons might undermine rather than stimulate sustainable action. For example, in response to positive feedback about one's group, people may conclude that they no longer need to take action because others have already done this on their behalf (consistent with the 'free-rider effect'; see Lorenzoni et al, 2007). Likewise, negative comparisons might sometimes stimulate relevant behaviour rather than discourage it, if people become motivated to repair their group's poor image (see Rabinovich and Morton, 2010). Consequently, although our initial studies show support for the self-categorization perspective on behaviour change, it also seems important to identify sources of variability in the effects of intergroup comparison context.

Do intergroup comparisons always lead individuals to shift their intentions away from the comparison standard? Or can this effect be altered, or even reversed, given certain circumstances? To address this question, in subsequent studies we explored how the focus of comparison might moderate the effects of intergroup comparison discussed above (see Rabinovich and Morton, 2009, for a full description). By the focus of comparison we mean which group (ingroup or outgroup) is foregrounded (i.e. taken as the reference comparator) in the specific comparison setting. Specifically, we expected that situations in which the *ingroup is compared to the outgroup* might trigger different processes from situations in which the *outgroup is compared to the ingroup* – even though both situations involve the same groups being compared.

To try and understand the possible differences between these situations, we draw on theorizing about normativity (e.g. Pratto et al, 2007). The basic point of this perspective is that certain groups are routinely perceived as more 'normative' (i.e. standard) than others (e.g. men are often seen to be more typical citizens than women). When two groups are being compared, normative groups are taken as the implied standard and less normative groups become the focus of explanation (i.e. the question is more often 'how are women different from men?' rather than 'how are men different from women?'). Normativity is something that can be determined by society as in the case of men and women, but it is also something that can shift subtly according to the framing of the comparison context and how this implies normativity of one group more than the other. Specifically, comparing the *ingroup to outgroup* implies that the outgroup is higher in normativeness than the ingroup, and therefore the outgroup becomes the standard for intergroup comparison. Conversely, comparing the *outgroup to the ingroup* implies higher normativeness of the ingroup and makes this the standard for comparisons (e.g. Hegarty and Chryssochoou, 2005; Pratto et al, 2007).

Linking this to our previous discussions, self-categorization theory often assumes that during intergroup comparisons ingroups will always be perceived as more normative than outgroups. And, as we illustrated above, research from this perspective shows that intergroup comparisons typically result in contrastive perceptions, whereby ingroup and outgroup stereotypes shift *away* from each other (i.e. contrast effect; see Turner et al, 1987; Hogg et al, 1990). However, while this may represent the general case, research from the normativity perspective suggests that the relative normativity of groups can shift according to features of the comparison context, even when comparisons involve ingroups (e.g. Hegarty and Chryssochoou, 2005). Moreover, comparisons between groups that differ in their normativity typically lead to assimilation of the less normative group to the standards of the more norma-tive group (see Markman and McMullen, 2003; Hegarty and Chryssochoou, 2005; White, 2008 – on the role of perceived normativeness in social com-parison). At the very least, then, it seems that when questions of normativity are taken into account, contrastive perceptions may not always follow inter-group comparisons.

To explore this possibility, we conducted a series of studies in which we again engaged participants in intergroup comparisons along the lines of our previous studies, but we also included a manipulation of the comparison con-text designed to shift the relative normativity of the ingroup versus the outgroup in that context (see Rabinovich and Morton, 2009). Specifically, three studies (total $N = 365$; all participants were British[3]) experimentally manipulated the focus of intergroup comparison such that either ingroup (Britain) or outgroup (another nation) was foregrounded in the comparison setting. In Study 1, we achieved this by varying the order of ingroup and out-group evaluation, asking participants to evaluate either ingroup or outgroup first (see Pratto et al, 2007, for a similar manipulation of comparison focus). In Studies 2 and 3, we manipulated the focus of comparison by varying the wording of the comparison task: participants were asked either to compare their ingroup (the British) to an outgroup, or, vice versa, to compare an out-group to the ingroup. As we suggest above, these syntactic variations, though subtle, convey information about which group is more normative and there-fore the standard for comparison. In addition to these manipulations of comparison focus, we again manipulated the nature of the comparison such that participants were comparing their group to an outgroup that was per-forming either better (a negative comparison, Sweden) or worse (a positive comparison, the USA) in the environmental domain. Intentions to behave sus-tainably were measured by asking participants how likely they were to perform a number of environmentally friendly actions during the next month (e.g. decreasing non-green fuel consumption).

The results of these studies revealed significant interactions between focus of comparison and standard of comparison on perceived ingroup environmen-tal norms and individual sustainable intentions. When participants were asked to compare Sweden or the USA to Britain (comparing *outgroup to ingroup*; implying greater ingroup normativity), the results conformed to our previous experiments: perceived ingroup norms and individual intentions shifted away from the outgroup comparison standard. Under these conditions, participants who engaged in positive comparison with the USA perceived their ingroup (Britain) as more environmentally friendly and reported stronger intentions to behave in a sustainable manner, but those who engaged in negative compari-son with Sweden perceived the ingroup as less green and their environmental intentions were reduced (see Figure 4.2). However, when participants were instead asked to compare Britain to Sweden or to the USA (*ingroup to out-group*; implying greater outgroup normativity), there were no significant differences between those participants who engaged in positive comparison and those who engaged in negative comparison: perceived ingroup norms and indi-vidual intentions did not change depending on whether participants compared

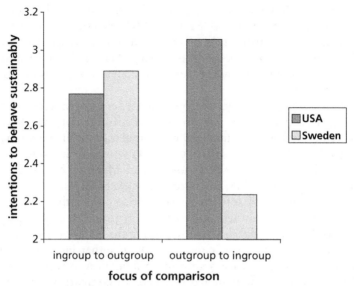

Source: Rabinovich and Morton, 2009

Figure 4.2 *The effect of comparison type and comparison focus on intentions to behave sustainably*

their group upwards and downwards. Importantly, additional analyses confirmed that shifts in the perceived normativity of ingroups and outgroups were responsible for these effects: participants who compared *outgroup to ingroup* perceived ingroup as relatively *more normative* than those who compared *ingroup to outgroup*, and perceived ingroup normativeness mediated the joint effect of comparison focus and standard on individual intentions to behave sustainably.

These results show how the outcomes of the intergroup comparisons are determined not just by the standards against which our group is compared, but also by which group becomes the focus of comparison in a given setting. When outgroups are compared to the ingroup, contrast effects are observed in a way that conforms to the principles of self-categorization theory (and the results of our earlier studies). However, when ingroups are compared to outgroups, the superior normativity of the outgroup implied by this setting may constrain the ability to contrast the ingroup and the self away from these standards. Accordingly, when outgroups 'set the standard', assimilation towards their standards may be more likely than contrast. This provides an important qualification to our original findings. Positive comparisons are not always encouraging and negative comparisons are not necessarily disengaging. Rather the focus of comparison can alter the overall meaning of the comparison situation, which has implications for both ingroup perception and individual behaviour.

Differentiation within: intragroup comparisons
So far we have discussed the effects of intergroup comparisons (comparing one's nation to other nations) on public engagement with environmental

issues. As we highlighted at the beginning of this chapter, intergroup comparisons of this kind are frequent and often provide a framework within which people consider their own behaviour. However, comparisons can also be carried out *within* rather than between groups. For example, the ingroup's present performance may be different to how it performed in the past, and performance at different points in time may come to be a source of comparison and evaluation, just as intergroup comparisons do. Indeed, intragroup comparisons are also frequently invoked in the public discourse on environmental issues; for example, by communicating the extent to which the collective performance on some dimension represents an improvement or a decline. Previously we have argued that positive intergroup comparisons are more motivating for behaviour than negative intergroup comparisons, especially when the ingroup is taken as the standard against which others are compared. Do intragroup comparisons function in a similar way? Specifically, are people similarly motivated by positive comparisons with their own past? Or does awareness of our own decline trigger reparative action as people try to live up to their group's previously higher standards?   Returning to the theoretical literature, it seems that both possibilities are viable. On the one hand, people may interpret the information about improvement as a positive (current) group norm and information about deteriorating performance as a negative group norm, and be motivated to adhere to it (e.g. Simon and Hamilton, 1994; Smith and Henry, 1996; Smith et al, 1999; Terry et al, 2000). This would lead to shifting one's behaviour away from the past performance standard and towards the behaviour that is perceived as the current norm. Specifically, improvement feedback would lead to intensification of individual efforts, and negative trend feedback would lead to disengagement.

On the other hand, individuals may interpret their group's performance in terms of meeting (or failing to meet) group standards. For instance, the group's improved performance in comparison with its past standards may convey information that group goals have been achieved. This is likely to lead to complacency and reduction in further effort. Consistent with this idea, Spoor and Schmitt (2009) have found that women who compared the current status of their gender group with its more negative past status perceived collective action as less necessary than when they engaged in intergroup comparison with men. This suggests that focusing on collective improvement over time may lead to complacency. In contrast, negative feedback about deteriorating performance may suggest to group members that they need to intensify their efforts in order to meet the group's previous standards (see, for example, Schultz et al, 2007).

In our final study (Duke et al, 2009), we stepped outside the intergroup context and explored the effects of intragroup comparisons on motivation to engage in sustainable behaviour. In this study, British participants ($N = 157$) received feedback about Britain's national CO_2 emissions either in comparison to an outgroup (i.e. an intergroup comparison, as per our previous studies), or to Britain's own past performance (i.e. an intragroup comparison). We also varied the specific information presented in these comparisons such that the current ingroup's performance compared either favourably or unfavourably to a comparison standard. In the positive comparison condition, Britain's current performance was presented as more favourable than the alternative performance standard, set either by the ingroup's own past or by an outgroup. Conversely, in the negative comparison condition, Britain's current performance was presented as less favourable than its own past or the comparison outgroup, depending on the condition. Importantly, the actual level of Britain's CO_2 emissions remained constant across the conditions. As in the previous studies, after participants read the comparative information, we measured intentions to engage in pro-environmental behaviours and the centrality of environmental values to the self.

Analyses revealed a significant interaction between the direction of comparison (positive or negative) and the type of comparison (intergroup or intragroup) on environmental intentions. In other words, the effectiveness of positive and negative comparisons depended on whether the standard for comparison was another nation or the past performance of one's own nation. Replicating our previous studies, intergroup comparisons (between Britain and another nation) resulted in contrasting intentions to act sustainably: when Britain was performing worse than another group, participants reported weaker intentions to behave sustainably than when Britain was compared to a group against which it was doing better. Again, these shifts in intention were driven by shifts in the centrality of environmental values to the self. In response to positive intergroup comparison, environmental values became more central to the self than in response to negative intergroup comparisons.

However, in the intragroup condition, where Britain's current performance was compared to its own past, these patterns reversed. Under these conditions, individual behavioural intentions shifted *towards* the comparison standard – becoming stronger when current performance was portrayed as worse than the past, and becoming weaker when current performance was portrayed as better than the past (see Figure 4.3). Value centrality displayed a similarly reversed pattern. Environmental values were reported as more central to the self after receiving feedback that current performance was worse than in the past, and less central after receiving feedback that current performance represented an improvement. Thus positive and negative comparisons resulted in different effects on individual intentions and the centrality of environmental values to the self, depending on whether they were conducted between Britain and other nations or within participants' own group.

These results suggest that intergroup and intragroup comparisons work differently. Intergroup comparisons activate individuals' motivation to differentiate one's own group from comparison outgroups. This results in higher effectiveness of *positive* comparisons: individuals shift their behaviour away from the (un-environmental) comparison standard, towards higher sustainability. However, intragroup comparisons do not activate the differentiation tendency, since there is not an outgroup standard to differentiate from. Instead, comparisons with ingroup's past performance may elicit feelings of responsibility for collective outcomes and concerns about the group living up to its own standards. These concerns result in higher effectiveness of *negative*

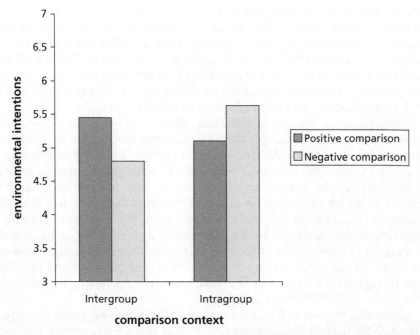

Source: Duke, Morton, and Smith, 2009

Figure 4.3 *The effects of positive and negative comparisons in intergroup and intragroup contexts*

intragroup comparisons: individuals are motivated to improve their behaviour when they compare unfavourably with their group's past (i.e. when they think performance is declining), but may become complacent when current performance is evaluated as an improvement on the past.

4. Policy implications

On the one hand, the programme of research we outline above has been motivated by theoretical concerns. That is, we were interested in better understanding how the context created by group-level comparisons might frame the behavioural decisions of individual group members, and which factors determine these effects. Indeed, we think our results provide an extension of theoretical ideas outlined in self-categorization theory by elucidating mechanisms through which intergroup comparisons influence behaviour (i.e. shifts in value centrality), conditions under which self-categorization processes are limited (i.e. when outgroups are more normative than ingroups), and conditions under which these effects reverse (in response to intragroup rather than intergroup comparisons).

However, in addition to these theoretical points, we believe that the results of our research have some important implications for policy making and communicating climate change, and other sustainability issues. First, and perhaps most importantly, the findings demonstrate that behaviour change does not have to start at an individual level. In order to produce a shift in individual environmental intentions, behaviour change agents do not have to target each individual's awareness, beliefs or attitudes. Instead, individual behaviour can change as a result of relatively subtle shifts in social context. Social identities can be harnessed to increase public engagement with specific norms and values, including environmental ones. Said differently, individual behaviour can be shifted by altering people's perception of who they are.

In particular, it seems that activating relevant outgroup stereotypes has a potential to alter the way people see the groups that they belong to, and themselves, and these contextually driven shifts in group- and self-perception may have consequences for individual behaviour. In other words, specific content of identities can be altered by social context. The way we see ourselves depends on which categories are salient in the social field. The fact that self-perception is socially rooted, and to a large extent flexible, opens up multiple opportunities for increasing public engagement with climate change through focusing on various aspects of the social context. Intergroup comparisons are one aspect of the social context that is open to manipulation, and therefore open to exploitation as part of interventions targeted at changing individual behaviour.

Generally, the research seems to suggest that activating positive comparisons (i.e. downwards comparisons with groups that are performing worse on the relevant domain) may be more productive than appealing to shame and guilt by making negative comparisons with groups that are performing better. The research has consistently demonstrated that participants engaging in positive intergroup comparisons are more likely to adopt a positive group image (in the domain of comparison) and to behave in a way consistent with this image. For example, in our studies, British participants who compared their own nation to the USA (stereotypically a less environmentally friendly group) were more motivated to act in a sustainable way than participants who engaged in comparison with Sweden (a more pro-environmental nation).

However, as we have also demonstrated, the effectiveness of positive social comparisons may depend on other factors, such as relative normativeness and status of the compared groups. Although generally ingroups are perceived as highly normative categories in intergroup context, when outgroup normativeness is increased, the positive effect of downward comparisons (and the negative effect of upward comparisons) may not hold. As our findings have demonstrated, when individuals perceive the comparison outgroup as a normative standard against which the ingroup is evaluated, they no longer shift their behaviour away from the outgroup norm. As such, positive intergroup comparisons are not invariably encouraging, and negative comparisons are not always disengaging. Rather, to predict the outcome of social comparison, behaviour change agents need to take into account relative status of the compared groups.

Notwithstanding this, our findings suggest that when outgroup stereotypes are strong (a comparison outgroup is perceived as strongly pro-environmental or strongly un-environmental), it may be easier to get ingroup members to shift their behaviour *away* from such stereotypes, rather than *towards* them. In this respect, using positive intergroup comparisons to encourage desirable behaviour seems more promising, as long as a downward comparison group is not highly normative.

Another factor that seems to alter, and even reverse, the outcomes of social comparisons is whether these comparisons are conducted *between* or *within* social groups. While in the intergroup context positive comparisons are more likely to lead to strengthening of environmental values and intentions, in intragroup settings where comparisons are made with the group's own past performance, negative comparisons may be more stimulating. The reason is that while intergroup comparisons define who we are by making clear who we are not, intragroup comparisons communicate whether we are meeting our own standards. In the latter case, feedback on improving performance (positive comparison with the past standard) leads to complacency, while the signal that the group's performance is deteriorating (negative comparison with the past) alerts group members that internal standards are not met and leads to intensification of individual efforts.

The fact that intergroup and intragroup comparisons seem to operate in different ways suggests that both types of comparison can be productively used by environmental campaigns designers. If the target group's environmental performance is already strong and the aim is to keep up the same level of engagement, the positive comparison information would be more effective if delivered in intergroup context (i.e. the group can be praised for achieving better results in comparison with other groups). Praising the group for improving on its own performance without activating intergroup comparisons may result in complacency and be counterproductive. However, if the target group's performance is not at its best and the aim of the intervention is to enhance engagement, criticism may be better delivered by highlighting the group's failing relative to its own standards rather than averting to intergroup comparisons with better-performing outgroups.

5. Conclusion

Are the kinds of negative intergroup comparisons that are frequently invoked in media an effective way of promoting public engagement with climate change? Or are there better ways in which agents might capitalize upon such comparisons to affect change? This chapter suggests that 'no' is the answer to the former question and 'yes' to the latter. Positive intergroup comparisons that encourage people to see green values as defining of their group, and by virtue of this their self, may be more effective in stimulating public engagement than negative comparisons that bring to the fore underperformance in comparison to more environmentally friendly outgroups. Of course, there are caveats to power of positive comparisons. When comparison outgroups have particularly high social value and are strongly normative, the power of positive comparisons is likely to be constrained relative to the pull of conforming to the normative (i.e. socially valued) position. Under these circumstances, environmental campaigners may instead choose to locate their persuasive messages in intragroup context. In intragroup settings, however, critical feedback that highlights the group's deteriorating performance may be more effective than positive feedback, which has the potential to create complacency.

To summarize, behaviour change agents have two tactics to choose from when designing comparative messages to stimulate public engagement. One is to use positive intergroup comparisons with underperforming and non-normative outgroups. The other is to inform the target group about its deteriorating performance in comparison with its past results (negative intra-group comparison). The specific choice would depend on the target group's current performance and salient outgroup stereotypes. It is important that communicators of persuasive messages anticipate and take into account the way that individuals construct the *meaning* of the comparative context, since this determines both self-perception and individual behaviour.

Notes

1. Britain lags behind on bioenergy, say MPs (18 September 2006). *The Guardian.* Retrieved 13 November 2006, from http://www.guardian.co.uk/environment/ 2006/sep/18/energy.greenpolitics
   'Charges needed' in war on waste (8 January 2007). *BBC News.* Retrieved 3 March 2007, from http://news.bbc.co.uk/1/hi/uk/6240119.stm
   Whipp, M. (2007, July 19). CPI: UK paper recycling relies too heavily on exports. Printweek.com. Retrieved 21 October 2007, from http://www.printweek.com /news/672431/CPI-UK-paper-recycling-relies-heavily-exports/
   Europe charged with recycling all batteries by 2008 (4 May 2006). *The Times.* Retrieved 13 November 2006, from https://www.timesonline.co.uk/article/0,,2-2164243,00.html
2. Participants in Study 1 were British first year psychology students (mean age = 20.00, SD = 5.69, 85 per cent female). Participants in Study 2 were 90 British adults (73 per cent female, mean age = 30.18, SD = 14.49) recruited via a partic-ipant pool.
3. Participants in Study 1 were British adults randomly approached in public spaces of a small English city (43 per cent female, mean age = 27.87, SD = 12.65). Participants in Study 2 were British adults recruited in the same public areas (59 per cent female, mean age = 20.91, SD = 7.17). Participants in Study 3 were British students recruited from a university participant pool (74 per cent female, mean age = 25.72, SD = 12.65).

References

Barr, S. (2006) 'Environmental action in the home: Investigating the "value-action" gap', *Geography*, vol 91, no 1, pp43–54

Barr, S. (2007) 'Factors influencing environmental attitudes and behaviors: A U.K. case study of household waste management', *Environment and Behavior*, vol 39, no 4, pp435–473

Duke, C. C., Morton, T. A. and Smith, J. R. (2009) Better or worse than who? Different types of comparison lead to different paths of environmental behaviour. Unpublished manuscript, University of Exeter

Fielding, K. S., Terry, D. J., Masser, B. M. and Hogg, M. A. (2008) 'Integrating social identity theory and the theory of planned behavior to explain decisions to engage in sustainable agricultural practices', *British Journal of Social Psychology*, vol 47, no 1, pp23–48

Gardner, G. T. and Stern, P. C. (2003) *Environmental Problems and Human Behavior* (2nd edn), Allyn and Bacon, Boston

Hegarty, P. and Chryssochoou, X. (2005) 'Why "our" policies set the standard more than "theirs": Category norms and generalization between European Union countries', *Social Cognition*, vol 23, no 6, pp507–544

Hogg, M. A. and Turner, J. C. (1987) 'Intergroup behavior, self-stereotyping and the salience of social categories', *British Journal of Social Psychology*, vol 26, no 4, pp269–348

Hogg, M. A. and Abrams, D. (1988) *Social Identifications: A Social Psychology of Intergroup Relations and Group Processes*, Routledge, London

Hogg, M. A., Turner, J. C. and Davidson, B. (1990) 'Polarized norms and social frames of reference: A test of self-categorization theory of group polarization', *Basic and Applied Social Psychology*, vol 11, no 1, pp77–100

Hopkins, N., Regan, M. and Abell, J. (1997) 'On the context dependence of national stereotypes: Some Scottish data', *British Journal of Social Psychology*, vol 36, no 4, pp553–563

Hornik, R. C. (1997) 'Public health education and communication as instruments for bringing about changes in behavior', in M. E. Goldberg, M. Fishbein and S. E. Middlestadt (eds) *Social Marketing: Theoretical and Practical Perspectives*, Lawrence Erlbaum, Mahwah, NJ

Jetten, J., Spears, R. and Manstead, A. (1997) 'Distinctiveness threat and prototypicality: Combined effects on intergroup discrimination and collective self-esteem', *European Journal of Social Psychology*, vol 27, no 6, pp635–657

Jetten, J., Postmes, T. and McAuliffe, B. J. (2002) 'We're all individuals: Group norms of individualism and collectivism, levels of identification and identity threat', *European Journal of Social Psychology*, vol 32, no 2, pp189–207

Kaiser, F. G., Ranney, M., Hartig, T. and Bowler, P. A. (1999) 'Ecological behavior, environmental attitude, and feelings of responsibility for the environment', *European Psychologist*, vol 4, no 2, pp59–74

Kollmuss, A. and Agyeman, J. (2002) 'Mind the gap: why do people act environmentally and what are the barriers to pro-environmental behavior?', *Environmental Education Research*, vol 8, no 3, pp239–260

Lorenzoni, I., Nicholson-Cole, S. and Whitmarsh, L. (2007) 'Barriers perceived to engaging with climate change among the UK public and their policy implications', *Global Environmental Change*, vol 17, nos 3–4, pp445–459

Markman, K. and McMullen, M. (2003) 'A reflection and evaluation model of comparative thinking', *Personality and Social Psychology Review*, vol 7, no 3, pp244–267

McAuliffe, B. J., Jetten, J., Hornsey, M. J. and Hogg, M. A. (2003) 'Individualist and collectivist norms: When it's ok to go your own way', *European Journal of Social Psychology*, vol 33, no 1, pp57–70

Nilsson, A., von Borgstede, C. and Biel, A. (2004) 'Willingness to accept climate change strategies: The effect of values and norms', *Journal of Environmental Psychology*, vol 24, no 3, pp267–277

Nordlund, A. M. and Garvill, J. (2002) 'Value structures behind proenvironmental behavior', *Environment and Behavior*, vol 34, no 6, pp740–756

Oakes, P. J., Haslam, S. A. and Turner, J. C. (1994) *Stereotyping and Social Reality*, Oxford, Cambridge, Blackwell

Ockwell, D., Whitmarsh, L. and O'Neill, S. (2009) 'Reorienting climate change communication for effective mitigation – forcing people to be green or fostering grass-roots engagement?', *Science Communication*, vol 30, no 3, pp305–327

Pickett, C. L., Bonner, B. L. and Coleman, J. M. (2002) 'Motivated self-stereotyping: heightened assimilation and differentiation needs result in increased levels of self-stereotyping', *Journal of Personality and Social Psychology*, vol 82, no 4, pp543–562

Pratto, F., Hegarty, P. and Korchmaros, J. (2007) 'Who gets stereotyped? How communication practices and category norms lead people to stereotype particular people and groups', in Y. Kashima, K. Fiedler and P. Freytag (eds) *Stereotype Dynamics: Language-Based Approaches to Stereotype Formation, Maintenance, and Change*, Lawrence Erlbaum Associates, Mahwah, NJ

Rabinovich, A. and Morton, T. A. (2009) 'The impact of comparative focus on assimilation and contrast effects in intergroup context', manuscript under review

Rabinovich, A. and Morton, T. A. (2010) 'Who says we are bad people? The impact of criticism source and attributional content on responses to group-based criticism', *Personality and Social Psychology Bulletin*, vol 36, no 4, pp 524–536

Rabinovich, A., Morton, T. A., Postmes, T. and Verplanken, B. (2009) 'Collective self and individual choice: The effects of intergroup comparative context on individual values and behavioral intentions', manuscript under review

Schultz, P. W., Nolan, J. M., Cialdini, R. B., Goldstein, N. J. and Griskevicius, V. (2007) 'The constructive, destructive, and reconstructive power of social norms', *Psychological Science*, vol 18, no 5, pp429–434

Simon, B. and Hamilton, D. L. (1994) 'Self-stereotyping and social context – the effects of relative ingroup size and ingroup status', *Journal of Personality and Social Psychology*, vol 66, no 4, pp699–711

Simon, B., Glassner-Bayerl, B. and Stratenwerth, I. (1991) 'Stereotyping and self-stereotyping in a natural intergroup context – the case of heterosexual and homosexual men', *Social Psychology Quarterly*, vol 54, no 3, pp252–266

Simon, B., Pantaleo, G. and Mummendey, A. (1995) 'Unique individual or interchangeable group member – The accentuation of intragroup differences versus similarities as an indicator of the individual self versus the collective self', *Journal of Personality and Social Psychology*, vol 69, no 1, pp106–119

Smith, E. R. and Henry, S. (1996) 'An ingroup becomes part of the self: Response time evidence', *Personality and Social Psychology Bulletin*, vol 22, no 6, pp635–642

Smith, E. R., Coats, S. and Walling, D. (1999) 'Overlapping mental representations of self, ingroup, and partner: Further response time evidence and a connectionist model', *Personality and Social Psychology Bulletin*, vol 25, no 7, pp873–882

Spears, R., Doosje, B. and Ellemers, N. (1997) 'Self-stereotyping in the face of threats to group status and distinctiveness: The role of group identification', *Personality and Social Psychology Bulletin*, vol 23, no 5, pp538–553

Spoor, J. R. and Schmitt, M. T. (2009) '"Things are getting better" isn't always better: Considering women's progress affects perceptions of and reactions to contemporary gender inequality', manuscript under review

Stern, P. C. (1999) 'Information, incentives, and proenvironmental consumer behavior', *Journal of Consumer Policy*, vol 22, no 4, pp461–478

Stern, P. C., Aronson, E., Darley, J. M., Hill, D. H., Hirst, E., Kempton, W. et al (1986) 'The effectiveness of incentives for residential energy conservation', *Evaluation Review*, vol 10, no 2, pp147–176

Tajfel, H. and Turner, J. C. (1986) 'The social identity theory of intergroup behavior', in S. Worchel and W. G. Austin (eds) *The Psychology of Intergroup Relations*, Nelson-Hall, Chicago

Terry, D. J., Hogg, M. A. and McKimmie, B. M. (2000) 'Attitude-behavior relations: The role of ingroup norms and mode of behavioral decision-making', *British Journal of Social Psychology*, vol 39, no 3, pp337–361

Turner, J. C., Oakes, P. J., Haslam, S. A. and McGarty, C. (1994) 'Self and collective: Cognition and social context', *Personality and Social Psychology Bulletin*, vol 20, no 5, pp454–463

Turner, J. C., Hogg, M. A., Oakes, P. J., Reicher, S. D. and Wetherell, M. S. (1987) *Rediscovering the Social Group: A Self-Categorization Theory*, Blackwell, Oxford and New York

White, J. B. (2008) 'Self–other similarity judgment asymmetries reverse for people to whom you want to be similar', *Journal of Experimental Social Psychology*, vol 44, no 1, pp127–131

5
Dismantling the Consumption–Happiness Myth: A Neuropsychological Perspective on the Mechanisms That Lock Us in to Unsustainable Consumption

Fiona Brannigan

1. Introduction

Concerns are growing that the level of consumption witnessed in western societies today is simply unsustainable (WWF, 2008; Jackson, 2009). In particular, the energy used to produce our consumer goods is making a significant contribution to climate change. It is becoming increasingly recognized that western societies need to take responsibility for these emissions and reduce them (e.g. Wang and Watson, 2007). Not all consumption is negative, of course; amongst other things, material possessions provide us with our basic needs. They can play a role in developing and bonding communities (Douglas and Isherwood 1979; McCracken, 1988), and they can help us to express our identities (Belk, 1988; Campbell, 1997). However, current rates of consumption are unprecedented and, many argue, environmentally and socially unsustainable (e.g. Jackson, 2005).

The theoretical models which provide insight into the motivations behind our consumer behaviours are many and varied. The models fall within a wide range of disciplines from social psychology to theories of economics. Several comprehensive reviews have been undertaken which provide an overview of the issues and concepts involved (e.g. Jackson, 2005). This chapter, however, does not attempt to offer such a review; rather, it seeks to weave a path through the complexities of several behaviour models and theories to offer a perspective on the mechanisms which may be locking us in to unsustainable consumption. Selected models and theories are merged to form an integrated perspective that reflects the 'eclectic' style adopted by marketing theorists and practitioners (Jackson, 2005). For ease, the central mechanism described in this chapter has been termed the Consumption–Happiness Myth. The term happiness here refers very specifically to the pursuit of pleasure and its role in motivating human behaviour (discussed in Sections 2 and 3). The term myth refers to the symbolic level at which the mechanism interacts with and influences our sense of self at the very deepest levels of consciousness.

This chapter argues that the Consumption–Happiness Myth locks us into specific patterns of consumption because of its impact on four key elements: affect regulation; conscious and unconscious input into decision making; habit formation; and psychological development.

Affect regulation

The concept of the duality of decision making – that is, that both emotions (affect) and rational thought have a role to play in the choices we make – has been widely discussed in recent years (Damasio, 1994; Epstein, 1994; Guillaume et al, 2009). Neuroscientist Antonio Damasio argues that emotions are not just involved in decision making, but are essential to the process (Damasio, 1994; Bechara and Damasio, 2005). Studies by Damasio and Bechara suggest that sound judgement first of all requires emotional processing. This emotional processing then merges with rational thought to enable the individual to choose the best course of action. Emotional processing is often felt as a 'gut feeling' or intuition; when this ability is impaired,, the effectiveness of decision making is reduced (Bechara and Damasio, 2005). Emotional input is only beneficial, however, when it is relevant to the task in hand. Studies suggest that it can be disruptive if the emotional input is unconnected (Bechara and Damasio, 2005). Further, the strength of the emotion can determine the extent to which emotional processing will influence the choices that are made: the stronger the emotion the greater its influence (Verdejo-Garcia and Bechara, 2008). So a strong, unrelated emotion could have a very detrimental effect on our ability to make sound judgements. To compensate for this, the degree to which emotions are able to influence decisions is normally moderated through a mechanism known as 'affect regulation' (Schore, 2001; Collins and Allard, 2004). Affect regulation involves the activation of areas of the brain which introduce a more reflective function, and which take into account circumstances and a variety of social judgements (Schore, 2001; Collins and Allard, 2004). This chapter will argue that our response to the marketing messages we receive has a direct impact on our ability to regulate affect, and as a result strong and often unrelated emotions are having too great an influence on our consumption behaviours.

Conscious and non-conscious processes

The influence that both conscious and non-conscious processes have on the choices we make has also been widely discussed in recent years as a result of the findings emerging from neuroscience (Overskeid, 2000; Bechara and Damasio, 2005). Many of these findings seem to confirm theories that are advocated by psychological practices such as psychotherapy and analytical psychology (e.g. Epstein, 1994; Fonagy et al, 2002; Knox, 2003). Several states of consciousness have been identified, including the conscious, the unconscious, and an intermediary stage that can be described as subconscious or pre-conscious (Kihlstrom, 1987; Bechara and Damasio, 2005). The gut feeling described by Damasio, for example, is neither fully conscious nor fully unconscious (Overskeid, 2000; Bechara and Damasio, 2005). The importance of the non-conscious states (i.e. unconscious and subconscious) in the decision-making process has been demonstrated by Benjamin Libet. Libet's (1993) findings suggest that we make decisions at an unconscious level before we become conscious of those decisions. Further, our decision making can be influenced by sensory input that is completely undetectable at a conscious level (Kihlstrom, 1987). Evidence suggests that emotions can also be experienced and processed at an entirely unconscious level (Berridge, 2004). If truly unconscious emotions exist, then our decisions and subsequent behaviours may be influenced by fears and desires without our knowledge. This chapter will argue that marketing directly influences our non-conscious emotional and cognitive processes, and by doing so motivates us to consume in ways that may be contrary to the rational choices we would otherwise make.

Habit formation

Neuroplasticity refers to the phenomenon by which areas of the brain that are used regularly are stronger, more developed and work more efficiently than those areas of the brain that are used less frequently (Siegel, 2007). As certain neural pathways are strengthened through regular activation, the processes involved move from being 'effortful' to being 'effortless' (Siegel, 2007; see also Chapter 1). In this way, neuroplasticity provides a mechanism by which habitual behaviours are formed. Recent evidence suggests that neuroplasticity is affected by our experiences and interactions with the external environment, and occurs throughout our lifetimes (Kolb and Whishaw, 1998). This chapter argues that through the constant triggering of certain neurological processes by the marketing messages that surround us, our brains are being shaped to operate in certain ways. Hence we are becoming locked in to unsustainable consumption in a very physical sense.

Psychological development

Disruption to our ability to regulate affect and the changes to the physical structure of our brains can have a significant impact on our psychological development (Schore, 2001). Psychodynamic theory and other self-development models suggest that an individual should progress through several stages; leading eventually to an advanced level of maturity (Maslow, 1943; Knox, 2003). This chapter will argue that the imbalances that are being created in terms of emotion versus rational thought and conscious versus unconscious processes, and the way in which we are being locked into these imbalances through habit formation, is disrupting this psychological development. As a result we are becoming locked into a psychological state that perpetuates our need for consumer goods. It also prevents us from reaching a level of psychological and emotional maturity that would allow us, as a culture, to deal with the enormous environmental challenges that we now face.

This chapter does not suggest that everyone is being affected by these mechanisms to the same extent. Rather, it argues that there is a continuum throughout society. Some of us will be affected a great deal, others not at all; but most of us will be affected to some degree. As marketing practices become increasingly sophisticated, however, the potential for more of us to become locked in to these mechanisms also increases. Of particular concern are the advances that are being made in neuromarketing. Neuromarketing is based on an emerging understanding of how our brains work at an unconscious level, and it attempts to develop techniques and marketing strategies to harness these unconscious processes (Lindstrom, 2008). This chapter argues that much of what is happening in terms of the Consumption–Happiness Myth would arise whether marketers were deliberately trying to manipulate these mechanisms or not, simply by the volume and nature of the messages encountered. The more skilled marketing becomes, however, the more effective their techniques will be, and the more strongly the mechanism will be reinforced.

The chapter will also consider the role that social marketing may have in helping to dismantle the Consumption–Happiness Myth. Kotler and Zaltman (1971) are credited with formally introducing the term 'social marketing'. They define social marketing as 'the design, implementation and control of programs calculated to influence the acceptability of social ideas' (Kotler and Zaltman, 1971, p5). One of the basic premises upon which social marketing is based is that it can adopt the same techniques so successfully utilized by general marketing to advance social issues for the common good (Institute for Social Marketing, undated). This chapter argues that such an approach should be treated with some caution. Importantly, however, social marketing also has a role to play in addressing the cultural context within which behaviours occur, and advocates suggest that it could contribute to 'socio-cultural evolution' (Levy and Zaltman 1975; MacFadyen et al, 1999). It is this aspect of social marketing which has the potential to make a significant contribution to dismantling the Consumption–Happiness Myth, particularly in relation to the role it can play in developing cultural mindfulness (discussed in Section 5).

2. The pursuit of pleasure

As new technologies allow neuroscientists to peer ever deeper into the workings of the human mind, the role that the pursuit of pleasure plays in motivating human behaviour has become an issue of increasing interest (Damasio, 1994; Penksepp, 1998; Berridge, 2008). Much of this discussion is based on the discovery of the 'reward circuit'. The reward circuit (also known as the reward system) is a complex network of neural pathways which connects several areas of the brain (Berridge, 2008). It has a key role to play in our experience of pleasure (Damasio, 1994). Clusters of neurons called the nucleus accumbens and the amygdala are particularly important to the functioning of the reward circuit, and its role in motivating behaviour and decision making (Schlaepfer et al, 2007; Cohen et al, 2009). At a physiological level, emotions and feelings arise from the release of neurotransmitters in the nucleus accumbens and associated circuitry. Recent evidence suggests that dopamine is instrumental to the anticipation of reward (the wanting), whilst opioids are instrumental to the enjoying of the reward itself (the liking) (Berridge, 2008). Further, the wanting and liking can be experienced at an entirely unconscious level (Berridge, 2004). Neuroscientist and psychologist Kent Berridge (2004) argues that the distinction between the wanting and liking phases of the reward system is very significant, because the two can become separated. If the system becomes disrupted, we can experience a strong 'want' or desire for something at an unconscious level that does not necessarily produce the 'liking' or pleasure reward that we anticipate. Despite this, however, the wanting does not reduce, in fact it can increase; the lack of satisfaction keeps us wanting more (Berridge, 2004; Small et al, 2008; Stice et al, 2008; Kessler, 2009). This view, although controversial, has been applied to understanding addiction, but also has significant implications for any consumption behaviours that are based on the pursuit of pleasure. It suggests that we can become locked into a never-ending cycle of high levels of wanting without any hope of satisfaction.

The amygdala, two small almond-shaped clusters located deep in the temporal lobe, have a significant role to play in assessing the emotional value of an external stimulus. The amygdala assesses whether the object should elicit fear and be avoided, or whether it should elicit the anticipation of pleasure and motivate an approach towards it (Paton et al, 2006; Belova et al, 2007, 2008). Marketers can activate the amygdala by creating associations (somatic markers) between consumer products and primary rewards (Lindstrom, 2008). The links in the chain can become quite abstract and distant from the original reward. So with respect to the consumption of goods, for example, the links in the chain might be designer watch–social status–money–security. The image of a designer watch in an advertisement would, therefore, be enough to activate the reward circuit (due to its association with primary reinforcers) and trigger the 'wanting'.

Antonio Damasio's theory of somatic markers describes the neurological process by which stimuli or cues are linked to primary rewards, and the ways in which they can influence cognitive decision making (Bechara and Damasio, 2005). Somatic markers are described as emotional states (that are 'tagged' to cues) which are constantly being created through our everyday experiences (Bechara and Damasio, 2005). Somatic markers often work at an entirely unconscious level, evoking strong emotional memories through the use of sensory stimuli such as colour and facial expressions (Lindstrom, 2008). Research suggests that both somatic markers and explicit knowledge are involved in decision making (Guillaume et al, 2009). However, the greater the emotional response to the stimuli, the greater its influence will be over the rational decision-making process (Verdejo-Garcia and Bechara, 2008). So the greater the emotional response that marketing campaigns can elicit, the more likely our decisions will be based on emotion rather than rational thought. If, through somatic markers, strong emotions are associated with a designer watch, for example, then these strong emotions have the potential to inhibit rational considerations such as 'I don't need it', 'I can't afford it', 'I've got two already'.

The amygdala can become hypersensitive as a result of constant activation by strong external stimuli. Further, the constant activation of the amygdala makes it hard-wired or conditioned to react to the same stimuli in the same way in the future. In other words, the constant triggering of the reward circuit by the external cues we encounter in our everyday lives has the potential to lock us in to habitual, automatic behaviour at an unconscious level (LeDoux et al, 1990; Phillips and LeDoux 1992; Kessler, 2009).

This phenomenon has recently been examined by David Kessler (2009) in his book *The End of Overeating*. Kessler, a former commissioner of the US Food and Drug Administration, demonstrates that the food industry is deliberately manufacturing food that has just the right amount of fats, salt and sugar to hit our 'bliss point'. In other words, the food is manufactured in such a way that it scores highly in the 'value' assessment of the amygdala and therefore triggers large amounts of dopamine to be released in anticipation of eating it, inducing a high level of 'wanting'. However, for many, the dopamine levels stay high even after consuming the product, preventing feelings of satisfaction and maintaining the 'wanting' in the eater. The highly palatable foods overstimulate the reward circuit, which conditions the consumer to seek more and more. Kessler calls this 'conditioned hyper-eating' (Kessler, 2009).

Is it possible that by the same mechanism we have 'conditioned hyper-consumption'? Are our reward circuits constantly being triggered by the cues that surround us every day, the billboards and the television advertisements, to the extent that we are left in a state of constant craving, albeit at an unconscious level? Thus when we see the advert for a designer watch our dopamine levels rocket and produce a high level of wanting, but when we buy it the sense of satisfaction doesn't occur or is very short lived. As a result, the 'wanting' only increases and is ready to be triggered again when we see the next advertisement.

3. Fear: the flip side of pleasure

The influential neuroscientist, Joseph LeDoux, suggests that 'the backside of every positive emotion is the fear you'll lose what makes you happy' (Dobbs, 2006). Perhaps we could add that the backside of every fear is the pleasure that arises if you manage to avoid it. Marketing theorists have identified the importance of these twin motivations in consumer behaviours (e.g. Bagozzi et al, 1999), whilst neuromarketer Martin Lindstrom argues that fear is a powerful tool in marketing and 'advertisers attempt to scare us into believing that not buying their product will make us feel less safe, less happy, less free and less in control of our lives' (Lindstrom, 2008, p138); the implication being that buying the product will therefore bring about the pleasurable feelings of being 'in control', 'safe', 'happy' and 'free'.

Whilst there is evidence to suggest that the reward circuit and the fear circuit are closely linked (Faure et al, 2008; Reynolds and Berridge, 2008), the specific processes that might cause one to 'flip' to the other are less well understood. Interestingly, the psychological theory of attachment may provide an insight into the neurological mechanisms involved.

The basic premise of 'attachment theory' is that when a fear or threat arises, an individual seeks proximity to a secure attachment figure or object (Bowlby, 1969; Collins and Allard, 2004; Shaver and Mikulincer, 2005). The attachment figure or object therefore acts as a safe haven from the threat, and as a result the individual experiences a strong feeling of love for them (Fonagy et al, 2002; Bartels and Zeki, 2004). At a neurological level, once a threat is perceived the attachment system de-activates areas of the brain associated with the processing of fear, allowing intensely pleasurable feelings to arise (Bartels and Zeki, 2004). It also de-activates areas of the brain involved in regulating our emotions (Bartels and Zeki, 2004). The level of fear aroused by the initial threat is determined by the value the amygdala places on the external event or stimulus, whilst the level of love for the attachment figure or object is determined by the corresponding release of opiates associated with the reward system (Fonagy et al, 2002; Bartels and Zeki, 2004). In other words, the greater the fear, the stronger the love (e.g. Fonagy et al, 2002).

We can become attached to people, experiences, events, objects and material possessions (McCracken, 1986, 1988; Belk, 1998; Kleine and Baker, 2004). Through relationship marketing we can also become attached to brands (Wolfe, 2002; Kleine and Baker, 2004; Park et al, 2006). Attachment to brands provides a very useful mechanism for marketing strategists. An attachment to a brand can be cultivated as a long-term 'committed relationship' (Fournier, 1998; Park et al, 2006), whilst an attachment to a product associated with the brand can be much more temporary. The attachment to a particular style of clothing, for example, may only last for a season before it is replaced with products from the next range (Park et al, 2006).

Constant triggering of the attachment system by external threats, however, can lead to the development of an anxious attachment style (Fonagy et al, 2002; Collins and Allard, 2004; Shaver and Mikulincer, 2005). Those with anxious attachment styles tend to be hypersensitive to fears, constantly scanning the environment for threats and responding with much stronger negative emotions than those with secure attachment styles (Fonagy et al, 2002; Collins and Allard, 2004; Shaver and Mikulincer, 2005). In response to threats, therefore, those with anxious attachment styles have a very strong desire for physical proximity to their safe haven (Fonagy et al, 2002; Collins and Allard, 2004; Shaver and Mikulincer, 2005).

Perhaps some people are more likely than others to develop anxious attachments because of the experiences they have had. If anxious attachments are developed in one area of life through insecure relationships, for example, it is more likely that anxious attachments will develop in other areas of life (Schore, 2001; Collins and Allard, 2004; Shaver and Mikulincer, 2005). It is important to recognize, however, that even though we may be generally secure in our attachments, we can still develop insecure attachment styles for specific relationships (e.g. for a brand or product) if the fear of loss of proximity is triggered often enough (Shaver and Mikulincer, 2005). If we develop anxious attachments for consumer goods, we are more likely to want to keep buying products in order to satisfy our deep need for this proximity. Once an anxious attachment response has been activated a few times it becomes a working model (Collins and Allard, 2004). A working model is a set of predetermined actions that automatically follow a certain set of circumstances (Fonagy et al, 2002; Shaver and Mikulincer, 2005). As a result, the constant activation of the attachment system through fear can lock us in to habitual behaviours (e.g. Fonagy et al, 2002), and the greater the emotional response to an external stimulus the more likely we are to call upon a pre-existing working model (Collins and Allard, 2004).

The value of attachments in motivating consumer behaviour has not been lost on marketers: 'attachment fosters strong behaviours ... that promote a competitive advantage, enable efficient growth through line and brand extensions, and hence enhance the equity of the brand' (Park et al 2006, p6). Somatic markers can be used to arouse strong fear emotions which tap into our deepest anxieties, particularly in relation to social status (Lindstrom, 2008). As with reward, fear-based somatic markers can be generated at an entirely unconscious level and can arise from the use of certain colours, shapes, aromas and sounds, or by fleeting facial expressions and other social indicators that have no significance at a conscious level (Lindstrom, 2008). Such unconscious triggers can impact on our thought process and emotions (Kihlstrom, 1987). The unconscious nature of this influence is significant: it suggests that we may experience fear without any awareness of it. So, when we really want that designer watch, we could have no idea that our desire has actually been prompted by the dread that without it the links in the chain might be: no designer watch–no social status–no money–no security.

In terms of consumption then, we could become conditioned to seek proximity to and ownership of consumer goods as a refuge from fear. The link between fear and consumption parallels the findings of a study which shows that thoughts of death increases the attractiveness of 'high-value' goods (Mandel and Heine, 1999). It also supports the findings of recent research which suggests that although fear images related to climate change have an initial impact, they are quickly 'forgotten' by the use of avoidance, distraction and denial techniques to overcome the unpleasant feelings generated (O'Neill and Nicholson-Cole, 2009). In 'Meeting Environmental Challenges: The Role of Human Identity', Tim Kasser and Tom Crompton (2009) provide a comprehensive review of a wide range of psychological defences that can arise when we are confronted by fears, including the impulse for immediate action to fix the problem.

It could be argued that we operate within a general culture of fear, from concerns about the latest flu epidemic to terrorism and job security. Marketing adds to this climate of fear by raising our stress levels with time-bound promotions, for example, that carry a warning to 'sign up to our fantastic promotion today or miss out'. Perhaps all these elements together keep our amygdala in a constant state of vigilance, predisposed to place a high value on anything that looks like a safe refuge. From a social marketing perspective, the use of fear within climate change campaigns may only serve to trigger the attachment system and push consumers to greater levels of consumption as a way of soothing the uncomfortable feelings that arise.

By activating neurological mechanisms associated with fear and pleasure, marketing can tap in to the very core of our identity. In fact, many neuroscientists argue that our very sense of self emerges from the pursuit of pleasure and the avoidance of pain (e.g. Damasio, 1994; Penksepp, 1997). Marketing is able to communicate with the deepest levels of our psyche through the use of symbols and identities. Identities can be understood as having both psychological and social functions, including promoting self-esteem, self-understanding, meaning, group membership, and so on (e.g. Sirgy, 1982; Dobbs, 2006). Marketers are able to associate products and brands which target particular 'ideal' selves or identities, and we buy the product as a way of incorporating a brand personality into our own sense of self (Pearson and Mark 2001; Wolfe, 2002; Lindstrom, 2008).

4. The balance is tipped

The neurological and psychological processes discussed in this chapter are not in themselves negative; in fact, they lie at the very heart of human experience. Constant manipulation by the marketing messages we receive, however, is tipping them out of balance, and it is this loss of balance that is bringing about profligate consumption. The activation of the amygdala through the promise of pleasure, for example, should allow us to experience desire followed by satisfaction, a normal and valuable part of life. Instead, the disruption of this system through the constant exposure to advertisements, which trigger powerful emotions, can lead to an endless cycle of consumption with no real pleasure beyond the momentary buzz of the acquisition.

Equally, the attachment system is a natural process which forms the basis of the bond between mother and infant. Our relationships with romantic partners, friends, family, and even our homes and possessions, rely on this system to function effectively. But when it is overactivated through fear marketing, this natural process is disrupted and we can become anxious, constantly on the look out for threats and in need of constant reassurance in the form of physical proximity to consumer goods. The fear that is generated through marketing is often quite unrelated to the product itself and is instead linked to primal fears through somatic markers (i.e. a designer watch is linked to security). To cope, we switch off the areas of our brain which should help us to moderate our response to strong emotions and actively suppress our fears, allowing our desires to go unchecked. By undermining our ability to regulate affect and by overdeveloping our capacity to suppress negative emotions, we may well be limiting or distorting the valuable input that arises from our gut instinct or intuition, an element considered by Damasio to be essential to sound judgement (Damasio, 1994).

The sheer volume of advertisements we encounter everyday means that marketing forms a kind of 'wallpaper' to our lives. We pass billboards by and flick through magazines without a second thought for the hundreds of messages coming our way. But the evidence suggests that our amygdala responds to each and every one (Kihlstrom, 1987; Lindstrom, 2009). It is the repeated activation of these neurological processes at a non-conscious level and the subsequent changes to the physical structures of our brain that locks us in to habitual behaviours.

These mechanisms do not of course affect everyone to the same degree, but it is probable that all of us are affected to some extent. It might be difficult for us to recognize this in our own lives because so much of what happens happens at an unconscious level. We may experience a desire to buy something without any knowledge of the unconscious associations our mind is making between the product and our sense of security, or the product and our ideal selves. Indeed, the actual desire itself may be unknown to us and could form the basis of the many impulse purchases we make each day, with no real emotion or thought. It might be the reason we reach for that last-minute purchase at the supermarket checkout.

The mechanisms that lock us in to the Consumption–Happiness Myth have implications for climate change behaviours other than the consumption of goods, but lie beyond the scope of this chapter. The role of the unconscious in the decision-making process may provide some insight into the 'value–action gap', for example. The value–action gap is the difference between what people say and what people do (e.g. Blake, 1999). Our rational thoughts could be overridden when choices are being made by strong unconscious emotions beyond our awareness. Could our sense of self play a role in our split-second decision about whether or not to turn a light off when leaving a room?

This chapter does not argue that the Consumption–Happiness Myth has been designed by one section of society (marketers) and imposed on another section of society (the rest of us). Rather, the Myth has been co-created. So, for example, the more our reward circuit is activated by the desire for consumer goods, the more we buy; the more we buy, the more that marketers will attempt to tap in to our deepest desires; and as a result, the more our pleasures (albeit transitory) will become linked to consumer goods. So the cycle continues. If as a culture we want to move towards more sustainable patterns of consumption, we need to consider how we might begin to dismantle the Myth. Social marketing could have a significant role to play.

5. Conclusions and implications for social marketing

The findings emerging from neuroscience could provide some useful insights for social marketers hoping to influence our climate change behaviours. From an ethical perspective, however, this is fraught with difficulties and extreme caution should be used. Observers have pointed to concerns about the implications for free will resulting from our lack of awareness, consent and understanding when neuromarketing techniques are employed (Wilson et al, 2008). Social marketers should also take care to avoid designing campaigns which inadvertently reinforce the Myth. The use of fear, for example, may only strengthen the very mechanisms which have locked us in to unsustainable patterns of consumption.

Significantly, social marketing has a role to play in addressing the social context within which our behaviours occur. Firstly, social marketing strategists should look to protect those who are particularly vulnerable to psychological conditioning by seeking legislation, which prevents marketing to children. Studies show that it is during the early years of development that we are most susceptible to the disruption of the attachment system, resulting in reduced affect regulation (e.g. Schore, 2001; Kessler, 2009). Further, neurological processes strengthened or underdeveloped in the early stages of life can have very long-term effects (Kolb and Whishaw, 1998).

Secondly, social marketing strategies should seek to limit the extent to which discoveries in neuroscience can be used to reinforce the Consumption–Happiness Myth. This could include an outright ban on neuromarketing research or at the very least a requirement that all the findings from such research should be made publicly available. In this way it may be possible to introduce legislation to limit the implementation of marketing techniques that can be used to tap into the very deepest levels of our unconscious processes and sense of self.

But perhaps the most significant impact that social marketing can make to dismantling the Consumption–Happiness Myth lies in its ability to contribute to the development of mindfulness. Mindfulness is an ancient practice of 'being aware of one's sensory experience in the present moment' (Siegel, 2007). It is a state of being that allows thoughts and feelings to be observed without judgement (Baer et al, 2006). Recent studies suggest that mindfulness can increase empathy (Segal et al, 2007), and has a role to play in treating obsessive-compulsive disorder (Baxter et al, 1992), anxiety (Hayes, 2004) and depression (Segal et al, 2002, 2007). It has also been demonstrated to improve our ability to develop secure attachments (Shaver et al, 2007) and has been suggested as a way to improve our capacity to cope with negative emotions (Crompton and Kasser, 2009).

Neurological studies demonstrate that the process of mentally labelling emotions as they arise (a key element of mindfulness) helps an individual to moderate their response to those emotions (Creswell et al, 2007). The development of this ability through practice and training could enable a consumer to first of all recognize the fears that are generated by marketing techniques, and by holding that fear without judgement or action, prevent it from unduly influencing the decision-making process. Further, mindfulness can help to undo habitual thought processes and patterns of behaviour (Siegel, 2007). Recent research has found that mindfulness meditation physically alters the structure of the brain through neuroplasticity. Lazar et al (2005) demonstrated that those who practise mindfulness meditation for long periods of time have significantly strengthened neurocircuitry in areas of the brain associated with cognitive and emotional processing.

Although mindfulness requires training and practice, studies indicate that mindfulness is also, to varying degrees, a 'naturally occurring characteristic' within cultures (Baer et al, 2006, p42). Social marketing could, therefore, play a role in encouraging a greater prominence of mindfulness within consumer societies. Mindfulness is about making the non-conscious conscious, and Farb et al (2007) suggests that one of the first steps is to develop the capacity to separate out our streams of consciousness. In this way we can tell the difference between the constant narratives that play out in our heads, the feelings that arise just below the level of consciousness and our own reflections (Siegel, 2007). In a marketing context, the 'constant narratives that play out in our heads' equate to the thoughts that pass through our minds at a conscious and non-conscious level in the seconds before we make a decision to buy. In raising awareness of the specific techniques used by marketing to activate the amygdala and trigger the reward circuit, social marketing could help to bring some of those subliminal conversations into consciousness.

Social marketing could also raise awareness 'about the feelings that are evoked at a non-conscious level by advertisements. This technique forms a key element of mindfulness training amongst practitioners. The Mindfulness-Integrated Cognitive Behaviour Therapy Institute (MiCBT), for example, encourages individuals to gain a better awareness of the sensations that are experienced in different areas of their body when habitual thought patterns, and the emotions that accompany them, are triggered. This increased awareness is coupled with an acceptance that the emotion will pass without the need to act or to judge.

Simply by observing the internal chatter and the emotions we experience just below the level of consciousness, we are able to adopt a more reflective approach, and we can slow down our decision making. By improving our ability to regulate affect and to address the balance between conscious and non-conscious decision-making processes, we can make sure that both these elements provide the valuable input we need to make sound judgements. In other words, we can develop our gut instinct and intuition to help us to make better decisions without being overwhelmed by intense and unrelated emotional triggers.

There is no doubt that some of the issue, we face in terms of climate change can arouse a strong sense of fear. Mindfulness suggests a method by which we can learn to hold this fear, pause and reflect. It also suggests a process by which cultures currently dominated by consumerism could begin to 'evolve'. Perhaps it is only by allowing a pause between thought and action, by being mindful, that we can mature sufficiently as a culture to meet the challenges that lie ahead. Of course, raising awareness about the mechanisms that lock us in to the Consumption–Happiness Myth, and the ways we can overcome them, is only part of the picture. For us to really bring about a cultural shift in the way we relate to consumer goods, our own emotions and the unconscious processes that drive our behaviour, we need to explore our deepest motivations and consider what kind of a society we really want to co-create.

References

Baer, R. A., Smith, G. T., Hopkins, J., Krietemeyer, J. and Toney, L. (2006) 'Using self-report assessment methods to explore facets of mindfulness', *Assessment*, vol 13, no 1, pp27–45

Bagozzi, R. P., Gopinath, M. and Nyer, P. U. (1999) 'The role of emotions in marketing', *Journal of the Academy of Marketing Science*, vol 27, no 2, pp184–206

Bartels, A. and Zeki, S. (2004) 'The neural correlates of maternal and romantic love', *NeuroImage*, vol 21, issue 3, pp1155–1166

Baxter, L. R., Schwartz, J. M., Bergman, K. S., Szuba, M. P., Guze, B. H., Mazziotta, J. C., Alazraki, A., Selin, C. E., Ferng, H. K. and Munford, P. (1992) 'Caudate glucose metabolic rate changes with both drug and behavior therapy for obsessive-compulsive disorder', *Archives of General Psychiatry*, vol 49, issue 9, pp681–689

Bechara, A. and Damasio, A. R. (2005) 'The somatic marker hypothesis: A neural theory of economic decision', *Games and Economic Behavior*, vol 52, no 2, pp336–372

Belk, R. W. (1988) 'Possessions and the extended self', *Journal of Consumer Research*, vol 15, issue 2, pp139–168

Belova, M. A., Paton, J. J., Morrison, S. E. and Salzman, C. D. (2007) 'Expectation modulates neural responses to pleasant and aversive stimuli in primate amygdala', *Neuron*, vol 55, issue 6, pp970–984

Belova, M. A., Paton, J. J. and Salzman, C. D. (2008) 'Moment-to-moment tracking of state value in the amygdala', *Journal of Neuroscience*, vol 28, issue 40, pp10023–10030

Berridge, K. C. (2004) 'Pleasure, unfelt affect and irrational desire', in A. S. R. Manstead, N. H. Frijda and A. H. Fischer (eds) *Feelings and Emotions: The Amsterdam Symposium*, Cambridge University Press, Cambridge, UK

Berridge, K. C. and Kringelbach, L. M. (2008) 'Affective neuroscience of pleasure, reward in humans and animals', *Psychopharmacology*, vol 199, no 3, pp457–480

Birnbaum, L. (2005) 'Adolescent aggression and differentiation of self: Guided mindfulness meditation in the service of individuation', *The Scientific World Journal*, vol 5, pp478–489

Blake, J. (1999) 'Overcoming the "value-action gap" in environmental policy: Tensions between national policy and local experience', *Local Environment*, vol 4, no 3, pp257–278

Bowlby, J. (1969) *Attachment and Loss*, Volume 1, Attachment, Basic Books, New York

Campbell, C. (1997) 'Shopping, pleasure and the sex war', in P. Falk and C. Campbell (eds) *The Shopping Experience*, Sage Publications, London, pp166–176

Cohen, M. X., Axmacher, N., Lenartz, D., Elger, C., Sturm, V. and Schlaepfer, T. E. (2009) 'Good vibrations: Cross-frequency coupling in the human nucleus accumbens during reward processing', *Journal of Cognitive Neuroscience*, vol 21, no 5, pp875–889

Collins, N. L. and Allard, L. M. (2004) 'Cognitive representations of attachment the content and function of working models', in M. B. Brewer and M. Hewstone (eds) *Social Cognition*, Blackwell, Oxford, UK

Creswell, J. D., Way, B. M., Eisenberger, N. I. and Lieberman, M. (2007) 'Neural correlates of dispositional mindfulness during affect labeling', *Psychosomatic Medicine*, vol 69, no 6, pp560–565

Crompton, T. and Kasser, T. (2009) *Meeting Environmental Challenges: The Role of Human Identity*, WWF-UK, Surrey

Damasio, A. (1994). *Descartes' Error: Emotion, Reason, and the Human Brain*, G. P. Putnam's Sons, New York

Dobbs, D. (2006) 'A Mastery of Fear Joseph LeDoux's Amygdala Complex', http://daviddobbs.net/page2/page10/ledoux.html, accessed 21 March 2010

Douglas, M. and Isherwood, B. (1979) *The World of Goods – Towards an Anthropology of Consumption*, Routledge, New York

Epstein, S. (1994) 'Integration of the cognitive and the psychodynamic unconscious', *American Psychologist*, vol 49, issue 8, pp709–724

Farb, N. A. S., Segal, Z. V., Mayberg, H., Bean, J., McKeon, D., Fatima, Z. and Anderson, A. K. (2007) 'Attending to the present: mindfulness meditation reveals distinct neural modes of self-reference', *Social Cognitive and Affective Neuroscience*, vol 2, no 4, pp313–322

Faure, A., Reynolds, S. M., Richard, J. M. and Berridge, K. C. (2008) 'Mesolimbic dopamine in desire and dread: Enabling motivation to be generated by localized glutamate disruptions in nucleus accumbens', *The Journal of Neuroscience*, vol 28, pp7184–7192

Fonagy, P., Gergely, G., Jurist, E. L. and Target, M. (2002) *Affect Regulation, Mentalization, and the Development of the Self*, Other Press, New York

Fournier, S. (1998) 'Consumers and their brands: developing relationship theory in consumer research', *Journal of Consumer Research*, vol 24, no 4, pp343–373

Goldin, P., Ramel, W. and Gross J. (2009) 'Mindfulness meditation training and self-referential processing in social anxiety disorder: Behavioral and neural effects', *Journal of Psychology*, vol 23, no 3, pp242–257

Greene, Y. and Hiebert, B. (1998) 'A comparison of mindfulness meditation and cognitive self-observation', *Canadian Journal of Counselling*, vol 22, no 1, pp25–34

Guillaume, S., Jollant, F., Jaussent, I., Lawrence, N., Malafosse, A. and Courtet, P. (2009) 'Somatic markers and explicit knowledge are both involved in decision-making', *Neuropsychologia*, vol 47, no 10, pp2120–2124

Hayes, S. C. (2004) 'Acceptance and commitment therapy, relational frame theory, and the third wave of behavioral and cognitive therapies', *Behavior Therapy*, vol 35, pp639–665

Institute for Social Marketing (undated) 'What is Social Marketing?', accessed from http://www.ism.stir.ac.uk/what_is_social_marketing.htm, accessed 10 May 2009

Jackson, T. (2005) *Motivating Sustainable Consumption*, a review of evidence on consumer behaviour and behavioural change, a report to the Sustainable Development Research Network, Policy Studies Institute, London

Jackson, T. (2009) *Prosperity Without Growth? The Transition to a Sustainable Economy*, The Sustainable Development Commission, London

Judith, A. (2009) 'Culture on the couch, western civilisation's journey from crisis to maturity', in S. Porter, K. Polette and T. F. Baumlin (eds) *Perpetual Adolescence: Jungian Analyses of American Media, Literature, and Pop Culture*, State University of New York Press, Albany

Kessler, D. A. (2009) *The End of Overeating, Taking Control of the Insatiable American Appetite*, Rodale, New York

Kihlstrom, J. F. (1987) 'The Cognitive Unconscious', *Science*, vol 237, issue 4821, pp1445–1452

Kleine, S. S. and Baker, S. M. (2004) 'An integrative review of material possession attachment', *Academy of Marketing Science Review*, vol 2004, no 1, pp1–39

Knox, J. (2003) *Archetype, Attachment, Analysis: Jungian Psychology and the Emergent Mind*, Brunner-Routledge, East Sussex

Kolb, B. and Whishaw, I. Q. (1998) 'Brain plasticity and behaviour', *Annual Review of Psychology*, vol 49, pp43–64

Kotler, P. and Zaltman, G. (1971) 'Social marketing: An approach to planned social change', *Journal of Marketing*, vol 35, pp3–12

Lazar, S. W., Kerr, C. E., Wasserman, R. H., Gray, J. R., Greve, D. N., Treadway, M. T., McGarvey, M., Quinn, B. T., Dusek, J. A., Benson, H., Rauch, S. L., Moore, C. I. and Fischl, B. (2005) 'Meditation experience is associated with increased cortical thickness', *Neuroreport*, vol 16, issue 17, pp1893–1897

LeDoux, J. E., Cicchetti, P., Xagoraris, A. and Romanski, L. M. (1990) 'The lateral amygdaloid nucleus: Sensory interface of the amygdala in fear conditioning', *Journal of Neuroscience*, vol 10, pp1062–1069

Levy, S. J. and Zaltman, G. (1975) *Marketing, Society and Conflict*, Prentice Hall, Englewood Cliffs, NJ

Libet, B. (1993) 'The neural time factor in conscious and unconscious events: Experimental and theoretical studies of consciousness', *Ciba Foundation Symposium*, vol 174, pp123–146, Wiley, Oxford, UK

Lindstrom, M. (2008) *Buy-ology, Truth And Lies About Why We Buy*, Doubleday, New York

MacFadyen, L., Stead, M. and Hastings, G. (1999) 'A Synopsis of Social Marketing', www.ism.stir.ac.uk/social_marketing.htm, accessed 13 December 2009

Mandel, N. and Heine, S. J. (1999) 'Terror management and marketing: He who dies with the most toys wins', *Advances in Consumer Research*, vol 26, pp527–532

Maslow, A. H. (1943) 'A theory of human motivation', *Psychological Review*, vol 50, issue 4, pp370–396

McCracken, G. (1986) 'Culture and consumption: A theoretical account of the structure and movement of the cultural meaning of consumer goods', *Journal of Consumer Research*, vol 13, issue 1, pp71–84

McCracken, G. (1988) 'Meaning manufacture and movement in the world of goods', in Grant McCracken (ed) *Culture and Consumption: New Approaches to the Symbolic Character of Consumer Goods and Activities*, Indiana University Press, IN, pp71–91

Mindfulness-Integrated Cognitive Behaviour Therapy Institute (MiCBT) (undated) 'Training', accessed from http://mindfulness.net.au/information/, accessed 10 December 2009

O'Neill, S. and Nicholson-Cole, S. (2009) '"Fear won't do it": Promoting positive engagement with climate change through visual and iconic representations', *Science Communication*, vol 30, no 3, pp355–379

Overskeid, G. (2000) 'The slave of passions: Experiencing problems and selecting solutions', *Review of General Psychology*, vol 4, no 3, pp284–309

Park, C. W., Macinnis, D. J. and Priester, J. (2006) 'Beyond attitudes: Attachment and consumer behaviour', *Seoul National Journal*, vol 12, no 2, pp3–36

Paton, J. J., Belova, M. A., Morrison, S. E. and Salzman, C. D. (2006) 'The primate amygdala represents the positive and negative value of visual stimuli during learning', *Nature*, vol 439, pp865–870

Pearson, C. and Mark, M. (2001) *The Hero and the Outlaw: Building Extraordinary Brands Through the Power of Archetypes*, McGraw-Hill, New York

Penksepp, J. (1998) *Affective Neuroscience: The Foundations of Human and Animal Emotions*, Oxford University Press, Oxford

Phillips, R. G. and LeDoux, J. E. (1992) 'Differential contribution of amygdala and hippocampus to cued and contextual fear conditioning', *Behavioral Neuroscience*, vol 106, no 2, pp274–285

Reynolds, S. M. and Berridge, K. C. (2008) 'Emotional environments retune the valence of appetitive versus fearful functions in nucleus accumbens', *Nature Neuroscience*, vol 11, no 4, pp423–425

Ryback, D. (2006) 'Self-determination and the neurology of mindfulness', *Journal of Humanistic Psychology*, vol 46, no 4, pp474–493

Schlaepfer, T. E., Cohen, M. X., Frick, C., Kosel, M., Brodesser, D., Axmacher, N., Joe, A. Y., Kreft, M., Lenartz, D. and Sturm, V. (2007) 'Deep brain stimulation to reward circuitry alleviates anhedonia in refractory najor depression', *Neuropsychopharmacology*, vol 33, pp368–377

Schore, A. N. (2001) 'Effects of secure attachment relationships on the development of right brain development, affect regulation and infant mental health', *Infant Mental Health Journal*, vol 22, pp201–269

Segal, Z. V., Williams, J. M. G. and Teasdale, J. D. (2002) *Mindfulness-based Cognitive Therapy for Depression: A New Approach to Preventing Relapse*, The Guilford Press, New York

Segal, Z. V., Williams, J. M. G., Teasdale, J. D. and Kabat-Zinn, J. (2007) *The Mindful Way through Depression*, The Guilford Press, New York

Shaver, P. R. and Mikulincer, M. (2005) 'Attachment theory and research: Resurrection of the psychodynamic approach to personality', *Journal of Research in Personality*, vol 39, pp22–45

Shaver, P. R., Mikulincer, M., Lavy, S. and Saron, C. D. (2007) 'Social foundations of the capacity for mindfulness: An attachment perspective', *Psychological Inquiry*, vol 18, issue 4, pp264–271

Siegel, D. (2007) 'Mindfulness training and neural integration differentiation of distinct streams of awareness and the cultivation of well-being', *Social Cognition and Affective Neuroscience*, vol 2, no 4, pp259–263

Sirgy, M. J. (1982) 'Self-concept in consumer behaviour: A critical review', *Journal of Consumer Research*, vol 9, no 3, pp287–300

Small, D., Veldhuizen, M., Felsted, J. A., Mack, Y. E. and McGlone, F. (2008) 'Separable substrates for anticipatory and consummatory food chemosensation', *Neuron*, vol 57, no 5, pp786–797

Stice, E., Spoor, S., Bohon, C., Veldhuizen, M. and Small, D. (2008) 'Relation of reward from food intake and anticipated food intake to obesity: A functional magnetic resonance imaging study', *Journal of Abnormal Psychology*, vol 117, no 4, pp924–935

Verdejo-García, A. and Bechara, A. (2008) 'A somatic marker theory of addiction', *Neuropharmacology*, vol 56, supplement 1, pp48–62

Wang, T. and Watson, J. (2007) 'Tyndall Centre Briefing Note: Who Owns China's Carbon Emissions?', tyndall.webapp1.uea.ac.uk/publications/briefing_notes/bn23. pdf, accessed 10 January 2010

Wilson, R. M., Gaines, J. and Hill, R. P. (2008) 'Neuromarketing and consumer free will', *Journal of Consumer Affairs*, vol 42, no 3, pp389–410

Wolfe, D. (2002) 'Brand Personality', www.boothmorgan.com/pdf_docs/, accessed 10 December 2010

WWF (2008) 'The Living Planet Report', Chris Hails, Sarah Humphrey, Jonathan Loh and Steven Goldfinger (eds) www.panda.org/about_our_earth/all_publications/ living _planet_report/, accessed 10 December 2010

6

Public Engagement with Climate Adaptation: An Imperative for (and Driver of) Institutional Reform?

Peat Leith

1. Introduction

The pace of human-induced climate change and its projected threats to liveli-hoods, lives, cultures and even nations creates an imperative to adapt rapidly across many parts of society. This imperative implies that adaptation will need to be a conscious and considered process of assessing and responding to threats and opportunities at various scales. Yet many impacts of climate change, at local and regional scales especially, will not be known until they have commenced or been in train for some time. Our limited ability to predict means the impacts of climate change will often be surprising. Threats that we have in our sights may not be the ones we need to be prepared for (Barnett and Adger, 2007). In agriculture, for instance, it is likely that farming systems developed over hundreds or thousands of years and geared to a particular climate regime will need to change. It is unlikely that anyone will be able to consistently predict the system changes that will be *most* adaptive. Nevertheless, adaptation will always proceed as a social process, informed variously by the knowledge of lay people, scientists and policy makers. In this chapter, I outline some fundamental aspects of the challenge of integrating knowledge for successful adaptation and what this means for engaging the public in assessing vulnerability and building adaptive capacity. I do so largely via description of a particularly instructive case: managing climate variability in Australian agriculture.

Building on the work of Cash et al (2003), I argue that interdisciplinary research for adaptation needs to be undertaken as action research with citi-zens, in order to develop knowledge that is locally credible, salient and legitimate (see Box 1). As I illustrate through analysis of how climate infor-mation was extended to Australian farmers and graziers, this often appears to require that scientists and science communicators need to be able to represent the natural world at the same time as representing the interests and ways of life of people. Where institutional conditions allow it, such communicative practice is evolving already.[1] Institutions that can support such action-oriented inquiry will need to be consciously developed in years to come and a key part of this process will be new forms of engagement with publics. Such engagement is central to understanding the human, social and cultural aspects of vulnerability, and therefore the context from which adaptation can proceed.

Viewed from this perspective, adaptation hinges on *knowledge systems* and the interaction between them as much as it is underwritten by knowledge itself. Knowledge systems can be thought of as socio-cultural ways of making and evaluating knowledge: the ways we construct the world in order to make sense of it and so make decisions. For instance, farmers and other resource dependent people will rarely think of climate in the same way climatologists do – in terms of meteorological data and mechanistic or statistical models (Leith, 2009). Rather, they curate their own, local climate through observation and talk that can span generations and wide geographical areas (McIntosh et al, 2000). Yet, although this sort of local conception of climate might be considered as a social construct, it is built up from the integration of diverse social, technological and environmental elements. Farmers may use satellite images at one moment, and at the next be observing and interpreting the behaviour of birds and animals, or listening to the 'theories' of their neighbours and family. Thus, unlike other chapters in this book, in this chapter publics are as much in the business of knowledge production as scientists. They are actively engaged in the process of shaping knowledge, and their interaction with scientists is seen in terms of its potential to transform the products of science, the scientists and even the process of science itself.

Research into climate change adaptation has drawn on various academic traditions. In Section 2, I briefly outline some central themes in adaptation research. A common aim of this research is *reducing* vulnerability; it thus moves beyond understanding to getting involved in the process of adaptation. This action-orientation implies that, in various ways, researchers become part of the system they are studying. In Section 3, I describe the case of managing Australian climate variability as an example of how such action research can operate, and suggest some interesting implications. I close the chapter by arguing that this case presents substantial possibilities and challenges for engaging the public with climate change adaptation, and that these challenges are central to the development of adaptation science, specifically, and more generally to scientific research for the public good.

2. Climate adaptation as action research in diverse social–ecological systems

Adaptation to climate change is a relatively new research domain, yet one to which many disciplinary perspectives have been applied. This cross-disciplinary attention, and the complexity and diversity of adaptation contexts, mean that definitions, objectives and methods for adaptation are not

---

Box 6.1 *Salience, credibility and legitimacy*

Synthesizing earlier scholarship in Science and Technology Studies (STS), Cash et al (2003) argued that in order for scientists to make knowledge which can be useful and useable in the public domain, there is a need to carefully balance salience, credibility and legitimacy of information. These terms can be briefly defined as follows:

- **Salience**: the relevance of information to a decision maker.
- **Credibility**: scientific plausibility and technical accuracy of information.
- **Legitimacy**: the fairness of the process that resulted in the information.

These dimensions of information are perceived differently across society. Farmers will often want information that is relevant to their patch. Scientists often prioritize more universal knowledge derived via methods considered credible in their particular research domain. In all communities, information and its sources are interpreted through lenses tempered by historical relationships, and the perceived interests and motives of particular organizations or individuals. These aspects of institutional legitimacy have substantial sway over the degree to which information, organizations and actors are regarded as trustworthy (Wynne, 1996).

Another important consideration in thinking about salience, credibility and legitimacy is that each of these dimensions of information can be traded off against the others. For instance, arguments for climate change scenarios in probabilistic terms are largely organized around assumptions that probabilities provide information that can be more easily interpreted by policy makers and is therefore more salient. However, many climate scientists have questioned the methodological credibility of the approaches used to derive such probabilities (Lempert et al, 2004). Having such arguments is crucial to dealing with uncertainty for decision making, yet can also be deployed by climate change contrarians to undermine the perceived legitimacy of climate research.

---

settled in the literature (Nelson et al, 2007). In the context of local adaptation, approaches that apply in one place may not apply elsewhere. Indeed, the understanding that adaptation will always be context-dependent is among the few widely agreed principles for intervention to assist adaptation (Nelson et al, 2007). Reviews of this literature on adaptation from various disciplinary perspectives are nevertheless beginning to define common ground.[2] In this section, I briefly outline some of this common ground via key terms and important discourses in adaptation research. These definitions (Box 2) and currents highlight the need for integration of expert-based and participatory forms of knowledge production and decision making.

Intentional adaptation in the face of climate change begins with some form of assessment of vulnerabilities, followed by development and implementation of strategies by which these vulnerabilities may be reduced. Thus, intentional climate adaptation is usually at least as pre-emptory as it is

Box 6.2 *Definitions of key terms relevant to adaptation*

The key concepts which tend to occupy research on climate adaptation are **exposure**, **sensitivity**, **adaptive capacity**, **resilience** and **vulnerability**.

Exposure is usually equated with the risks or hazards associated with the biophysical impacts of climate change. **Sensitivity** may relate to physical or socio-economic susceptibility of individuals or groups to such hazards. For example, the resource-dependence of subsistence farmers often makes them particularly sensitive to changes in climatic conditions (Brooks et al, 2005). **Adaptive capacity** is often considered as a function of the resources available to individuals or groups and their ability to utilize these resources to adapt to changing conditions (Nelson et al, 2007). It is thus a very particular form of capacity which is tied up with the ability of an individual or group to innovate, experiment and adapt to novel or emerging conditions. Folke et al (2003) argued that adaptive capacity implies four interrelated factors: communities must learn to live with change and uncertainty; foster reorganization of systems through nurturing diversity; combine different forms of knowledge in order to learn; and generate opportunities for self-organization. This definition of adaptive capacity is closely linked to the idea of resilience, which Holling (1973) defined in terms of the degree to which a system is buffered from shock, coupled with the ability of that system to maintain its critical function following a change to a different state. These concepts of adaptive capacity and **resilience** are often considered in terms of the ways they mediate (ameliorate or intensify) the biophysical impacts of climate change and sensitivities to them. Thus, **vulnerability** to climate change can be defined as a function of these parameters (Figure 6.1).

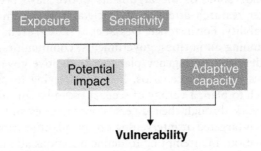

Source: Allen Consulting, 2005, p21

Figure 6.1 *A definition of vulnerability*

reactive. Although literature on adaptation stresses the importance of stakeholder participation (Füssel, 2007), two very different streams of research are distinguishable as ways of pre-empting change. At the most basic level, these approaches can be considered on a continuum from biophysical to societal approaches, with the former focusing more on questions of risk, exposure and sensitivity, and the latter considering the human, cultural and socio-economic aspects of adaptive capacity and resilience. In reality, any given project focusing on vulnerability assessment and adaptation will tend to move back and forth along this continuum. However, these streams of research are rarely well integrated, in part because the substantial interdisciplinary commitment necessary for such integration is rarely achieved.

To date, the biophysical impacts, risks or hazards associated with climate change have been the primary focus of adaptation research (Dessai et al, 2009). Such approaches are usually based on statistical and/or dynamic models underpinned by monitoring of biophysical systems. In essence, risk-oriented approaches aim to reduce uncertainties in order to define and hence manage risk. The basic reasoning is simple: if we can predict the impacts of human action on climate, then we can make informed decisions about how to control the risks associated with our actions, whether through mitigation of the causes of the hazard or adaptation to its consequences. Unfortunately, the complex, non-linear systems in question are rarely well-represented by biophysical models, such that modelled future risks may not be the most pressing concerns to eventuate (Holling et al, 1998). The paradoxes that more scientific effort can increase rather than reduce uncertainty (Dessai et al, 2009) and exacerbate controversy (Sarewitz, 2004) also present substantial challenges. Technical focus on reducing uncertainties can also stall decision making if policy makers and the public take the position that they need better clarification of risks in order to act. None of these criticisms of technical approaches to adaptation are meant to imply that biophysical research should not be central to climate adaptation. Rather, as a whole, they suggest that biophysical research needs to be applied in concert with other forms of research and practice as a means to an end: reducing vulnerability in a given context.

In recent years some of the arguments above have been mobilized to encourage greater research attention to societal and governance issues surrounding vulnerability. For instance, Dessai et al (2009) argue that adaptation requires that planning authorities, governments, communities, businesses and others need to develop contingency plans and adaptive governance arrangements for various plausible scenarios. Instead of trying to pick a particular scenario for which to plan, a variety of scenarios can be considered as thought experiments to work through their diverse consequences and trade-offs. Such work is very much targeted at intervening on the adaptive capacity side of the vulnerability equation. In attempting to define questions about loss and trade-offs in particular contexts, this sort of work is explicitly value-oriented, and needs to be undertaken in collaboration with the communities of interest or place whose futures are at stake (e.g. Turner et al, 2003). This work also requires interdisciplinary thinking which can pre-empt and curtail unforeseen impacts of adaptation strategies, or even vulnerability assessments themselves. For example, vulnerability assessments of small island nations have resulted in substantial reductions in foreign investment in those nation states, which in turn constrain their adaptation options (Barnett and Adger, 2003). These sorts of considerations highlight that power, knowledge and the institutions of governance can be as integral to adaptation as finance and other forms of capital.

This brief summary of some central considerations and trends in adaptation research is too cursory to do justice to this complex new field. Nevertheless, I have used it to highlight some of the reasons that action-oriented, interdisciplinary and collaborative research is gaining momentum. In such research, public engagement is a core aspect of fostering the trust necessary to develop useful and useable collective understandings of these socio-environmental systems. Such research will ideally move back and forth between technical questions and those relating to values; researchers will also work across scales, and attempt to be inclusive, adaptive and reflective about the processes they employ (Kates et al, 2001). This work differs markedly from traditional approaches to scientific research, not least because it explicitly aims to represent socio-environmental systems, and foster social learning and decision making based on these representations. How such work can be done in practice is explored below through the informative case of communicating seasonal climate prediction in Australia.

3. Communicating climate risk in the 'Land of Droughts and Flooding Rains'

During the late 1980s, the Australian government started to review its Drought Policy. At about the same time, the El Niño Southern Oscillation (ENSO) became the basis for seasonal climate prediction in Australia. Prior to this time, drought had been included under the Natural Disaster Relief Arrangements and declaration of drought in any region sparked injections of public monies to provide relief for drought-stricken farmers. The Drought Policy Review Taskforce (DPRTF, 1990a) viewed these arrangements as anachronistic, reflecting bygone socialist intervention, and encouraging poor management of recurring and inevitable drought. The fluctuations of ENSO had provided a scientific explanation of a much older national identification of Australia as 'a land of droughts and flooding rains'.[3] In a distinct move towards the neo-liberal ideal that individuals and communities ought to manage their own risks, drought became a 'normal risk' for agriculture (Higgins, 2001).[4] Yet climate risk was not fully knowable to each and every farmer. Where earlier governments had funded research and development for the agricultural sector and paid for public extension to ensure the information was delivered to the farm gate, the emerging neo-liberal vision was more entrepreneurial and individualistic. Public extension, a long-standing discipline with a goal of enabling innovation and change in rural communities and among farmers, was substantially cut back during the 1980s and 1990s. Where an earlier view propounded extension as a means of encouraging innovation through extending scientific knowledge to agriculture, from a neo-liberal perspective the benefits of better risk management were private benefits, which, under this ideology, made its adoption appear as the natural responsibility of industries and individuals.

Beyond the demise of public extension, the ability of scientists to communicate climate risk generally was limited by some factors that reflect the challenges of communicating climate change. Several different (and sometimes conflicting) seasonal rainfall forecasts were produced by different agencies of Commonwealth and State governments. They were presented as maps showing the probability of receiving above median rainfall over the next three months. These probabilities varied across the landscape. Maps were often accompanied by media releases indicating the state of the Pacific Ocean. These states – El Niño or La Niña – were described by scientists respectively as decreasing or increasing the likelihood of wetter than average conditions, in some regions at least. Despite climate scientists' inclination towards a cautious language, El Niño quickly became synonymous with drought in the public lexicon. Even a lexicographer has suggested we refer to drought in Australia as the 'El Niño season' (Arthur, 2003, p181). The awkwardness of caveats attached to ENSO took some getting used to. Such phrases as 'not all droughts are caused by El Niño, just as not all El Niños cause drought' were applied repeatedly by climate scientists and extension agents, as they attempted to make climate states distinct from agro-economic ones.

It also appeared that, despite presenting information as an objective analysis of risk, probability forecasts were often poorly understood or were misinterpreted. A key difficulty for climate scientists in convincing the public or policy makers of the usefulness of their knowledge is summed up by the oft-repeated notion that 'humans are poor intuitive statisticians' (Hayman, 2001, p231). This claim is based on influential psychometric research (e.g. Kahneman and Tversky, 1996). However, to understand how scientists try to get around these psychological stumbling blocks to communicating climate information requires a more social, qualitative analytical approach. One such approach is to analyse how language and artefacts are used to create particular understandings of phenomena such as El Niño, La Niña, or their effects across social and cultural boundaries.

Over the past three decades, STS scholars have developed a variety of conceptual devices that are particularly useful for this sort of analysis at the boundaries of scientific, policy and public understanding. These devices originate from the concept of 'boundary work', which refers to the work done by people, via language, to assist in settling what Gieryn (1999, p5) refers to as 'credibility contests'. Analysis of boundary work has been applied to understanding how knowledge is made robust within and among scientific disciplines (Gieryn, 1999), and across the domains of science, policy and lay publics (Jasanoff, 1987; Shackley and Wynne, 1996). For getting to grips with the boundaries between sciences, policy and the public, STS scholars have developed three particularly useful concepts relating to boundary work.

Firstly, 'boundary objects' such as maps and graphs can serve to stabilize particular understandings of phenomena across communities (Star and Griesemer, 1989). These are often used over and over again to drive home a particular message. Their meaning is developed through negotiation or dialogue between different communities such that they become key points of discussion and understanding across these communities. For example, the so-called 'hockey stick' graph was a fundamental boundary object demonstrating increasing surface temperature in the northern hemisphere. Such objects can become significant points of public and policy interest (or controversy, in the case of the hockey stick), and as such are usefully considered in analysis of social negotiation of information.

Secondly, boundary organizations occupy a space between different sectors of society, are accountable to both, and serve a role of mediating the relationship between them (Guston, 2000). An example of this sort of organization was the research funding body developed in response to Australia's National Drought Policy (DPRTF, 1990b), the Climate Variability in Agriculture Program and its various successors. The coordinator of this programme sought funding for research from Rural Research and Development Corporations (which fund research relevant to particular farm sectors and are themselves funded through mandatory farm levies). These private monies were then matched to a specified limit by tax revenue from the Commonwealth Government, and research priorities were defined by government and industry partners. This model for funding agricultural research ensures that research is developed to serve both public and private goods through particular forms of accountability of the programme to its sponsor organizations (Cash and Buizer, 2005).

The final form of boundary work, boundary ordering language, refers to language that is used to shore up authority, often by creating and stabilizing particular stories about phenomena, institutions or practices (Jasanoff, 1987). The communicative work required to develop an appropriate public understanding of a concept such as ENSO, as implied above, is not trivial. Analysing such communication can help to make things explicit that are often implicit in the ways scientists and lay people talk about climate, risk, uncertainty and knowledge. It can also help researchers to reflect, for example, on how they construct practices and identities of farmers in specific ways alongside their representations of the climate. Of course, while such qualitative research provides detailed and informative accounts, it does not pretend to be representative. Nevertheless, what follows illustrates how analyses of boundary work can help to understand what is going on with engagement between scientists and farmers in the context of extending climate information to agriculture.

In the rest of this chapter, I examine how 35 Australian climate scientists, agricultural systems researchers and extension agents communicated climate variability, prediction, risk and uncertainty. This description is based on a discourse analysis of interviews, media transcripts and other public documents, which were collected between 2003 and 2005 (see Leith, 2009). The participants were employees of national and state agencies, and often collaborated across these agencies and their disciplines to develop improved applications of climate prediction for Australian agriculture. For simplicity, I refer to these participants generically as agro-climatologists (or just researchers) for the remainder of this chapter. In some instances, I refer to disciplinary backgrounds (climate scientists, systems modellers, extension agents) to distinguish the different ways these groups talked about engaging farmers with climate information. I detail three categories of engagement and communication which were identified as particular 'modes of extension' (see Leith, 2009): discursive extension, conceptual extension and contextual extension (see also Table 6.1).

Discursive extension of climate

Discursive extension of climate operates largely at the level of societal discourses and narratives, and might be summed up by this optimistic quote from one agro-climatologist: 'We have actually gone a long way in [terms of] the mental map of most Australians, of improving understanding of the shape of climate.' If climate is what you expect and weather is what you get, then clearly one of the roles of agro-climatologists has been to try to foster realistic expectations of the climate among the broader public. ENSO has been important in this regard, as it provides the capacity to ground the notion that Australia is *naturally inclined to experience extremes* and that *average conditions are not normal*. Yet, as a boundary object, ENSO appears in many different ways, and this is, partially at least, reflected in the different roles and mandates of institutions.

The Australian Bureau of Meteorology (hereafter, the Bureau) and its National Climate Centre play a substantial role in constituting the climate for the nation. During interviews, participants from the Bureau tended to describe their research and communication focus as being national. As Kestin (2000, p192) points out, this national focus limits the Bureau's capacity to contextualize information in relation to the needs of particular geographical areas or industries. These climate scientists also tended to be committed to communicating climate forecasts as probabilities and emphasizing that the probabilities describe the risk as best as possible. From this perspective the onus is on individuals to work out how to use the probabilities of above or below median rainfall. The meanings of probabilities are left as neutral objects which simply summarize scientific understanding of current conditions as a number. Further translation of these numbers was seen as a task for farmers, industry bodies and, importantly, state government agencies. In short, Bureau scientists emphasized 'improving products, rather than improving publicity', while employees of state agencies tended to want to work towards improved application of climate information.

Some of the most interesting lessons about discursive extension of climate in state agencies come from the Australian state in which agriculture is politically important, and ENSO's impacts on agriculture are most obvious and pronounced: Queensland. Many of these stories about communicating climate prediction reflect an intimacy with primary producers and their experience that has developed over years of interaction:

> *What I do, ... [is] set up the risk management profile that primes these guys [farmers] to be aware of the problems. Rather than just saying the forecast is good – they might say, 'I will go and buy more cattle' or something – you prime them to be watching. And then I say things – 'let's watch it together over the next months. I don't know if there is an El Niño coming, but if the SOI [the Southern Oscillation Index] keeps dropping, and the Pacific continues to warm up, then you have got problems. So let's watch that together over the next month.' So they get ownership over the situation, and say: 'Oh, there is actually a*

website, you can watch it. Is that right?' And they watch it. So they become participants in the whole process. That's what I do. I don't put out the forecast. I actually involve them in – this is participative stuff, I suppose – so I say this on the radio: 'let's watch it together'.

This researcher is not presenting a prediction per se. Rather, he defers interpretation to the autonomous risk manager who is given the keys to unlocking the system. The object of concern is no longer the forecast, but the construction of the Pacific Ocean and atmosphere – the physical system. This system becomes the thing that can or cannot be trusted. This performance of climate prediction not only recreates climate as partially predictable, it builds individuals as autonomous agents who only need to be pointed to the right indices in order to understand and so manage ENSO-related climate risk. An intimacy with agricultural publics and their concerns, in the quote below, moves a step further to constitute human choice in the face of adversity:

> *[Dr Roger] Stone [a prominent agro-climatologist from Queensland] says most farmers across Queensland would be already preparing for the possibility of another El Niño weather event. He says there is only a 10 percent chance of drought-breaking rain during spring. 'Many parts of the state are actually suffering enough as it is,' he said ... 'It's yet again another pretty careful approach to risk management, as we say, and it's a pretty cautious approach to the whole farming system at the moment to dig down and survive another fairly dry period' (ABC Radio National, 2006).*

Here, farmers are constructed as cautious survivors who consider El Niño as a matter of course. The percentage chance provided is not the relatively high probability of above median rainfall. Rather, the emphasis is on the chance of a subjectively variable concept of 'drought-breaking rain'. With conditions already dry, El Niño becomes an object that will prevent the reparation of a difficult situation. In such a predicament, when hope is thwarted by scientific forecasts, the option remains to persevere, to 'dig down and survive', calling on all the reserves available: financial, psychological, social, emotional. Thus in the matter of a brief media grab, ENSO is brought to bear on the well-being of the primary producers across Queensland, and in the same breath, those managers are constituted as risk managers out of necessity. They are 'preparing for the possibility' of El Niño: for the possibility of a high probability of below median rainfall, and for the uncertain likelihood of continuing drought!

Conceptual extension of climate
In histories of rural Australia, drought and deluge appear as punctuation in the lives of industries, communities and individuals. The overlayering of rainfall records with the history of ENSO and its mechanisms creates a conceptual climate that can renovate the sense of uncertainty that has historically

pervaded understandings of what the future holds, climatically speaking. Despite the limited and declining budget for public extension in Australia, substantial effort has gone into extending information about this linkage between ENSO and rainfall, especially in Queensland. This form of extension has tended to take a fairly traditional approach: scientists or extension agents explain some of the statistical and mechanistic aspects of ENSO and its association with Australian rainfall to groups of farmers in a workshop setting. Together, these statistical and mechanistic aspects of the conceptual climate can redefine what might be deemed appropriate for agricultural and ecological management.

Explaining the mechanisms of ENSO was described in interviews as a necessary grounding for establishing public credibility of statistical forecasts. Such explanation often proceeds from explaining how particular weather systems bring rain (e.g. cyclones, fronts, monsoonal troughs) and how these can be affected by different ENSO conditions. In itself, a basic mechanistic understanding of climate via weather was described as an absolutely necessary step in making the very idea of climate prediction tenable to decision making. As one extension agent put it:

> You've got to make the connection between a warm patch of ocean in the Pacific and rain at somebody's backyard, and without the weather we couldn't do that, so we had to put in the weather stuff, yeah, and that's still the case.

According to this line of thinking, it is by explaining mechanism in terms of local impact that credibility of climate forecasting is built for particular places. Describing weather processes, and then climate as the sum of those processes, pays dividends in seeing 'people's eyes light up'. Such descriptive work was seen as preparing people to more readily engage with seasonal climate forecasting; it was equally regarded as equipping decision makers with tools to interpret weather maps, to reconfigure their knowledge of the agro-ecosystems they manage in climatic terms, and to engage with the language and boundary objects of climate and weather.

A mechanistic association may be at least partially explanatory; historical association can be convincing. A major effort for agro-climatologists has been extending analyses of climatic history as a means of demonstrating the strength of associations between rainfall and ENSO indices. For instance, the phases of the Southern Oscillation Index allow each year of the historical record to be allotted to a specific climate state (Stone and Auliciems, 1992). This in turn provides farmers with a familiar way to think about the current conditions, in relation to history and the rainfall distribution in analogous years (Leith, 2009). These distributions allow for computation of odds or probabilities of receiving a given amount of rainfall. Agro-climatologists often suggested that these probabilities, once understood and trusted, make decisions easier through formally rationalizing the decision process. As one researcher put it:

There's some exercises where you get people to, you know, write down options and look at even simple probabilities [which] actually I think can be liberating for them sort of thing in terms of that. ... I think it's often a useful way of thinking about the uncertainty ... and being probably explicit about what it is ... I think some notion of rainfall and seasonal forecasts and so on ... can be an empowering thing to think about. 'Well we don't know what's happening in the future, but these are the odds of going this way or that way.' Also so that people don't beat up on themselves too much if things do go wrong because they still know that, well, that was probably the right decision at that time.

This account is an informative one; it is explicitly concerned with the well-being of decision makers, not just their decisions. This researcher suggests that transforming uncertainty into probability can externalize or at least neutralize self-blame for results of decisions by emphasizing the apparent objectivity of using 'the best available information'. The decision made on the basis of the best available information recreates the local decision and decision maker within a risk assessment framework.

Yet, hidden behind the publicly purported objectivity of probabilities were quiet concerns among some scientists that the bases of seasonal rainfall forecasts were being eroded. As one climate scientist put it: 'It would be easier to make seasonal forecasts if the "background" climate was not changing so rapidly. I suspect that this is changing the relationships on which we base our forecasts.' Human-induced climate change, on this account, could be undermining the stability of climate associations between ENSO and Australian rainfall, at least theoretically. These concerns present a substantial challenge for agro-climatologists: how should they translate multiple forms of uncertainty associated with climate variability without entirely undermining the salience, credibility and legitimacy of their forecasts?

From the interviews it appears that researchers from different disciplines have very different approaches to these questions. For climate scientists, appropriate application of climate predictions was often talked about in terms of ensuring that forecast systems are credible using the most widely accepted methods of developing forecast schemes and evaluating their performance. Systems scientists and extension agents had a more pragmatic approach to building boundary objects and balancing the uncertainties with the imperatives of application. Among extension agents and some systems scientists, for example, there was a pervasive argument that decisions will be made by farmers on the basis of highly unscientific assessments, and that some science, albeit provisional, is better than none at all. Rather than being solely concerned about the scientific credibility of the information they were putting out, they were also interested in how information is, and can be, used by farmers. Extension agents, whose core work is social engagement and communication, are also always interpreting responses to information and adjusting how objects are framed, in order to try to produce very specific meanings *and effects* among audiences and individuals.

The extension of conceptual climate can thus be described as a process of creating useful and useable boundary objects and ensuring they are not misused. Extension of a conceptual climate might, at first glance, appear to be agro-climatologists attempting to explain their understanding of climate in ways that are meaningful to farmers and graziers. Viewed through the conceptual lens of boundary work, it is clear from the interviews that stabilizing the boundary objects of climate science requires substantial negotiation. This extension, far from preaching science to the masses, relies on iterative interpretations of how boundary objects of science are and should be constituted. Questions need to be addressed and redressed across scientific disciplines. For example: What information can and should have traction for decision makers? How should such information be framed so it is useful but not misused?

Without a conceptualized climate, the boundary objects of climate prediction may well be free-floating, relatively meaningless, and so have little traction on either strategic or tactical decisions among primary producers. Worse yet, without conceptual extension, these boundary objects might be stabilized among primary producers in a form that is completely incongruous with scientists' understandings. The process of translation of the risks and uncertainties of climate via framing boundary objects throws into relief the interdependence of the legitimacy, salience and credibility of information for potential 'end-users'. Extension of the conceptual climate therefore comes to be seen as an interpretive and negotiated process of the translation of scientific concepts for particular contexts, and the management of the risks of this translation.

The contextual extension of climate

Applied climate forecasting tools for agriculture began to proliferate in the early and mid-1990s. These tools were largely based on agronomic systems models initiated with outputs from statistical climate forecasting models (McCown, 2001). They integrated diverse variables relating to soils, pests, management options and climate. Some were further developed into decision support systems (DSSs) to assist farmers to make tactical and strategic decisions. This integration of risk factors at local or farm scale allowed the history of ENSO impacts to be relived and re-managed in a virtual setting. Such modelling expresses climate prediction in context, in relation to place, history, productivity, profit and management options.

In terms of applying climate forecasts to agriculture, the argument for a research focus on these contextual approaches to climate variability, above and beyond the extension of conceptual climate information, is perhaps most succinctly summed up by Hammer et al (2001, p531): 'the leap directly from a seasonal forecast to a decision is too great to be done (well) intuitively'. This value, however, is difficult to quantify and tends to rely on primary producers' own estimations of the validity of the model. I argue that this value is importantly mediated by the work agro-climatologists do in representing biophysical and social systems simultaneously.

In Australia, the transformation of *Decision* Support Systems to *Discussion* Support Systems (Nelson et al, 2002) marks an important shift in thinking among agricultural systems researchers. It is, firstly, an acknowledgement that rather than formal validation, which bestows some scientific credibility to models (cf. Oreskes et al, 1994), models are made salient, credible and legitimate to primary producers through their ability to produce qualitatively realistic hindcasts and forecasts (Meinke and Stone, 2005). Yet, secondly and perhaps more importantly, it acknowledges that these models need to be mediated by discussion between scientists and farmers in order that both can better learn how the socio-environmental system really functions. Once sufficiently legitimate, credible and salient, the transaction costs of the modelling experiments are negligible compared to the economic risk associated with real, on-farm experiments over a considerable number of seasons (Carberry et al, 2002; Meinke et al, 2006). Yet this salience and legitimacy may be as much a product of the social engagement as it is a product of the hard science underpinning the DSSs. Nevertheless, such work has often engaged very few, usually highly educated or motivated farmers who had 'graduated' from conceptual extension programmes. Because adoption of these modelling technologies relies on close interaction and discussion to develop trust in models via trusting their developers, they have tended to be adopted only by a small proportion of farmers.

Where systems researchers have engaged in the close collaborative work of contextual extension, they gain a deeper understanding not only of the biophysical aspects of a farmer's work, but also the social and cultural ways of being and thinking that are crucial to understanding the functioning of farms (e.g. Vanclay, 2004). This understanding enables some agro-climatologists to convert their own language of risk and uncertainty into colloquial or locally appropriate forms, as described above in relation to discursive extension. These approaches are also part of a broader shift in extension and engagement to social learning, which emphasizes a participatory and collegial approach to knowledge production among scientists and farmers (e.g. Ison and Russell, 2000). For one systems scientist, such participatory research had provided insights into the diversity of farmers and the enigma of their decision making, which had reoriented their understanding of their own role:

> *Some people are only at the stage of just needing to be excited into the possibility that there's a decision to be made. Others are a long way down the track and know exactly what the decision is, and they really want quite technical responses to it. And cutting across all of that, some people just want to talk about it, and will never put pen to paper, or whatever, and so you need real rules of thumb and things you can just transmit like that [clicks fingers]. Other people want to engage with other human beings and do it in a workshop sort of situation. There's still others that don't like doing that and want to sit privately and do it on paper, and still others might do that, but are happy to actually get on to a computer. And so the idea that you have a computer decision support system as the only output was stupid. That's just one tool in a pantheon of things which*

> *altogether can actually contribute to this decision-making process.*

Though it is not useful or useable to all farmers, contextual extension has the potential to build understanding and trust across communities of researchers and farmers. Among the key lessons from such work is an understanding that researchers and policy makers are part of the complex systems that they analyse (Stafford Smith, 2003). Taking this view, the broad socio-environmental system is seen as a contingent experimental space, in which learning is required in order to adapt to changing circumstances and surprises. Thus, some agro-climatologists have argued that scientific institutions and governance structures need to be made adaptive such that they can shift to respond to emergent socio-environmental phenomena at various scales (Stafford Smith, 2003). By trying to open up natural systems to improved management with the assistance of modelling technologies, biophysical systems scientists have repeatedly been drawn to examine the social, cultural and political contexts that animate these open and complex systems. In some instances, interdisciplinary teams work across the old social and biophysical divides to engage and reflect more deeply on the processes of their action research. In turn, such groups often need to push against institutional and political constraints which limit the capacity of scientists to participate in ongoing social learning with farmers, which tends to be viewed institutionally as extension rather than research per se. Yet, the integration of extension and research is fundamental to such research. Only through such integration can the careful balancing of salience, credibility and legitimacy be achieved.

4. Weighing up salience, credibility and legitimacy in engagement for adaptation

Managing for climate variability is an imperative for agricultural adaptation to climate change (Howden et al, 2007). The key elements of the Australian experience of managing for climate variability described above are likely to be relevant to broader engagement for adaptation. This will especially be the case where people are substantially affected by climate variability and change such as in farming communities, flood prone areas, or places frequented by extreme and partially predictable events such as hurricanes and heatwaves. In such places, people will probably have established mental and social constructions of their climate which may differ substantially from understandings of scientists.

The important lessons from analysing how Australian agro-climatologists made their uncertain climate knowledge useful and useable to farmers hinge on their ability to weigh up the imperatives of making information locally salient and legitimate, while maintaining its scientific credibility. Such work requires connections between scientists and the public by which boundary objects can be framed and reframed for particular contexts. I have typified the diverse forms of engagement as generally occurring in three modes: discursive, conceptual and contextual extension, summarized in Table 6.1. While these modes

Table 6.1 Summary of the characteristics of the three modes of extension, their requirements, benefits and translation risks

Mode of extension	Form of intervention	Role of agricultural publics	Technical complexity	Number of people engaged	Publics appear to gain	Extension requirements of researchers	Translational risks	Potential benefits
Discursive	Rhetorical	Interprets representation and performance	Low	Many	A 'feel' for climate variability drivers and predictability. A sense of who is a good representative of climate variability and who understands their predicament in relation to climate.	Ability to succinctly perform identities of and relations with audience at the same time as representing climate variability and predictability through effective metaphors and signs.	Overemphasizes boundary-objects as signs, the meaning of which can be easy to mistranslate. Scientists rather than science gain credibility. Performance of public identities may backfire unless at local or regional scales with which a climate representative is very familiar.	Allows for wide-reaching extension of a 'feel' for the Australian climate that scientists have gained through their research. Success depends on the proximity of researchers to potential users of information, because it requires their performance of this proximity. Thus, emphasizes the need for close engagement.
Conceptual	Didactic	Develops understanding of climatology (statistical and mechanistic)	Moderate	Few	Basic scientific understanding of weather and climate as it affects their productivity and life. Familiarity with boundary objects and some ability to interpret their meaning.	Ability to engage small groups and represent climatic history and mechanism such that it is relevant considerations in decision making.	Creates meaning of boundary-objects and can unwittingly encourage do-it-yourself interpretation of signals or patterns, by-passing forecast systems, especially where engagement is sporadic or one-off.	Can lead to good understanding of boundary objects in public domain. Iterative engagement builds technical understanding among publics, and socio-cultural linkages among scientists and publics. Can generate trust and reciprocity.
Contextual	Co-learning	Becomes part of socio-technical network of agroclimatic modelling	High	Very few	Transformation of relations with scientific understanding of their 'system' and renovation of relationships between experience and experiment. Connection with boundary objects, and an extended lay-scientific community of practice.	Ability to link diverse technical and social aspects of productivity, profitability, sustainability, climate variability, decision making and identities; including ability to run and modify models for different contexts, and interpret model outputs.	Risks of engaging with only one cohort of technically literate agricultural publics and thus not broadening ways of knowing. Instead, can create alignment among scientists and a particular cohort of technically-oriented primary producers, leading to marginalization of other ways of knowing and agricultural knowledges.	Can result in extended communities of practice across disciplines and sectors. Builds socio-technical alignment among publics and scientists. Generates ability for publics and scientists to respectively represent each other in their own epistemic communities. Leads to co-learning and, if continued to more adaptive societies.

of extension serve different audiences and operate at different levels, they also build on one another in important ways. In the discursive mode of extension, to make El Niño meaningful yet not synonymous with drought, substantial rhetorical work was required. For the rhetorical work to be effectively salient and legitimate, story-lines about drought and identity were deployed. These narratives ensured the gravity of farmers' predicaments was not glossed over, while their autonomy as decision makers and risk managers was highlighted. Developing the capacity to get these story-lines right appeared to require close engagement between researchers and farmers so that the former understood the knowledge systems of the latter. The processes of conceptual and especially contextual extension made such engagement possible.

Linking cultural identities with scientific notions of climate risk and uncertainty is not accidental. Rather, it appears as a pragmatic choice that has been made by some agro-climatologists in order to make scientific information more useful and useable. If such linking of social and natural representations is necessary for application of climate knowledge more broadly, we might expect work on climate adaptation to require similar efforts. Yet such work is not straightforward or unproblematic. The work of representing cultural identities is usually associated with politics and implies particular power relations which should not be left unexamined. In recent years, STS scholars have developed a useful approach for thinking about such complexes of the natural, technological and social. It is summed up by the term *co-production*: 'natural and social orders are produced together' (Jasanoff, 2004, p2). Jasanoff (2004, pp2–3) describes co-production as 'shorthand for the proposition that the ways in which we know and represent the world (both nature and society) are inseparable from the ways in which we choose to live in it. Knowledge and its material embodiments are at once products of social work and constitutive forms of social life; society cannot function without knowledge any more than knowledge can exist without appropriate social supports.' Co-production by this definition takes on a much deeper significance than scientists and the public producing knowledge together: it means more than collaboration. In the context of climate adaptation, it implies that engagement needs to be considered as a process not only of communicating with a public, but of building a polity and contributing to the construction of identities, discourses and institutions. This sort of work will require substantial reflection and commitment to ethical conduct to ensure that public trust in scientific organizations is increased and adaptation can proceed as a genuinely collective endeavour.

Notes

1. In many cases the largest impacts of climate change will be indirect. Where water supplies supporting large populations diminish rapidly, the socio-political fallout associated with mass migration could lead to conflict, which in turn could spiral into regional warfare. Unfortunately, such extreme situations are seen as increasingly plausible (Barnett and Adger, 2007), and substantial scientific and political work will be required to ameliorate the scale of human tragedy they may precipitate. The scale of adaptive measures needed to avert such issues is not covered in this chapter.

2. Detailed reviews from various disciplinary perspectives are available as follows: economic perspective (Adger, 2003) social–ecological systems approaches (Nelson et al, 2007); policy and planning approaches (Füssel, 2007; Hallegatte, 2009).
3. This line is from the emblematic poem, 'My Country', by Dorothea Mackellar, which Australians have long-embraced for breaking the adoring ties with the land-scapes of 'the Mother Land' and forming a new identity with the 'sunburnt country', as Mackellar put it: 'a land of sweeping plains/ Of ragged mountain ranges/ Of droughts and flooding rains'.
4. This neo-liberal shift is apparent in other countries. For example, Butler and Pidgeon (2009) note a change in UK flood management from policies of 'flood defence' to 'flood risk management', with increasing responsibility being borne by individuals and communities.

References

ABC Radio National (2006) 'Radio National News', http://www.abc.net.au/news/newsitems/200609/s1731912.htm, accessed 6 September 2006

Adger, W. N. (2003) 'Social capital, collective action and adaptation to climate change', *Economic Geography*, vol 79, no 4, pp387–404

Allen Consulting (2005) *Climate Change Risk and Vulnerability*, Australian Greenhouse Office, Department of Environment and Heritage, Canberra, Australia

Arthur, J. M. (2003) *The Default Country: A Lexical Cartography of Twentieth Century Australia*, University of New South Wales Press, Sydney

Barnett, J. and Adger, N. (2007) 'Climate change, human security and violent conflict', *Political Geography*, vol 26, pp639–655

Barnett, J. and Adger, W. N. (2003) 'Climate dangers and atoll countries', *Climatic Change*, vol 61, pp321–337

Brooks, N., Adger, W. N. and Kelly, P. M. (2005) 'The determinants of vulnerability and adaptive capacity at the national level and the implications for adaptation', *Global Environmental Change*, vol 15, no 2, pp151–163

Butler, C. and Pidgeon, N. (2009) Climate Change Adaptation, Floods and the City: Governing for sustainable living? Paper presented at *Sustainable Cities and Regions: Enabling Visions or Empty Talk?*, Örebro University, 11–13 March 2009

Carberry, P. S., Hochman, Z., McCown, R. L., Dalgliesh, N. P., Foale, M. A., Poulton, P. L., Hargreaves, J. N. G., Hargreaves, D. M. G., Cawthray, S., Hillcoat, N. and Robertson, M. J. (2002) 'The FARMSCAPE approach to decision support: farmers, advisers, researchers monitoring, simulation, communication and performance evaluation', *Agricultural Systems*, vol 74, no 1, pp141–177

Cash, D. W. and Buizer, J. (2005) *Knowledge-Action Systems for Seasonal to Interannual Climate Forecasting*, National Research Council, Washington, DC

Cash, D. W., Clark, W. C., Alcock, F., Dickson, N. M., Eckley, N., Guston, D. H., Jager, J. and Mitchell, R. B. (2003) 'Knowledge systems for sustainable development', *Proceedings of the National Academy of Sciences of the United States of America*, vol 100, no 14, pp8086–8091

Dessai, S., Hulme, M., Lempert, R. and Pielke Jr, R. (2009a) 'Do we need better predictions to adapt to a changing climate?', *EOS Transactions of the American Geophysical Union*, vol 90, no 13

DPRTF (1990a) *Managing for Drought*, Australian Government Publishing Service, Canberra

DPRTF (1990b) *National Drought Policy*, Australian Government Publishing Service, Canberra

Folke, C., Colding, J. and Berkes, F. (2003) 'Synthesis: Building resilience and adaptive capacity in socio-ecological systems', in F. Berkes, C. Folke and J. Colding (eds), *Navigating Social–Ecological Systems: Building Resilience for Complexity and Change*, Cambridge University Press, Cambridge

Füssel, H. M. (2007) 'Adaptation planning for climate change: concepts, assessment approaches and key lessons', *Sustainability Science*, vol 2, pp265–275

Gieryn, T. F. (1999) *Cultural Boundaries of Science: Credibility on the Line*, The University of Chicago Press, Chicago

Guston, D. H. (2000) *Between Politics and Science: Assuring the Integrity and Productivity of Research*, University of Chicago Press, Chicago

Hallegatte, S. (2009) 'Strategies to adapt to an uncertain climate change', *Global Environmental Change*, vol 19, no 2, pp240–247

Hammer, G. L., Hansen, J. W., Phillips, J. G., Mjelde, J. W., Hill, H., Love, A. and Potgieter, A. (2001) 'Advances in application of climate prediction in agriculture', *Agricultural Systems*, vol 70, nos 2–3, pp515–553

Hayman, P. (2001) *Dancing in the Rain: Farmers and Agricultural Scientists in a Variable Climate*, Sydney, University of Western Sydney

Higgins, V. (2001) 'Calculating climate: "Advanced liberalism" and the governing of risk in Australian Drought Policy', *Journal of Sociology*, vol 37, no 3, pp299–316

Holling, C. S. (1973) 'Resilience and stability of ecological systems', *Annual Review of Ecology and Systematics*, vol 4, pp1–23

Holling, C. S., Berkes, F. and Folke, C. (1998) 'Science, sustainability and resource management', in F. Berkes and C. Folke (eds) *Linking Social and Ecological Systems: Management Practices and Social Mechanisms for Building Resilience*, Cambridge University Press, London

Howden, S. M., Soussana, J. F., Tubiello, F., Chhetri, N., Dunlop, M. and Meinke, H. (2007) 'Adapting agriculture to climate change', *Proceedings of the National Academy of Sciences of the United States of America*, vol 104, pp19691–19696

Ison, R. and Russell, D. (eds) (2000) *Agricultural Extension and Rural Development: Breaking out of Traditions*, Cambridge University Press, Cambridge, UK

Jasanoff, S. (2004) 'The idiom of co-production', in S. Jasanoff (ed) *States of Knowledge: The Co-production of Science and Social Order*, Routledge, London and New York

Kahneman, D. and Tversky, A. (1996) 'On the reality of cognitive illusions', *Psychological Review*, vol 103, no 3, pp582–591

Kates, R. W., Clark, W. C., Corell, R., Hall, J. M., Jaeger, C. C., Lowe, I., McCarthy, J. J., Schellnhuber, H. J., Bolin, B., Dickson, N. M., Faucheux, S., Gallopin, G. C., Grubler, A., Huntley, B., Jager, J., Jodha, N. S., Kasperson, R. E., Mabogunje, A., Matson, P. and Mooney, H. (2001) 'Sustainability science', *Science*, vol 292, no 5517, p641

Kestin, T. (2000) *Variations of Australian Climate and Extremes*, Melbourne, Monash

Leith, P. B. (2009) *Knowing El Nino: integrating knowledges of managing climate variability in the eastern Australian rangelands*. Hobart, University of Tasmania, http://eprints.utas.edu.au/9529/

McCown, R. L. (2001) 'Learning to bridge the gap between science-based decision support and the practice of farming: Evolution in paradigms of model-based research and intervention from design to dialogue', *Australian Journal of Agricultural Research*, vol 53, pp549–571

McIntosh, R. J., Tainter, J. A. and McIntosh, S. K. (2000) 'Climate history and human action', in R. J. McIntosh, J. A. Tainter and S. K. McIntosh (eds), *The Way the Wind Blows: Climate History and Human Action*, Columbia University Press, New York

Meinke, H. and Stone, R. (2005) 'Seasonal and inter-annual climate forecasting: the new tool for increasing preparedness to climate variability and change in agricultural planning operations', *Climatic Change*, vol 70, pp221–253

Meinke, H., Nelson, R. A., Kokic, P., Stone, R., Selvaraju, R. and Baethgen, W. (2006) 'Actionable climate knowledge: from analysis to synthesis', *Climate Research*, vol 33, pp101–110

Nelson, D., Adger, W. and Brown, K. (2007) 'Adaptation to environmental change: Contribution of a resilience framework', *Annual Review of Environment and Resources*, vol 32, pp395–419

Nelson, R. A., Holzworth, D. P., Hammer, G. and Hayman, P. (2002) 'Infusing the use of climate forecasting into crop management practice in North East Australia using discussion support software', *Agricultural Systems*, vol 74, pp393–414

Oreskes, N., Shrader-Frechette, K. and Belitz, K. (1994) 'Verification, validation, and confirmation of numerical models in the earth sciences', *Science*, vol 263, pp641–646

Sarewitz, D. (2004) 'How science makes environmental controversies worse', *Environmental Science & Policy*, vol 7, pp385–403

Shackley, S. and Wynne, B. (1996) 'Representing uncertainty in global climate science and policy: boundary ordering devices and authority', *Science, Technology and Human Values*, vol 21, no 3, pp275–302

Stafford Smith, M. (2003) 'Linking environments, decision-making and policy in handling climatic variability', in L. Botterill and M. Fisher (eds) *Beyond Drought: People, Policy and Perspectives*, CSIRO Publishing, Collingwood, Victoria

Star, S. L. and Griesemer, J. R. (1989) 'Institutional ecology, "translation", and boundary objects: Amateurs and professionals in Berkeley's Museum of Vertebrate Zoology', *Social Studies of Science*, vol 19, no 3, pp387–420

Stone, R. and Auliciems, A. (1992) 'SOI phase relationship with rainfall in eastern Australia', *International Journal of Climatology*, vol 12, pp625–636

Turner, B. L., Kasperson, R. E., Matsone, P. A., McCarthy, J. J., Corellg, R. W., Christensene, L., Eckley, N., Kasperson, J. X., Luerse, A., Martellog, M. L., Polskya, C., Pulsiphera, A. and Schillerb, A. (2003) 'A framework for vulnerability analysis in sustainability science', *Proceedings of the National Academy of Sciences of the United States of America*, vol 100, no 14, pp8074–8079

Vanclay, F. (2004) 'Social principles for agricultural extension to assist in the promotion of natural resource management', *Australian Journal of Experimental Agriculture*, vol 44, pp1–10

7
Ecological Citizenship as Public Engagement with Climate Change

Johanna Wolf

1. Ecological citizenship and climate change

The eroding role of the nation state and the globalization of environmental problems have sparked an evolution in citizenship theory towards alternative and non-traditional conceptualizations of citizenship. One such non-traditional theory is ecological citizenship (Dobson, 2003), a normative green theory of citizenship that emphasizes citizens' responsibilities over citizens' rights, similar to civic-republican conceptions of citizenship. Ecological citizenship, according to Dobson, extends beyond traditional notions of citizenship because it strongly emphasizes responsibilities, suggests that these responsibilities are non-reciprocal and non-territorial, and because it includes the private sphere in its remit (Dobson, 2003, p82). These characteristics make this theory of citizenship unconventional and have been a cause for criticism (Drevensek, 2005; Luque, 2005; Valdivielso, 2005; Hayward, 2006a, 2006b). Yet, despite criticisms, ecological citizenship has been found to have some traction in empirical studies conducted in the UK (Horton, 2005; Seyfang, 2006), Canada (Wolf et al, 2009) and Sweden (Jagers, 2009).

According to these studies, ecological citizens not only exhibit knowledge and concern about environmental problems, but also perceive a need for their engagement and either express willingness to act or have already undertaken activities to help mitigate the problems. Characteristic green lifestyles among green activists in the UK, negotiated collectively to seek consistency between political positions and personal preferences, were found to be promoted by a culture of environmental citizenship (Horton, 2005). Also in the UK, consumers involved in local organic food networks exhibited 'ecological citizenship values' in their activities (Seyfang, 2006, p389). Among participants of the study, ecological citizenship seemed to be a strong motivating force that drove behaviour (Seyfang, 2006). A study in Canada suggests that participants perceived an individual civic responsibility for acting on climate change, and that this has led them to change behaviour (Wolf et al, 2009). In a study in Sweden, 25 per cent of 1724 participants fit the definition of an ecological citizen (Jagers, 2009). The results suggest that four major factors affected the Swedes' willingness to act: ideology, interest in the environment, perceived severity of environmental problems and age (Jagers, 2009).

Together, these studies not only show that ecological citizens do exist, but depict such citizens as at least cognitively and behaviourally engaged in environmental issues. As argued by Dobson, there should be at least theoretically an element of care in the attitudes of ecological citizens, suggesting that there may be affective (emotional) components to their engagement. Dobson suggests that 'ecological citizens care because they want to do justice' (2003, p123), implying that virtues of care and compassion are motivated by a desire for equity and justice among people (and indeed between people and other species). As Jagers puts it, ecological citizens subscribe to the motto 'When I live my life I affect others, and to these others I have obligations (regardless of whether or not I know them)' (2009, p20). Evidence from Canada supports this notion of care for others, as participants articulated a sense of interconnectedness among people who may not know each other, but whose lives are nonetheless affected by individuals, albeit collectively, making everyday decisions (Wolf et al, 2009). Therefore, it seems that ecological citizens know about, care about and act on environmental issues. As will be discussed below, it has been suggested that whether an individual is engaged meaningfully depends on just these factors: cognition, behaviour and affect (Lorenzoni et al, 2007).

This chapter examines to what extent and how ecological citizens are engaged in climate change. Drawing on empirical research conducted in Canada, various aspects of engagement in climate change, as defined in this book, are examined in the perceptions and activities of study participants. The next section defines public engagement. The methods section outlines how the empirical research was conducted. A two-part analysis of the results first examines ecological citizenship as a form of engagement, and then analyses the barriers and limitations in operationalizing this type of citizenship as a form of public engagement. In the discussion, the characteristic features of ecological citizens' engagement in this research are examined and set against the backdrop of literature on public perceptions, attitudes and behaviour. The chapter concludes that ecological citizens are indeed engaged affectively, cognitively and behaviourally in climate change.

2. Public engagement

Given the severity of the problem of climate change, and the time lag in the climate system that commits the world to significant changes in climate in the near future, many acknowledge that the public has an important role to play in reducing emissions and adapting to impacts (see Introduction chapter). Despite urgent calls for emission reductions, however, effective behavioural change that would lead to sufficient cuts to greenhouse gases remains elusive to date (e.g. Lorenzoni et al, 2007). Ambitious targets to cut emissions have been set by some countries such as the UK, but it is still unclear just how, and how much, the public can and should contribute to this effort. As a result, there is debate about how best to reach these targets and how best to mobilize and engage the public in this effort effectively.

Lorenzoni et al (2007, p446) define 'engagement' as 'a personal state of connection' with the issue of climate change. This definition therefore contrasts with engagement as a process of participation. A state of engagement comprises cognitive, affective and behavioural aspects, and this conceptualization therefore implies that knowing about climate change is insufficient in order to be engaged. People also need to care about it, be motivated and be able to take action (Lorenzoni et al, 2007). And yet, according to this definition, effective emission reduction approaches may still be elusive. Even if people know and care about the issue, and are able to act, they may still decide to do nothing, or their actions may be ineffective in terms of reducing net emissions. Consequently, according to this definition, even if a person is engaged in climate change, he or she may not achieve *de facto* effective personal emission reductions.

It has been argued that more knowledge, improved information dissemination and more effective communication will not necessarily lead to the required social changes for effective emission reduction (Moser and Dilling, 2007). While it is undeniable that a certain level of knowledge about climate change can be helpful for individuals to reduce emissions, it has been demonstrated that knowing about the problem, even being exposed to an information campaign, may not lead to a change in behaviour (McKenzie-Mohr, 2000). Hence, knowledge is necessary but alone insufficient to effectively change behaviour to reduce emissions.

Affect and emotion play an important role in individuals' perceptions of and responses to climate change. The experiential system of risk perception, which operates in parallel to the analytic system, contributes significantly to decision making about and response to risk (Slovic et al, 2004). Experiential factors, including affect, have been found to influence risk perception of and policy support for climate change in the USA (Leiserowitz, 2006). The affect heuristic (i.e. an unconscious 'rule of thumb' that biases decision making and may produce an apparently 'irrational' decision) suggests that emotional reactions to a situation affect the way we respond (Marx et al, 2007). For example, affective risk perception shapes how Ugandan farmers respond to seasonal forecasts (Marx et al, 2007). When presented with scientific forecasts, farmers voiced fears that unusually scarce rains might lead to hunger for their households and they recall similar years in which they experienced such events (Marx et al, 2007).

Behavioural responses to climate change have only recently been investigated in research. In the UK, studies on energy efficiency behaviour suggest that the types of actions employed by households include using lower energy lightbulbs, recycling, reducing car use and utilizing public transit more frequently (Poortinga and Pidgeon, 2003; Norton and Leaman, 2004). However, only a small part of the UK population has resorted to these measures and overall energy consumption is still rising. Furthermore, a study from the UK suggests that there is a divergence between intent-oriented actions (i.e. activities intended to reduce environmental impact) and impact-oriented actions (i.e. those which reduce environmental impact irrespective of intention) (Whitmarsh, 2009). Crucially, actions taken with the intention to tackle climate change (e.g. recycling) are often not the most effective in reducing energy consumption and rarely extend beyond private-sphere behaviours (Whitmarsh, 2009; see also Chapter 3). As will be discussed below, this result resonates with the findings of the current research.

Numerous barriers to engaging the public have been identified. Based on empirical studies, the public perceives both individual and social constraints to engagement (Stoll-Kleemann et al, 2001; Lorenzoni et al, 2007). Lack of knowledge about causes, consequences and solutions, perceived scientific uncertainty, distrust of media, externalizing responsibility, remoteness of the threat of climate change, competing priorities, fatalism, reluctance to change lifestyles, and individual helplessness, make up only some of the public's perceived barriers at the individual level (Lorenzoni et al, 2007). Perceived political and industrial inaction, the free-rider effect, social norms and a lack of enabling initiatives have been identified as barriers at the social level (Lorenzoni et al, 2007).

Considering the evidence on ecological citizenship, however, it seems there are groups in society that do engage with climate change despite the widely perceived barriers noted above. Bearing in mind the three components of engagement (knowledge, affect, behaviour), are ecological citizens engaged in climate change meaningfully and, if so, to what extent? Does their behaviour extend beyond the role traditionally assigned for individuals as 'consumers' to encompass civic and community engagement? The sections that follow will provide some answers to these questions.

3. Methods

The empirical evidence in this chapter stems from a larger study (Wolf et al, 2009) examining perceptions of and responses to climate change, in a case study of two communities in British Columbia in western Canada, using Q-methodology (Brown, 1980; McKeown and Thomas, 1988). The research used semi-structured interviews; these were followed by a Q-sort ranking exercise and then by two focus groups, one in each community. The participants were recruited selectively and purposively. Selectively recruited participants included key actors and decision makers on climate change and other environmental issues locally, and those recruited purposively represented a spectrum of local residents at large. Purposive participants were recruited at four locations in each community; a sailing club, a golf course, a shopping mall parking lot, and a mother and toddler group. The sample of participants is likely more environmentally conscious than the general population of Canada.

This chapter draws on the interview portion of the study, semi-structured interviews conducted with 86 participants in 2004 and 2005. The interview questions explored participants' knowledge and perception of climate change, their views on what should be done about the problem, whether they felt affected by climate change in any way, whether they changed any behaviour in response to hearing about climate change, and who they felt had responsibility to act. Participants were also asked about their weekly routine, their energy use and their involvement in any community volunteer initiatives. In this research, 85 of 86 participants felt they had an individual civic responsibility for acting on climate change that characterizes the traits of ecological citizenship (Wolf et al, 2009). In studying the responses of these participants, this paper gleans insights into the cognitive, affective and behavioural engagement in climate change of ecological citizens. The analysis of interview data below concentrates on evidence for these three aspects of engagement and considers only evidence regarding greenhouse gas mitigation, not both mitigation and adaptation as in the original research.

4. Ecological citizenship as engagement: evidence from Canada

Civic engagement and cognition
Clearly, knowing about climate change is a crucial prerequisite for intentional action on the problem. Without knowledge that the problem exists, no purposeful action can take place. There is, however, not one knowledge of climate change; rather, there are varying levels, and culturally mediated ways, of understanding the scientific evidence of the warming globe, including the greenhouse effect, the human contribution to emissions and the changes in behaviour that would result in reduced emissions from personal activity. What then do ecological citizens know about climate change?

Participants consulted a wide variety of sources in learning about climate change, including television, radio, newspapers, newsletters of NGOs and a variety of online resources. As has been suggested elsewhere, active knowledge acquisition, as part of a conscious process of learning, is subject to biased assimilation (Rachlinski, 2000), and these participants were no exception. Individuals' knowledge was augmented by further information only in those ways that minimized conflicts with pre-existing related concepts. This was most clearly evident in the sceptic who sought sources of information that were highly unlikely to challenge the view that climate change is merely environmentalists' scaremongering.

A spectrum of knowledge and understanding is discernible in the responses of participants. Everyone interviewed knew of climate change; some called it global warming. The vast majority of participants accept the scientific evidence of climate change and that human contributions to emissions are warming the world. Three participants held sceptical views of varying degrees. Two believed the atmosphere is warming, yet were uncertain about humanity's contribution to the problem. Both still felt action should be taken as a matter of precaution. Only one participant denied the science of climate change and any human contribution to it. This was the only participant who felt that no action should be taken to reduce emissions and who perceived no personal civic responsibility.

Knowledge of the science of climate change among participants showed varying degrees of differentiation. The majority of participants knew about gases warming the atmosphere; some called this pollution. Those who did not know about the greenhouse effect showed significant confusion between climate change and stratospheric ozone depletion, a common misconception (Bostrom et al, 1994; Stamm et al, 2000; Ungar, 2000). Participants who knew about the greenhouse effect did not confuse climate change with ozone depletion, but not all of these participants were able to name greenhouse gases beyond carbon dioxide and methane.

Few participants had a good understanding of how much greenhouse gases' individual and household activity collectively contributes relative to other sources. Equally mixed was knowledge about what behavioural change results in effective emission reductions (cf. Lorenzoni et al, 2007). The majority of participants identified driving a car as a significant source of personal emissions, but did not know that flying is one of the most emission-intensive individual activities. As will be discussed below, this lack of understanding constitutes a barrier to effectively reducing emissions through voluntary changes in behaviour.

What level of knowledge then was common to all participants who perceived an individual civic responsibility for acting on climate change? The lowest common denominator of understanding about climate change among this group was simply knowing the problem exists and is human-made. Even those participants who did not know about the greenhouse effect, and were confused about ozone depletion, still felt a civic responsibility to reduce their emissions. This suggests that even basic awareness of anthropogenic climate change, recognized as a problem, may be sufficient in shaping a sense of personal responsibility and willingness to act.

Civic engagement and affect

Knowledge of climate change has been identified as a necessary but insufficient prerequisite for acting on the problem. Indeed, knowledge and affect seem related to each other. Participants described emotions in response to climate change ranging from concern to fear, helplessness, hopelessness and depression to frustration and anger. They also felt compassion for those affected by the impacts of climate change and a sense of guilt for contributing to the problem. Fear, helplessness, hopelessness and frustration were particularly common among participants. Many different dimensions of climate change induced fear. The thought of humans interfering with the atmospheric system was marked by a sense of unpredictability on an unprecedented scale. The nature of some of the severe effects of climate change, such as melting polar ice caps or large-scale flooding in low-lying countries, also induced fear. The scale of climate change as a global problem means that people may feel helpless, mirroring what Lorenzoni et al (2007, p450) call the 'drop in the ocean' feeling. Hopelessness was linked to the perception that there is no political leadership at national and global levels, but also to uncertainty about whether effective emission reductions are technologically and politically possible in a meaningful timeframe. Participants who expressed feeling depressed by climate change were scientists who have actively followed the science of climate change for at least two decades, and who felt no progress has been made to mitigate effectively. Frustration was mentioned by participants in the context of discussions they have in their social circle with people who feel that, while a solution may be technologically feasible, it is politically and socially elusive, possibly rendering the problem intractable.

As the impacts of climate change were largely perceived to occur elsewhere, in particular in developing countries, participants articulated a sense of compassion for those affected. Many participants were insightful regarding the underlying context of poverty and inequality in developing countries, and believed that these countries suffer disproportionately from the burden of climate change. This realization caused a sense of guilt tied to activities they perceived as emissions-intensive and therefore contributing to the problem. This perceived inequity in part induced the feeling of individuals' civic responsibility in the absence of political leadership on the issue (cf. Wolf et al, 2009). Table 7.1 below summarizes the emotional responses to climate change that participants articulated in their interviews.

Some participants reported that they have to manage their emotional engagement with climate change. They suggested that their commitment to making a difference would be negatively affected if they let the discouraged sentiments of others take hold:

> I am affected by other people getting emotional as well. [W]e have a number of people here who are … doomsayers and that does affect me. I try not to let it … because it would incapacitate me. … I would be much less effective as an advocate. So I have to really try and temper my own emotional engagement.

This highlights that a strong emotional response to climate change can command action among ecological citizens, and that this emotional response has to be managed in order to be effective as an engaged citizen. In particular, participants dealt with negative emotions like fear, helplessness and hopelessness in ways that supported rather than encumbered them in their action.

Behavioural responses also had affective aspects, especially when participants felt they had acted to reduce their emissions, whether or not they have effectively reduced net emissions. These feelings were not singular emotions, such as fear and anger discussed above, but rather included motivational sentiments of empowerment, affirmation of personal identity and purpose, righteousness, and urgency. These feelings were invoked when participants engaged in a particular activity. Especially among activists, but generally among those participants who changed behaviour, such feelings combined with serious concern about climate change and its effects to motivate action.

Empowerment plays a particularly important role in shaping behavioural responses of ecological citizens. Participants who changed behaviour felt empowered, that is able and motivated to act, even if the change in behaviour resulted in only a small amount of emission reduction. Feeling affirmed in one's personal identity is an important sign of acting in congruence with one's values and ethics. When action on climate change is in line with an individual's underlying values, the cognitive dissonance often associated with climate

Table 7.1 *Emotional responses to climate change among participants*

Type of emotion	Example quote
Fear	'I guess the thing is that it is a concern at the back of one's mind.' (Salt Spring Island participant, female)
	'I worry about it [climate change] on the whole, how it affects me personally. I am very nervous about it. I can perceive it.' (Salt Spring Island participant, female)
	'I am scared about long term sea level rise living on the coast … And the melting Arctic. That's what the scientists are saying, it's scary, the melting in the Arctic.' (Victoria participant, female)
	'[Interviewer: Do you feel you have been affected by climate change?] Oh yeah – directly affected. Definitely emotionally affected because it freaks me out, and uhm, it definitely motivates me just by realizing that it's a problem and that it affects my life.' (Victoria participant, male)
Helplessness	'I have been hearing that [climate change] for 30–40 years, it is all bad news. I don't read much of it anymore. I guess I feel helpless to do anything. So I am just trying to work on Salt Spring to try and save what we have here. As much as I can.' (Salt Spring Island participant, female)
	'There is no public leadership, so people just think it is like helping famine in Ethiopia or something. They just think "what can I do, the problem is so huge".' (Salt Spring Island participant, female)
Hopelessness	'[Interviewer: Is there a typical end to those conversations [about climate change]?] Ya, a feeling of hopelessness, really … [T]here is just so many other elements playing in that story that you can't just say mankind is going to pull it together and we are going to fix the problem. Because all the other things, with media, and corporations and money, … industry, there is no way you can fight that tiger. And politicians – that isn't what they care about.' (Victoria participant, female)
Depression	'I have been depressed by it, yes. I have to fight to stop going into permanent depression.' (Salt Spring Island participant, male)
Frustration	'I have talked to people about this kind of stuff for 20 years and nothing has changed … Some people get frustrated and angry … I don't like when people get angry about it. I don't like the energy of that. It has negative effects on you.' (Salt Spring Island participant, male)
	'I think people have a lot of frustration and disillusionment about this [climate change].' (Salt Spring Island participant, female)
Compassion	'I feel affected, I feel for them. I feel "Ok what can I do?" Or what should I not do so not to contribute to their problems?' (Victoria participant, female)
	'[I]t is not just the people, it is the entire world, the animals and all the creatures … So I would say yes, definitely affected emotionally …, but not just for people, but for everything else as well.' (Victoria participant, female)
Guilt	'I feel incredibly guilty when I travel by plane. I just know, because the air planes are high, the emissions are going straight into the higher atmosphere and they do an incredible amount of damage.' (Victoria participant, female)
	'[W]e live about an hour outside of Victoria and I … ride the bus. And occasionally I do bring my vehicle but I always feel guilty.' (Victoria participant, female)

change (i.e. an uncomfortable psychological state arising from knowing about, but not acting to address, anthropogenic climate change; see Stoll-Kleemann et al, 2001) is reduced. The sense of righteousness participants described relates to enacting normative responses they perceive as right and legitimate. The vast majority of participants perceived a sense of urgency about acting on climate change, even if they did not identify or feel personally affected by local climate change impacts. Table 7.2 below summarizes the emotional motivations for behaviour undertaken in response to climate change.

What then are the emotions and sentiments that most or all participants have in common? All participants showed some level of concern about climate change, but not necessarily fear. The strongly negative emotions of hopelessness, helplessness and depression are articulated only by a few participants, who nevertheless adjust behaviour in an attempt to reduce their emissions. Frustration was only mentioned explicitly when participants talked about how others might feel about climate change. While it seems unlikely that none of the participants were frustrated about the lack of progress on emission reductions, they did not articulate this frustration. One reason for this could be that their focus of attention was primarily on their own behaviour, and hence their explanations about how they feel mostly related to their behaviour. Predominantly, the majority of participants perceived the impacts of climate change as occurring elsewhere, in developing countries, and as a result, feelings of compassion for those affected were common. Tied to this realization

Table 7. 2 *Emotional drivers for behaviour undertaken in response to climate change*

Type of emotion	Example quote
Empowerment	'I am really feeling quite desperate … how badly we have mucked up things. And as a Canadian … I see the energy consumption that goes on, and I realise that I am one of the early adopters and it has taken me a long time to get it. And I think to myself "Oh my God, there is so much to be done!" And … this pushes me onward.' (Salt Spring Island participant, female) '[1:] It feels like it's helping. It … feels empowering to actually be making a conscious decision about how one is going to live this life and I think it does make a difference. And I think that people would feel good if they did it too. [2:] And I think in a world where I sometimes think that I don't have a lot of control over the air I breathe …, in the smallest way that is some sort of control I have.' (Two Salt Spring Island participants, female) '[Is this about a negative message rather than a positive message?] Yes. Saying that there is something that can be done [about climate change]. Definitely people are going to want to change if the message is empowering. I don't think that anyone ever changes something significant about how they live their lives unless it actually feels good to do this on some level.' (Victoria participant, male)
Affirmation of identity	'It is a question about being able to live in a way that reflects your values and ethics, and I guess that is about identity. Because … values and ethics are about identity. So, being able to live in a way that allows me to be part of the solution, or at least not be part of the problem, is important.' (Victoria participant, male)
Righteousness	'I guess it wasn't a huge decision [to ride the bus], it was just the right thing to do. … For me, this was just the right thing to do … [I]t just feels right.' (Victoria participant, female)
Sense of urgency	'It [The Day After Tomorrow movie] had a huge emotional impact, I just thought "My goodness, my God, what are we doing to ourselves?" We have nobody to blame but ourselves so … We have to get out there and reduce greenhouse gases somehow, but how to do it … how to change the world I don't know.' (Victoria participant, female)

were feelings of guilt for participating in the societal system that causes climate change and results in negative impacts on others living elsewhere.

Feeling empowered by enacting some behaviour in response to climate change was very common. Regardless of the scale of behavioural change and actual emission reductions, empowerment was almost always a component of action. It is difficult, however, to disentangle whether empowerment happens before or after action is taken. Some participants, as seen in Table 7.2 above, suggested that their empowerment stems from their belief that action is needed urgently. Other participants clearly felt empowered after having acted to reduce emissions. Empowerment was also named in the context of communicating to the public how best to reduce emissions in a way that encourages them to act. Most commonly, participants were empowered in the sense that they felt able to act, and this applied to everyone who participated in the study except for the sceptic.

The degree to which participants felt affirmed in their identity by acting on climate change depended both on how serious they felt the problem of climate change is, and on their values. When participants felt the problem was very serious and urgently required action, and their value orientations emphasized altruism or ecocentrism (i.e. ecologically centred values), they seemed to derive significant comfort or intrinsic satisfaction from the congruence between their values and their actions, and they articulated this explicitly. Others simply suggested that they had to act so as not to feel guilty and part of the problem. As a result, it seems that while identity played a role for some, the more important force in determining behaviour may be individuals' underlying value systems (cf. Whitmarsh, 2009).

Many of the participants' responses suggest that a sentiment of righteousness played a role in how and why participants act, but this was not common to all. Those who did express some degree of righteousness emphasized that their behaviour was the 'right' way to act on climate change. Others were more cautious and underscored that they could and should not patronize others by prescribing a course of action or a particular lifestyle. As the sentiment was not common to all participants, it does not seem to play a major role in shaping behaviour of ecological citizens.

Participants in this research showed varying degrees of concern over the severity of climate change and consequently perceived differing levels of urgency for action. It is clear, however, that every ecological citizen felt that action is required, and some level of urgency was attached to the problem. The differences among participants relate primarily to the scale and timeframe at which they felt action was needed. Therefore, common to all ecological citizens was the perception of at least some urgency for action.

Based on these results, ecological citizens are affectively engaged with climate change. But rather than a set of emotions common to all, ecological citizens may feel different emotions in relation to climate change. Every participant except the sceptic was at least concerned, perceived some level of urgency and suggested some affective component to their behaviour.

Civic engagement and behaviour

Ecological citizens in this study changed their behaviour in attempts to reduce their greenhouse gas emissions. Whether the change in behaviour resulted in net emissions reduction, however, depended on citizens' knowledge of emission-intensive behaviour. The effectiveness of the changed behaviour also depended on the extent to which the original behaviour that participants perceived to be emission-intensive was resistant to change. These two factors determined whether the behavioural change was effective in reducing emissions. While it was not the objective of this study to quantify how effective changes in behaviour were, the results indicate that often good intentions and changes in behaviour do not actually result in meaningful net emission reductions.

The types of behavioural changes employed by participants ranged from broad environmental activities, such as recycling, to reducing energy use; for example, by turning down the thermostat, using energy efficient light bulbs and selling the household car. While climate change was never the sole reason for changing behaviour, it almost always featured as a cause for behavioural response. Table 7.3 below summarizes the behavioural responses by participants.

By far the most common activity undertaken by 98 per cent of participants was recycling, a behaviour that could be considered iconic for helping the environment. The majority of participants who mentioned recycling either did not know whether it effectively reduces emissions or did not say whether they knew. Roughly half to one-third of participants engaged in reducing car use, composting, changing home heating, eating less or no meat, and buying organic food. All of these activities were brought into the context of effective emission reductions by participants, indicating that they thought these behaviours would help address climate change. Between one-fifth and one-third of participants changed lightbulbs, grew food, conserved water, bought local products, reduced ferry use and cycled. It is important to note that these activities were not undertaken in isolation; rather, participants employed numerous behaviours in conjunction with each other. All behavioural change was dictated in part by perceived emission intensity, and not actual emission intensity. The most common highly emission-intensive activity that was most resistant to change was flying for business or leisure. Clearly, this has consequences for overall emissions and makes effective reductions much less likely.

Over one-third of participants were involved in some local informal community network. This participation included volunteering for local NGOs, but most commonly involved some form of engagement in informal associations with a specific, mainly environmental, but also social, mandate. These associations included a water preservation society, two watershed stewardship groups, a car-share cooperative, a community energy strategy task force, two neighbourhood associations, a transportation society, a cycling association and a ferry advisory committee. Participants involved in these efforts felt disappointed by and disengaged from decision making on climate change at the provincial and federal level in Canada. They perceived a lack of leadership on climate change at the federal political level in Canada and believed they were

Table 7.3 *Behaviours and activities employed by participants*

Behaviour/activity	No. participants (percentage)	Exemplary quote
Recycling	84 (98)	'Recycling is great! Our kitchen is taken over by recycling.' (Victoria participant, male)
Selling car/ reducing car use/ downsizing vehicle/ driving hybrid vehicle	39 (45)	'My sixteen year old car finally died, after driving it as long as I could, to reduce having to spend money on another car and all the embodied energy that comes with that. I looked around for the most fuel efficient car I could find, and I bought a Toyota Prius.' (Victoria participant, male)
Composting	36 (42)	'We compost. I get immense satisfaction out of taking the compost out after a couple of years.' (Victoria participant, male)
Changing heating system/turning down thermostat/ reducing heating fuel use	34 (40)	'We use a heat pump. And the heat pump saves on fossil fuels. ... It is economical, and also because we are contributing less carbon to the air.' (Victoria participant, male)
Eating less meat Vegetarianism Veganism	16 14 (36) 1	'It's better for your health. And raising cattle needs a lot of water, and energy, and the energy contained in red meat is much less than what has to be spent on raising it ... a vegetarian diet is much better for the environment.' (Salt Spring Island participant, male)
Buying organic food	29 (34)	'We ... buy local organic food ... [T]he organic soil stores much more carbon ... .' (Victoria participant, male)
Community engagement	29 (34)	'I am on the board of the Victoria Care Share Co-op.' (Victoria participant, female)
		'I am part of the Salt Spring Island Water Preservation Society.' (Salt Spring Island participant, female)
Changing lighting	26 (30)	'Almost all of our light bulbs are the new [compact] fluorescent light bulbs.' (Salt Spring Island participant, female)
Growing food	24 (28)	'We produce a lot of our own food.' (Victoria participant, female)
Conserving water	22 (26)	'Every little bit counts: conserving water, living communally, buying recycled products ... made locally.' (Victoria participant, female)
		'And also I am careful about the use of water, and I start nagging everybody where I work too about "turn the water off!". 'Cuz we may seem like we live in a water-rich province but it is an illusion.' (Salt Spring Island participant, female)
Buying local products	20 (23)	'I like to buy local as much as possible.' (Salt Spring Island participant, female)
Reducing ferry use	18 (21)	'We combine all our reasons to go to Victoria or Vancouver [by ferry] and then we do them all in one go.' (Salt Spring Island participant, male)
Bicycling	16 (19)	'I bike. It's quicker to bike and better for me.' (Victoria participant, male)

not afforded sufficient agency as citizens. As a result, participants sought agency on the issue by participating in informal networks, but also as individuals that are part of a household.

The evidence presented here suggests that ecological citizens in this research were able to take action, and indeed actively employed or changed behaviours to reduce emissions. As the wide range of behaviours and activities shows, citizens' responses were guided by perceived, not actual, emission intensity, and it is unclear how their net emissions may have changed as a result. Their engagement also included participating in certain civic activities, which provides evidence that ecological citizens perceive participation in the democratic process (via community groups or networks) as important. Civic involvement, therefore, is part of their behavioural engagement with climate change.

5. Barriers and limitations to civic engagement

Despite the active cognitive, affective and behavioural engagement among participants of this study, numerous barriers to effective engagement can be identified. Some of these barriers exist at the individual level, and the others are due to structural and institutional factors. At the individual level, a lack of appropriate knowledge of effective emission reduction strategies was the most common, not lacking awareness of, or knowledge about, climate change per se. As the evidence outlined above suggests, a change in behaviour, even among these engaged participants, did not necessarily translate into net emission reductions because of insufficient knowledge of emissions associated with specific activities. A prominent example was reducing car use while continuing to fly. Unlike other and more systemic barriers, this lack of relevant knowledge could be addressed in part by disseminating information about greenhouse gas emissions from flying, driving a car, and other activities such as changing lightbulbs and turning down the thermostat (although *willingness* to change these behaviours may not follow from this knowledge).

In this study, there was no evidence that a lack of knowledge or awareness about climate change as an urgent and human-made problem was a significant barrier to action. One reason for this could be that this sample of participants was environmentally engaged and aware. Recent surveys of the Canadian public, however, suggest that while nearly two-thirds of the population believe that climate change is a significant threat, 7 per cent of Canadians believe climate change is no threat at all (Harris Decima, 2009). In the case of climate change sceptics, a disbelief in the severity of the problem, combined with a disbelief of the human contribution to it, shape an obvious lack of engagement, but this does not constitute a lack of knowledge. Reaching and further affectively engaging the latter fraction of Canadians, among them sceptics, will therefore likely be difficult.

Barriers that prevent or encumber affective engagement among ecological citizens include specific emotions that have to be managed, such as fear. These emotions themselves can encumber action and reduce motivation to engage. As the quote from a participant on Salt Spring Island earlier shows, feelings of fear and doom can affect the ability to engage effectively in action on climate change. She stated explicitly that she tempers her 'emotional engagement'. Similarly, another participant suggested that:

> you can't let yourself, or don't let yourself live with the panic about a future situation, because I couldn't possibly live that way worrying so much about the future. I just try to do the best with my life, and ... one thing I worry about is how to increase awareness in other people, how to get the message out, and having to change culture, but I don't know how to do that yet.

Both hopelessness (or what the above participant called 'doom') and fear are viewed as potentially disengaging from the issue, and both participants actively counter this by responding to these emotions consciously.

Even the most engaged ecological citizens interviewed here face behavioural barriers. These barriers are primarily structural and institutional factors that prevent or encumber well-meaning attempts to reduce emissions. Participants identified regulations and standards that pertain to home and car insurance as barriers to emission reduction. For example, building code regulations that are strictly enforced prevented one participant from installing exclusive wood heating. Instead, the household had to install a propane backup central heating system because without it the home would not have passed the building inspection. Two participants complained that car insurance incentivizes driving through discounted longer insurance periods, rather than providing coverage based on time or distance driven, a system that would provide incentives for driving less through the combining of multiple trips. A number of participants complained about the lack of incentives available for installing alternative energy sources such as photovoltaics and solar hot water. Top-down government efforts were viewed as a necessary component of reducing emissions through strict regulation. But in the absence of leadership on the issue at the federal level, and in a liberal culture that is often at odds with government intervention, ecological citizens felt it is left up to them to act. Ecological citizens also perceived a lack of political leadership at the provincial and federal level as an obstacle to engaging the Canadian public at large. Widespread consumerism, corporate interests and a western living standard being taken for granted were also perceived as barriers for the public.

6. How do ecological citizens compare to the general public?

There are some similarities between ecological citizens' knowledge, affective connection and behaviour, and that of the general public. The type and detail of knowledge among ecological citizens is similar to that found in studies of the general public, as there is evidence for some confusion about ozone depletion and climate change (Bostrom et al, 1994; Kempton et al, 1995; Stamm et al, 2000), about which gases cause climate change (Read et al, 1994; Brechin, 2003) and knowledge about how to address the issue is mixed (Lorenzoni et al, 2007; Whitmarsh, 2009). This suggests that perhaps the only consistent difference to the general public may be a serious concern about climate change as an urgent problem among every ecological citizen (e.g. Dunlap et al, 1993; Kempton, 1993; Kempton et al, 1995; Stamm et al, 2000).

Since most of the research on affect and emotions with respect to climate change focuses on risk perception, it is not possible to comprehensively compare ecological citizens' affective engagement with that of the public. Participants here were not disengaged by fear, as has been suggested elsewhere (O'Neill and Nicholson-Cole, 2009), to the extent that they would have stopped acting on climate change. Instead, fear motivated some to do more about the problem. These participants likely felt some degree of personal agency. However, most participants perceived climate change as a geographically remote problem, suggesting that their concern is not shaped by perception of local or personal impacts. Indeed, the finding that ecological citizens are seriously concerned about and act on climate change, despite perceiving it as a remote problem, suggests that feeling affected by the impacts may not be a necessary condition for engagement including behavioural change (cf. Whitmarsh, 2008).

The majority of activities undertaken by ecological citizens in response to climate change are similar to those identified by other research (Whitmarsh, 2009), but there are some important differences. Citizens engaged in NGOs and informal networks, such as community associations, as a means to increase their individual agency, and thus demonstrated interest in changing the structures that govern their agency (cf. Luque, 2005). They also cited climate change as one among numerous reasons for changing behaviour, suggesting citizens perceive an explicit link between their individual activities and some associated greenhouse gas contributions. While this research suggests that perceived, not actual, emission intensity in part determines how behaviour is changed, ecological citizens interviewed here did adjust behaviour with the explicit, but not sole, intention of reducing emissions. Research in the UK has suggested that only 31 per cent of the public have taken action explicitly out of concern for climate change, but often this is not the most effective action to cut emissions (Whitmarsh, 2009). Ecological citizens therefore may distinguish themselves by acting on climate change in response to both a sense of responsibility and affective engagement, rather than by the effectiveness of their behavioural change in terms of reducing emissions.

7. Conclusion: towards meaningful and effective engagement

In addition to exhibiting the characteristics of ecological citizens put forward by Dobson (2003; emphasizing responsibilities, non-reciprocity, non-territoriality and including the private sphere in citizenship's remit; cf. Wolf et al, 2009), the ecological citizens in this study were cognitively, affectively and behaviourally engaged in climate change. Their depth of knowledge and affective responses to climate change varied widely, and resulted in behaviours that were believed to reduce emissions. According to this analysis, ecological citizens do not exhibit a specific set of knowledge, emotion and action in response to climate change, but rather demonstrate a suite of knowledge, affect and behaviours as part of their engagement with the issue. Unlike in other research that suggests ecological citizens understand themselves as activists whose lifestyles embody a culture of green living (Horton, 2005), lifestyles of participants in this research are relatively diverse and do not embody a homogeneous culture of sustainability. They seem to be empowered rather than disempowered by their knowledge and subjective perception of climate change, and distinguish themselves by feeling responsible and acting on the problem with explicit intention. Their engagement, however, goes beyond changing behaviour as a result of knowing and being concerned about the problem, and includes civic engagement that aims to enhance their agency as individuals. In this respect, ecological citizens exhibit a commitment to changing the structures and institutions that govern their engagement. Yet despite this engagement, the obstacles and barriers highlighted here suggest that even ecological citizens may not reduce their emissions effectively. A lack of knowledge about how to achieve effective emission reductions, accompanied by structural impediments and a less than pervasive culture of low-carbon lifestyles, are critical obstacles in making engagement meaningful. This suggests that information campaigns should focus on emissions associated with carbon-intensive activities, and that broader policies should enable and encourage a culture of more sustainable, low-carbon lifestyles so that individuals' sense of ecological citizenship can be translated into effective action. The evidence examined here therefore suggests that ecological citizenship theory may benefit from explicitly accounting for the active engagement by citizens in environmental issues such as climate change, including in particular the affective dimensions. Further, ecological citizenship should consider citizens' sense of agency and empowerment in explaining the relationship between the sense of responsibility and behaviour. Future research could explore ecological citizens' value systems to explain their lack of disempowerment and the reason for their engagement in more depth, as well as considering whether, and in what ways, ecological citizens may be taking action to adapt to the impacts of climate change.

References

Bostrom, A., Morgan, M. G., Fischhoff, B. and Read, D. (1994) 'What do people know about global climate change? 1. Mental models', *Risk Analysis*, vol 14, no 6, pp959–970

Brechin, S. R. (2003) 'Comparative public opinion and knowledge on global climatic change and the Kyoto Protocol: the US versus the rest of the World?', *International Journal of Sociology and Social Policy*, vol 23, no 10, pp106–134

Brown, S. R. (1980) *Political Subjectivity: Applications of Q Methodology in Political Science*, Yale University Press, New Haven, CT

Dobson, A. (2003) *Citizenship and the Environment*, Routledge, London

Drevensek, M. (2005) 'Negotiation as the driving force of environmental citizenship', *Environmental Politics*, vol 14, no 2, pp226–238

Dunlap, R. E., Gallup, G. H. and Gallup, A. M. (1993) *Health of the Planet Survey: A George A. Memorial Survey*, Gallup International Institute, Princeton, NJ

Harris Decima (2009) *2009 Climate Change Debate Surveys (Part I of II) – A Harris*

Interactive/Financial Times study conducted for the Munk Debates, retrieved 11 December 2009, from http://www.munkdebates.com/media/MunkDebatesPoll_ HarrisInteractive_Monday30November.pdf

Hayward, T. (2006a) 'Ecological citizenship: A rejoinder', *Environmental Politics*, vol 15, no 3, pp452–453

Hayward, T. (2006b) 'Ecological citizenship: Justice, rights and the virtue of resource-fulness', *Environmental Politics*, vol 15, no 3, pp435–446

Horton, D. (2005) 'Demonstrating environmental citizenship?', in A. Dobson and D. R. Bell (eds) *Environmental Citizenship*, MIT Press, Cambridge, MA

Jagers, S. C. (2009) 'In search of the ecological citizen', *Environmental Politics*, vol 18, no 1, pp18–36

Kempton, W. (1993) 'Will public environmental concern lead to action on global warming?', *Annual Review of Energy and the Environment*, vol 18, pp217–245

Kempton, W., Boster, J. S. and Hartley, J. A. (1995) *Environmental Values in American Culture*, MIT Press, Cambridge MA

Leiserowitz, A. (2006) 'Climate change risk perception and policy preferences: The role of affect, imagery and values', *Climatic Change*, vol 77, pp45–72

Lorenzoni, I., Nicholson-Cole, S. and Whitmarsh, L. (2007) 'Barriers perceived to engaging with climate change among the UK public and their policy implications', *Global Environmental Change*, vol 17, pp445–459

Luque, E. (2005) 'Researching environmental citizenship and its publics', *Environmental Politics*, vol 14, no 2, pp211–225

Marx, S. M., Weber, E. U., Orlove, B. S., Leiserowitz, A., Krantz, D. H., Roncoli, C. et al (2007) 'Communication and mental processes: Experiential and analytic processing of uncertain climate information', *Global Environmental Change*, vol 17, no 1, pp47–58

McKenzie-Mohr, D. (2000) 'Fostering sustainable behaviour through community based social marketing', *American Psychologist*, vol 55, pp531–537

McKeown, B. F. and Thomas, D. B. (1988) *Q Methodology: Quantitative Applications in the Social Sciences*, Sage, Thousand Oaks, CA

Moser, S. and Dilling, S. (eds) (2007) *Creating a Climate for Change: Communicating Climate Change and Facilitating Social Change*, Cambridge University Press, Cambridge

Norton, A. and Leaman, J. (2004) *The Day after Tomorrow: Public Opinion on Climate Change*, MORI Social Research Institute, London

O'Neill, S. and Nicholson-Cole, S. (2009) '"Fear won't do it": Promoting positive engagement with climate change through visual and iconic representations', *Science Communication*, vol 30, no 3, pp355–379

Poortinga, W. and Pidgeon, N. (2003) *Public perceptions of Risk, Science and Governance. Main findings of a British survey on five risk cases*, Centre for Environmental Risk, University of East Anglia, Norwich

Rachlinski, J. J. (2000) 'The psychology of global climate change', *University of Illinois Law Review*, vol 1, pp299–319

Read, D., Bostrom, A., Morgan, M. G., Fischhoff, B. and Smuts, T. (1994) 'What do people know about climate change – Part 2: survey studies of educated lay people', *Risk Analysis*, vol 14, pp971–982

Seyfang, G. (2006) 'Ecological citizenship and sustainable consumption: Examining local organic food networks', *Journal of Rural Studies*, vol 22, pp383–395

Slovic, P., Finucane, M., Peters, E. and MacGregor, D. G. (2004) 'Risk as analysis and risk as feelings: Some thoughts about affect, reason, risk, and rationality', *Risk Analysis*, vol 24, no 2, pp1–12

Stamm, K. R., Clark, F. and Eblacas, P. R. (2000) 'Mass communication and public understanding of environmental problems: the case of global warming', *Public Understanding of Science*, vol 9, pp219–237

Stoll-Kleemann, S., O'Riordan, T. and Jaeger, C. C. (2001) 'The psychology of denial concerning climate mitigation measures: evidence from Swiss focus groups', *Global Environmental Change*, vol 11, no 2, pp107–117

Ungar, S. (2000) 'Knowledge, ignorance and the popular culture: climate change versus the ozone hole', *Public Understanding of Science*, vol 9, pp297–312

Valdivielso, J. (2005) 'Social citizenship and the environment', *Environmental Politics*, vol 14, no 2, pp239–254

Whitmarsh, L. (2008) 'Are flood victims more concerned about climate change than other people? The role of direct experience in risk perception and behavioural response', *Journal of Risk Research*, vol 11, no 3, pp351–374

Whitmarsh, L. (2009) 'Behavioural responses to climate change: Asymmetry of intentions and impacts', *Journal of Environmental Psychology*, vol 29, no 1, pp13–23

Wolf, J., Brown, K. and Conway, D. (2009) 'Ecological citizenship and climate change: Perceptions and practice', *Environmental Politics*, vol 18, no 4, pp503–521

PART 2

METHODS, MEDIA AND TOOLS

*How can we more effectively communicate
with the public about climate change and
energy demand reduction?*

8
Engaging People in Saving Energy on a Large Scale: Lessons from the Programmes of the Energy Saving Trust in the UK

Nick Eyre, Brooke Flanagan and Ken Double

1. Introduction

Direct personal carbon emissions from homes and transport account for almost half of the UK's carbon emissions (HM Government, 2009a). The choices people make, from turning off lights to installing microgeneration, have the potential to make a significant contribution to meeting the UK's climate change targets. As a result, behavioural change is the key to unlocking significant carbon savings in the UK economy.

The Energy Saving Trust (EST), through its mission to lead 60 million people to act on climate change, has put behavioural change at the forefront of tackling personal carbon emissions. Typically, behavioural change that the EST seeks to influence includes the following:

1   One-off discretionary behaviours (e.g. installation of cavity wall insulation and microgeneration), which is usually very infrequent.
2   Choices in purchasing behaviour (e.g. purchase of A++ rated appliances).
3   Conscious and common substitution behaviour (e.g. travel by bus instead of car).
4   Routine habitual behaviour (e.g. turning the room thermostat down; turning off standby).

Increasingly, EST awareness raising activity has focused on the last area, influencing changes to habitual household energy behaviour. This has largely been based on the assumption that behavioural change is linear, and if a person starts with the easier behaviours they will move along a path of increasingly more difficult and/or costly changes. Whilst recent evidence based on evaluation of EST advice suggests this assumption has some merit, behavioural change is far more complex and not always based on conscious, rational decision making (see Chapter 1). It is influenced by a range of factors, both internal and external, which provide a significant challenge to those seeking to change behaviour as it relates to climate change.

With efforts to persuade, coerce, advise and provide information achieving only limited success, practitioners decided on a different approach, based on understanding and overcoming the barriers to behavioural change. The Energy Efficiency Innovation Review (HM Treasury and Defra, 2005) highlighted several key barriers to the wider take-up of cost-effective household energy efficiency measures, including:

- up-front costs of measures;
- transaction costs, or the 'hassle factor' of getting measures installed, in part due to the disparate nature of energy efficiency offers (e.g. grants, energy supplier obligations);
- distrust of energy suppliers and installers to fit measures properly;
- lack of information, interest and the perception that costs are higher than they actually are.

At the same time these barriers were being acknowledged, moves were being made in the UK Government to understand better what drives behaviour change. Since 2005, the UK Government has increasingly engaged with the theory and practice of behaviour change, firstly through their Sustainable Development Strategy (HM Government, 2005), then the contribution of the Sustainable Consumption Roundtable (2006), which was followed up by extensive work on pro-environmental behaviours by the Department for Environment, Food and Rural Affairs (e.g. Defra, 2008). This change in the broader policy landscape provides the context for the EST's focus on behaviour change.

2. EST history

Formation and finding a role
The EST was established in the aftermath of the Rio 'Earth Summit' in 1992. The incumbent Conservative government was in the process of reshaping energy markets. A decade earlier, the Secretary of State for Energy, Nigel Lawson, famously rejected the Government's role in planning 'the future shape of energy production and consumption'. This set the tone for a decade of privatization and liberalization in the UK energy sector, in which a free market was the goal.

However, environmental challenges did not disappear; indeed, the Prime Minister, Margaret Thatcher, was one of the earliest politicians to show an interest in climate change in 1989, so the UK played an active role in the Rio process. However, in energy efficiency, the Government's role was seen to be to ensure fair competition in the energy market with the assumption that this would result in free market-based solutions to energy efficiency investment, despite the evidence that market barriers outside the energy sector might prevent this.

The EST was created in this political environment. Already there was pressure on the Government and energy companies (still largely retail supply monopolies at that stage) to act, and be seen to act. Government ownership or direct control was not considered appropriate and the governance reflected this. The EST was created as a public/private partnership, with some directors from energy companies, but a majority of independent directors, and Government involvement only as an observer on the board. Initial links to energy companies were strong, with some early staffing provided via energy supplier secondments. But as the EST developed and its role changed, although good relationships were maintained, there was more detachment. The organizational culture remained commercially aware, but new staff recruited were primarily attracted by environmental goals, and from diverse backgrounds in management, marketing, public and third sector organizations.

Developing the programmes

The same broad pressures for action on energy efficiency via the energy market had led to the energy privatization legislation, including provisions for energy efficiency funding by household energy suppliers. There were early schemes in gas (E-factors schemes) and electricity (Energy Efficiency Standards of Performance, EESoP), although the former were abandoned by the second gas regulator, Clare Spottiswoode, who variously claimed that they constituted a tax and that they were regressive (although neither claim was correct). The problems of relying on regulatory discretion were eventually resolved in the Utilities Act 2000, which placed the schemes under ministerial control, allowing the Labour Government to reinstate schemes in gas and massively increase their scale.

EST was a strong proponent of energy supplier schemes on both sides of the 1997 Election. The early schemes were effectively a major source of funding, as the EST acted as scheme manager for both national schemes (involving all suppliers) and framework schemes (opt-in programmes). But this was short lived, as energy suppliers soon recognized the competitive and brand benefits of managing their own energy efficiency programmes.

In this context, the EST reoriented itself as primarily a deliverer of advice and awareness raising programmes, where independence from direct commercial pressures had an acknowledged role. However, the implications for funding were severe, and could have been terminal but for some neat political footwork by the Conservative Secretary of State for the Environment, John Gummer. In the midst of a crisis in December 1994, precipitated by the defeat in Parliament of proposals to levy the full rate of VAT on household fuels, he successfully argued that retaining the rate at 8 per cent would require greater direct effort on energy efficiency and injection of Government funding into EST, initially of £25 million per year.

Direct government funding provided the basis for a set of publically funded EST programmes that still persist – an advice network, a marketing programme, and support for both 'supply chain' (the energy efficiency industry) and 'community' (local authorities and voluntary organizations). The advice programme has become the EST's most distinctive feature through the national network of EST advice centres (ESTACs). The marketing programme created a new 'Energy Efficiency' brand, initially purely as a marketing device, but then linked to an 'on product' accreditation system 'Energy Efficiency Recommended' (now renamed 'EST Recommended').

Changing focus

The EST's historic role – energy saving in households – is very focused and remains contentious. The Government created a separate Carbon Trust in 2002, notionally funded from hypothecated receipts of the Climate Change Levy, to play a similar role for business and technology development. This separation is not mirrored in agencies promoting sustainable energy in other countries. The organizational cultures and staff backgrounds of the two Trusts are very different, reflecting their target markets. But potential overlaps remain; for example in local authority advice, household technology development, promotion of 'product carbon footprints' and mass market advertising.

The focus on household energy has always been a little restrictive given the high (and growing) level of personal emissions from transport. Early EST programmes featured grants for fuel switching (to gas and electricity), but these suffered a number of problems and were found to be not cost-effective. The more logical development, a holistic approach to personal carbon emission advice, was until recently resisted by the Department for Transport. The EST now provides consumer transport advice through the ESTACs, although this remains a small activity. This institutional context has led to the EST broadening its activities to include microgeneration, waste and water saving – essentially a more joined up approach to supporting 'greening' citizen behaviour, but with carbon saving remaining the main policy driver.

3. Measuring the impact of the EST

From the early days of the EST it was recognized that, as a not for profit independent organization using direct government funding, it was important to determine and understand the impact of its activities. An evaluation programme was established in 1993–94 initially to assess the energy advice provided to householders through the energy advice centres. The scope of evaluations has increased with the expansion of EST activities, with evaluations undertaken on a regular basis in recent years to cover the broad range of EST activities. This includes advice provided to households through the advice centres, the website and advertising activities, work with the supply chain, local authorities and communities. A consistent mission of the EST has been to achieve reductions in carbon dioxide (CO_2) emissions from households, and this has been the main metric used to measure impact.

In the mid-1990s there were several grant-based schemes supporting the early adoption of improved heating systems (condensing gas boiler scheme, heating controls, small-scale combined heat and power; CHP), and these were successful, particularly the condensing boiler scheme, in gaining acceptance of newer technologies. High-efficiency condensing boilers are now part of Building Regulations for new and replacement gas heating systems. Subsidy schemes are important for newly available technology in order to encourage market growth at the early stage of the transformation of the market for the adoption of new products.

The main grant schemes now are for microgeneration technologies (such as solar thermal water heating and solar photovoltaics), through schemes such as the Low Carbon Buildings Programme. The evaluation of these schemes uses the grant information to establish the measures that have been installed and the associated expected CO_2 savings.

The majority of EST activity is now focused on awareness raising and provision of advice to consumers, together with assisting the infrastructure to deliver household energy savings through local authorities and the supply chain. Evaluation of the impact of advice provision is more problematic, as it requires an understanding of action taken as a result of the advice given. The approach taken is to undertake surveys of a representative sample of customers receiving advice using a structured questionnaire to determine what they recall about the advice, whether any and what action has been undertaken and energy efficiency measure installed. In undertaking the surveys, account is taken of the time required from the point of advice provision to the implementation of measures, and typically, for the significant installed measures in households, it takes three to four months from advice to completed action. The evaluation is undertaken annually in four quarterly survey waves.

The EST is the largest provider of energy saving advice, but not the only source. Thus, an understanding of what other information sources are used is gained from the survey, including whether other EST advice channels are used such as advice centre customers using the EST website. Where more than one EST advice channel is accessed, the survey determines the most important in leading to action being taken. This avoids double counting of customers accessing EST services through various routes.

It is important to understand what would have happened anyway if EST advice provision had not been available, so that the added value of EST activities can be assessed. This is another challenge for the evaluation, since it is not practical to set up a parallel universe of identical customers who are not provided advice (the counterfactual) and see what they do. As part of the customer survey, for each action taken the customer rates how influential the advice provided by the EST was in the decision to take action; this ranges from 'crucial to taking action' to 'would have done it anyway'. Only where the customer has indicated that the EST has influenced the decision to take action is the resulting CO_2 saving attributed to the EST.

Once the specific attributed energy saving measures have been determined for the sample of customers surveyed, the CO_2 savings arising from the actions are determined using standard average expected savings by house type (ex ante estimates) for each specific measure. These average CO_2 values are determined through detailed modelling of the impact of each measure (and combination of measures), using the physical characteristics of the measure and house type and construction. The modelled values are verified through physical measurements of energy savings achieved through in-house trials. The CO_2 savings by measure are expressed in terms of an annual saving and a lifetime saving, which takes account of the number of years that the impact is expected to persist. For instance, cavity wall insulation is assumed to have a lifetime of 40 years. The methodology used is consistent with the CO_2 values used for the operation and evaluation of the Government's Carbon Emissions Reduction Target (CERT) scheme. At this stage, the sample results are grossed up to the total population of customers receiving advice, allowing for any differences in the profile of the sample compared to the overall population to determine the overall annual and lifetime CO_2 savings.

This generic quantitative approach is applied to the evaluation of the advice centres and the EST website. The broad approach is also used for the evaluation of consumer advertising, but in this case a survey of a representative sample of the general public is undertaken using a face-to-face survey technique which incorporates showing examples of the advertising to ensure correct recognition of the campaign. The effectiveness of advertising is measured in terms of awareness of the EST and the actions taken as a result of the campaign. In terms of impact, compared to individual advice and other channels, advertising tends to influence a greater proportion of habitual behaviour change rather than one-off or purchasing behaviours.[1]

The same broad approach is used for other infrastructure and capacity building activities such local authority and supply chain support. The sample of survey respondents in these other evaluations reflect the audience that the EST is seeking to influence. For instance, the local authority survey samples local authority officers with responsibility for sustainability or energy efficiency in about 40 per cent of the local authorities with which the EST engages. This is to determine what energy efficiency schemes have been undertaken by the local authority and measures installed, as a result of the advice and support provided from the EST.

The evaluation approach is robust, but there are challenges and uncertainties that need to be addressed that differ by the advice channel. Some of these are as follows.

Do customers accurately remember what they did following interaction with the EST?

The results of the evaluation surveys are dependent on customer recollection of the interaction and its relationship with the decision-making process. This in turn is influenced by the time lapse between the provision of advice and the survey. A significant time lapse may result in lack of recall of the importance of the advice. However, it is important to establish that action has actually taken place rather than an intention to act, which is more likely to elicit a positive response. This is because respondents may wish to give a socially acceptable response rather than having a real commitment, creating a positive bias to the survey responses. So, there is a balance in the judgement for the timing of surveys in relation to the advice provision.

Representation of the client base?
For advice provision where there is a recorded database of customers, such as customers of the advice centres, it is relatively straightforward to secure a representative sample of customers. However, for the EST website, registration is only required for the use of specific tools. This gives a reliable database of customers for those specific tools. However, for the general user of the EST website, it is much more difficult to establish a representative sample. A sample is generated from respondents to an invitation to participate in research to improve the website, but this is likely to be a sub-set more likely to take action or interested in environmental websites. Web access statistics are used to relate dwell times on the site for respondents to the research invitation, with action taken determined by the survey. Then, using this profile to apply to the dwell time profile of general users, an overall assessment of actions taken is obtained. However, it is recognized that there is still some uncertainty in the representativeness of the sample in relation to the general web user population.

Interaction with other policies?
A key function of EST advice is the signposting of customers to the subsidies and special offers available for the installation of energy efficiency measures under such schemes as CERT or its predecessors, fuel poverty or local authority schemes. The EST is a fundamental part of the infrastructure to guide customers to these schemes and in stimulating action. As such, the EST provides benefits in reducing transaction costs for these schemes so that more savings can be delivered, and increases the scope for savings by reaching customers who would not otherwise participate. However, it is difficult to separate the impact of the intervention of advice and signposting from the delivery mechanism to install energy efficiency measures. The CO_2 savings that the EST has influenced or stimulated are those that have been attributed by customers to EST activities, but include those that are delivered through other government policies.

In addition to quantitative surveys, small-scale qualitative studies are also commissioned to understand and probe specific issues identified through the quantitative surveys. This informs and guides future surveys, and provides a means of identifying learning and insights through understanding 'how and why' EST activities have impact.

4. Results of the EST's evaluation research

In principle, the savings deriving from EST activities can be measured in terms of energy, money and carbon. Because of the EST mission and funding source, carbon has been the main metric.

Over the last 15 years, EST programmes have invested over £300 million in engagement with energy users to save energy. The regular evaluations to measure the impact show that the EST during that period has influenced or stimulated over 120Mt of lifetime CO_2 savings at very good cost-effectiveness. Over that time, the programmes have developed and expanded, resulting in increasing impact and CO_2 savings. The annual impact has grown to over 1Mt CO_2, which is approximately 0.8 per cent of annual UK emissions and far exceeds the impact of any other public engagement activity in climate change mitigation. The cumulative lifetime impact over that period is shown in Figure 8.1.

The scope of activities in recent years is demonstrated through the results for 2007–8, the most recent complete year of evaluation results. In 2007–8, the EST stimulated or influenced annual CO_2 savings of nearly 1.2 million tonnes and lifetime savings of over 24 million tCO_2. The average cost-effectiveness (government expenditure per tonne of lifetime CO_2 saved) is £1.5/tCO_2. The main areas of activity generating the savings are shown in Table 8.1.

The cost-effectiveness figure in Table 8.1 represents the cost to government of saving one tonne of tCO_2. The associated energy savings benefits to consumers generally outweigh this cost significantly, so that the total national cost-effectiveness is positive; +£50/tCO_2 was reported in the UK Climate Change Programme Review (Defra, 2006), and this has now risen to +£115/tCO_2.

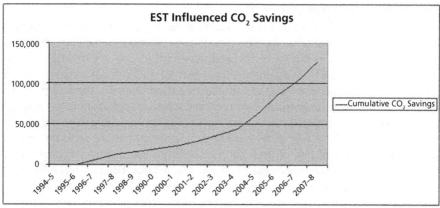

Figure 8.1 *EST influenced CO_2 savings in cumulative $ktCO_2$*

Table 8.1 *EST evaluation results summary for 2007–8*

	Funding £m	Annual CO_2 saving $ktCO_2/a$	Lifetime CO_2 savings $ktCO_2$	EST cost-effectiveness £/tCO_2
Energy efficiency				
Consumer	18.7	770	10,930	£1.7
Local Authority and Housing Association	3.5	304	9665	£0.4
Supply chain	1.3	40	1173	£1.1
Communities	0.6	54	1885	£0.3
SMEs	0.7	3	46	£15
Total energy efficiency	**24.8**	**1172**	**23,698**	**£1.1**
Renewables	**7.9**	**5**	**121**	**£65**
Transport	**2.9**	**17**	**217**	**£13**
Total EST	**35.6**	**1194**	**24,036**	**£1.5**

The consumer (household) audience is the main focus of EST activities directly through advice centres, the website and advertising activities, or indirectly through local authorities, housing associations or supply chain partners. The direct advice consumer audience accounts for about 65 per cent of annual CO_2 savings and over 45 per cent of lifetime savings. The vast majority of savings continue to be through energy efficiency actions by households, although increasing impact has been seen in renewables and transport activities compared to previous years.

The impact of energy efficiency activities forms the majority of CO_2 savings achieved, and measures installed in households provide the most significant proportion. The breakdown of the types of the main energy efficiency measures that have been installed in 2007–8 is shown in Figure 8.2.

The main routes through which advice is effective are the installation of key energy efficiency measures; for example, loft and wall insulation (see Figure 8.2). Behavioural measures with lower probable persistence are secondary, comprising 2 per cent of the total. The benefits of advice programmes therefore interact with other policies designed to encourage energy efficiency measures, notably financial support via CERT. However, it is well established that advice and finance address separate barriers to investment, and therefore that they are synergistic (OXERA, 2006).

The policy focus on reducing energy demand has led to increased interest in the extent to which improvements in energy efficiency are offset by consequential changes to demand. The evaluation of carbon emissions reductions due to EST programmes set out above takes account of this, in so far as individual users increase comfort levels as efficiency improves. In general, direct rebound effects due to these consumer decisions are relatively small (15 per cent for insulation being the largest effect). A recent comprehensive review indicates that there is more uncertainty about the size of macroeconomic effects arising from the consequential improvements in total factor productivity of the

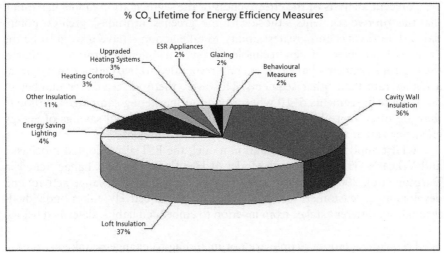

Figure 8.2 *EST savings from energy efficiency in 2007–8*

economy (Sorrell, 2009). These more complex effects cannot be assessed at individual programme level.

Consumer marketing

Consumer marketing has been a key part of the EST's activity. Initially, it was used to raise the profile of energy efficiency as a concept, then to support energy supplier schemes and drive uptake of no-cost/low-cost measures such as the installation of compact fluorescent lightbulbs (CFLs). As the scale of operation of the EST expanded, particularly in energy efficiency advice, the purpose of consumer marketing changed. It predominantly was designed to raise awareness of climate change and of the need to act. However, much of the consumer marketing and advertising at the time, both from the EST and government, demonstrated a mismatch between the enormity of the challenge of climate change and the relatively small actions being suggested as a response. The juxtaposition of the apocalyptic and the trivial were not well suited to empowering behavioural change (Segnit and Ereaut, 2006).

Following a period of mass marketing, the EST chose to develop a market segmentation model in order to target messages more effectively. The segmentation model was developed specifically for the EST in 2005, linking attitudes and behaviour through objective measures such as energy use and car travel. The decision to add behaviour as a key component was based on previous experience of segmentation models, which demonstrated that attitudes were not a good predictor of actual behaviour.

The segmentation looked for areas of greatest potential for carbon saving by comparing average expected energy usage and car usage with that actually reported. A third dimension of segmentation was introduced – that of attitude – so that more versus less willing-to-listen groups could be identified. The result was a ten-segment model based on the Experian Mosaic typology,[2] still in use in 2009, which has provided the basis for targeting consumer marketing messages as well as advice delivered through the ESTACs.

A recent analysis of the effectiveness of the segmentation model has found that the top two segments – those with the 'greenest attitudes', greatest potential carbon savings and greatest ability to take action – have proved to be the likely early adopters of new technologies, such as microgeneration. Similarly, the top four segments have consistently responded to marketing campaigns at a higher rate than other segments. However, there are a greater number of households in segments 5–10 who respond to marketing campaigns, although they are often more likely to be motivated by the financial savings of energy efficiency rather than by the benefits to the environment.

Whilst applying the segmentation model, the EST also adopted Prochaska and Velicer's 'Transtheoretical Model of Health Behaviour Change' (cited in Darnton et al, 2006), as a means of framing its behaviour change activity and developing a 'customer journey'. This model effectively takes individuals through six different stages from inaction to embedded habits, described below:

1 Pre-contemplation: people are not intending to change or take action.
2 Contemplation: people are intending to change within the foreseeable

future, but are not ready to take action; doubts about the effectiveness of action, and of uneven costs and benefits, may stall people at this stage for some time.

3   Preparation: people are intending to take action in the immediate future; they are very aware of the costs and benefits of change, and are likely to have taken some related action recently, including having a plan of action in place.

4   Action: people have made or are making specific overt modifications to their behaviour.

5   Maintenance: people are working to prevent lapsing back into old behaviour; they are becoming more confident about their effectiveness.

6   Termination: the changed behaviour has become habit and there is no chance of relapse.

However, in applying this model, the EST has encountered a challenge in overcoming the attitude–action gap inherent within it. As Figure 8.3 illustrates, over an 18-month period of quarterly surveying, there was very little movement between the key stages. This continues to present a challenge in moving people from an awareness and acknowledgement of the need to act onto making larger behavioural changes.

Energy advice

Methods

Energy advice is defined to be information that is relevant to the personal circumstances of the individual. It is different from the provision of general information. For example, it is providing information to tell someone about cavity wall insulation, what it usually costs and what the typical annual savings might be. However, this only constitutes providing advice if they own

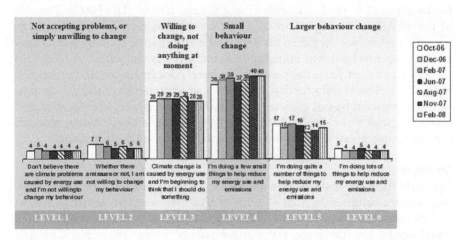

Figure 8.3 *Changes in UK consumer attitudes to energy behavioural change, 2006–8*

the property and the work has not already been undertaken, and is supplemented by advice on how to undertake cavity wall insulation, what support there is, and the expected financial costs and savings for their type of house. Unsurprisingly, general information is usually less effective than advice, and the effectiveness of advice increases if it is more specific and trusted (Darby, 2003).

In principle, a number of routes may be used to provide advice. Shop-front 'advice centres' were fairly common in the 1980s, but are now rarely used because the propensity of most people to seek advice actively in this way is limited. Delivery of advice to large numbers of people generally involves taking the advice to the people, not vice versa. The traditional options are face-to-face and via phone, although web-based services have increasingly become an option in recent years as their accessibility and familiarity increases. Different advice routes appeal to different demographics – 65 per cent of phone advice customers are over 50 years old, whereas online information on new technologies is likely to be accessed by a younger demographic (see Chapter 13 on new media and engagement).

Home energy advice has its roots in the social goals that drove most of the original advice services in the aftermath of the energy price rises of the 1970s. EST's initial advice programme supported the existing, rather patchy, provision of energy advice centres that were in existence in the early 1990s, largely due to local authority and voluntary initiatives. Providing additional funding allowed the EST to expand the network, eventually to full UK coverage after 1995. This allowed the EST to increase its influence over the advice provision, but not to own the advice providers. Increasingly, big differences in the quality and effectiveness of advice became apparent, and to address this the EST introduced a standardized system of support for the contracted energy efficiency advice centres (EEACs). A standardized set of advice outcomes was ensured by using a centralized computer-based system to assess cost-effective opportunities, based on inputs of key household characteristics by the householder through a 'Do It Yourself Home Energy Check' (DIYHEC). The role of the EEACs was to generate DIYHECs, with payment by results, and to provide a telephone service. This provided a transparent funding mechanism and quality threshold, but arguably little incentive to innovate.

In more recent years the network has been reformed again and rebranded as ESTACs. This is fully funded, but with a smaller number of larger centres, generally regional based, allowing more professional advice, management and marketing staff to be employed. The goals are more strongly geared towards carbon saving, creating a new incentive structure for advice provision.

Message

The early focus on home energy advice has its roots in social goals. The message was the same as the goal – saving energy saves money. Advice provision and its targeting was geared to lower income groups with the most pressing social needs, and the basic training for energy advice providers (City and Guilds Energy Awareness 6176) has been developed and delivered by the fuel poverty charity National Energy Action (NEA).

With a brief to address carbon savings, the link between message and goal becomes more complex. The research identified above indicates that money saving is the most powerful driver for many households, but environmental messages are of importance to the market segments with higher propensity to act. EST advice has adapted to this in a number of ways. ESTACs are focused primarily on carbon saving and therefore tend to target households with a higher saving potential (i.e. with higher incomes). And web-based tools, including the EST's own (EST, 2009a), have been developed as 'carbon calculators', primarily to support more proactive, environmentally aware groups (Bottrill, 2007).

Two-fifths (40 per cent) of the direct emissions of the average UK household relate to transport, but until recently the EST has not undertaken consumer facing transport advice because it did not secure funding to do so from government, which has tended to prefer national information campaigns in this sector. However, the EST has been successful in now broadening its advice message to include both transport and microgeneration, and is piloting integrating advice on water use.

The EST has focused on direct consumer emissions, and therefore not addressed issues of energy and greenhouse emissions 'embedded' in products (e.g. in food). This is because funding has not been available for these objectives, and because of the difficulties in defining appropriate and effective messages for these objectives.

Local authorities and community

The EST has been supporting local authorities and communities for several years, initially through centralized support services such as Community Action for Energy (now Green Communities) and Practical Help. Recently, however, more in-depth localized support is provided through the local authority '1:1 programme' and Low Carbon Communities, reflecting the EST's recognition of their importance in influencing behavioural change.

Local authorities have a key role to play, leading their communities to act on climate change. They are in a strong position to provide this leadership due to the following:

- Local knowledge – a much better and more detailed understanding of their communities and local conditions than central government. They can target areas, homes and/or people more effectively.
- Trust – local government is considered more trustworthy than central government and many other sectors, both in general (Lyons, 2007) and in the field of home energy efficiency (EST, 2009b). It holds a position of authority and is generally well regarded by the people who live in the area.
- Lead by example – the key to any leadership role is leading by example. Many local authorities have been working hard to get their own house in order, working with the Carbon Trust's Local Authority Carbon Management Programme, which provides a good springboard for wider community action.

- Partnerships – an opportunity to bring key stakeholders in energy, housing and transport in an area together. This includes businesses, supply chain, schools, voluntary sector, etc. All these parties are key to action across a local area. Local Strategic Partnerships, with clear guidance on how to use them, are integral to this.
- Engagement – all of these combined put local government in a strong position to engage with their communities and individuals to tackle climate change.

The capacity and performance of local authorities on climate change has, to date, been highly variable. Whilst there are several innovative authorities that have led the way, this has not necessarily resulted in wide-scale improvements across the sector. In many instances, climate change has not been a political priority at the local level, and thus has not received the necessary resources and support. The introduction of National Indicator 186 (NI 186[3]), which is one of the set of performance indicators for local authorities in England, and its inclusion in the Comprehensive Area Assessment audit regime, has helped to raise the profile of community climate change action and raise it on the political agenda locally, but there is still a proportion of authorities not taking action and without the capacity to do so (Audit Commission, 2009).

The EST provides a range of advice and support to local authorities to improve their performance, and put them on track to achieve their carbon reduction targets. In particular:

- An advice line open to officers and Councillors providing detailed technical support on climate change, and the offer of training events in the authorities' offices. This typically handles about 3500 queries per year and delivers around 100 local events.
- In-depth consultancy support to 80 authorities to help them benchmark their current performance and develop a prioritized climate change action plan.
- Software tools to help authorities deliver on their climate change national indicators, including developing Tracking Action on Carbon Emissions (TrACE), a tool designed to assist local authorities in collating an evidence base of activity undertaken to meet NI 186 targets in a standardized format (thus also assisting the Audit Commission in assessing activity).
- Work with a number of authorities to help them with their fuel poverty reporting. Local authorities also work with ESTACs to support local awareness raising and delivery schemes, including area-based approaches.
- Behavioural research also shows that friends and family are key agents in normalizing action on carbon emissions reduction (Welsch and Kühling, 2009).

Communities are an essential part of normalizing and embedding behavioural change (see Chapters 9 and 14). Not only do they provide an effective support network for increasing behaviour change amongst individuals and households, but the third sector is also active in the provision of sustainable energy and transport in its own right.

Communities – both geographic communities and communities of interest – are an important channel to reach citizens, and provide reputable information and advice on low-carbon households and transport. The Energy Saving Trust's Green Communities programme operates at both the local and national level. At the local level, it provides targeted support and outreach for specific community projects, from improving the energy efficiency of a community hall to installing renewable energy. Nationally, Green Communities is a network of local community organizations and practitioners working with groups. The network is supported by a range of tools, including community carbon footprinting, technical advice and training.

Supply chain

Over the years of its existence, the EST has established close links with some of the trades, professions and companies that deliver energy efficient products and services. The aim has been twofold – to influence and up-scale their activities and to use them as an additional route to influence consumer behaviour, essentially gearing the EST's own marketing resources.

Some of the earliest work focused on the retailers responsible for sales of white goods. Following the introduction of the EU Energy label, it indicated that many shop floor staff were unable to explain it to customers. The EST undertook an extensive training scheme to address this. Following the development of the 'Energy Efficiency Recommended' label, the EST promoted the appropriate use of this to key retail outlets.

In 2000, the EST led the establishment of the Energy Efficiency Partnership for Homes. This brings together key groups across society to address home energy saving issues (EEPfH, 2009). The 'supply chain groups' have been amongst the most active of these. These broad alliances have been important in addressing some trade barriers to energy efficiency. Most notably, condensing boilers suffered for many years from a lack of enthusiasm amongst gas installers (Banks, 2001). This was potentially a major barrier to the successful implementation of their mandatory use from 2005, following an announcement to that effect in 2003 Energy White Paper. However, a training programme covering more than 60,000 registered gas installers transformed industry attitudes over a short period.

More recently, EST supply chain programmes have focused on joint marketing with industry; for example, through the 'wash at 30' campaign for lower temperature clothes washing with a leading detergent manufacturer. Initial evidence indicates there are moves towards lower temperature washing, including at 30°C, but there is a lack of publically available detailed data.

5. Future trends

The Climate Change Act 2008, and the statutory carbon reduction targets of 80 per cent by 2050 and 34 per cent by 2020, have brought the challenge of behavioural change to the fore. In February 2009, the Government published, for consultation, the Heat and Energy Saving Strategy (DECC, 2009), which contained ambitious targets for the insulation of 'all cavity walls and lofts where practicable' by 2015, and flagged the likelihood of the need to reduce emissions from the household sector to almost zero by 2050.

These targets pose an unprecedented challenge to achieve significant behavioural change within a relatively short period of time. Changes to habitual behaviour are still necessary, particularly with a predicted increase in electricity use from appliances in the home, but the challenges beyond this to ensure the uptake of more complicated and more costly measures, such as microgeneration and solid wall insulation, need far more attention.

The introduction of financing options for energy efficiency and microgeneration measures, such as the 'Home Energy Pay as You Save' pilots, along with feed-in tariffs and renewable heat incentives, will go some way to overcoming the financial barriers to installing these technologies and measures (HM Government, 2009a). However, other barriers, such as mistrust of new technologies and the hassle factor of installing solid wall insulation, are great. There are 6.6 million solid wall properties in England alone. During the first 15 months of the CERT, just over 14,000 solid walls were insulated, almost entirely in the social housing sector. Currently, there are just over 100,000 microgeneration installations across the country, with a target of 800,000 household installations by 2020 (HM Government, 2009b).

This challenge is set against an increasingly complex backdrop with more players in the market, more messages and advertising campaigns being run by both the public and private sectors (see Chapter 11), and a period of financial constraint. Advice is now being delivered by energy suppliers through the CERT, as well as by high-profile retailers and even some local authorities.

Local authorities are likely to play an increasing role in changing behaviour and delivering household energy saving. The Department for Communities and Local Government recently consulted on the future role of local authorities, and floated the concept of devolving some part of the national carbon budgets to the local level (CLG, 2009). This is likely to be a longer-term prospect, but will, in all likelihood, lead to greater engagement on carbon emissions reduction at the local level, with local authorities in the lead.

The Government is also reviewing how household carbon-saving programmes are delivered after 2012. This is an explicit recognition of the need for a step change in installation rates (DECC, 2009) and these may ultimately involve new ways of compelling people to take action, including the possibility of regulation in the future. This will, no doubt, result in an even greater role for behavioural change, and greater innovation and joining-up of the delivery of such programmes.

6. Conclusions

The EST was founded in a period in which the role of the market was seen as predominant in the energy sector, but has emerged into a situation where the importance of climate change means that energy saving is widely acknowledged as a public good. Because of its relatively long history, scale of operations and focus on energy use by individuals, the EST is a unique organization.

The impact of EST programmes has been measured with methodologies developed for evaluating the role of engagement and advice. The focus has been to change behaviour rather than attitudes. The total annual savings influenced by the EST are approximately 0.8 per cent of UK household emissions, with most of these resulting from implementation of cost-effective physical measures, particularly insulation, in the housing stock.

Direct engagement with individuals makes the largest contribution, within the EST programmes, to energy saving and is synergistic with financial support for householders. In particular, the effectiveness of household energy advice is now well established.

Programmes that deliver energy savings indirectly through engagement with key businesses (the energy efficiency supply chain), and a broader set of housing providers and influencers (local authorities, housing associations and community groups), are extremely cost-effective, demonstrating the importance of change to broader socio-economic systems in delivering climate change mitigation.

Despite the successes reported, it would be unwise to assume that models for individual engagement are now fully developed. The scale of carbon emissions reduction from personal energy use that is required to meet climate change goals implies more substantial change than has yet been achieved, both in physical changes to buildings and products and in everyday behaviour. This everyday behaviour includes not only household energy use, but also transport, both of which are often strongly habitual (see Chapter 1). It seems very probable that more intensive interaction with individuals will be required (as discussed elsewhere in this book – e.g. Chapter 10), as well as changes to social attitudes, public policy and business models.

Notes

1   In terms of impact, EST evaluation shows its own advertising tends to influence a relatively greater proportion of habitual behaviour (53 per cent) rather than one-off or purchasing behaviours (47 per cent), compared to individual advice and other channels. The equivalent numbers for Advice Centres are overall 10 per cent habitual behaviour and 90 per cent one-off/purchasing, and for the website over-all 18 per cent behaviours and 82 per cent one-off purchasing behaviours. This is measured in terms of annual CO_2 savings and is within the consumer impact shown in Table 8.1.

2   In this model developed by Experian for the EST, UK households are divided into one of ten segments according to their household energy bills, car usage and atti-tudes towards the environment. Built from a wide variety of socio-demographics and market research data, the segmentation can be applied at the most granular of geographic levels to help understand the geo-demographic variation in key environmental attitudes and behaviours. The segmentation is derived by overlay-ing household and transport energy consumption and attitudinal data across Experian's Mosaic model, and grouping Experian's 61 Mosaic types into ten EST bespoke segments.

3   The indicator is reduction in per capita CO_2 emissions in the local authority area, from homes, transport, services and industry outside the EU Emissions Trading Scheme.

References

Audit Commission (2009) *Lofty ambitions: the role of councils in reducing domestic CO₂ emissions*, http://www.audit-commission.gov.uk/housing/nationalstudies/loftyambitions/Pages/Default_copy.aspx, accessed 21 March 2010

Banks, N. (2001) 'Socio-technical networks and the sad case of the condensing boiler', in P. Bertoldi, A. Ricci and A. T. de Almeida (eds) *Energy Efficiency in Household Appliances and Lighting*, Springer Verlag, Berlin

Bottrill, C. (2007) Internet-based tools for behaviour change, *Proceedings of the European Council for an Energy-Efficient Economy 2007 Summer Study*, France

CLG (2009) *Strengthening Local Democracy*. Department of Communities and Local Government, http://www.communities.gov.uk/publications/localgovernment/localdemocracyconsultation, accessed 21 March 2010

Darby, S. (2003) 'Making sense of energy advice', *Proceedings, European Council for an Energy-Efficient Economy*, Paper 6, no 157

Darnton, A., Elster-Jones, J., Lucas, K. and Brooks, M. (2006) *Promoting Pro-Environmental Behaviour: Existing Evidence to Inform Better Policy Making*, Chapter 1: *Theory*, Andrew Darnton and the Centre for Sustainable Development at the University of Westminster

DECC (2009) *Heat and Energy Saving Strategy Consultation*, Department of Energy and Climate Change, http://hes.decc.gov.uk/, accessed 21 March 2010

Defra (2006) *Synthesis of Climate Change Policy Evaluations*, http://www.ccevaluation.org/inventory/g2/300-GEF.html, accessed 21 March 2010

Defra (2008) *A Framework for pro-Environmental Behaviours*, Defra, http://www.defra.gov.uk/evidence/social/behaviour/documents/behaviours-jan08-report.pdf, accessed 21 March 2010

EEPfH (2009) Energy Efficiency Partnership for Homes, *Annual Review 2008/09*, http://www.eeph.org.uk/uploads/documents/partnership/FINAL%20eeph%20web.pdf, accessed 27 October 2009

EST (2009a) EST Carbon Calculator, http://www.energysavingtrust.org.uk/calculator/start, accessed 21 March 2010

EST (2009b) Unpublished results of on-line market research survey by ICM for Energy Saving Trust

HM Government (2005) *Securing the Future: UK Government Sustainable Development Strategy*, TSO, London

HM Government (2009a) *The UK Low Carbon Transition Plan: National Strategy for Climate and Energy*, http://www.decc.gov.uk/en/content/cms/publications/lc_trans_plan/lc_trans_plan.aspx (accessed 21 March 2010)

HM Government (2009b) *The UK Renewable Energy Strategy*, http://www.decc.gov.uk/en/content/cms/what_we_do/uk_supply/energy_mix/renewable/res/res.aspx, accessed 21 March 2010

HM Treasury and Defra (2005) *Energy Efficiency Innovation Review*, HMSO, Norwich

Lyons, M. (2007) *Place Shaping: A Shared Ambition for the Future of Local Government: Final Report of the Lyons Inquiry into Local Government*, The Stationery Office, London

Oxera (2006) *Policies for Energy Efficiency in the UK Household Sector, Report to Defra*, Oxera Consulting Ltd, Oxford

Segnit, N. and Ereaut, G. (2006) *Warm Words: How are we Telling the Climate Story and can we Tell it Better?*, IPPR, London

Sorrell, S. (2007) *The Rebound Effect: an assessment of the evidence for economy-wide energy savings from improved energy efficiency*, UK Energy Research Centre, http://www.ukerc.ac.uk/support/tiki-index.php?page=ReboundEffect, accessed 21 March 2010

Sustainable Consumption Roundtable (2006) *I Will if You Will*, Sustainable Development Commission and National Consumer Council

Welsch, H. and Kühling, J. (2009) 'Determinants of pro-environmental behaviour: the role of reference groups and routine behaviour', *Ecological Economics*, vol 69, pp166–176

9
Keeping Up with the Joneses in the Great British Refurb: The Impacts and Limits of Social Learning in Eco-renovation

Jo Hamilton

1. Introduction

Since 2007, there have been an increasing number of community organized 'Open Eco-Homes' events across the UK, where eco-renovated and eco-new build homes are open to the public. These events have proved extremely popular, and have provided unrivalled opportunities for social learning about energy and greenhouse gas reductions from the homes. They have translated the 'one size fits all' approach of national information campaigns into meaningful and appropriate renovations according to the house type, shown the full potential of renovations possible, and brought out the aspiration in insulation.

Whilst this chapter focuses on some specific UK Open Homes events, the principles of social learning from these events can be applied more widely. Similar events have taken place in other countries,[1] and whilst policies will be different, similar opportunities and barriers for engagement and behaviour change exist.

The achievements of Open Homes events are evaluated against the crucial need for step change to the UK's approach to eco-renovation. What barriers and opportunities need to be addressed to ensure interest at the Open Homes translates into action and reduction in greenhouse gas emissions at home? Could replicating this model contribute to a greater understanding and uptake of eco-renovation across the UK – and if so, at what scale? What are the perceived shortcomings, and the opportunities for further development? Is 'preaching to the converted' a fair criticism, when most of the 'converted' still need to convert their homes? What else is needed?

Throughout this chapter, 'Open Homes' refers to the variety of Open Eco-Homes events. 'Eco-renovation' covers home renovation and refurbishment to reduce energy consumption (e.g. insulation) and other environmental impacts (water conservation, waste reduction, indoor air quality, environmental and recycled materials), as well as the inclusion of microenergy-generation technologies (microgeneration) such as solar thermal, solar photovoltaic and ground source heat pumps. 'Eco-renovators' and 'home owners' refer to the people who have eco-renovated, then opened their homes in the Open Homes events.

In this chapter, the scale of the challenge is outlined in Section 2, with a focus on the barriers, opportunities and trigger points to eco-renovation in Section 3. The relevance of social learning is introduced in Section 4, whilst Section 5 is an overview of policy to 2009. The range of Open Homes events, and analysis of the feedback and evaluation data, is examined in Section 6, with limits to the approach and conclusions drawn in Sections 6 and 7.

2. The scale of the challenge

The Intergovernmental Panel on Climate Change (IPCC) state that 'mitigation efforts and investments over the next two to three decades will have a large impact on opportunities to achieve lower stabilisation levels' (IPCC, 2007). The Stern Review of the economics of climate change states that 'ultimately, stabilisation – at whatever level – requires that annual emissions be brought down to more than 80 per cent below current levels' (Stern, 2006). This figure is now widely accepted as the minimum reduction target necessary by 2050, and reflected in the UK Climate Change Act 2008 (DECC, 2008).

The household sector represents 27 per cent of the UK's total carbon emissions (Defra, 2007). Whilst ambitious policies to make all new build homes zero carbon by 2016 is welcome (DCLG, 2007), the main challenge is renovating the existing housing stock, as outlined by Boardman: 'Of the homes we will inhabit in 2050, around 80 per cent are already standing today, and these have to be the main focus for carbon reduction policies' (Boardman, 2007, p6).

Reducing housing sector emissions, and meeting the target of transforming 26 million homes by 2050, requires 500,000 low-carbon refurbishments every year (Killip, 2008a). Installing insulation has been identified as one of the most cost-effective energy-saving actions which individuals can take, yet, despite policies and grants to increase the uptake of insulation, only 16.3 per cent of the UK housing stock is considered to be fully insulated, and at least 80 per cent of UK homes would benefit from improvements in insulation (Utley and Shorrock, 2008). However, energy efficiency measures alone will not be sufficient to achieve the reductions needed; they will need to be combined with the adoption of low- and zero-carbon technologies (Boardman, 2007, p63).

3. Barriers, opportunities and trigger points for eco-renovation

Improving the fabric, thermal envelope (the sum total of the building elements that provide a thermal barrier between the interior and exterior – namely walls, floor, roof and windows) and including suitable microgeneration technologies of many millions of UK homes is not straightforward. Even with cost-effective measures, there are many barriers which are further compounded when more complex renovations are needed. The barriers, opportunities and trigger points to eco-renovation are now briefly examined.

Barriers to eco-renovation

The following barriers to eco-renovation have been identified in previous research:

- *Perception and engagement of public.* Energy efficiency is not seen as top of many people's priorities (CASE, 2008), and is associated with a 'compromise on the style or liveability of a home' (Ipsos Mori, 2009).
- *The hassle factor.* Often the perception of the disruption and time taken for eco-renovation outweighs the reality, although major works such as installing some solid wall and underfloor insulation, and whole house approaches, can be disruptive.
- *Cost.* Financial disincentives are one of the most often cited barriers to efficiency and microgeneration. High upfront costs of substantial eco-renovation and microgeneration often have long payback times, so the perceived costs outweigh the expected energy savings (Caird et al, 2008).
- *Unfamiliarity.* Many microgeneration products are innovative, with no chance to 'try before you buy' (Bergman et al, 2009). This can also apply to more complex eco-renovation, such as external solid wall insulation.
- *Information gaps.* Bergman et al (2009) assert that there is a lack of clear, practical information addressing crucial subjects such as cost, how the microgeneration technologies are installed, and their compatibility with other systems (p32). Householders do not always know the associated carbon reduction from different technologies, nor how to compare them with other approaches to eco-renovation. Reputation and familiarity of the technology are important.
- *Fragmented market.* The energy efficiency and eco-renovation market is complex and fragmented, with the funding dominated by a small number of large players, whilst being delivered through a large number of small and medium enterprises (UK Green Building Council, 2008). Installing efficiency and microgeneration technologies often cross traditional trade areas, causing a lack of joined-up capacity. This is compounded by a lack of independent, trusted suppliers (Caird et al, 2008; Bergman et al, 2009) who can advise on a whole house renovation.

Eco-renovation opportunities and trigger points

Opportunities for eco-renovation include:

- *Independent advisers and suppliers.* Meeting the demand for independent, trusted suppliers as opposed to installer and manufacturers (CASE, 2008; Bergman et al, 2009, p34; NHER, 2009), could stimulate a greater uptake of eco-renovation and microgeneration.

- *Housing slump.* The global financial crisis has had an impact on the UK housing market. People are staying in properties for longer, giving an opportunity to upgrade instead of move (UK Green Building Council, 2008).
- *Energy prices.* Energy and fuel price fluctuations and increases can make energy efficiency and microgeneration more attractive. Related to this, energy efficiency can help address fuel poverty and energy security policy agendas.
- *More jobs.* The economic potential of new jobs created in the construction and building services industry could be worth £3.5–6.5 billion per year (Killip, 2008a), and help meet the growing demand for information and advice about different eco-renovation.

Whilst the opportunities to completely renovate a house may be few and far between, trigger points (Caird et al, 2008; Ipsos MORI, 2009) can be capitalized on, such as the following:

- *Moving house* provides an ideal opportunity to renovate – either before selling or after moving in. The Sponge Network, a network of professionals sharing an interest in a sustainable built environment, have produced a 'Buyers guide for a greener home' (Sponge, 2008) for this purpose.
- *Repairs, maintenance and upgrades* offer many opportunities to upgrade the fabric and thermal properties of the building alongside planned works, thus minimizing the 'hassle factor'.
- *Changes of life*, such as becoming a parent or retiring, are times when behaviours in the home change, and there is the opportunity to make improvements to the home. This is consistent with the notion of 'habit discontinuity' discussed in Chapter 1. Linked to this, a room-by-room approach to eco-renovation may be appropriate: focusing renovations around energy intensive rooms such as kitchens and bathrooms, which tend to get overhauled more frequently.

4. Why social learning?

Whilst existing policies, incentives, education and awareness are important, they are failing to stimulate the scale of action required, as identified by the barriers in Section 3. Reaching energy demand reduction targets and increasing the uptake of efficiency measures and policies, alongside ambitious renovation and installation of appropriate microgeneration technologies requires top-down action – that is, legislation, carbon budgets, building regulations, Carbon Emissions Reduction Target – and bottom-up approaches, which rely more on informal networks and community-led approaches such as the Eco Homes events (see also Chapter 11 and Ockwell et al, 2009). Thus, in addition to removing the structural barriers, there is a need to exemplify the benefits of energy efficiency and eco-renovation, and present them as integral parts of an aspirational lifestyle. According to the Domestic Energy Fact File, double glazing has more than twice the uptake of cavity walls, despite the cost being considerably more (Utley and Shorrock, 2008, p26). This may be due to double glazing being more aggressively marketed, but also being more aspirational than cavity wall insulation.

Theories of social learning could help address the barriers and negative perceptions outlined in Section 3. Although a broad term, the notion of 'social learning' has been widely applied in the environmental context (e.g. Social Learning Group, 2001). Drawing on this notion, Jackson (2005) explains that: 'we learn most effectively from models who are attractive to or influential for us, such as our parents (at certain ages), celebrities, people who are successful or powerful, or people who are simply like we are' (p110). Similarly, Rise et al (in Muro and Jeffrey, 2008, p326) suggest that: 'actors ... can be encouraged to learn by creating a learning environment', which is the environment the Open Homes events try to create to encourage replication of eco-renovation.

Albert Bandura's (1977) Social Learning theory suggests that people learn through observing others' behaviour, attitudes and outcomes of those behaviours. It is worth considering his four key learning stages with regard to the Open Homes events here:

1 *Attention:* an enjoyable and unusual event with a high degree of interactivity and 'hands on' opportunities is more stimulating than another 'ten top tips' leaflet.
2 *Retention:* people need to remember what they've learnt, which is more likely if they've enjoyed the experience, but follow up to the events is crucial.
3 *Replication:* Visitors need to be given the ability to replicate what they've learnt (a combination of determination, opportunity and available funding). They are more likely to replicate if the person 'modelling' or demonstrating the behaviour (in this case eco-renovating their home) is similar to the observer, and, with regard to Open Homes events, if the building is similar.
4 *Motivation:* giving people positive models can be an important motivator, and they also meet many others who share their concerns.

This four-stage approach can be applied to different types of energy-saving actions. Behaviour change to reduce regular (habitual) energy consumption can be reinforced and 'locked in' by (one-off) eco-renovation actions, thus showing visitors the importance of replicating larger-scale actions, such as installing insulation, when the opportunity arises.

However, new learning experiences which might lead to changes in beliefs and intentions do not necessarily lead to changes in behaviour (Muro and Jeffrey, 2008, p327). This view is widely described as the 'value-action' gap: where people's behaviour doesn't necessarily match or follow their values (Defra, 2008). Jackson (2005) asserts the difference that 'Having pro-social or pro-environmental values or attitudes is not the same thing as engaging in pro-social or pro-environmental behaviour', and that 'pro environmental intentions and behaviours do not necessarily correlate with reduced energy consumption in the household' (p53).

In recent years, policies to change behaviour and overcome the value–action gap have increasingly focused on social marketing (see, for example, Defra's 'Framework for pro-environmental behaviours: Defra 2008), and Bergman et al (2009) highlight that 'networks of friends and acquaintances could play an important role in the significant and complex decision of microgeneration' (p31).

5. The need for a step change in home renovation

The need for a step change to improve the energy performance of homes has been recognized in a number of recent UK reports. UK government household carbon saving schemes such as The Home Energy Saving Programme, carbon emission reduction targets (CERT), and new household energy ratings such as Energy Performance Certificates (EPCs),[2] are hindered by the 'cost-effective efficiency trap', whereby the range or type of efficiency measures suggested are 'overly restrictive', and achieve a limited reduction in CO_2 emissions (see Banks, 2008; CSE et al, 2008; Killip, 2008a). To be an effective lever for improving the housing stock of the UK, EPCs need to be more visible, more accurate and incorporate higher cost, non-standard improvement measures as recommendations (NHER 2009), and coupled with an awareness programme to 'show the benefits of moving up the EPC bands' (Boardman, 2007, p47).

The need to show the range of eco-renovation and microgeneration possibilities which could be applied to a variety of homes is reflected in the findings from the UK government's 'Big Energy Shift' public deliberative consultation (Ipsos Mori, 2009, p17). The report calls for demonstrations of retrofit properties which look similar to mainstream types of houses, in order to overcome the perception that eco-renovation is only for particular types of home or 'green' people. The report goes further to say that whilst demonstration homes can convey the technical possibilities of eco-renovation and eco new build,[3] the realities of living in a home are best conveyed by those who have carried out the renovation themselves. It highlights the importance of a strong policy hand from government in the form of legislation, new financing packages, social marketing and targeted information tailored to the occupants of diverse housing stock.

The Department for Energy and Climate Change (DECC)'s Low Carbon Transition Plan (DECC, 2009) builds on this consultation, setting out an ambitious policy of packages, including:

- extending the Carbon Emission Reduction Target (CERT) to benefit 1.5 million additional households with cost-effective energy efficiency measures;
- pay as you save models for microgeneration;
- feed-in tariffs for electricity generation;
- smart meters in homes;

- more proactive services from the Energy Saving Trust;
- upgrading the Energy Performance Certificates (EPCs).

At the same time, the Committee on Climate Change (2009) have outlined that new approaches are required in home energy efficiency improvements, such as a 'whole house approach' policy.[4] Solid wall insulation was identified as a key area, with the aim of insulating 2.3 million solid walls by 2022 (about 200,000 per year). However, this could present significant problems for the construction industry, as solid wall insulation retrofits involve significant disruption and expense to the householder.

The Committee on Climate Change also strongly supported the need for long-term financing packages, including pay as you save and renewable heat incentives. Existing schemes to encourage the uptake of microgeneration such as the Low Carbon Buildings Programme (LCBP), whilst helping to incentivize the uptake of some technologies, could have had a more far-reaching impact. Bergman and Jardine (2009) question whether the LCBP is able to deliver the holistic approach to carbon reductions, such as combining energy efficiency measures and microgeneration installations in the same development, which was one of its aims. The report mentions that: 'lack of holistic specialist advice forces householders to research, evaluate and choose between the different technologies, which have different attributes, costs and carbon saving potential. Such trade offs are not trivial calculations to make, and householders are generally unqualified to make such a decision' (p40).

Similarly, Bergman et al (2009) note that the uncertainty surrounding grants leads installers to focus on maximizing sales. They might not be aware of their ability to influence consumer's behaviour, and this limited interaction reduces energy-saving possibilities; reaping the full benefits requires a supportive socio-technical system to be in place.

Thus, while a step change in home renovation is being recognized, the potential to achieve this is currently limited by various factors. The need for networks, and communications and communities between existing and potential adopters, could be partly met by the Open Days, which are now examined.

6. Open Homes events

Between September 2007 and September 2009, over 18 different Open Homes events took place across the UK, demonstrating a range of home energy efficiency and eco-renovation, primarily focused on eco-renovated homes.[5] These events ranged in style and format from single tours around an eco-renovated home, eco-renovated homes being open on a regular basis prior to being occupied, to an area-wide approach over a number of days.

Over 150 different properties took part, with the events attracting over 27,000 visitors. More people were reached through online case studies and videos of eco-renovated homes. Visitor numbers were highest where the marketing of the events was 'piggy-backed' on established programmes that allow public access to historic or otherwise interesting buildings which are normally not open, such as 'London Open House' and 'Heritage Open Days'.

The selection process for homes taking part in the Open Homes events was for the most part informal, primarily determined by the local event organizers. In most cases it was enough to have installed one or more energy-efficiency measures or microgeneration, and to be willing to take part and share experiences. In some cases, monitored energy consumption data confirmed the emissions reductions achieved, and a smaller number of events detailed post-occupancy evaluations through working with local university students. In the case of the events organized by the Sustainable Energy Academy's Old Home Super Home project,[6] a national home energy rating (NHER)[7] scheme was used to assess the effectiveness of the changes made to the building to achieve at least 60 per cent reductions in CO_2 emissions.

Experience at the Oxfordshire Open Homes events

The Oxfordshire events are now focused on, with reference to other events where evaluation data is available. In the three Oxfordshire events (2007, 2008 and 2009), over 30 eco-renovated homes, covering a variety of ages and types, were open to the public from between two hours and two days over a weekend. Visitors were given tours or allowed to wander through the houses. They were provided with information about the house, the renovations, materials and technologies used, potential suppliers, and sources of funding. Average energy consumption and resultant energy reduction was given where available. At some locations, tours were given by the architects and builders (who were in some cases also the home owner) involved with the renovation.

All Oxfordshire-wide events were jointly organized by Oxfordshire ClimateXchange and Climate Outreach Information Network's (COIN) Ecovation project. Event marketing used a variety of channels: website, email lists, posters and leaflets, local television, radio and newspapers, the eco-renovators' own networks, and other local networks. Through being part of the National Heritage Open Days, publicity was widened locally and nationally. Other events have been similarly organized by local organizations and initiatives, and used similar marketing strategies.

Oxfordshire visitor numbers were calculated by totalling the approximate number of visitors per house, and allowing for visitors going to more than one property. A conservative estimate of both Oxfordshire events are 500 unique visitors per event, who visited on average 2–3 properties; 291 visitor feedback forms were completed by visitors in 2007, 135 in 2008, and 167 in 2009, making a total of 593 visitor responses.

Most eco-renovators encouraged completion of feedback forms at their homes, but factors influencing their completion included a lack of time and space available during the visit, and self-selection, which could result in a positive bias. Almost all visitor respondents were home owners themselves, although learning from the events could be applied across other housing sectors.

As the feedback results show (Figures 9.1 and 9.2), opportunities for social learning were high and showed marked trends. New learning was highest in the areas of insulation and energy efficiency (Figure 9.1), which were

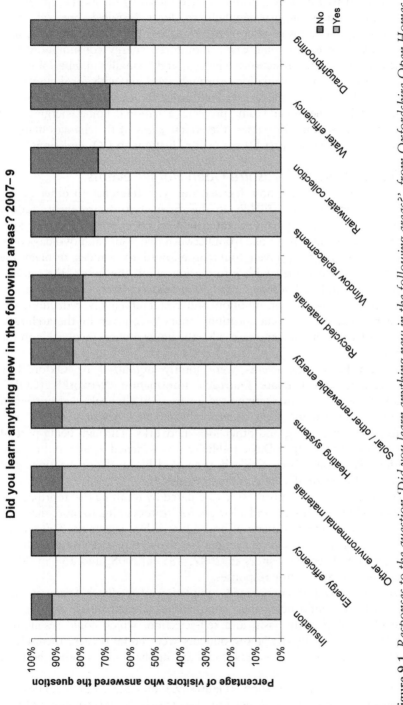

Figure 9.1 Responses to the question 'Did you learn anything new in the following areas?', from Oxfordshire Open Homes in 2007 and 2008 (N=593). Note that 100 per cent represents 100 per cent of responses to the specific question, not the percentage of all respondents or all visitors.

features included in every home. Given the relative accessibility of information around insulation and efficiency, it could be inferred that seeing insulation and efficiency as part of a suite of more popular technologies elevated the visitors' understanding of their role and importance.

Visitors were also attracted to novel materials such as straw-bale building, lime and hemp insulation, together with renovation tailored to specific building types such as 1930s semi-detached homes, Victorian terraces and traditional Cotswold cottages. A self-reported measure of understanding indicated that 60 per cent of participants felt their knowledge of the impacts of homes on climate change had improved (see Figure 9.2). However, more information and action is required both at and after the events, to help people become clearer about how to tackle improvements to their own homes, with just over 50 per cent of visitors saying that they are 'clear about how they might tackle improvements to their own home', and they 'have an appreciation of the costs involved'. This feedback supports the relevant barriers highlighted in Section 3.

For the Open Homes events to stimulate greater replication of eco-renovation, clearer information about all sectors of the renovation supply chain would need to be included, together with the potential costs. For the 2008 and 2009 Oxfordshire Open Homes, a directory of local suppliers was available to facilitate this, and in some cases the presence of expert advisers to show visitors around increased visitors' understanding and experience of the Open Homes.

General feedback on the Oxfordshire Open Homes experience was over-whelmingly positive, with 98 per cent pleased they had come. Almost all participants in the Open Homes considered that 'touch and feel' visits were a good way of learning about eco-renovation (Figure 9.2).

Oxfordshire visitor comments ranged from overall appreciation of the concept and experience ('Wonderful idea – very inspiring and valuable to get feedback from people who have done it') to appreciation of the scale involved ('Inspiring but also somewhat daunting'). The opportunity for replication of renovation is captured in comments like: 'It shows there are things which can be done even without money: using an emergency, perhaps, to make eco-improvements.' Other comments highlighted practical next steps: 'Really interesting talking with the building contractor.'

This correlates with other events. Reports of the 2008 and 2009 Stroud Open Homes (Booth, 2008; Royall and Booth, 2009), and the Mendip Open Green Homes and Gardens (Solloway, 2009), demonstrated a 'huge thirst for knowledge of eco-renovation and lower carbon technologies'. Examples of personal feedback address the range of key issues such as the importance of insulation: 'I had not appreciated that my insulation measures could be improved significantly'; the importance of demonstrating a particular type of house: 'Very useful to see the reality of "greening" a Cotswold cottage' and 'so nice to be able to see a property like mine'; the realities and decisions made about eco-renovation: 'Good to see we all need to make compromises'; and an introduction to more ecological building techniques: 'Seeing and touching lime plaster has now clarified how I'm going to approach it in my own home.'

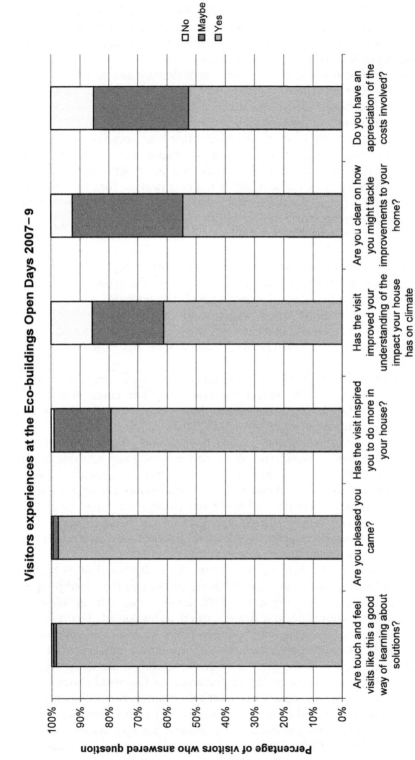

Figure 9.2 *General feedback from the Oxfordshire Open Homes, 2007–9 (N=593). Note that 100 per cent represents 100 per cent of responses to the specific question, not the percentage of all respondents or all visitors.*

Analysis from the Norfolk events (CPRE, 2007, 2008) demonstrates that visitors rated their experience highly, with 95 per cent increasing their understanding of energy efficient technologies. Visitor comments from the 2007 event (CPRE, 2007) showed a breadth of experience gained from householders who were considering both minor improvements and major refurbishments, to professionals (architects, planners and developers): 'We found it invaluable having access to first hand experience, to hear recommendations of particular technologies and approaches.' Myth-busting was also evident, as one visitor commented: 'you hear so much hype in the media (about green technologies) ... it's great to hear what it's actually like'.

The Open Homes events seem an ideal way to help people who are already planning to eco-renovate their homes, and overcome some negative perceptions that it would be too difficult or couldn't be done by people like themselves. Comments from two home owners who had recently eco-renovated their homes, and took part in the 2009 Oxfordshire Open Homes events, reflected this:

> I found the events encouraging to see other people's efforts at a later stage than I was at ... I found it useful to help me clarify my own thinking and hear other people talking about their decisions and processes.

> We found the 2008 Open Homes events very helpful, seeing and handling physical examples of specific materials in houses and talking to eco-renovators about the reality, costs, compromises, what they would do differently. It was particularly helpful to be able to take away information about materials, technologies, facts on the energy saved.[8]

Many other anecdotal comments received at the Oxfordshire Open Home events reinforced that they were useful in finding out about the technologies, processes and, crucially, that other people are going through similar decisions.

Taking part in the Open Homes events could also help to increase the influence of the homeowners, as they realize that many people value their experiences. An eco-renovator mentioned from her first involvement in 2009 that: 'what stood out was the buzz of talking to real people with (mostly) no commercial incentive. Not preaching, simply sharing experiences with those who have self-selected to walk through the door.'

With reference to Defra's (2008) '4E's Model' (Enable, Engage, Exemplify, Encourage) of behaviour change, feedback from the Open Homes suggests that the 'hands on' approach helped to:

1   enable visitors: through removing informational barriers and showing viable options;
2   engage visitors through trusted messengers: home owners, 'people like them', delivering the information, focusing on local homes and initiatives, through local networks and media channels, informal settings;

Figure 9.3 *Visitors at an eco-renovated house in Oxford*

3 exemplify homes and good decisions: demonstrating local people leading by example, sharing learning, appropriate renovation and microgeneration technologies for the building types;
4 encourage visitors: through highlighting the viability and benefits of achieving eco-renovation, helping potential renovators with information and decisions.

Behaviour change from the visitors

Whilst this data suggests that the Open Homes are a good way of learning, with between 75 and 80 per cent feeling inspired to do more in their own house, more in-depth research is required to investigate the subsequent actions visitors take as a result of visiting the homes, the information they receive, and if they put their intentions into action.

In Brighton and Stroud, visitors made pledges to take action. If every action pledged on the Brighton pledge forms were taken, all the households concerned could together save 4000 tonnes of carbon dioxide, and £475,000 from heat and £31,000 from electricity bills in just three years (Impetus, 2009). Analysis of the Stroud event in 2009 (Royall and Booth, 2009) showed that: 'even the enthusiasts or pioneers need or want examples and guidance before acting'; 596 pledges were received in total, ranging from the easy (turning the thermostat down) to the more complex (exterior solid wall insulation). The pledges also showed that there is interest in all of the key heating, insulation and renewable energy measures, with the relative difficulty of achieving some of the measures not reflected in the pledges. Verification of the resultant action from the pledges made is not possible at this time, but it does demonstrate a willingness to take action.

Other evaluation findings provide more concrete evidence of behaviour change. Analysis of the Norfolk events (CPRE, 2008) noted that 50 per cent of visitor respondents said that they had applied simple measures to conserve energy, 29 per cent said they had increased the insulation in their home, whilst 8 per cent had installed renewable energy technology. Similarly, Sustainable Energy Academy's 'Old Home Super Home' project analysis found that 54.9 per cent of visitor respondents had installed energy efficiency measures or renewable technologies in their home following their visit to an exemplar home. What is perhaps more interesting is that 26.7 per cent of the respondents thought they had spent over £5000. Only 4.5 per cent had done this to increase saleability of their property, whilst 81.8 per cent had done it to save money on fuel and water bills. Two-thirds (67.6 per cent) were inspired to make 'lifestyle' changes following their visits (SEA, 2009).

Turning the inspiration into action can occur within a small or larger time frame, depending on the opportunities available. A home owner and solar photovoltaic installer who opened his 'Solar Electric' house in the 2009 Oxfordshire event received 25 follow-up requests from visitors, resulting in six contracts to install solar photovoltaic systems on their homes in under a month. Follow-up actions can take much longer though.

Many eco-renovators who opened their homes referred to the opportunistic nature of their renovation work, and almost all experiences of the eco-renovators support Boardman's (2007) assertion: 'The rate of improvement in the energy efficiency of the general housing stock is largely dependent on the initiatives of the owners' (p42). Demonstrating the variety and scope of renovation could help more people to seize the eco-renovation opportunity when it arises, thus bringing the cost of the 'eco' part of the renovation down (Killip, 2008a). This message is important in countering the perception, and potential barrier, that eco-renovation is out of most people's budget, especially given the global financial crisis.

The eco-renovated properties, taken collectively, demonstrate a much fuller range of the technically possible interventions, and not just those measures which are supported by government grants and advice services. They show visitors how eco-renovators have tackled complex, interconnected issues to do with property maintenance and improvement, often including problems which are not directly related to energy conservation (e.g. damp walls). The actual houses – as well as the stories told by the eco-renovators – enable participants to feel that eco-renovation can be done by them.

7. Limits to the Open Homes approach

The Open Homes events have clearly been valued and enjoyed by the visitors, but there are limits and drawbacks. The approach is labour- and time-intensive for organizers and hosts. A common reflection among hosts has been that the experience is rewarding and exhausting in equal measures: 'It was tough, but also exhilarating, like a good party should be' (home owner in the

2007 Norfolk Green Buildings Open Days); but that people were 'pleased to participate ... it was fantastic to be part of the eco-homes camaraderie' (home owner, Oxford). Follow-up enquiries can be an ongoing drain on people's time, and it is in the nature of the event (largely voluntary and community-focused) that each homeowner has to make their own decisions about how much time to give.

Eco-renovators are not selected for their technical knowledge or communication skills, nor are most participating properties selected against published criteria or technical standards, with the exception of the 'Old Home Super Home' exemplar homes. This has a positive aspect, the persuasive power of a story told by the people involved, but it also means that there is no quality control or attempt at consistency. The visitors are left to reflect on what they have heard, provided with further information, and in many cases given the opportunity to opt into an email list for similar events and discussions. Volunteers were used to help out at the events, which in many cases has helped some of them achieve their own eco-renovations. Encouraging eco-renovation professionals to volunteer at the events seems to work well both for the visitors' experiences and the numbers of new commissions coming to the professionals.

A further limitation relates to lack of data about energy consumption and energy reduction for the eco-renovated homes. Such data was used where available, but generally there was no quantitative energy data for visitors to see. This is reflected in visitors not having an appreciation of the costs involved (Figure 9.2).

The programme of Open Homes events has thrown into vivid relief some of the structural barriers that exist to greater replication, examined in Section 3. Social learning may be an excellent route to raising awareness and inspiration about the technical potential of home eco-renovation, but it does not necessarily help with queries about finding good products, suppliers and contractors for projects which the visitors may be inspired to undertake.

Where hosts are able to make specific recommendations, these are very highly valued by visitors: the strength of 'word-of-mouth' recommendations from a trusted source; and a house that people can relate to. It would be instructive to follow where these interactions lead in terms of work to other properties and the level of satisfaction achieved.

From anecdotal evidence, and analysis of the feedback forms, visitors to the Oxfordshire Open Homes events could be identified as relatively environmentally conscious individuals.[9] Although this accounts for a relatively narrow sector of society, enabling those poised and most able to renovate their homes could help replication of eco-renovation. To encourage wider participation and learning across population, a wider variety of homes and people could be reflected in the Open Homes, combined with other 'show home' opportunities aimed at different sectors of the population, such as the UK Centre for Sustainable Energy's '100 ideas home' (Rose, 2007). Widening visitor participation (and possibly resultant actions) at the Open Home events could be achieved through estate agents, as the information and experience would be delivered to people who often have the immediate opportunity to eco-renovate.

8. Conclusions

Open Homes events have been excellent examples of social learning, raising awareness and inspiring visitors about the opportunities and potential for energy-conscious refurbishment. The events can increase the opportunity for replication by demonstrating what an eco-renovated home is like to live in. As found in the Big Energy Shift (2009, p21) 'seeing real life examples was one of the most compelling incentives for individuals to take up new ideas'.

However, this activity is not a guarantee of widespread replication. The impact of these events needs to be seen in context, including how they relate to Government-backed programmes (grants, advice services) and the role of tradespeople in guiding the decisions, and spotting eco-renovation opportunities for householders during property maintenance and improvement. For maximum impact, other parts of the supply chain need to be inspired about the technical potentials of eco-renovation, and peer support is needed for householders who are embarking on eco-renovation. A wider policy framework, providing not just education but also financial incentives, training, quantified energy performance standards and accurate energy labelling, needs urgent attention, as outlined in Section 5. While policies do not support the actions required, their effectiveness for behaviour change is hindered.

Further areas of study to assess the effectiveness of Open Homes include a deeper analysis of feedback from other Open Homes events, a consideration of how energy prices and the current housing market influence visitors actions, how Open Homes events could encourage the take-up of measures by a wider sector of the population across other housing sectors (e.g. Registered Social Landlords), and if they could demonstrate climate adaptation.

Most of the data presented here examines feedback from visitors at a particular time. How visitors to Open Homes process the information and experience, and what they do as a result of it, remains a subject for further research and signals the need for a coordinated follow-up strategy to maximize the actions from social learning. How do the Open Homes events help enable the process of eco-renovation and, if so, does this make replication more likely? How will we know if the Open Homes events played a decisive role in replication? Did it help those on the eco-renovation path achieve their actions more quickly and with more confidence, or did it inspire eco-renovations that would have been unlikely before attending the event? How can we assess the impacts of the events from people who didn't visit, but read about the events or saw the publicity?

Whilst most events have taken place at the completion of a project, there is enormous value for construction workers and avid home improvers to see the 'work in progress'.

The greatest strength of the Open Homes events seems to be the power of real-life experience and the telling of a 'story' by an ordinary citizen about their own home, combined with the visitor's experience of being in, seeing and touching the home. There is undoubtedly scope to more fully integrate these events with other existing sources of information, and to target other parts of the housing supply chain.

Acknowledgements

An earlier version of this chapter was co-authored by Gavin Killip and first presented as a poster and short paper in the ECEEE 2009 Summer Study, under the title of 'Demonstration, inspiration ... replication? Assessing the impact and limits of social learning from Eco-homes Open Days in the UK' (www.eceee.org/conference_proceedings/eceee/2009).

The author would like to thank all the funders for both Oxfordshire events, including Defra's Climate Communications Fund, Fund for the Environment and Urban Life, Sustainable Energy Academy, plus Open Home owners and volunteers for help in organizing the events; other Open Homes organizers across the country for sharing their insights and feedback and Gavin Killip at the Environmental Change Institute for ongoing advice and significant input into earlier versions of this chapter. The feedback questions are based on a template provided by Sustainable Energy Academy's 'Old Home Super Home' project

Notes

1   Some US events include:
    Sierra Club National Weatherization Day: www.sierraclubgreenhome.com/
    Northeast Sustainable Energy Association Green Building Open Day: www.nesea.org/greenbuildings/
    Green Home Tours in Seattle: www.greenhometours.net
2   Home Energy Saving Programme (HESP): UK Government measures announced to help families on middle and modest incomes cut their energy bills, www.number10.gov.uk/Page16807
    Carbon Emission Reduction Targets (CERT): UK Government's Household sector energy and carbon saving scheme, with obligations on energy suppliers to meet household carbon saving targets, www.decc.gov.uk/en/content/cms/consultations/open/cert/cert.aspx
    Energy Performance Certificates (EPCs): EPCs contain information and give a rating on home energy use and carbon dioxide emissions, and a recommendation report. They are required as part of the Home Information Packs, and are issues whenever a building is built, sold or rented out, http://epc.direct.gov.uk/index.html
3   For example, Centre for Alternative Technology (www.cat.org.uk), Building Research Establishment's (BRE) Innovation Park (www.bre.co.uk/page.jsp?id=634).
4   DECC's definition of a whole house approach – considering a household's energy needs and carbon dioxide impacts as a whole, and establishing a comprehensive package of measures to address them ... 'a key benefit of the "whole house approach" is that it ensures that the needs of the property are assessed as a whole, that they happen in the right order, and that disruption is minimised' (DECC, 2009).
5   Events have taken place across the UK. These include Sustainable Energy Academy (SEA) 'Old Home Super Home' project 2008, and also as part of the Civic Trust's 'Heritage Open Days', and London Open House. www.sustainable-energyacademy.org.uk/
    Oxford Open Eco-houses 2007, 2008, 2009, www.ecovation.org.uk
    Faringdon (Oxfordshire) Eco-Trail June 2008, http://www.ecoweek.info /Find_Out_More_/ECOTRAIL/ecotrail.html

Green Buildings in Norfolk Open Days 2007, 2008, 2009, http://www.cprenorfolk.org.uk/news-events/

Llanidloes Eco-homes Open Weekend 2008, 2009, http://www.lles.co.uk/

Brighton Open Homes 2008, 2009, www.ecoopenhouses.org/index.html

Stroud Eco-homes 2008, 2009, www.stroudopenhomes.org.uk/

Lewes 2009, http://transitiontowns.org/Lewes/ECO-HOUSES

Mendip Environment Open Green Homes and Gardens 2009, http://mendip.ourenvironment.org.uk/node/70

Totnes. Eco-construction Walk 2009, http://totnes.transitionnetwork.org/building andhousing/ecotourreport

In addition, there are many other similar types of events that have taken place.

6 Sustainable Energy Academy's Old Home SuperHome – a network of exemplar, old dwellings which have undergone an energy-efficiency retrofit, www.sustainable-energyacademy.org.uk

7 NHER National Home Energy Rating scheme – Europe's first domestic energy labelling scheme, established by the National Energy Foundation, www.nher.co.uk

8 Responses gained through conversations and email correspondence by the author from some eco-renovators who opened their home in the 2009 Oxfordshire event.

9 According to Defra's (2008) environmental segmentation model, visitors are mostly likely to fall into the top two pro-environmental segments: 'Positive Greens' and 'Concerned Consumers', which Defra estimate account for around 32 per cent of the population.

References

Bandura, A. (1977) *Social Learning Theory*, General Learning Press, New York

Bergman, N. and Jardine, C. (2009) *Power from the People: Domestic Microgeneration and the Low Carbon Buildings Programme*, Environmental Change Institute, Oxford

Bergman, N., Hawkes, A., Brett, D., Baker, P., Barton, J., Blanchard, R., Brandon, N., Infield, D., Jardine, C., Kelly, N., Leach, M., Matian, M., Peacock, A., Staffell, I., Sudtharalingam, S. and Woodman, B. (2009) 'UK microgeneration. Part I: policy and behavioural aspects', *Energy*, vol 162, no 1, pp22–36 [online], available from http://www.atypon-link.com/telf/doi/abs/10.1680/ener.2009.162.1.23, accessed 17 September 2009

Boardman, B. (2007) *Home Truths: A Low Carbon Strategy to Reduce UK Housing Emissions by 80% by 2050*, Environmental Change Institute, Oxford

Booth, P. (2008) *Open Homes for a Sustainable Future Report*, [online] Transition Stroud, available from http://www.stroudopenhomes.org.uk/?page_id=34, accessed 7 November 2008

CASE – Centre for Analysis of Social Exclusion (July 2008) *'Teach in' on Energy and Existing Homes – restoring neighbourhoods and slowing climate change'*, Seminar Report, LSE / CASE report 56 [online], available from http://sticerd.lse.ac.uk/case/_new/news/year.asp?yyyy=2008#169, accessed 2 November 2008

Caird, S., Roy, R. and Herring, H. (2008) 'Improving the energy performance of UK households: Results from surveys of consumer adoption and use of low- and zerocarbon technologies', *Energy Efficiency*, vol 1, no 2, pp149–166 [online], available from http://www.springerlink.com/content/c5320x0118j36123/, accessed 22 September 2009

Committee on Climate Change (2009b) Meeting Carbon Budgets – the need for a step change. Progress report to Parliament Committee on Climate Change, Executive

Summary October 2009, available from http://www.theccc.org.uk/climate-change-act, accessed 19 October 2009

CPRE (2007) Norfolk Open Days Newsletter 2007 [online], available from http://www.cprenorfolk.org.uk/news-events/newsletter-opendays07.pdf, accessed 12 February 2009

CPRE (2008) Green Buildings in Norfolk – Open Days 2008, Evaluation Results from Vivid Interface Ltd. Forwarded by personal communication with event organizer

DCLG (2007) Building a Greener Future: Policy Statement [online], available from http://www.communities.gov.uk/documents/planningandbuilding/pdf/building-greener.pdf, accessed 3 October 2009

DECC (2008) *UK Climate Change Act*, HMSO, London [online], available from http://www.decc.gov.uk/en/content/cms/legislation/en/content/cms/legislation/cc_act_08/cc_act_08.aspx, accessed 12 November 2009

DECC (2009) UK Low Carbon Transition 2009, p85 [online], available from http://www.decc.gov.uk/en/content/cms/publications/lc_trans_plan/lc_trans_plan.aspx, accessed 22 July 2009

Defra (2007*) e-Digest Environmental Statistics Key Facts about: Climate Change Carbon dioxide emissions by end user: 1990–2006 United Kingdom* [online], Defra, available from http://www.defra.gov.uk/environment/statistics/globatmos/gakf07.htm, accessed 2 November 2008

Defra (2008) *A Framework for Pro-environmental Behaviours* [online], Defra, available from http://www.defra.gov.uk/evidence/social/behaviour/index.htm, accessed 7 November 2008

Jackson, T. (2005) *Motivating Sustainable Consumption: a review of evidence on consumer behaviour and behavioural change* [online], A report to the Sustainable Development Research Network by Centre for Environmental Strategy, University of Surrey, available from http://www.compassnetwork.org/images/upload/MotivatingSCfinal.pdf, accessed 4 November 2008

IPCC (2007) Fourth Assessment Report, Summary for Policy Makers [online], IPCC http://www.ipcc.ch/pdf/assessment-report/ar4/syr/ar4_syr_spm.pdf, accessed 7 November 2008

Impetus Consulting (2009) *Eco Open Houses – Showing and Telling*, South East Excellence [online], available from www.ecoopenhouses.org/media/OpenEco Houses_report.pdf, accessed 30 October 2009

Ipsos Mori (2009) *Big Energy Shift Summary Report from Citizens' Forums* [online], available from http://www.big-briefs.com/big_energy_shift/Big_Energy_Shift_Summary_Report.pdf, accessed 30 August 2009

Killip, G. (2008a) *Building a Greener Britain: Transforming the UK's Existing Housing Stock*. A report for the Federation of Master Builders, Environmental Change Institute, Oxford

Killip, G. (2008b) 'It's the size of the Reduction Target, Stupid! The need for a whole-sale rethink of Energy Efficiency Policy in UK Housing', *ACEEE Summer Study on Energy Efficiency in Buildings*, September 2008, USA, 6-111-121

Muro, M. and Jeffrey, P. (2008) 'A critical review of the theory and application of social learning in participatory natural resource management processes', *Journal of Environmental Planning and Management*, vol 51, no 3, pp325–344

NHER (2009) Energy Performance Certificates: Seizing the opportunity [online], available from http://www.nher.co.uk/pages/insight/seizing_the_opportunity.php, accessed 10 January 2010

Ockwell, D., Whitmarsh, L. and O'Neill, S. J. (2009) 'Reorienting climate change communication for effective mitigation: Forcing people to be green or fostering grass-roots engagement?', *Science Communication*, vol 30, no 3, pp305–327
Rose, C. (2007) Campaign Strategy Newsletter No 37, 28 December 2007: Feedback on Reaching Prospectors, available from http://www.campaignstrategy.org/newsletters/campaignstrategy_newsletter_37.pdf, accessed 15 January 2009
Royall, H. and Booth, P. (2009) *Eco-renovation Open Homes for a Sustainable Future*, Transition Stroud Energy Group [online], available from www.stroudopenhomes.org.uk, accessed 10 January 2010
SEA (2009) Old Home Super Home. Personal correspondence with G. Mallett, 26 October 2009
Social Learning Group (2001) *Learning to Manage Global Environmental Risks: a Comparative History of Social Responses to Climate Change, Ozone Depletion and Acid Rain*, MIT Press, Cambridge, MA
Solloway, H. (2009) Report on Mendip Open Green Homes and Gardens 2009, Mendip Environment Community Interest Company [online], available from http://mendip.ourenvironment.org.uk/node/121, accessed 6 January 2010
Sponge (2008) Buyers Guide to a greener Home, available from www.spongenet.org/buyersguide/
Stern, N. (2006) *Stern Review on the Economics of Climate Change* SHORT executive summary, HM Treasury [online], available from http://www.hm-treasury.gov.uk/d/CLOSED_SHORT_executive_summary.pdf, accessed 7 November 2008
UK Green Building Council (2008) Low Carbon Existing Homes report, available from http://www.ukgbc.org/site/resources/show-resource-details?id=316, accessed 14 April 2009
Utley, J. and Shorrock, L. (2008) *Domestic Energy Fact File 2008*, Building Research Establishment [online], available from http://www.bre.co.uk/filelibrary/pdf/rpts/Fact_File_2008.pdf, accessed 15 October 2009

10
Up-scaling Social Behaviour Change Programmes: The Case of EcoTeams

Scott Davidson

1. Introduction

A quick look at the pro-environmental behaviour movement today reminds one of the views of London City from the top of Parliament Hill in Hampstead Heath park – a bustling arena of seemingly random activity as planes sketch patterns across the sky, helicopters cruise over St James' Park, buses and taxis zip around everywhere, and everything seems frantically busy. As one gets more involved in this energetic field, a greater realization dawns on the incredible number and variety of initiatives going on across the UK, aimed at getting individuals to shift either individual behaviours or whole lifestyles in a pro-environmental direction. The passion and commitment of the individuals attempting to drive this change is evident, and within their own small spheres, they are indeed often making a genuine and long-lasting difference to the individuals their programmes reach. Despite all of this energy, passion and busyness, however, these behavioural shifts are not making their effect weighty enough to register on the radar of mainstream society and culture.

Whilst the growth of sales in environmental products continues to outgrow many other areas of the market, significant behavioural change in more challenging areas, such as diet or transport, is still evident amongst only relatively small pockets of individuals (DEFRA, 2008b). Yet to create a sustainable society, we will need to engage a critical mass to take up sustainable lifestyles before the rest will follow; a social tipping point will need to be reached. To achieve this, effective behaviour change programmes will require, along with regulation and other changes, a large move towards up-scaling.

The aim of this chapter, using Global Action Plan's EcoTeams as a case study and findings from a series of interviews with behaviour change practitioners, is to briefly outline key barriers which explain why this frantic activity is not achieving greater impact, and suggest some potential ways to overcome those barriers. Specifically, I will discuss issues around the lack of evidence base for pro-environmental approaches, the focus on small impacts, and the difficulty in up-scaling these programmes, as well as wider barriers to pro-environmental behaviour change caused by central government policy.

2. Global Action Plan's EcoTeams

EcoTeams is one of the largest pro-environmental behaviour change pro-grammes in the world. To date it includes over 150,000 participants worldwide and has reduced carbon emissions by tens, if not hundreds, of thousands of tonnes (Moser and Dilling, 2007). EcoTeams was originally designed in the USA by environmental psychologists and practitioners, who wanted to create an environmental behaviour change programme based on the socio-psychological research available. It employed three main principles from the literature which will be described shortly, and found its first traction for the programme on a reasonable scale in the Netherlands. It arrived in the UK initially involving 200 households in Nottingham, with the original eight-month programme running in the Netherlands shortened to a five-month programme spread across four major themes: waste and shopping, energy, transport and water.

EcoTeams essentially involves the recruitment of an EcoTeam leader, who then recruits six to eight individuals from different households to form an EcoTeam. Across the five-month programme, the EcoTeams meet once per month and are provided with a set of resources for each of the themes. These resources outline ways to reduce individual environmental impacts within each area, and participants measure their waste, recycling, electricity, gas and water usage throughout the programme. As such, they can see the impacts their behaviours are having as they make behavioural changes. At the end of the EcoTeams process, participants are presented with their overall impact reduc-tions through the programme, a United Nations Environment Programme certificate, and have a final celebratory meeting. A more in-depth discussion of the underlying principles of EcoTeams follows.

Information, but effectively delivered

There is a wealth of literature on the variable efficacy of certain message types and formats according to context, audience and content. Principles of persua-sion and influencing people's behaviour through appeals to social norms and other social mechanisms have been extensively described by Cialdini amongst others (e.g. Goldstein, Martin and Cialdini, 2007). Another area of focus has been on the effects of tailored information (e.g. Abrahamse, 2007; Abrahamse et al, 2007), whilst the effectiveness of peer-to-peer communication has also received attention in research specifically around EcoTeams as part of the group process (e.g. Burgess and Nye, 2008). Finally, the marketing 'foot in the door' strategy (i.e. gaining commitment to undertake a simple behav-iour, after which larger changes are more likely to be agreed to) is also being relied upon by some in the environmental behaviour change field (Crompton, 2009). EcoTeams' information format, style and delivery is designed around principles outlined in the literature above, including:

1 using social norm messaging (e.g. '70 per cent of people just like you [name desirable action / behaviour]');
2 using tailored feedback for each participant on the impacts of their actions;
3 asking for small behaviours first, before asking for more complex changes further into the programme;
4 peer-to-peer information delivery, tailored to the local environment.

The tailored delivery method is critical in overcoming specific local barriers such as places to source environmentally friendly produce or recycle certain products (Burgess and Nye, 2008). The importance of the way information is delivered within EcoTeams is further reinforced by Hobson (2001), when she highlights the positive impact on EcoTeams' participants of the encouraging and creative way that facts are presented. Hobson argues that this is essential in making environmental impacts accessible, so that they will resonate with the personal changes that participants make (Bickerstaff and Walker, 2001; in Hobson, 2001).

Measurement and feedback

Measurement and feedback are seen as key to both facilitating the actual changes taking place within the programme, and in helping these behaviours become new pro-environmental habits. Burgess and Nye (2008) describe in detail the effect that measurement and feedback has in helping to create initial behaviour change through two main processes of 'competence and control', and a 're-materialization' of the resources we use. Firstly, they propose that resource consumption has become automated, and requires 're-materialization' into consciousness where it can be considered, before being acted upon (for more on breaking habits, see Chapter 1). Consistent with this, Hobson (2001) notes that EcoTeams' participants seem to experience 'why do I do that?' revelations about their behaviours. Secondly, they propose that participants' ability to see the impacts that their behavioural changes are making through meter readings and waste weighing allows them to feel like the actions they take do make a difference, hence increasing their sense of 'competence and control' over their personal resource use. This suggested increase in relevant self-efficacy has been highlighted within the wider behavioural change literature as an important factor in successful change in the form of perceived behavioural control (Bandura, 1977; Stern, 2000; Feltz et al, 2007).

In addition to measurement and feedback's ability to help initiate change through increasing perceived behavioural control and 'rematerializing' automated behaviours, it is also argued that feedback is critical in ensuring the behaviour lasts (De Young, 1996; Hobson, 2001; Staats et al, 2004; Burgess and Nye, 2008). This may work through positive reward mechanisms and reinforcement (De Young, 1996).

The importance of social groups

The importance of social groups in the EcoTeams process should not be underestimated. In research with EcoTeams' participants, the importance of the social group aspect is consistently highlighted. Stories of EcoTeams going on beyond the five-month process or moving onto other projects together are common within Global Action Plan.

Supporting this is a wealth of external and independent research which supports the importance of the use of social groups. In the largest academic study conducted with EcoTeams within the UK, Burgess and Nye (2008) explain the importance of social groups in terms of reinforcement and confirmation of participants' lifestyles, along with social group pressure to conform and change in line with others. They suggest this works through confirmatory information and positive examples, along with well-researched mechanisms outlined by Social Identity Theory (SIT; Tajfel and Turner, 1979). The sizeable literature on SIT suggests that group social pressures can act on powerful levers such as self-esteem in order to motivate individuals to emulate the behaviours and attitudes of other members of the in-group (Hunter et al, 2005; see also Chapter 4). These group mechanisms when coupled with confirmatory information being delivered through other group members, and the positive examples being provided, act as a potent force for change. The strength of social influence within EcoTeams is also supported by Staats et al (2004). They found that where social influence was strong in an EcoTeam, habit strength had no significant moderating effect on the positive relationship between intention and behaviour.

Similar to the re-materialization concept, Hobson notes that participants start to break down daily routines into their constituent behaviours through EcoTeams, and as a result begin to question the way (and why) they do things. Using Giddens' (1984) structuration theory, Hobson argues that this breaking down of behaviours, when coupled with the integration of new environmental information, allows participants to view their behaviours from a new 'discursive lens'. This discursive lens describes a less rigid behavioural routine, which is more flexible to change due to the process ongoing within EcoTeams. It suggests a constant increased level of open-mindedness, where the participant is better able to incorporate new information and use this to alter behaviours on a more consistent basis than would be normal, due to the way habits attenuate attention to new information and thus are resistant to change (see Chapter 1). The concept of a 'discursive lens' is supported by the concept of practical and discursive consciousness, outlined by Spaargaren and Van Vliet's (2000) model of pro-environmental behaviour. Thus, another important aspect of EcoTeams relates to bringing automated behaviour into conscious thought, where habits can be broken and re-formed into new pro-environmental habits (Staats et al, 2004; Burgess and Nye, 2008). Hobson (2001) explains this new pro-environmental behaviour 'stickiness' in terms of the durability of the 'discursive lens' that is formed through the EcoTeams process. The importance of social groups from a variety of perspectives is important then, and acts to break old habits and form new ones through several strong behavioural levers.

EcoTeams – the overall mechanics

In considering the overall EcoTeams process from a wider perspective, Burgess and Nye (2008) argue that through a process of 'reflexive lifestyle examination', 'bundles of behaviours' can be examined and changed together. Staats et al (2004) support this assertion highlighting the importance of the wide range of options for change provided within the EcoTeams literature. Burgess and Nye further argue that through changing bundles of behaviours rather than individual behaviours, it is more likely that new routines can be formed where new behaviours complement each other. Certainly where certain individual behaviours rely on other changes for success, this argument seems to make sense. Take the example of Bob who works in an isolated area with no local lunch facilities, and normally uses the car to drive and get lunch. Bob now decides, having been part of an EcoTeam, that he is going to cycle to work instead. There is a group of behaviours which are going to be key for this to work, including remembering to bring shower gear and lunch to work, and preparing for various weather conditions too. Potentially helpful behaviours may also include having working clothes at work, but leaving some smart clothes at home for evenings out. This may change dry cleaners used, diet, shopping lists and washing routines at home and so forth. We see that the transport change is difficult to consider in isolation, and instead needs to be considered as part of a wider network of interlinked habits which need to switch as a 'bundle of behaviours'. Burgess and Nye (2008) argue that the new information coming through the social groups that are EcoTeams should reflect this consideration of current everyday routines.

We can see that through the three underlying factors outlined above, and their interaction, EcoTeams has the ingredients according to the socio-psychological literature to be an effective behaviour change programme. Indeed, hints above suggest that it is effective in changing behaviours and holding this change long enough to create new pro-environmental habits. It is worthwhile now, briefly considering the evidence around just how effective EcoTeams are.

EcoTeams' impacts

Findings from two major studies of EcoTeams (Staats et al, 2004; Burgess and Nye, 2008), alongside one MSc thesis (Baxter, 2009) and some initial findings from core EcoTeams' programme evaluation (Global Action Plan, 2009), are now briefly discussed. These studies comprise multiple methods conducted across a significant and varied sample, and provide mutually supportive evidence of EcoTeams' efficacy.

In general, in both Burgess and Nye (2008) and Staats et al (2004), EcoTeams' participants report behaviour change across all targeted areas, and to have maintained changes up to three years after the programme had ended (see Figures 10.1 and 10.2). Changes were generally made of easy uptake behaviours (e.g. recycling more or switching off appliances) which fit with already existing lifestyles, and less frequently of more difficult behaviours such as installing microgeneration. The longitudinal research points towards more changes being made up to three years after the programme ended, often of a more difficult nature. Further research by Baxter (2009) and Global Action Plan (2009) further supports this in suggesting participants go onto more difficult behaviours towards the end of the programme or after its end, and that

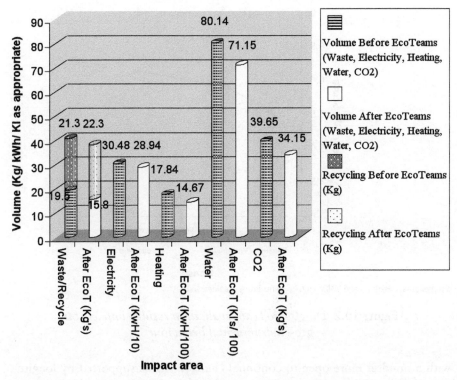

Figure 10.1 *Average UK EcoTeam impacts (per household per month). Usage level of each resource per household before and after EcoTeams in units adjusted to fit within one scale. That is, waste and recycling are measured in kilograms; electricity is measured in kilowatt hours divided by ten (KwH/10); and energy used for heating in kilowatt hours/100 (Kwh/100) for heating energy. Water is displayed in kilolitres divided by 100 (Kl/100). Carbon dioxide emissions are displayed in kilograms*

a significant number may go on to join other environmental groups as a direct result of EcoTeams' participation. Figures 10.1 and 10.2 illustrate changes made during and after the programme.

As Figure 10.1 shows, significant resource reductions were achieved in every area by UK EcoTeams, and can be expressed in percentage terms as an increase in recycling as a proportion of waste of 5.1 per cent, a reduction in electricity consumption of 7 per cent, and a reduction of heating energy consumption of 20.8 per cent. Water consumption is reduced by 14.9 per cent and overall CO_2 by 16.6 per cent. Similarly, as Figure 10.2 shows, Staats et al (2004) found significant increases in pro-environmental behaviour (using a pro-environmental behaviour scale focused on eight key behaviours) during the programme (T0–T1) when compared to a control group, and a continued acceleration of uptake beyond the end of the programme.

All of the evidence points towards EcoTeams as an effective programme, not only in the sense of motivating behaviour change, but as a programme which seems to unfreeze habitual routines across lifestyles, replacing routines

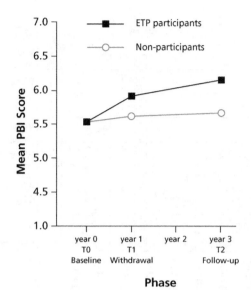

Source: Staats, Harland and Wilke, 2004 – permissions obtained (2010)

Figure 10.2 *Dutch EcoTeam evaluation results: impacts on pro-environmental behaviour*

with a mindset more open to continual change. This is supported by longitudinal follow-up research showing a continued increase of behaviour change, and a move towards more difficult behaviours up to three years after the project end and potentially beyond.[1] Despite this evidence base, however, and the documented effectiveness of EcoTeams, successful behavioural change initiatives are still in the minority, and still not being employed at the scale required to meet the challenging targets being set around lifestyle related carbon reductions (e.g. DEFRA, 2008a). A discussion of the barriers to this up-scaling of successful behavioural change initiatives follows.

3. Up-scaling: building an evidence base

There are few who currently envy government ministers their position. Government debt and environmental pressures soar alongside each other, in a way which cannot help but remind one of the story of Icarus, whose home-made wings melted upon flying too close to the sun, with inevitable consequences to follow.

Environmental impacts remain inextricably linked to the economy, rising as the economy grows, whilst the ideology of endless economic growth seems immovable. With imminent and unavoidable public spending cuts situated within the context of endless economic growth and linked rising environmental impacts, the financial pressure on government has never been higher. Subsequently, effective demonstration of the returns of investment from behaviour change programmes has never been so important, and this demonstration relies upon a robust evidence base of the full impacts of the field's programmes.

This need is emphasized further when coupled with issues of political capital. As McKenzie-Mohr (2008) and Jackson (2005) repeatedly highlight, mass marketing is often a minimally effective tool in changing behaviours in a pro-environmental direction. Regardless, the political lure of the mass media marketing approach continually sees funding directed towards this, instead of more effective behaviour change programmes.

Despite this, a glance across the UK at the myriad of frantic behavioural change initiatives under way reveals a severe lack of activity relating to building an evidence base. Indeed, whilst the 10:10 campaign (discussed in Chapter 11) represents one of the most successful and largest environmental awareness raising campaigns of the last few years, the major criticism currently being levelled at the project is that it has no key measurable outcomes; 10:10 is exceptional in having wedged its foot in the door of the UK's consciousness. However, unless it proactively moves to more effective behaviour change than a mass pledge system, and in doing so captures its impacts, it runs the risk of becoming another 'Make Poverty History' – a fantastic awareness-raising campaign that provides evidence of only a tiny proportion of long-lasting change compared to its potential.

EcoTeams is one of the very few programmes which has been extensively evaluated, and yet on its own has not proved large enough thus far to attract significant enough funding to genuinely up-scale. Many more will need to develop the evidence base and collaboratively engage policy makers if genuine expansion is to be achieved.

Shining a small light of hope in this area, the Sustainable Behaviours Unit (SBU) within the UK Department for Environment, Food and Rural Affairs (DEFRA) is to be commended for its efforts to support robust measurement within pro-environmental behaviour change programmes. Under their Environmental Action Fund, Action-Based Research Fund and Greener Living Fund projects, they demand a minimum level of evaluation of pro-environmental behaviour change projects and in most cases more extensive in-depth research. The funding within these projects helps small organizations involved in the pro-environmental behaviour change field build capacity around measurement and reporting. Despite these efforts, the SBU is small and with limited funding, and as such is inadequately resourced to equip, evaluate or support the variety of behaviour change initiatives occurring in the UK to an extent where they might up-scale. With this in mind, it is important each organization builds their evidence base and seeks support to do so. As such, here are six related wishes for members of the pro-environmental behaviour change field:

1   Use online survey software (e.g. 'Survey Monkey')[2] to do at least basic evaluation. Such software is cheap or free, incredibly simple to use, and will design, send out, remind, capture data and allow basic analysis.
2   Utilize Dillman's *Mail and Internet Surveys* (2008) to make surveys as robust as possible, and especially to capture unanticipated impacts. This book is easily accessible, readable, and full of easy and practical tips.
3   Get acquainted with the behaviour change literature. As starting points, there are online guides[3] and accessible summaries (e.g. Goldstein et al,

2007) outlining the many things organizations can do to make their programmes more effective at zero or low cost.

4   Spend at least some small amount in training on social research skills such
    as survey design, evaluation methods and basic research methodology.
    This can be as simple as an introductory course or evening workshops.
5   Press government for more funding for sustainable behaviour projects and
    research (e.g. to support the SBU and equivalents in other countries).
6   Ask behaviour change project funders (including government) to set, and
    publicize in advance, minimum basic levels of evaluation, and mandate
    that they have been in existence for at least six months before any bid
    application could be accepted relating to that programme. This would
    help encourage the wider field to begin building their evidence base.

Up-scaling: as far as we can, as far as they can

When EcoTeams started, it was all about focusing on small steps which,
together, make a big difference. A recent paper in this area by Tom Crompton
(2009), of the World Wide Fund for Nature (WWF), has highlighted the
potential problems with this approach. Crompton argues that as long as the
pro-environmental behaviour change field relies on a 'virtuous escalator' of
people *automatically* moving on from small to big behaviours, we will fail in
our aims. The 'virtuous escalator' idea, as Crompton points out, underlies
many of today's major environmental campaigns. It is based on the assumption that if we can only get people to start doing some simple things like
recycling, switching off lights or appliances, and changing their lightbulbs,
then these behaviours will begin *automatically* to spill over into other areas,
leading to gradual wider lifestyle change. The evidence around this is inconsistent, and sometimes even suggests that doing small things allow people to
justify not doing the big things; for example: 'I don't need to drive less, I recycle' (Crompton, 2009). The key difference between this and the foot in the
door technique is that the latter makes a large request following a small, compared to the former which assumes the person will move onto larger action
without being requested (i.e. automatically).

Recent UK campaigns to reduce plastic bag use are one example. Certainly
it is admirable to reduce needless waste, a category within which the plastic
bag certainly sits comfortably. However, it is important to look at the side
effects of these campaigns too. Firstly, with limited resources, and big targets,
it is vital the pro-environmental movement works *efficiently*. Efficiency
demands exclusive focus on the things which will meet the target and as such
excludes campaigns focused solely on 'small impact behaviours' (unless they
are explicitly and meaningfully used as a hook to later *actively move* people
onto larger impact behaviours). Secondly, as mentioned above, research suggests that in motivating only small behaviours, individuals will sometimes
justify not initiating more meaningful change, as 'they've done their bit'. Being
purely speculative, the devil's advocate may suggest it is possible that plastic
bag campaigns might have actually done *more* harm to the environment than
good, through drawing attention and resources away from more action that
actually makes a significant difference (also again highlighting the need for

evaluation of programmes). Focus must be linked to relative emissions reductions, to be able to move beyond potential 'token' gestures such as reducing plastic bag use.

GAP have taken the criticisms of the WWF paper (Crompton, 2009) seriously, and set out to undertake focused research into quantifying just how much of the low impact behavioural uptake has led to higher impact behaviour change within EcoTeams, how spill-over occurs, and how they can optimize spill-over behaviours. As mentioned, results show that some EcoTeam participants move on to the most difficult behavioural changes, including dietary changes, reducing flights, reducing car use, and installing microgeneration or retrofitting their home (Baxter, 2009; Weeks, in progress). In addition, research suggests around 30 per cent of GAP participants move on to join other pro-environmental groups, campaigns or collective action after EcoTeams has finished (Global Action Plan, 2009), showing the programme's additional value in promoting wider environmental citizenship (see Chapter 7). Further research is currently focusing on quantifying what *proportion* of participants is moving on to higher impact behaviours and the reasons for this spill-over.

In realizing that EcoTeams are moving participants on to higher impact behaviours, but that they could potentially do more, programmes are being redesigned accordingly. EcoTeams no longer uses the message of 'small changes' for engagement. Rather, it leaves the level of change open whilst highlighting and contrasting the small-impact behaviours with the high-impact behaviours. It attempts to engage and motivate people to make the small changes and stresses that these are still important, whilst ensuring that participants do realize that there is much more they can do. It does this mainly through an 'impact hierarchy', which was developed to grade behaviours using explicit and transparent assumptions according to their carbon- or water-saving potential.[4] The feedback from participants so far has highlighted this as one of the most useful and liked aspects of EcoTeams (Global Action Plan, 2010).

The challenge to moving people on, without de-motivating and losing participants along the way, involves an intricate balance. Push too much, and EcoTeams may lose participants all together; push too little, and EcoTeams risk relying on the non-existent 'virtual escalator' (Crompton, 2009) and thus being inefficient. Ultimately, this will differ for each individual, and so the need for differentiated programmes which take this into account is also increasingly important if the programmes are to be effective enough to warrant up-scaling. This may involve differing levels of programme intensiveness with appropriate shifts in language, motivating factors, knowledge level, behavioural suggestions and commitment requirements. Behaviour change programmes must advance so that they *actively move* participants *as far as possible*, whatever their pro-environmental behaviour starting point.

I have four wishes on my 'as far as they can, for up-scaling' wish-list: I wish for every behaviour change programme to:

1   Give clear information on the impacts of each behaviour being encouraged relative to the other behavioural options available. Information on

impacts should be based as closely as possible on credible, official data (e.g. from government bodies or peer reviewed academic research), so programmes across the field are consistent.

2 Stop using 'small steps make a big difference' type messaging. Dave Mackay (2008, p114) argues: 'Don't be distracted by the myth that "every little helps". *If everyone does a little, we'll achieve only a little.* We must do a lot. What's required are *big* changes in demand and in supply.'

3 Design behaviour change programmes that *actively move* their participants as far as possible.

4 Not be scared to question what each other is doing in the behaviour change field, constructively and honestly, to ensure we are working *efficiently.*

I am aware that the above may come as a little hard-edged to some readers. I make no apologies though: if we are to make our targets, we are all going to need a lot more edge, focus, and efficiency to what we do.

Up-scaling: government policy as a barrier

Certain government policies act as a barrier to pro-environmental behaviour change, making behaviour change programmes less effective, and so reducing the chance of up-scaling. Further, criticism of government and of politicians is endless, in every sector and across every major decision they make. At times it is constructive, though often it is destructive, and this distinction is important. Criticize a politician and it is unlikely they will engage; however, approach them saying that 'we have a problem, and I believe I have thoughts that may help us solve that problem', and a more accommodating ear may be discovered. I want to focus in this section on what the pro-environmental behaviour change field could do, to more often find that accommodating ear in discussing policies that act as a barrier to programme up-scale; that is, engaging policy makers not only more frequently and with more effort, but more *effectively.* As such, this section outlines first three major criticisms of central government from the pro-environmental behaviour change field, and then offers ways in which we can all be better at helping our governments address these criticisms and so increase the potential to up-scale.

Considering criticism of direct policy implications first, there is a list too long to review here policies which make it difficult to 'be green'. Obvious examples include planning laws which make installing microgeneration labour-intensive, and tax systems which help to make flying cheaper than train travel and driving a car cheaper than public transport. These specific barriers were reiterated in the recent research on EcoTeams by Baxter (2009), and seem to limit the effectiveness of behaviour change programmes, hence damaging the case for up-scaling.

A second major criticism is regarding explicit government leadership. The UK Sustainable Development Commission report 'I will if you will' (SDC, 2006) outlines the significant barrier that government not leading by example poses, as individuals repetitively state they are not willing to change while they see government taking little action. The report called for the Government to 'set a visible example to the public, by making all central government buildings and transport carbon neutral by 2012, and putting a priority on changes such as sustainable food and on-site renewable energy in public settings like schools and hospitals' (p2). Unfortunately, the UK Government has made little progress on these issues relative to the potential for action. Additional difficulties for fostering public trust and willingness to act arise from contradictory policy-related messaging. For example, DEFRA's 'Act On CO_2' campaign asks individuals to 'switch off', or cycle instead of drive, whilst the Department for Transport approve airport expansion and fund road building at exponential levels compared to that for cycling facilities. Confusing messages from government present another barrier to pro-environmental behaviour change, its programmes and their up-scaling (see also Lorenzoni, Nicholson-Cole and Whitmarsh, 2007).

Potentially dwarfing these two previous areas, however, is the policy of endless economic growth. An in-depth discussion of this important area is not possible here, although a brief summary follows. Endless economic growth necessitates continuing and significant material throughput and waste production (including carbon), driven by increasing consumption by individuals. Jackson (2009) clearly and comprehensively argues that efficiency gains will only at best slow this throughput and waste production. In taking today's trends of efficiency gains, population and economic growth, and extrapolating them forward to 2050, Jackson shows that rather than emissions being at the IPCC's target of 80 per cent lower than 1990 levels, they will be 80 per cent higher! Further, Jackson shows that if we were to make IPCC targets in an equitable world where everyone earned roughly the same, the carbon intensity per dollar would have to be less than zero! The economy would somehow have to be generating money, whilst taking more carbon out of the atmosphere than it puts in. Consequently, it seems that in a planet with finite resources and waste-holding capacity, sustainability is genuinely a mathematical impossibility in the context of endless economic growth.

Why include this section within criticisms of government policy? It is perhaps unfair to label this as solely a central government policy, as it is more an ideology of the modern age, held central to our entire economic model, and so the businesses form the engine room, and the consumer and marketing provide the fuel. Nevertheless, it is central government, more than any other area in society, which holds the potential to change this. Unfortunately, at the moment, the understanding of the necessity, and indeed the benefits, that such a change could bring is not common within government. Yet the evidence in favour of change is stark. As shown in Figure 10.3, perceived well-being, happiness and levels of contentment in 'wealthy' nations are no longer rising with growth, and in some cases may be declining (Kasser, 2002).

Stress levels, time affluence (the feeling that one has sufficient time to pursue activities that are personally meaningful), mental illness and other quality of life indicators are moving in a negative direction, as the economy grows and people work harder, faster and longer hours, and communities dissolve in the age of individualism (Kasser, 2002).

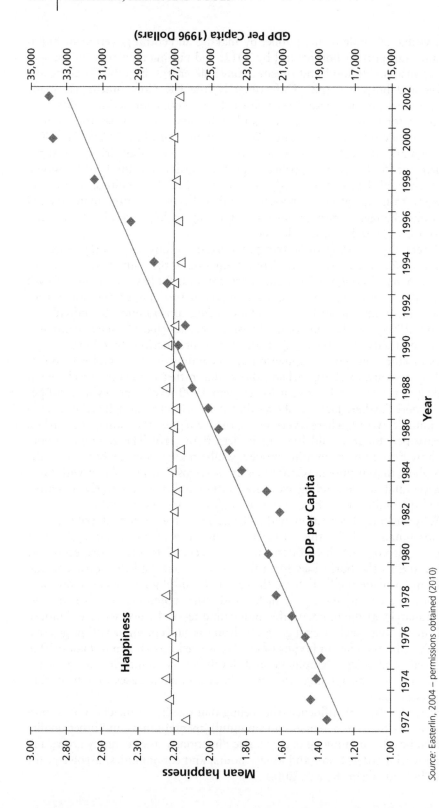

Source: Easterlin, 2004 – permissions obtained (2010)

Figure 10.3 *Perception of well-being against economic growth*

Helpfully, there is a momentum of discussion gathering around this topic as models are developed for zero- or low-growth economic models (Victor, 2008), and the evidence base demonstrating the inefficacy and unsustainability of endless economic growth in delivering prosperity is built (Kasser, 2002, 2004; Jackson, 2009). *Redefining Prosperity* (Jackson, 2009) presents a compelling argument for not only a change to our economic system as being necessary if we are to achieve a sustainable society, but as preferable on the basis that an alternative model would lead to a healthier and more prosperous society. Yet, economic growth – and associated individual consumption and waste production – remains a central ideology driving in some way or another all of government policy, and as such is probably the largest central government policy barrier to pro-environmental behaviour and thus the up-scaling of behaviour change programmes.

Up-scaling: helping government to help us

I have outlined three main areas of government policy which act as barriers to pro-environmental behaviour change, and to the efficacy and up-scaling of behaviour change programmes. These were contradictory policy, an inappropriate focus on information-only approaches and economic growth. How might our field help government in overcoming these barriers? To answer this question, I conducted informal interviews with five high-level individuals working in the behaviour change field within and alongside government. Surprisingly, the suggestions were incredibly simple, and yet included things which as a field we do not actively seek out to do. The suggestions include both getting effective behaviour change onto the policy makers' decision table directly and garnering policy makers' attention indirectly.

Firstly, it is important that we begin communicating more **collectively** with policy makers. As highlighted earlier, EcoTeams is an extremely effective programme, with a reasonably good evidence base, but is not strong enough by itself to attract the attention required to allow mass up-scaling. Other similar programmes could add collaborative and complementary weight to each other's voices. Such a lobby group would actively seek out and engage policy makers potentially using existing channels (e.g. in the UK, the charity Green Alliance). They would work on specific issues relevant to the field. These may include, for example, the importance of 'evidence-based behaviour change' versus 'information only' campaigns, or the need for additional funding for behaviour change programmes and evaluation. This lobby group would also be able to add its voice to calls for 'redefining prosperity'. Engaging policy makers collaboratively can offer a stronger voice to the concerns and successes of the behaviour change field, and gain support for the rationale to up-scale.

Expanding on the point briefly mentioned above, the field should assume that policy makers have not fully realized and internalized the message that information alone is necessary but not sufficient to create the kind of changes that they seek in individual behaviour. To do this they will need to support effective behavioural change programmes. The second suggestion in this section then is for the behaviour change field to *actively* engage policy makers, and repeatedly and directly utilize events and questions during conferences, meetings and events to make this message absolutely clear. The more it is discussed, the more prevalent it will be within policy makers' minds. This, I realize, may sound simplistic, but the behaviour change field is not making this message clear enough at the moment for policy makers to take it seriously. We are not doing the basics, and without the basics, we will not gain the traction needed to up-scale.

Finally, in terms of direct engagement, a suggestion is to invite relevant policy makers to round-tables with senior business leaders who support your behaviour change programme. It is important to be clear at this point, though, precisely how government might be involved with definite propositions. Bringing business and government *together* to share costs and match funding is a win–win situation. The behaviour change field must actively make these things happen to increase the chance of achieving the kind of up-scaling needed. Focusing on grassroots only will never be enough.

Similarly though, focusing on policy makers only will never be enough either, and in terms of considering both policy and individual behaviour change together, there is an opportunity to engage both areas in helping the other. Ockwell, Whitmarsh and O'Neill (2009) outline how this might work in an attempt to address the kinds of barriers to behaviour change discussed here. They argue that government information campaigns are ineffective in motivating behaviour change, and that given the difficulties around up-scaling and behaviour change itself for some behaviours, regulation may be a better option. At the same time they do, however, note that regulation will not be able to cover all behaviours (e.g. switching off lights, heating levels) and so call for the appropriate use of both government messaging and behaviour change programmes. This is outlined firstly as using government communication to gradually persuade citizens of the benefits of environmental regulation instead of motivating them to change behaviour. Secondly, Ockwell et al argue for the behaviour change field to aid this communication process in expanding their persuasion efforts to motivate individuals towards 'environmental citizenship' and engagement in the political process (see Chapter 7).

The pro-environmental behaviour change field has access to some of the most pro-environmentally motivated individuals in the UK. Moving participants on to be active participants in the democratic system and the community, once they have achieved the big behavioural wins in their own lifestyle, may be an excellent follow-up activity. It maintains engagement with programme participants longer, it adds value to the programme, and it begins to help tackle the infrastructural barriers that prevent or make difficult further change for both those individuals and the wider community. Behaviour change programmes which specialize in moving people onto new behaviours would barely need adapting other than in terms of added content, to move people onto engaging with local or central government. There may, in fact, be some potential for the pro-environmental behaviour change field to forge stronger links with the political activism movement (e.g. in the USA, Moveon.org, the campaign which helped motivate thousands of people to support Barrack Obama in his run for presidency). Research into EcoTeams suggests this is possible in two main ways. Firstly, it suggests that participants are eager to be involved further following participation in EcoTeams and may actually go on to join other programmes (Hobson, 2001; Staats et al, 2004; Burgess and Nye, 2008; Baxter, 2009; Global Action Plan, 2009). Secondly, specific research into the 'livable neighbourhood programme' in the USA (a second-generation EcoTeam aimed at 'effective neighbourhood mobilization') has shown that EcoTeams' participants go on to influence what products local stores are stocking (by applying pressure and demanding more ethical products), and develop actions to improve their neighbourhood (Van den Burg, Mol and Spaargaren, 2003). It is clear that EcoTeams' participants, at least, are keen to do more. Moving them on to politically engaging activity whilst strongly highlighting the links between their behaviours (and others they may seek to change) and government legislation, again may help in the eventual up-scaling of behaviour change programmes through the removal of policy barriers.

Alongside moving participants onto political involvement is ensuring that the behaviour change sought is contextualized within a journey towards a lifestyle which is in line with low or zero economic growth, or even 'de-growth'. Through making this desired lifestyle end point explicit, practitioners can begin to raise awareness of this crucial facet of sustainable development. This may aid a value shift helping to prepare the way for a less materialistic lifestyle for participants, though more importantly will help extend the debate around economic growth from beyond the academic and third sector walls to the public domain. This is an important step if low, zero or de-growth is to gain the political traction it needs to become a serious political issue.

Finally – and this extends beyond simply helping government – a further suggestion is for behaviour change practitioners to seek media partners. This may help in two main ways: firstly, it raises policy makers' awareness, if done effectively, of effective behaviour change programmes; secondly, it offers the policy maker an opportunity for the kind of public exposure gained through mass media information-only approaches. Using media partners and gaining mass media exposure for our programmes provides policy makers a win–win of both efficient cost per tonne of carbon savings and cost per capita reached with positive political messaging.

As such, practitioners should not be ashamed to use celebrities (see Boykoff and Goodman, 2008, for an excellent commentary) or standard marketing practices to gain exposure for their programmes, as long as their programme exemplifies good behaviour change practice. Marketing is a multi-billion dollar business for a reason: marketers are good at what they do. There is a vast range of possibilities for reality TV shows based around celebrities and their green behaviours. I would urge any pro-environmental behaviour change programme with the ideas and contacts to pursue this as a valuable option, ensuring that the behavioural change techniques involved be explicitly part of any such media exposure. The leverage this might have in moving the debate on from information-only could be significant in opening the doors for up-scaling for the pro-environmental behaviour change field.

In summary, then, my wish-list for the pro-environmental behaviour change field in engaging policy makers is to:

1   form a lobby group and speak with one voice rather than the frantic, pas-
     sionate and energetic individualism with which it currently does;
2   focus significant efforts on making visible to policy makers the inefficacy
     of mass media communication with evidence-based arguments, whilst
     contrasting it against effective behavioural change mechanisms;
3   apply pressure for significant funding for government-funded behavioural
     change research to build capacity for this field;
4   actively plan to bring policy makers and big business together around the
     field's agenda of good pro-environmental behaviour change initiatives,
     and actively find the angles, do the sums, and make the propositions that
     can make co-funded initiatives an attractive and cost-effective proposition
     for all stakeholders;
5   use media partners to highlight the effectiveness of behaviour change and
     the need for it to be up-scaled;
6   slightly expand their programmes not only to engage participants in indi-
     vidual pro-environmental behaviour change or community-based change,
     but to move participants on to be actively involved in the political process
     (see also Chapter 3).

4. Conclusion

In conclusion, there is a frenzy of disconnected yet fantastic behaviour change
programmes buzzing in isolated pockets all over the UK and in many other
countries. These contain models of excellent behaviour change programmes,
grounded on social psychological principles of behaviour change (e.g.
EcoTeams), which are genuinely making significant impacts. As long as these
initiatives remain small-scale and isolated, however, the potential this field
has to make a significant contribution to lifestyle change and carbon reduction targets will remain unrealized. To change this we, as a field, must do three
main things:

• we must develop a robust evidence base and we must move away from
  focusing solely on small behaviours or giving the impression that we only
  need to do small things to make a big difference;
• we must also collaborate as a field and with our programme participants;
• we must use this collaboration to effectively engage the policy makers in
  our area to help overcome policy barriers.

I hope this chapter has been helpful (and hopefully not patronizing) in highlighting the simple things that we have to do as a field, but that we are
currently not doing. To make a step change in the impacts we can achieve, we
are going to have to get back to some of the basics and do them not just effectively, but exceptionally. As Dave Mackay (2008, p114) says, in facing the
challenge of a sustainable energy supply: 'we cannot do a little, we must do a
lot'.

Notes

1   It is important to distinguish between the impact of EcoTeams and the impact of simple spill-over effects assumed to result from the foot in the door approach (discussed later). The EcoTeams approach engages participants at a depth and duration through powerful social mechanisms that seem sufficient to lead to a change of mindset. The foot in the door approach assumes that by simply motivating a small change, regardless of the depth, duration and strength of mechanism employed, a larger change may later happen: 'the virtuous escalator'. Clearly the latter is a very different approach and, as discussed in more detail later, has only inconsistent evidence in support of it.
2   www.surveymonkey.com
3   www.cbsm.com
4   Available within the EcoTeams programme at www.ecoteams.org.uk

References

Abrahamse, W. (2007) *Energy conservation through behavioural change: Examining the effectiveness of a tailor-made approach*, University of Groningen, Faculty of Behavioural and Social Sciences, available at http://dissertations.ub.rug.nl/faculties/ppsw/2007/w.abrahamse/, accessed 13 January 2010

Abrahamse, W., Steg, L., Vlek, C. and Rothengatter, T. (2007) 'The effect of tailored information, goal setting, and tailored feedback on household energy use, energy-related behaviors and behavioral antecedents', *Journal of Environmental Psychology*, vol 27, pp265–276

Bandura, A. (1977) *Social Learning Theory*, Prentice Hall, Englewood Cliffs, NJ

Baxter, M. (2009) What are the main motivators and barriers to the uptake of difficult pro-environmental behaviours within the EcoTeams setting? Unpublished MSc thesis, The Centre for Environmental Strategy, The University of Surrey

Bickerstaff, K. and Walker, G. (2001) 'Public understandings of air pollution: The "localization" of environmental risk', *Global Environmental Change*, vol 11, pp133–145

Boykoff, M. and Goodman, M. (2009) 'Conspicuous redemption: promises and perils of celebrity involvement in climate change', *Geoforum*, vol 40, no 3, 395–406

Burgess, J. and Nye, M. (2008) An evaluation of EcoTeams as a mechanism for promoting pro-environmental behaviour change at household and community scales. Unpublished report, Global Action Plan

Crompton, T. (2009) *Simple and Painless: The Limitations of Spillover in Environmental Campaigning*, WWF, http://assets.wwf.org.uk/downloads/simple_painless_report.pdf, accessed 3 February 2010

DeYoung, R. (1996) 'Some psychological aspects of reduced consumption behavior. The role of intrinsic motivation and competence motivation', *Environment and Behavior*, vol 28, pp358–409

DEFRA (2008a) *Climate Change Act*. Available at: http://www.opsi.gov.uk/acts/acts2008/ukpga_20080027_en_1, accessed 13 January 2010

DEFRA (2008b) *A Framework for pro-environmental behaviours*, available at http://www.defra.gov.uk/evidence/social/behaviour/pdf/behaviours-jan08-report.pdf, accessed 9 February 2010

Dillman, D. A., Smyth, J. D., Christian, L. M. (2008) *Internet, Mail, and Mixed-Mode Surveys: The Tailored Design Method*, Wiley, New York, http://www.websm.org/

2009/09/Bibliography/Internet_Mail_and_MixedMode_Surveys_The_Tailored_Design_Method_/?&page=1&avtor=15, accessed 13 January 2010

Easterlin, R. (2005) 'Feeding the illusion of growth and happiness: A reply to Hagerty and Veenhoven', *Social Indicators Research*, vol 74, no 3, pp429–443

Feltz, D., Short, S. and Sullivan, P. J. (2008) 'Self-efficacy in sport: Research strategies for working with athletes, teams and coaches', *Human Kinetics*, vol 3, no 2, pp293–295

Giddens, A. (1984) *The Constitution of Society*, University of California Press, Berkeley

Global Action Plan (2009) Internal Research conducted as part of the City Bridge Trust EcoTeams Project, 2009. Unpublished report

Global Action Plan (2010) Internal research on effectiveness of EcoTeams. Unpublished report, Global Action Plan

Goldstein, N. J., Martin, S. J. and Cialdini, R. B. (2007) *Yes! 50 Secrets from the Science of Persuasion*, Profile Books, London

Hobson, K. (2001) 'Sustainable lifestyles: Rethinking barriers and behaviour change', in M. J. Cohen and J. Murphy (eds) *Exploring Sustainable Consumption: Environmental Policy and the Social Sciences*, Pergamon, Oxford, pp191–209

Hunter, J. A., Cox, S. L., O'Brien, K., Stringer, M., Boyes, M., Banks, M., Hayhurst, J. G. and Crawford, M. (2005) 'Threats to group value, domain-specific self-esteem and intergroup discrimination amongst minimal and national groups', *British Journal of Social Psychology*, vol 44, pp329–353

Jackson, T. (2005) *Motivating Sustainable Consumption – A Review of Evidence on Consumer Behaviour and Behaviour Change. A report to the Sustainable Development Research Network*, Policy Studies Institute, London

Jackson, T. (2009) *Prosperity Without Growth: Economics for a Finite Planet*, Earthscan, London

Kasser, T. (2002) *The High Price of Materialism*, MIT Press, Cambridge, MA

Kasser, T. (2004) 'The good life or the goods life? Positive psychology and personal well-being in the culture of consumption', in P. A. Linley and S. Joseph (eds) *Positive Psychology in Practice*, Wiley, Hoboken, New Jersey, pp55–67

Lorenzoni, I., Nicholson-Cole, S. and Whitmarsh, L. (2007) 'Barriers perceived to engaging with climate change among the UK public and their policy implications', *Global Environmental Change*, vol 17, nos 3–4, pp445–459

MacKay, D. J. C. (2008) *Sustainable Energy – Without the Hot Air*, UIT, Cambridge

McKenzie-Mohr, D. (2008) 'Fostering sustainable behaviour: beyond brochures', *International Journal of Sustainable Communication*, vol 3, pp108–118

Moser, S. C. and Dilling, L. (2007) *Creating a Climate for Change: Communicating Climate Change and Facilitating Social Change*, Cambridge University Press, Cambridge, UK, p294

Ockwell, D., Whitmarsh, L. and O'Neill, S. (2009) 'Reorienting climate change communication for effective mitigation – forcing people to be green or fostering grass-roots engagement?', *Science Communication*, vol 30, no 3, pp305–327

SDC (2006) *I Will if You Will*, The Sustainable Development Commission, London

Spaargaren, G. and Van Vliet, B. (2000) 'Lifestyle, consumption and the environment: the ecological modernisation of domestic consumption', *Society and Natural Resources*, vol 9, pp50–76

Staats, H., Harland, P. and Wilke, H. A. M. (2004) 'Effecting durable change: A team approach to improve environmental behavior in the household', *Environment and Behavior*, vol 36, no 3, pp341–367

Stern, P. (2000) 'Toward a coherent theory of environmentally significant behavior', *Journal of Social Issues*, vol 56, no 3, pp407–424

Tajfel, H. and Turner, J. C. (1979) 'An integrative theory of intergroup conflict', in W. G. Austin and S. Worchel (eds) *The Social Psychology of Intergroup Relations*, Brooks-Cole, Monterey, CA

Van den Burg, S. W. K., Mol, A. P. J. and Spaargaren, G. (2003) 'Consumer-oriented monitoring and environmental reform', *Environment and Planning C: Government and Policy*, vol 21, pp371–388

Victor, P. A. (2008) *Managing Without Growth: Slower by Design, Not Disaster*, Edward Elgar Publishing, Cheltenham, UK

11
The Role and Effectiveness of Governmental and Non-governmental Communications in Engaging the Public with Climate Change

Gemma Regniez and Savita Custead

1. Introduction and context setting

This chapter aims to provide a practitioner's view of current climate change communications, primarily focusing on the UK context. We discuss the ways in which governmental and non-governmental approaches can engage individuals with relevant issues, and indicate the extent to which some of these efforts have been successful. In the following sections, we discuss examples of communications aiming to engage the public with climate change, drawing on evidence of their objectives and efficacy from various documentary sources. Subsequently, in order to provide the reader with wider understandings and interpretations of approaches in this area, we present perspectives from a selection of leading communicators before concluding with our key findings and recommendations.

For the purpose of this chapter, we broadly distinguish governmental approaches, at both national and local level, from non-governmental efforts, including 'grassroots' movements such as the Low Carbon Communities Network (LCCN) and more campaign-centric examples by not-for-profit organizations such as the 'Not Stupid' campaign. The latter category also includes national media and recognized business brands such as UK high street chain Marks and Spencer. In many cases, these major commercial organizations are positioning themselves alongside numerous not-for-profit organizations (e.g. the association of the *Guardian* and the *Sun* newspapers with the 10:10 campaign). For this reason, we have grouped these organizations into one (albeit heterogeneous) category, while recognizing the diversity of interests, resources and approaches that exist amongst non-governmental organizations. We also acknowledge that governmental and non-governmental organizations often do (and should) work together to engage the public.

As mentioned in the Introduction to this book, political leaders appear to welcome the pressure that grassroots approaches are bringing, namely because it provides them with a mandate to do what they need to do to make real changes in key situations. In December 2009, the UK Secretary of State for Energy and Climate Change, Ed Miliband, called for the creation of a global 'popular mobilization' campaign to pressure world leaders into tackling climate change, while recognizing: 'There will be some people saying, "we can't go ahead with an agreement on climate change. It's not the biggest priority." And therefore, what you need is countervailing forces. Some of those countervailing forces come from popular mobilization ... Political change comes from leadership and popular mobilization. And you need both of them' (Miliband; as cited in Adam and Jowit, 2009).

In this chapter, we distinguish our criteria for evaluating the campaigns we review into four areas, to reflect impacts on the public and the objectives of the organizations involved, namely: (a) levels of public engagement (e.g. increased awareness, attitude change, behaviour change); (b) ability of the public to influence policy; (c) sustainability (i.e. durability/longevity); and (d) relations to policy, social, economic or other objectives.

We look at examples of communications-based initiatives that have resulted in a clear positive action on the part of the audience they have aimed at. For governmental communications, this could be the number of those people reporting to have insulated their homes (a key policy priority for reducing the UK's carbon footprint[1]). For non-governmental approaches we can look to examples like the LCCN, and in particular identify where grassroots approaches can help achieve national policy objectives as well as produce other, broader (e.g. social) benefits, and how they can be better sustained as part of wider initiatives with numerous partners.

We argue that key to any successful communication to engaging the public with climate change will be the development of a consistent approach which incorporates complementary messaging and imagery across all activities. We look in particular at examples of organizations who have grouped together to engage the public in a communications activity wider than their own organization, offering a consistent and clear approach. This collaborative model could provide communications professionals with the scope to combine the best of governmental, social and commercial approaches, resulting in empowerment of the community they serve to support their own efforts against climate change.

2. Examples of communicating climate change

To provide the reader with a broad overview of the current campaigns running in the UK at the time of writing, we have chosen to review some of the most high-profile government and business-led campaigns, community projects and networks in relation to climate change issues. This review does not attempt to cover every initiative; rather, it provides a review of a selection of illustrative governmental and non-governmental examples. They have been chosen on the basis of their levels of sustainability, engagement and abilities to feed into policy, including relation to national indicators, and direct or indirect connection with policy initiatives.

All the examples that follow are similar in that they all aim to engage the public in the issue of climate change and initiate some form of action, be it behavioural change through turning household appliances off standby to an overall cut of individual emissions by 10 per cent. What differentiates them is the means in which they try to instigate that change and the form of advice they provide concerning what makes the most difference. Key questions that this review should help to answer include: Who is best placed to communicate climate change messages to the public? Who are the experts in this field? Whom do the public trust for advice in this area and whose voice is loudest?

National government

Campaign	ACT ON CO$_2$ www.direct.gov.uk/actonco2

Background	Launched as the Government's vehicle for communicating climate change messages to the public in 2007. Two departmental campaigns were launched in parallel: one designed to raise awareness of 'smarter' driving led by the Department for Transport; one designed to inform the public of the new government brand and the ways in which they could minimize their individual impacts on the UK's carbon emissions. The longer-term plan at its launch was to provide the ACT ON CO$_2$ branding to 'badge' all government departments wishing to communicate messages in relation to their policies to the public (pre the elections in 2010). This aims to provide consistency to any messaging coming from within government and highlights links across related issue areas like water and energy (e.g. the Department of Environment, Food and Rural Affairs (Defra)'s 'Water, use it, don't waste it' campaign). It also provides a link to credible partnerships with stakeholders funded by government departments such as the Energy Saving and Carbon Trusts, and the private sector such as Asda, Little Chef, John Lewis and Total. The most recent campaign approach uses a combination of everyday tips for saving money and energy with a more controversial emotional appeal-based approach. By using a child as the main character who is being read a bed-time story describing devastating impacts of climate change, it emphasizes our responsibility to our children to leave them with a 'happy ending',[2] along with providing practical advice on how we can make a difference. ACT ON CO$_2$ has focused on a mass media approach through television, online and press presences. A sub-brand of the campaign 'ACT ON Copenhagen' was created to provide the public with a 'one-stop shop' for information on the UK's standing for the COP15 discussions in December 2009.
Level of public engagement	The campaign evaluation (TNS, 2009) involving face-to-face interviews with the public throughout the campaign duration (September to December 2008), combined with Defra's regular attitudes survey (2009), found that in respect of interest and attitudes towards energy saving activities, the campaigns achieved:

- *More people, compared with two years ago, say they have thought about saving energy in the home*; 77 per cent of respondents disagreed with the statement 'I don't really give much thought to saving energy in the home', compared with 62 per cent in 2007.
- *Most participants claimed to have taken some action as a result of seeing the campaign*, most commonly low-investment behaviours such as turning off lights (53 per cent) and checking/inflating tyres (51 per cent).
- *Higher impact from the home energy component is in part attributed to greater advertising*, including on TV (TNS, 2009). Other recent surveys (Defra, 2009) suggest awareness about climate change and key terms (e.g. carbon footprint) is rising, but that a sizeable minority (28 per cent) agree that 'I don't believe my everyday behaviour and lifestyle contribute to climate change', unchanged from 2007.

In terms of energy use and home insulation, the majority of people reported they have adopted energy saving behaviours in the home, with an overall increase in those cutting down on energy use, compared with two years ago; for example:

- 76 per cent said they were cutting down on the use of gas and electricity at home, compared with 58 per cent in 2007.

Although not all of these results can or should be attributed solely to the campaign, the larger majority of the public are reported to be acting on the key behaviours prescribed by the campaign and the policies it supports. This is a positive outcome, with the caveat that 'reported' behaviour change is not necessarily 'actual' change. Evidently, the campaign still has work to do in convincing the public of the effects of their own everyday behaviour and, some would say, their ongoing reluctance to accept the existence of climate change.

The campaign has also had a marked effect on those challenging the effects of climate change, causing numerous bodies to challenge the methods and statistics used within the more hard-hitting element of the campaign (the Advertising Complaints Authority received over 100 complaints for the depiction of devastation detailed in the 'Happy Ending' creative). Is this the lead the Government should be taking, using a clear message to the public of what the worst case scenarios could be if no action is taken? Our interviewees discuss this issue further in the following section.

Ability to influence policy	The campaign was not intended to provide a role for the public in shaping policy, but influence rather to encourage low-carbon lifestyle change. The campaign itself works in support of particular government policies (see below).
Sustainability	The top-down approach here is highly sustainable given the UK Government's ongoing commitment to tackling the causes of climate change and ongoing need for a 'badge' for government campaigns. Partnering this with private sector partners is a better fit than with a credible grassroots approach, and any attempt to link with non-government initiatives will depend upon how best this campaign can be used to support more locally-based initiatives.
Relations to policy, social, economic or other objectives	The UK was the first country to commit to internationally binding carbon targets and must meet an 80 per cent reduction in carbon emissions by 2050. The 40 per cent of the UK's CO_2 emissions that are a result of personal choice (individuals) form a key part of the Government's strategy to reduce carbon emissions, and the ACT ON CO_2 campaign is aimed specifically at combating that 40 per cent. In particular, the campaign has been designed to support policy delivery, and rollout, for example, the 'great British refurb' announced in February 2009 (see footnote 1) that encouraged

the public to take up offers on discounted insulation and double glazing and benefits available to specific members of the public (e.g. the elderly).

The campaign also aims to raise awareness of policies such as the Carbon Emission Reduction Target (CERT) launched in April 2008, which has helped five million households install insulation.

NGO national campaigns

Campaign	Not Stupid Campaign, www.ageofstupid.net/

| Background | Not Stupid is the global campaigning arm born out of the film *Age of Stupid*, released in March 2009. The brainchild of Franny Armstrong, Director of 'McLibel', and producer John Battsek (*One Day In September*), the film stars Pete Postlethwaite as a man living alone in the devastated future world of 2055, looking at old footage from 2008 and asking: 'why didn't we stop climate change when we had the chance?'.

Not Stupid developed as the call to action for people viewing the film, independent of any top-down influences. The campaign began with an aim to turn 250 million global viewers into climate activists via their oneclimate.net network. |
|---|---|
| Level of public engagement | Reportedly 250 million viewers were at premieres in the UK, USA, Australia, India, Canada, Belgium and many other countries; the *Age of Stupid* film and the ensuing call to action are reaching a vast audience across the world. What specific action is stemming from this approach is more difficult to quantify. |
| Ability to influence policy | Despite retaining a grassroots approach, the Not Stupid campaign successfully engaged Ed Miliband (Secretary of State for Energy and Climate Change 2008–10) on a number of occasions. The campaign claims, as a result of the high-profile challenge to the Secretary of State made by Pete Postlethwaite (the star of the film) at the film's premiere in London in March 2009, that UK Coal Policy was amended – but it is unclear how. |
| Sustainability | This was a campaign aimed very specifically at getting a positive result at the climate change discussions held in Copenhagen in December 2009. It is unclear whether it will have a legacy post the negotiations. Although a credible campaign in itself, its founders have now moved on to develop the 10:10 campaign with other partners (see next example). |
| Relations to policy, social, economic or other objectives | The Not Stupid campaign is aligning itself with another grassroots campaign: the 10:10 campaign, which focuses on higher reductions in a shorter time-frame than the 80 per cent by 2050 announced by the Government. |

Campaign	10:10, www.1010uk.org

Background	A partnership between public and private sectors and individuals, the 10:10 campaign was developed as a result of the findings from the Climate Safety report, published by the Public Interest Research Centre (2008). This research identified the urgent need for more immediate targets – namely 10 per cent by 2010 – as research points to shorter time-frames for turning the effects of climate change around.[3]

10:10 is another project born out of the team from Age of Stupid, but has successfully engaged partners from governmental and non-governmental institutions alike, obtaining support from celebrities, politicians, the media including tabloid press (Jackson, 2009), and the private sector. The campaign is mainly PR focused, with a concentration on obtaining high-profile spokespeople (the lead singer of the band Radiohead signed up during the talks at Copenhagen) and media channels to spread messaging concerning lowering carbon emissions by 10 per cent per individual.[4]

Level of public engagement	At the time of writing, 10:10 was still an online campaign, which limited the range of individuals and organizations drawn to sign up. With support from the *Guardian* and other liberal media sources, initial supporters very much reflected the traditional readership of the source by which they had been introduced to the campaign. When asked, the campaign leaders were satisfied with the progress of the campaign, recognizing the role that local and neighbourhood champions could play as 'early adopters' of the principles of the campaign. In addition, a number of prominent 'big business' representatives signed up, as well as local councils – many of whom saw 10:10 as a way to reach targets on national government-set indicators.
Ability to influence policy	10:10 is an illustrative example of an engineered bottom-up campaign, with a route to government and policy that is straightforward (at least for the campaign if not necessarily for those who have signed up to it), in addition to having access to policy makers by having them sign up to the campaign directly. Early on, the Cabinet signed up to the pledge and the Shadow Cabinet quickly followed. Less than ten months after its inception, the UK's Liberal Democrat party tabled a motion to debate 10:10 in the UK parliament. All parties were voicing great interest in the potential for mass engagement and direct democracy.
Sustainability	Even with all of the publicity, high-profile signatories and support from government, campaign leaders were saying at the approach to 2010 that there were no plans on the table to continue the campaign after one year. The programme has been deliberately created as a short-term project with temporary staff. For those supporting, such questions of legacy may still linger, with a possibility that the contacts may be passed along to active partners such as the Low Carbon Communities Network and the Sustainable Development Commission. Professional communicators will be watching to see the impact of the short-term campaign, and how levels of commitment and enthusiasm continue into the following years.
Relations to policy, social, economic or other objectives	This campaign looks to a closer deadline to achieve results, aiming for a 10 per cent reduction in the UK's carbon emissions by 2010 unrelated to the Government's 80 per cent by 2050. It is unclear whether it has wider more socially orientated objectives; however, by its very nature, it has succeeded in capturing the attention of a wider mix of partners both nationally and locally.

NGO local initiatives

Campaign	*Low Carbon Communities Network, www.lowcarboncommunities.net/*

Background	The Low Carbon Communities Network (LCCN; see also Chapter 14) was formed in 2007 and provides an illustrative example of the potential impact of bottom-up campaigning, as well as a key case study on the organizational trajectory that such organizations might take. The LCCN's current mission statement is 'to link, network and support the rapidly growing movement of climate change groups that are

forming at a local and community level'. Like many initiatives, the development of this body represents the evolution of a 'top-down' structure (in this case a coordinating network) to bring together and try to augment grassroots activity. In the initial phases, back in 2007, the founders of the network were seeking a model to support existing communities in their climate reduction activities. The network grew organically as additional communities joined who felt they would have a stronger voice in an umbrella structure. In October 2008 an open and democratic vote of members was held, and the network unanimously agreed to seek legal status for the structure, with a result that the LCCN gained official Not for Profit status.

Level of public engagement
Tracey Todhunter, one of the founding directors of the network, was interviewed about the project, and noted the diversity of the members and the variety that this brings to engagement interventions with the public. She notes that LCCN members have a common starting point – selecting actions and schemes which they feel are appropriate for their own community – but with strong differences in method. There are no set indicators or parameters for action, and the groups have the license to think creatively and imaginatively about what will work well on their own doorstep.

Ability to influence policy
There appears to be a shared sense of frustration among members with local authority approaches to the threat of climate change, traditional policy initiatives and the pace of policy making. This has had a positive outcome, leading to a commitment to move forward at a faster pace with community projects and individual action. As Tracey Todhunter describes, the prevalent sentiment is 'we want to do it for ourselves'.

When it came to showcasing this community work and connecting it with policy, the network played a key role. One of the key developments for the LCCN was commissioning a website, which gave it a visible presence to the outside world. From this, community members began to be invited to policy events, could access consultation documents, and had a recognizable form that they could point to and claim membership of. The network played a strong brokering role connecting communities to policy and relevant consultations. At each stage it promoted communities giving direct feedback to policy initiatives, rather than responding with a diluted or averaged response. Although the network may have been a type of imposed top-down structure, it did not hinder bottom-up activity or the direct voices of community members.

Another way this grassroots activity connected with policy, particularly in the early days, was their involvement in the development of government National Indicators – particularly Indicator 186 (reduction of domestic emissions). A number of local authorities joined the network itself with an aim of connecting with communities who were interested in taking part. It could be that local authorities were looking for a cost-effective way of achieving their targets, yet a more positive view would be that they recognized the potential of supporting grassroots activity. Throughout the process, a number of communities began to understand the language of indicators and process of policy; in short, a common language began to emerge.

Two years after its inception, the LCCN members witnessed the development of the Government's Low Carbon Communities Strategy, a strong recognition of the potential for community led activity. In addition, the Energy Saving Trust outlined its strategy for 'Green Communities' – a policy that bore a strong resemblance to the LCCN model and was likely influenced by it. 2009 was an exciting time for the network, who could continue to play a brokering role between individual communities and departments such as DECC and Defra, and continue to support communities who had found their own voices and were continuing to influence policy, as well as drive change in their communities. Yet the developments at a national level, and the addition of more top-down programmes, also raised the issue of the sustainability of the LCCN itself.

Sustainability Reviewing the work of the LCCN over time, one realizes that the role of the network itself may be short lived, but soon after the creation of the network the grassroots activity it represents has not only been strengthened, but led to a number of unexpected policy outcomes as mentioned above.

The political aims of the network make it difficult for it to obtain charitable status, and the future at the time of writing is uncertain. The founders have a sense of pride that the network has taken on a life of its own, and do not necessarily see any difficulty in any direction the LCCN members may choose for the network, especially as they are now strong, influential and growing. While both community and local authority members had been strengthened by the network, and policy makers were beginning to recognize the impact of community led action, in some senses the LCCN had completed the task it had been set up to do.

Relations to policy, social, economic or other objectives
As described in Chapter 14, the aims of the network are not solely (or even primarily) to support policy objectives to reduce carbon emissions. Rather, there are clear social reasons for individuals' involvement, including support from and interaction with like-minded people, providing them with a base from which to launch their own initiatives.

Private sector

Campaign	Marks and Spencer (M&S) Plan A, http://plana.marksandspencer.com/

Background M&S launched Plan A in January 2007, setting out 100 commitments to achieve in five years. Through Plan A, they are working with their customers and suppliers on delivering their 'five pillars': combat climate change, reduce waste, use sustainable raw materials, trade ethically and help customers to lead healthier lifestyles:

'We're doing this because it's what you want us to do. It's also the right thing to do. We're calling it Plan A because we believe it's now the only way to do business. There is no Plan B.'[5]

Level of public engagement
Prior to launching Plan A, M&S ran its 'Look Behind the Label' education campaign. This engaged their customers in their products and policies, prior to introducing the changes Plan A has brought. By running this activity prior to Plan A, M&S aimed to help their customers understand and therefore appreciate the changes being instigated. As John Grant (2007) writes in his book *Green Marketing Manifesto*: 'there is an interesting psychology to this. M&S is letting customers be ethical consumers, through products they may have already bought; it is therefore a much smaller psychological step to do more' (p144).

Reportedly 17,201 people (businesses and customers related to M&S) had committed to pledges with Plan A since January 2007 (at the time of writing). They have partnerships with key non-government organizations such as WWF, but no obvious public-facing partnership with government.

Reportedly 39 of the 100 commitments under Plan A had been completed; of these, 24 of the targets had been raised and, after 12 months, the decision to charge 5p for single-use food carrier bags cut the use of bags by 83 per cent from 464 million to 77 million bags – the £1.2 million profit generated from the charge has gone to the environmental charity Groundwork.

Ability to influence policy	Plan A has become an integral part of company policy for M&S and others within the business sector look to this model for inspiration. However, M&S does not appear to have looked to influence wider government policy with the campaign.
Sustainability	In its latest sustainability report, 'How We Do Business 2009',[6] M&S states that, prior to launching, they were prepared to invest £200 million over five years in Plan A, but that two years on it has already become cost positive, making it good business sense. In the words of Sir Stuart Rose, Managing Director: 'Plan A isn't a project, it's the modern expression of how we do business. It builds on core values that have underpinned the business from the beginning – Quality, Value, Service, Innovation and Trust. Trust is a value that is ever more important in today's economic climate. By doing what we believe is right, we will continue to build strong, trustworthy relationships with our customers, our partners, and our people – long into the future.' As indicated below, the environmental and economic benefits of this work suggest it represents a sustainable approach to engagement.
Relations to policy, social, economic or other objectives	M&S have pledged to make their operations in the UK and the Republic of Ireland carbon neutral by 2012, and help their customers and suppliers reduce their emissions too. The company has reduced CO_2 emissions in its stores, offices, warehouses and delivery vehicles by nearly 100,000 tonnes, an 18 per cent decrease on their 2006–7 baseline. They have also brokered the UK retail sector's biggest renewable energy contract with NPower. The six-year deal will see NPower provide M&S with 2.6TWh of renewable electricity from April 2009 – enough to ultimately power all of the retailer's stores and offices in England and Wales.

These illustrative examples showcase a number of common themes across programmes engaging the public with climate change. First, each of the examples demonstrates an increasing commitment to working in partnership, particularly across sectors. Another theme – specific to the focus on climate change – is the role of targets, baseline data and recognizing achievement. In setting targets – or positioning a campaign to achieve targets faster than another group – an engagement body relies on available baseline data, as well as methods for measurement and tracking of emission reductions. One of the most interesting threads here, central to any review of related programmes, is how the call to action (whether awareness raising, lobbying or individual action on climate change measures) is achieved. National and local government programmes are most likely to inform, legislate, or offer financial incentives to promote action. Non-governmental and locally centred programmes are more likely to appeal to intrinsic or community-based motivating factors. Both approaches may have the same result, and practitioners may choose an approach based on speed of the outcome, resources available, motivations or desires of the target audience, or previous successes.

All of the initiatives featured are effective and innovative in their own right. It would be interesting to see how they could be drawn together to further complement each other. Some work is already being done to identify partnerships and 10:10 exists as a result of a number of partners joining together to connect climate change messages with the public. Arguably, more needs to be done to join up messaging across all of these initiatives, and moving forward this could be a key indication of success for this form of communication.

As to our earlier questions concerning who is best placed to communicate climate change messages to the public and who are the experts in this field, there is definitely no consensus at this stage. Government is trying to respond to public demand to take a strong lead with its two-phased approach, and research suggests this is where the public turn to for advice (TNS, 2009). Currently, this remains criticized and challenged by wider stakeholders who choose to run their own separate initiatives. Whom do the UK public trust for advice in this area and whose voice is loudest? Arguably it is the Government. However, recognized and trusted brands such as M&S also have a key role to play in communicating and facilitating the availability of alternatives to a public who remain confused and increasingly exasperated with the plethora of messages aimed at them in this area.

3. Views on climate change communications by key communications professionals

To provide the reader with alternative viewpoints of what makes a successful climate change campaign, the following section reports on interviews carried out in October and November 2009 with recognized experts within the communications and engagement sector. The interviewees lend their thoughts on governmental and non-governmental approaches to communicating climate change, and what denotes success and/or failure for them. We had hoped to also provide a balanced political viewpoint to this selection; however ministers and shadow ministers were unavailable for comment. Interviewees were probed on their views of governments creating movements behind public issues, the dangers of mixed messages and unrelated campaigns targeted at the public, their own suggestions for what is currently working in the UK in this area, and what channels should be used to effectively engage the public moving forward.

The interviewees were provided with a series of questions in face-to-face or telephone meetings, and the following is a summary of those interviews. All the accounts that follow represent the views of the interviewee and not the authors of this book.

Government perspectives

Paddy Feeny
Paddy Feeny, Communications Director for the Department for Energy and Climate Change, holds responsibility for overseeing the latest government communications approaches concerning climate change to the general public. His view is that government's 'top-down' communications on climate change are just as important as grassroots campaigns in maintaining the ongoing debate and driving the action needed to obtain the 80 per cent targets that government is working towards for 2050.

For Feeny, the Government's role is four-fold:

- to provide people with clear information about the problem (in an environment where numerous voices are trying to be heard, government can play the part of the authority figure);
- to provide consumers with the means of changing their lifestyles, with a sliding scale from exhortation to regulation;
- by publicly encouraging wider grassroots 'movements' and supporting 'coalitions of the willing'; and most importantly
- by providing the sign-off for the larger decisions required for the development of sustainable infrastructure; for example, the investigation and use of nuclear and/or renewable energies as alternatives.

Feeny asserts that many of those who claim to be most concerned about the environment are against the use of nuclear and don't like the 'aesthetics' of wind farms, but still want low-carbon energy. For Feeny, it is down to the Government to lead and make the hard decisions that are in the interests of the public.

When considering government's involvement in bottom-up approaches, Feeny is clear: government can provide public support in the guise of turning up to events and will encourage groups to create pressure and raise awareness, but to provide overt support or attempt to 'create' a bottom-up approach would be the 'kiss of death' to any genuine grassroots attempts to galvanize the public.

In the example of the 'Make Poverty History' campaign, government acted as a mediator between the various charities and non-government organizations involved, but did not move to own the approach in any way. Similarly, in the various grassroots campaigns such as 10:10 and the 'Tck Tck Tck' campaign, Feeny welcomes the engagement of ministers, but cautions this should be without losing the organization's independence, the very thing that gives bottom-up approaches the opening to be challenging and debate the status quo.

For Feeny, the key role for government is leadership; the job of ministers and government departments is to tell the public what they need to know, even if it is not necessarily what they want to hear. Playing the authoritative role in communicating climate change related messages can take three key approaches:

1 Providing the expert voice of science and ensuring it has a place at the table of communicating climate change. The Chief Scientist plays a key role in government decision making, and provides a lead authority on the science of climate change and government thinking over and above any other voices.
2 Managing individual behaviour: helping consumers make the journey to low-carbon living, and showcasing the positive benefits in skills, economic growth and lifestyle.
3 Providing independent, impartial help and advice to consumers, especially the vulnerable, through schemes like Warmfront and carbon offsetting.

For Feeny, the future for the Government's ACT ON CO_2 campaign, at least within the Department for Energy and Climate Change, should be rooted in the science of climate change, filling the hole that currently exists where the 'chief medical officer' for climate change would sit. This could see an ongoing move away from the focus on the individual, which features in the campaigns already in existence from various organizations across the UK and more of a focus on the effects, much like the messages featured in the 'Happy Ending' creative featured in the government campaign in December 2009. He mentions in particular the need for consistency in all messages aimed at the public.

Feeny believes evidence is beginning to show that confusion surrounding the existence of climate change appears to be abating as more evidence arises; however, there remains doubt around how serious the issue may be. The UK Government will need to be responsible for delivering the bad news as well as the good, with a balance between 'exhortation and regulation'; in his view, a hard job for any Minister for Energy to handle.

Mark Lund

Mark Lund is Chief Executive of the government agency the Central Office of Information, and formerly Chief Executive of the advertising agency Delaney Lund Knox Warren, responsible for the hard-hitting stroke awareness campaign for the Department for Health. In the case of government communications for climate change, Mark Lund's view is clear: government must set the agenda, the scope of the problem and identify ways in which to solve it. The issue is whether setting out the problem automatically gets people to do something about it as a result. For Lund, the essential ingredient for behavioural change communications is what he calls the 'man in the mirror' element: any activity needs to probe the viewer to ask 'what am I going to do about it?', and this is where bottom-up can play a role. A partnership between government and grassroots can facilitate a flow of message solutions which, if coming directly from the top-down, would otherwise seem too 'preaching', and could result in a loss of credibility or appeal.

Although many grassroots campaigns on the surface are opposing government, digging deeper reveals many common objectives which Lund feels is an opportunity for consistency in the overcrowded 'green' marketplace. Government should not aim to create social movements, but grassroots can and should provide pressure that can direct government policy, even if it goes against the current status quo.

For Lund, the Government's ACT ON CO_2 campaign has the potential to meet the Government's leadership requirement as long as it maintains consistency. Splitting the campaign creative across the departments, rather than pooling resources and creating one larger campaign, for him risks its overall ability to impact. A more inclusive partnership with organizations outside of government will be the key to influencing a confused and reticent public.

Lund's experience working with the private sector means he is well aware of the potential consumer brands could have in this area. For example, working in partnership with government and pressure groups, using brands such as Ariel, M&S and Persil, who have an everyday affinity with family life, can produce clear results. Ariel's 30 degree campaign has been celebrated as one of the key ways in which to instigate simple behaviour change in a short time-frame. Lund encourages us to imagine the impact if this influence joined a tripartite alliance with the government and non-government sector. He main-tains government should lead this partnership, working to galvanize the commercial sector behind one goal. He mentions the Change4Life campaign, led by the Department of Health, as an example of how this kind of approach can work well. Success in this area requires that tribal mistrust across the pub-lic and private sectors will need to be overcome, and Lund's view is that it should be the Government that makes this work.

From a channel's perspective, Lund sees clear roles for government and other sectors. Mass media with an immediate reach, such as television, is a key top-down technique which can grab public attention quickly. Television, com-plemented by more disruptive approaches preferred by the grassroots element, can create a two-pronged approach to raise awareness levels. Once engaged, the conversation between the public and more bottom-up levels can begin via social media platforms such as Twitter, where the rule of six degrees of sepa-ration (i.e. individuals who would normally be several steps removed in a social network and not in direct contact) has been completely broken down. Again, the tripartite partnership between government, grassroots and the pri-vate sector works well here. Brands can set up the interest levels, but are unable to build the form of relationship with the public grassroots organiza-tions can, or the authority and guidance that government provides. For Lund, a successful partnership between the three groups and their chosen channels is key to achieving effective and consistent climate change communications.

Business and grassroots perspectives

Chris Powell

Chris Powell is Chairman of BMP-DDB – the advertising agency producing numerous highly regarded advertising campaigns (e.g. Barclaycard) – and was a key member of Labour's Shadow Communications Agency from 1972 to 1997.

Chris Powell is puzzled. Until now, all behaviour change initiatives from government have come with a behaviour complemented by a law regulation, the two moving together to help get the message across to the public and make sure there is enforcement to back it up. He gives two recent examples of where this has occurred in other areas of policy: the smoking ban in public places that came into being in July 2007 followed years of 'propaganda' concerning the health risks of smoking and tips on how to give up, all funded by govern-ment; the THINK! drink–drive road safety campaign combines advertising that reminds us of the awful social consequences of killing someone, and actu-ally seeing the police pulling people over for breath tests (i.e. 'I am in real danger of getting caught if I do it'). But when it comes to climate change, this pattern has not yet been replicated, and for Powell this is what is missing.

There is a plethora of behaviours being championed by a plethora of organizations, including the Government; too many to achieve any real changes in the long term. Contradictory messages are also preventing any real progression towards a positive result. For Powell, concentrated action across government and non-government approaches is the key to working towards tackling the confusion over climate change:

> At a minimum there will need to be a single clear, much repeated, message that is credible and is realistically likely to lead to action. It is hard enough to get over one idea, especially if it is unwelcome, so there's no chance of success with a myriad. (Powell, 2008)

Powell feels that the science of climate change is no longer being questioned, but people are still unsure (or unwilling?) to do something about it. Powell's view is that so far all campaigns, particularly at a grassroots level, have targeted the 'keenies', those with a predisposed interest in the issue. The wider public remain disengaged from the 'Do the Green Thing' and 10:10 campaigns currently running.

So for Powell, what sorts of messages should be used to illustrate climate change and encourage a change in behaviour? He is clear that there should be just one message, and when that has achieved behaviour change, and only then, should communicators move on to another one. He gives the Maldives as a very real example of climate change happening now and sending a clear message to those that are watching that this is just the first casualty, in what could be a long line of casualties. Clever PR work has already put the Maldives on the front pages of UK papers (an underwater cabinet meeting was featured on a number of the national front pages in October 2009). Social pressure for Powell is a tool worth using, when it comes to getting the message across. His view is that the approach should look to the imminent changes that will have to be made, such as passenger taxes going up which will enforce less use of flights.

Powell views government as the ones who should be taking the lead from a top-down perspective, and agrees with Paddy Feeny that governments should avoid taking responsibility for grassroots organizations. The key for him is long-term investment, with a single message, led by government and supported with legislation; another challenge for any Minister for Energy.

4. Discussion and conclusions

At the beginning of this chapter, we distinguished government communications at national and local levels from other communications initiatives by 'grassroots' movements such as the Low Carbon Communities Network, and more campaign-centric examples by not-for-profit organizations such as the 'Not Stupid' campaign. In this chapter, we also touched upon business-sector approaches, and have provided a mixture of views from the communications industry and not-for-profit sectors of the ways in which we can more effectively engage the public in the issue of climate change and facilitate behaviour change. We focused on UK examples, but consider the approaches used and conclusions we now draw from these to have wider resonance and application.

It is clear that any approaches aimed at engaging and inciting action in members of the public must be consistent, and any tripartite alliance such as those advocated by Mark Lund will need to reach consensus on what they are asking the public to do as a result of the communications. But how can government, grassroots and commercial messaging complement one another to support goals such as the Government's 80 per cent reduction in carbon emissions by 2050, or the more imminent ambition of the 10:10 faction?

In the Central Office of Information's book, *How Public Service Advertising Works* (COI, 2009), Matthew Parris comments: 'from the public's point of view, "here's how you can" comes rightly and naturally from public service advertising; "here's why you should" needs to be handled with more care and, "never mind why: just do as your told" must be consigned to advertising history.' He also notes: 'We should not overlook one potent weapon in the public service advertiser's armoury: fear. Fear is a great persuader; few commercial advertisers can trade on fear as reliably as government information does' (COI, 2008, p6).

The use of fear is reflected in the television campaign launched by DECC's ACT ON CO_2 team at the end of 2009. Playing on parents' fears for their children is a tried and tested method for public service messages, and it may well be the best way to spur a still-reticent public into individual action. But as Parris goes on to note, fear only works on diminishing returns and shock fatigue can be a risk to such approaches. Indeed, research in this area suggests fear will be ineffective in provoking behavioural response unless accompanied by clear and motivating information about action to reduce the risk (e.g. O'Neill and Nicholson-Cole, 2009), which is why the two-phased approach (i.e. fear appeals coupled with action strategies) which the ACT ON CO_2 campaign is currently pursuing may reap results.

This is also where grassroots approaches can help. Where governmental information about climate change is provided, local initiatives can help provide the means and motivations by which the public can engage in the issues, both locally, with a direct dialogue with governments nationally and on a global scale. In addition, those working at grassroots levels often use government messages as a way of framing their own context-specific messages attuned to a diverse range of motivations for low-carbon living, such as improved health and greater social cohesion. Indeed, certain campaign messages may be targeted around working towards more immediate and community-oriented outcomes than towards long-term, national policy targets. It is not that these initiatives work in isolation from policy, but depending on the origins of the campaign, the relationship can be complex.

Business also has a key role here. The 'I will if you will' concept, coined by the Sustainable Development Commission (SCR, 2006), comes into play, with businesses such as M&S providing the opportunity needed by the public to change their behaviours. At the same time as changing the way their business works (and thus producing economic benefits for the organization), they are also giving the public an alternative to the energy-consuming, packaging-producing norm.

National media in all countries also have the opportunity to play a positive or a negative role in developing dialogue with their respective publics on this issue. By getting behind one message, they can effectively transport it into a wider arena and give it a sense of momentum it otherwise would not achieve, much like the UK media's support behind the 10:10 campaign. Equally, controversial coverage challenging the reality of climate change can have just as powerful an adverse effect as reflected post the airing of the UK Channel 4 programme 'The Great Global Warming Swindle' in March 2007. Research into the UK public's attitudes to climate change (e.g. Downing and Ballantyne, 2007) reveals that the persuasive climate sceptic message contained in this documentary left a lasting impression on public perceptions of the issue, and fuelled existing doubt about the reality and severity of anthropogenic climate change. This suggests that 'getting the science right' and then communicating this to the public is insufficient to persuade the public, who are exposed to a range of competing (and often more palatable) views. In the current context of multiple discourses about climate change and without a clear consistent message across all sectors, individuals' trust in the communicator, and their evaluation of the credibility and attractiveness of the message, will be crucial for determining how the public respond to this issue.

Finally, communications is purely one tool that can highlight the consequences of climate change and act as a catalyst for behaviour change. As with all public information campaigns, it cannot work without the support of effective policies within government and businesses alike; for example, the eco-homes activity covered within Chapter 9. The key to successful policy and communications responses will be greater collaboration across government, grassroots and business networks, with an acknowledgement from all parties of what each can bring to the table and, despite how hard it may be, an agreement on what key areas all sides can get behind, to achieve the shared impacts they are working towards. The M&S model for Plan A is one example of how government and business could work together to yield impressive results in this area.

Notes

1   In February 2009, The Department of Energy and Climate Change announced its intention to make all UK homes produce near zero carbon emissions by 2050. The new 'heat and energy saving strategy' (hes.decc.gov.uk/) aims to make improvements available to householders in every home in every street by 2030, with cavity wall and loft insulation available for all suitable properties by 2015.

2   http://actonco2.direct.gov.uk/actonco2/home/campaigns/Change-how-the-story-ends.html

3   PIRC (2008) p22: 'Short term solutions: As an immediate, short-term objective, the UK should aim to cut its greenhouse gas emissions 10% by the end of 2010. Delivering short-term actions provides the essential foundation for mid-term policies and long-term targets. Without short-term action, the real work has yet to begin. Work by researchers from the Tyndall Centre for Climate Change Research

(Anderson et al, 2008) has made clear that: 'focusing on a long-term transition to low carbon technologies is misguided, with real and substantial cuts being necessary in the short- to medium-term ... Consequently, if the UK is to demonstrate effective leadership on climate change and actively pursue a 450 ppmv pathway, it is incumbent on the Government to redress the balance of its policy agenda in favour of an early transition to a lower energy-consuming society' (p3721).

4   http://www.1010uk.org/
5   http://plana.marksandspencer.com/about
6   http://corporate.marksandspencer.com/file.axd?pointerid=f3ccae91d1d348ff8
    f523ab8afe9d8a8&versionid=fbb46819901a428ca70ecf5a44aa8ddc

References

Adam, D. and Jowit, J. (2008) People power vital to climate deal, *Guardian*, 8 December 2008, http://www.guardian.co.uk/environment/2008/dec/08/ed-miliband-climate-politics-environment, accessed 19 August 2010

Anderson, K., Bows, A. and Mander, S. (2008) 'From long-term targets to cumulative emission pathways: Reframing UK climate policy', *Energy Policy*, vol 36, pp3714–3722

COI (2008) *How Public Service Advertising Works*, COI/World Advertising Research Center

Defra (2009) Public attitudes and behaviours towards the environment – tracker survey. A research report completed for the Department for Environment, Food and Rural Affairs by TNS, www.defra.gov.uk/evidence/statistics/environment/pubatt/index.htm, accessed 19 August 2010

Downing, P. and Ballantyne, J. (2007) *Tipping Point or Turning Point – Social Marketing and Climate Change*, IPSOS MORI, www.ipsos-mori.com

Grant, J. (2007) *The Green Marketing Manifesto*, John Wiley & Sons Ltd, West Sussex

Jackson, B. (2009) 'Starter for 10:10', *The Sun*, 1 September 2009

O'Neill, S. and Nicholson-Cole, S. (2009) '"Fear won't do it": Promoting positive engagement with climate change through visual and iconic representations', *Science Communication*, vol 30, no 3, pp355–379

Powell, C. (2008) 'Marketers need a clear message on the environment', *Market Leader*, Spring issue, World Advertising Research Center

Public Interest Research Centre (PIRC) (2008) *Climate Safety – In Case of Emergency*, http://climatesafety.org/download/climatesafety.pdf, accessed 19 August 2010

Sustainable Consumption Roundtable (SRC) (2006) *I will if you will: Towards sustainable consumption*, http://www.sd-commission.org.uk/publications/downloads/I_Will_If_You_Will.pdf, accessed 19 August 2010

TNS (2009) *Act on CO$_2$ Campaign Evaluation Q1 08/09. Prepared for DfT, Defra/DECC*, TNS, London

12
Communicating Energy Demand: Measurement, Display and the Language of Things

Sarah Darby

Civilization advances by extending the number of important operations which we can perform without thinking about them.

Alfred North Whitehead, *Introduction to Mathematics* (1911)

1. Introduction

This chapter begins by looking at energy-related practices with an innocent eye, asking what energy users might be expected to know about the nature of their demand from the signs available. Focusing mainly on energy use in the home, it draws attention to some of the things that we notice, do not notice and cannot notice when we use different fuels or energy sources, and connects these with the infrastructures and networks of things, people and practices that make up energy systems. This forms the background to a discussion of the changes in gas and electricity metering that are now under way. I touch on how 'smarter' meters relate to government, utility and customer objectives, and discuss some of the ways in which new metering arrangements may take their place in energy systems. They will do so by not only recording consumption but giving it a new dimension (time of use), and acting as a form of communication between end-users, suppliers and even appliances. What potential do new meters and associated communication technologies hold for improving energy literacy?

2. Reading the signs

Climate change is a vast phenomenon, difficult to observe systematically and to analyse. The existence of this book in itself tells a story of difficulty – not just difficulty in communicating the realities of climate change, but in engaging people with possible responses. In this chapter, I attempt the simpler task of looking at the communication of energy demand. While energy issues in the 21st century are closely related to climate change issues, and are also politically and socially contentious, there are, at least, some points of contact and understanding for the individual. Everyone buys energy services in some form; everyone has experience of using different energy sources in a variety of ways; and most people have formed some general views on how their energy demands are met, as well as on possible forms of supply.

Having said that, though, the specifics of energy demand are often hidden from view. This limits our understanding of the daily realities of energy use, and of the options for change to lower-impact energy systems. While we know that information alone tends to be of little use in bringing about change, especially where established habits and interests are under threat (see Chapter 1), it is clear that tacit knowledge or know-how (learned from practical experience) is a powerful and necessary element of any system managed by and for humans (Sternberg et al, 2000). This type of knowledge is often derived from a range of sources. Many or most of these sources are not explicit, not found in books or formal repositories of knowledge. They are conversations, demonstrations of how to carry out particular tasks or advertisements. Or they may lie coded in the design of artefacts: push this button in order to see this information; pull this lever in order to open that window. We are surrounded by signs and indications of how to go about everyday life: What do the signs tell us about our energy demand? And what might they more usefully communicate to us? Before considering these issues, it is worth taking a brief look at the nature of energy systems.

3. Energy systems: things, people and practices

Energy systems, Walt Patterson reminds us, are 'arrays of physical assets – mostly infrastructure' (Patterson, 2007). The infrastructure is not only the extraction and conversion equipment, pipes and wires that bring us heat, light and other energy services. It is also, crucially, the buildings, vehicles and appliances that use energy in order to bring us the services that we want and expect. By transforming the nature of these systems, we can also transform the nature and scale of demand for fuel. Figure 12.1 illustrates some of the connections between fuel source, conversion technologies, networks, users and end-uses.

Energy is available to us constantly in the form of sunlight, wind and moving water – something that can be harnessed if we have the right infrastructure. Fuel is a *stored* form of energy. Fossil fuel is most closely associated with accelerated climate change, and it can seem as though a 'solution' to climate change lies solely with the rapid phasing out of fossil fuel use. The centrality of carbon trading in international climate policy reinforces this. But biofuels are also highly problematic on a planet facing deforestation and food insecurity. Uranium brings its own, extreme, difficulties, such as waste disposal, the need for large quantities of cooling water for reactors and reactor safety requirements. Even renewable energy without fuel can involve difficult trade-offs on a finite planet; for example, is river water best used for

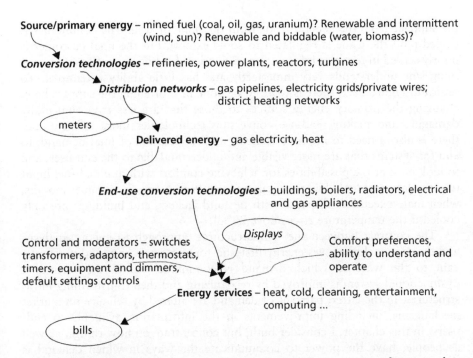

Figure 12.1 *Things, processes and outcomes in energy systems: between the mine and the clean clothes, the wind and the home office*

hydropower or for crop irrigation, or for maintenance of biodiversity? A systems view of energy quickly teaches that there are no easy and sustainable solutions that rely entirely on changes to supply, popular though these might be. Moving towards low-climate-impact energy systems means, inevitably, reining in demand and matching it more closely to the most suitable sources of supply: not simply adapting a growing demand to non-fossil sources of supply. That, in turn, means changing energy infrastructures as outlined in Figure 12.1 and, with them, the practices of millions of individuals.

That is an outline of the big picture. But from the standpoint of individuals in an industrialized part of the world, the most noticeable characteristic of energy systems is likely to be the arrival of bills for fuel and electricity at regular intervals. This is when they discover that they have managed to use x kilowatt-hours (kWh) or 'units' of energy over the period since the previous bill. Again it is time to pay. They do not, normally, have any means of tracking their consumption in detail, whether in real time or retrospectively. Someone paying for fuel and electricity through a prepayment meter is spared unpleasant surprises when the bill arrives, but, even then, there is no itemizing of consumption. As Kempton and Montgomery commented, buying kWh from a utility is akin to buying goods in 'a store without prices on individual items, which presented only one total bill at the cash register' (1982, p817). In such a market, fuel and electricity are seen primarily as commodities rather than elements in ecological, physical, social or systems. They are bought by the supplier from the generator, or from the mine or well. The commodity is traded (and the trade is regulated to some extent), but the final customer is poorly served in terms of information, dependent for home comforts on something s/he understands very imperfectly and has little ability to control. To return to Figure 12.1, there is work to be done in shortening the supply chain, changing the primary energy sources to those that are less environmentally damaging and making end-use conversion technologies more efficient. But there is also a need to improve controls and moderators of final demand, to aim for systems that are more visible and understandable to the end-user, and to look hard at the possibilities for achieving comfort with minimal fuel input (e.g. the Japanese 'cool biz' requirement for offices during the summer months, when male executives dispense with ties and jackets, and buildings are only cooled if the temperature rises above 28°C).

The contrast between the 'infrastructures' approach to energy analysis, and the approach that sees energy first and foremost as a commodity, is relevant to the ways in which demand is communicated. In the former, a dysfunctional system is improved by recognizing and then transforming infrastructures. In the latter, patterns of demand are altered by reliance on market mechanisms, including improvements in the information available to end-users. In this chapter, I consider both, but concentrate on how things, as well as people, have the power to communicate the ways in which demand is shaped. I argue that transformation of our energy systems towards lower environmental impact will require us to make both usage and supply more visible, and the connections between them more obvious.

I focus on electricity and natural gas for two reasons. First, they are characteristic sources of power in industrial or post-industrial societies; and they are largely invisible in everyday use. Those who rely on charcoal, wood, dung or coal for most of their fuel needs are unlikely to need to learn much about their usage patterns, or about how best to manage their fuel stocks. They will easily be able to observe the size of the woodpile, the quantity of charcoal left in the sack, the oil or kerosene reserve in the lamp; and will be able to draw on experience of how much fuel is needed to carry out tasks with their available equipment: cooking a meal on a stove, heating a room for the day, lighting with candles or oil-lamps. City-dwellers who use solid fuel may only be indirectly aware of the ecological impact of their demand, but they will normally have a clear enough picture of what they are using in their own home.

Gas and electricity, though, are different. They enter the house almost invisibly, through pipes and wires that are largely concealed within the walls, floor or roof, or that are camouflaged to make them blend in with the decor. The Centre Beaubourg in Paris, boldly displaying the heating, water piping and ventilation systems that are the guts of the building, is a rare type of construction – and an adventurous public building, not designed as a home.

Far more common is the building that gives away little about what is going on within, in terms of energy flows. Pipes, wires and radiators are painted over discreetly or hidden within the walls. The small lights and digital clocks that indicate standby consumption are easily disregarded. Radiant heaters, gas fires and lights provide visible and tangible heat, but are fed from

Figure 12.2 *The Centre Beaubourg, Paris*

invisible sources. The main indicator of potential electricity demand is likely to be the number of lights, appliances and power points; the main indicators of potential heating load will be the building's size, layout and insulation (the insulation arrangements, again, being largely invisible). Gas, electricity and air for ventilation pour through these buildings, with little to indicate the rate or extent of usage. If occupants leave without switching off these systems, the heaters, air-conditioning and appliances continue to do their work, drawing on reserves of fuel and power that are normally only interrupted in emergencies. Only homes with solid fuels, those that are not on an electricity grid, or those on prepayment meters, have a *finite* source of energy services; the rest rely on supplies that are bought on credit and are, from the householder's standpoint, virtually infinite.

As we become more accustomed to complex systems to deliver our energy services, an interruption in supply becomes a major disruption, not just an inconvenience. A man who lived 36 floors up in a Toronto apartment block once described to me what it had been like to live in his well-appointed home for three days during the 2003 power blackout that affected the north-east USA and most of Ontario. There were no functioning water pumps, lifts or sewage systems in the building, and, of course, none of the appliances were working. Water had to be carried up the stairs from ground level. The experience was not all bad, he said. The family talked together more than they usually did, found more time for reading and, for the first time in years, were able to enjoy the stars at night. But it was not sustainable for long and it illustrated a wider truth: it is not sustainable, either, to construct building shells that are only habitable when supplied with unending streams of cheap fuel and power.

4. Agency, control, communication and visibility

The processes of 'civilization', as defined by Alfred North Whitehead in the epigraph to this chapter, have introduced technologies and processes with little thought as to what the ecological effects will be. Almost a hundred years after that statement, it seems clear that 'performing operations ... without thinking about them' is, at best, a mixed blessing. For example, we have seen a combination of new materials, artefacts, standards, construction practices and increased wealth lead to housing designs that are markedly different from those of a century ago. Yet it is only relatively recently that we have begun to think seriously and systematically about the environmental impact of our building practices, and about the impact of what we do within the home. A dramatic illustration of the combined impact of changes in construction and the marketing of air-conditioning in Kerala is given by Wilhite (2008). He uses this and other examples to point out that technologies, as well as people, have agency, and that they combine to alter practices, sometimes with far-reaching impacts.

Simple energy systems, such as candles, typically give way to more complex and centralized systems such as large electricity generation stations and their fuel supply lines, transmission and distribution networks, and the complexes of wiring, switches, light fittings and bulbs that deliver lighting to us in buildings. As consumers, we make the transitions to more complex systems of provision smoothly enough, enticed by the promise of more attractive and convenient services. Yet the transitions are rarely smooth for the people who pioneer them, and they may require many agents. Some are human: inventors, designers, manufacturers, publicists, retailers, early adopters, repairers. But the non-human agents or actants are just as vital; for example, raw materials, machine tools, transport networks and accounting infrastructures. Moving from candles to electrical lighting is in fact a lengthy and complex process. But once achieved, it becomes harder to imagine moving away from a complex, high-energy system than it is to think of adapting the new infrastructure in ways that increase the end-use efficiency (e.g. low-energy bulbs and better voltage control); or perhaps automating some processes (e.g. using sensors to switch off lights in unoccupied spaces).

The legacy of North Whitehead's 'without thinking' approach to human and social development lives on in the movement to automate energy systems: to take control or agency out of people's hands and vest it in technologies and systems. But this clearly has limitations. There are enthusiasts for automated homes, for example, but automation is likely to be a costly and ineffective alternative to installing simpler energy conservation and efficiency measures; to date, it has been aimed at high-end dwellings and sold on the basis of remote control and security, rather than energy savings (Green and Marvin, 1994). Furthermore, there are limits to the extent to which even technophile householders want decisions about how and when they use energy services to be taken out of their hands. What can be done to communicate demand more effectively, to encourage thinking? To return to Figure 12.1 again, what can be done to improve the situation from one in which the consumer only has the limited information offered by the bill, along with a meter that gives limited information on cumulative usage?

Understanding all the variables in the average home, let alone managing them to best effect, is not straightforward and relies on a good deal of tacit knowledge (practical know-how), built up over time. Energy management in most homes, too, is not purely an individual activity, but involves the activities and preferences of all household members. It is also a reflection of how each individual thinks about the concept of 'home' and goes about living there (Aune, 2007).

What householders understand about the energy system (allied to what they have in the way of housing and appliances, and what they do in terms of purchasing and daily practices) is going to be affected by the 'language of things' and, in particular, the extent to which they make energy use explicit, rather than hidden. In what follows, I outline some actual and potential changes in communicating energy to end-users. There is a great deal to be written about the energy-related messages and practices that are 'scripted' into the design of buildings, appliances and controls (the implied message on a thermostat that indoor temperatures of 25°C are 'normal', because the dial shows figures from 10°C right up to 30°C, for example; or whether the design of washing machine control panels favours low-temperature choices). But here I shall concentrate on more direct communications, on ways in which it is possible to measure, sense and evaluate energy uses, so that householders are able to move from being passive consumers to more active managers. This relates immediately to the nature of energy-as-commodity, something packaged and measured. But it also, in the longer term, relates to energy-as-infrastructure.

5. Measurement and display

In a motor vehicle, we take measurement and clear display for granted. Speed has to be known, for legal and safety reasons, and it is prominently displayed on the speedometer. A satnav system can warn drivers when they are passing a speed camera, but even without a satnav the driver is constantly made aware by road signs of the appropriate speed for a given area (which affects the rate of fuel consumption). In addition, car users are shown how far they have travelled in the vehicle (and, if they wish, on a given trip), and how much fuel remains in the tank. The Toyota Prius broke new ground by showing drivers their rate of consumption in real time, something that is being adopted as part of a move towards 'eco-driving', credited with improvements in fuel economy of 5–10 per cent (UKERC, 2009). It also displays miles-per-gallon over the previous half an hour in a series of five-minute interval bars, giving the driver additional feedback that s/he can relate to variables such as whether the engine has warmed up, terrain, road and weather conditions, the state of traffic, speed of driving, and the load which the vehicle is carrying. The driver is able to build up a picture of the situations and actions that affect consumption, and to adapt it over time.

Householders have to deal with a more complex set of energy flows in the home than those in a car, but with much less useful information to guide them. Some of the information may even be negative, saying, in effect, that there is little point investigating further: this lighting is automatically controlled ... there is no power rating label on this appliance ... it is impossible to alter the default settings without time and expertise that you don't have. What is available can be summarized as:

- *what is taken in by the senses* (heat, cold, light, sound);
- *what is conveyed by the utility bill* (which may or may not be estimated rather than measured); and
- *what can be deduced from reading the meter*, if the householder is diligent enough to go there and to keep records.

However, this situation has been changing in recent years, for three main reasons: increased demand for useful information from building users; developments in metering and ICT; and the need to control peak electricity demand more effectively.

The increased demand for useful information from building users stems from concern about energy costs and environmental impact, and, increasingly, the need to comply with new policies such as the EU Energy Services Directive (ESD) and the Energy Performance of Buildings Directive. The ESD itself was influenced by experimental evidence on the effectiveness of improved consumption feedback in reducing demand: accurate, clear information on recent or current consumption in written form (including bills), or on some form of electronic display. The recipient typically sees actual usage along with some standard of comparison: previous usage in a comparable period of time or the usage of households of similar size (see Chapter 4 for discussion of social norms and behaviour change), or consumption broken down into different end-uses. This very specific information is then combined with the recipients' knowledge of their daily routines and practices, to raise awareness of energy, encourage experimentation, and reduce demand. Participants in these experiments or trials have typically made energy savings of up to 10 per cent from feedback given more or less indirectly – for example, via bills or websites – and of up to 15 per cent when the feedback is more readily available via a display. There is also evidence that at least some of the effect is durable, as the feedback encourages the formation of new habits. (See Darby, 2006; Abrahamse et al, 2007; and Fischer, 2008, for reviews.)

Developments in measuring and display technology and in ICT have brought down the unit costs of 'smart' meters at the same time as they have increased the possibilities: these are discussed below. The third motive force behind development of metering and display has been electricity suppliers' increasing need to control the timing of demand. This has effectively endowed 'energy' with a new dimension, as far as the user is concerned: electricity can now be expressed in terms of quantity, fuel source, carbon content and timing. Suppliers are beginning to introduce variable tariffs to encourage their customers to use electricity more evenly through the day, cutting down at peak times. In order to do this effectively and credibly, they need to be able to measure consumption over short time-periods using 'interval metering', and to record the information for billing purposes.

Developments in metering and display

The notion that a utility meter might perform more complex operations than simply recording cumulative units of energy first took hold in the late 1970s, but it is only in the last decade, with developments in communications technology, policy, commerce and regulation, that 'smart' metering has become a reality. At the time of writing, Italy and Sweden are the only countries where almost every building has a smart meter, but many other countries and regions are beginning to adopt some form of smart metering, and many trials are in progress throughout the world.

Yet in spite of all the recent activity in testing and implementing advanced metering infrastructures (AMIs), there is still no generally agreed definition of what a smart meter is. Broadly, it is best understood as a basic meter plus some form of communication technology: it is the communication that confers the smartness. Here, I will adopt the UK convention of referring to meters with one-way communications (from customer to supplier) as 'advanced', while those with two-way communications are 'smart'. At the time of writing, the UK Government is developing a definition by envisaging the following functions for smart metering systems:

1 remote provision of accurate reads for defined periods of time;
2 two-way communications between meter (customer) and supplier;
3 a Home Area Network based on open standards to provide real-time information to an in-home display (for electricity), and the potential to link other devices such as thermostats and appliance switches to the meter;
4 multiple registers within the meter to support time-of-use tariffs (electricity);
5 ability to control electricity load remotely, for demand-side management;
6 ability to disconnect and reconnect remotely, and to switch the customer between credit and prepayment;
7 ability to measure net exports of electricity to the grid and to communicate with devices measuring the total generation from a microgenerator, for billing purposes (DECC, 2009).

From the point of view of communicating energy demand directly, 3 and 7 are the most significant elements in a new meter. The former provides for readily visible information to the householder on consumption, while the latter paves the way for more widespread in-home generation. It stops short of specifying a display giving details of the rate and scale of generation, something which can also influence consumption (Keirstead, 2005), but there seems to be an intention to take the householder seriously as a producer or 'prosumer', rather than a consumer with a hobby. Without some form of display in the home, there is only the more accurate billing as a mechanism by which the house-holder can learn, day by day, about what is effective in managing usage. So this inclusion of displays in the definition of what constitutes a smart meter is highly significant. Anderson and White (2009) give a useful insight into what such a specification might include, based on qualitative work with house-holders, emphasizing the importance of what is shown on the default screen, the popularity of an analogue 'speedometer' display to show electrical demand in real time, and the importance of using money units.

Less directly, requirement 1 – the remote provision of accurate meter reads for defined periods of time – allows for timely, accurate bills. This is now required by the Energy Services Directive, as discussed below, and it removes estimated bills from the landscape – arguably the single greatest source of cus-tomer discontent with energy suppliers. Enabling the use of the same meter for both credit and prepayment (6) is also an important provision: prepayment is a simple and underrated means of bringing about changes in consumption pat-terns. It gives energy users more control over their spending on energy, and freedom from unpleasant surprises in their bills. Prepayment also alters the psy-chology of consumption – the user is paying for finite amounts in advance, bringing the experience closer to that of buying coal, firewood or oil – and there is evidence that this, in itself, tends to bring down demand (Darby, 2006). Time-of-use tariffs (4) are of most use at present in parts of the world with sharp peaks in load, but even in temperate regions, peak electrical load is usu-ally rising at a faster rate than overall load. The ability to manage this, and to match demand to intermittent supply from renewables, is becoming more desir-able. This can be done through agreements between customer and supplier to pay time-variable rates for electricity (or even real-time rates, within given boundaries); or it can be done by direct (utility) load control of appliances such as water and space heaters, air-conditioning or refrigeration. There can there-fore be some combination of conscious response to price signals by the customer, and remote control or automation. There appears to be a useful syn-ergy between customer displays and time-varying tariffs, with some evidence that a display increases the impact of time-of-use tariffs through raising cus-tomer awareness of usage patterns and their cost, and that the impact of a display can double if the householder is also prepaying (Faruqui et al, 2009).

Policy objectives and changes in metering

Many policy documents and instruments relating to changes in metering have emerged over the past decade, but the single most significant policy driver of change in the European Union has probably been the Energy Services Directive of 2006 (directive 2006/32/EC). The overall aims of the Directive are broad: to improve security of supply, mitigate carbon dioxide emissions and create stronger demand-side incentives to reduce emissions. The first paragraph of the preamble states the urgency of improving efficiency, managed demand and renewable supply. Article 13 of the Directive requires Member States to ensure that energy consumers have frequent and informative billing, along with meters that reflect consumption accurately and provide information on time of use, and Article 11 empowers them to set up 'a fund ... to subsidize the delivery of energy efficiency improvement programmes and ... measures ... These shall include the promotion of energy auditing ... and, where appropriate, improved metering and informative billing.'

The ESD is often seen as a 'smart metering directive', although the requirements of the Directive, and Article 13 in particular, are for provision of better feedback information to energy users, rather than for specific new technologies: encourage meter-reading; provide individual meters reflecting actual consumption and actual time of use; provide billing that is frequent enough to enable customers to regulate their consumption; and show prices and consumption on bills, along with historic comparisons and comparisons with other users.

There are escape clauses in the Article, too: 'where appropriate', 'in so far as technically possible, financially reasonable and proportionate in relation to the potential energy savings'. However, Article 13 is a significant development in that it relates 'efficiency' to energy services, and improvement of communications between customer and supplier. It recognizes the significance of end-users' behaviour in the scale and timing of energy demand, and the need to use feedback to improve their understanding of how to manage energy. The novelty lies in using new metering technology to make feedback more accessible, presenting the data over short intervals of time and/or in real time; in allowing the user to see, or to estimate easily, the relative significance of different end-uses; and in making it possible for customers to understand and control usage either for their own ends, or to assist the network operator by shifting load from one time of day to another. These issues are discussed in more detail in Darby (2009).

6. Potential for engagement through better communication in energy systems

Figure 12.3 shows a range of in-home energy displays available at the time of writing; more are constantly appearing. Are they here to stay? How do new meters and displays take their place in energy systems, as 'things', as communicators and as symbols? And what potential do they hold for better public engagement with energy issues?

Along with the virtues of improved feedback and resource literacy, it is worth remembering the limitations. To give an extreme example, the Easter Islanders are extremely isolated in the Pacific Ocean even now, and were even more so in the days before steamships and aeroplanes. They were entirely reliant on their own resources, on a small island. Their flourishing civilization, in the early medieval period, could hardly have had better feedback to assist them in managing their resources: it was very obvious how many trees were on the island, for example, and how necessary they were for construction of homes and fishing-boats, for shelter, fuel and food. Yet the islanders did not manage to maintain their prosperity. By the time that James Cook visited the island in 1774, the people were much reduced in numbers, no longer able to go out fishing and in a pitiable condition. Counter-examples also exist of collective resources being effectively managed (e.g. Ostrom, 1990), but these

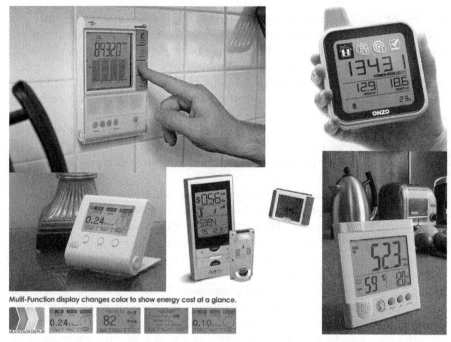

Multi-Function display changes color to show energy cost at a glance.

Figure 12.3 *Examples of in-home energy displays*

do not undermine the point that informational feedback and ecological knowledge do not inevitably generate appropriate behavioural responses (see also Chapter 1).

But if better feedback – that is to say greater visibility – is not *sufficient* for low-impact energy systems, it is a *necessary* element. Whatever our future energy systems look like in terms of hardware and software, they will fail in ecological terms unless they communicate the nature and scale of demand to the people who use them. Without this, there will not be the capacity to manage effectively, whether this is at the household level or at the level of political decision making. Even those who are not at all interested in managing their energy use might concede that total automation (removing the need to think about all 'important operations') is not workable without a degree of informed consent. The debate is now likely to centre around the most desirable forms of communication and knowledge-sharing, and the most appropriate uses of automation; not over whether one approach should completely replace the other.

A relatively recent development is the resurfacing of a supply-side interest in managing demand, in order to increase operational efficiency and meet environmental commitments. For electricity, the network needs to be managed in such a way as to minimize peak demand and to balance intermittent renewable supply with demand; that is, customers can ideally either shift their own load, in line with available supply, or allow their supplier to do it for them. (Abaravicius et al, 2005, give an insight into what is involved when the supplier takes control.) For both electricity and gas, most utilities still have little incentive to reduce their overall sales: decoupling sales from profits is still limited to a few jurisdictions, mostly in North America. But the introduction of policy measures to mitigate climate change, such as tradable 'white certificates' for reduced consumption, is bringing about some change in utility priorities (Bertoldi et al, 2010). Over and above these aims, utilities in a liberalized market have an incentive to try to maintain customer loyalty through good service. Good communication does not guarantee success in customer retention or in demand management, but we do know that poor communication is an ingredient of failed and failing systems.

At the end of the supply line, in the home, changes in the design of appliances and controls, along with the advent of energy displays and smart meters, offer a more comprehensive and ecological way of looking at energy use. To adopt the terminology of the psychologist James Gibson, the 'affordances' of appliances and meters are altering:

> The affordance of anything is a specific combination of the properties of its substance and its surfaces taken with reference to an animal ... It is equally a fact of the environment and a fact of behaviour ... [it] points both ways, to the environment and to the observer. (Gibson, 1977, p130)

An affordance thus has physical properties, but these only have meaning in relation to the animal, or person, using it. To give a pair of domestic examples, a freezer which has an auto-defrost feature has the affordance of saving work for the owner, while a computer with a range of power-down and start-up features has the affordance of potential energy savings (provided that the user can find and operate the necessary features). A very significant part of recent developments in energy display and in metering lies in their offer of affordances that go against the 'without thinking' trends of the last century. The new affordances connect our energy-using activities more closely and obviously to physical infrastructures, and to our activities. The primary impact is likely to be a change in our awareness of, and spending on, energy-as-commodity. More widely, though, the new affordances can influence our view of energy-as-infrastructure. The significance of different infrastructure elements (e.g. buildings, appliances, controls), and different practices, can become clearer. Energy users and microgenerators can be in a better position to make decisions on purchases and practices. At the same time, large-scale suppliers now have a technical means of engaging customer support in managing electrical load.

7. Summary

We learn from both people and things throughout our daily lives, and, in this chapter, I have explored some aspects of what it means to communicate energy demand to householders through the agency of things. Our homes can host a great range of activities, some of them extremely sophisticated and energy-intensive. Yet, at the same time, many of the energy implications of our activities have become less visible and less easy to understand over time. The advent of better electronic and written feedback, with or without 'smart' meters, offers a way of comprehending and countering this trend, and the indications are that better feedback is altering perceptions of energy, improving the ability of householders to manage it and beginning to alter their relationship with their energy suppliers (who are now under pressures of their own to manage demand more effectively).

There is a lot of hyperbolic talk about the promise of smart meters, and it is important to remember that all we know at this stage is that they open up new possibilities and that they have been used to manage electrical demand successfully in some circumstances. The extent to which they can also *engage* customers in demand management and demand reduction will depend on the quality of the customer interface – on the extent to which new metering systems allow for interaction with all of the people who use them, not only the utilities. The development of displays is helping with this. Engagement will also depend on the options open to customers for taking action, and on the extent to which their usage is automated or controlled directly by the supplier. And it will depend on the willingness of regulatory bodies to make changes in the governance of energy systems.

To communicate climate change is to convey something on a mighty scale, in space and time. As Shellenberger and Nordhaus commented in their controversial essay on the 'death of environmentalism' (2004), it is difficult to gain support for effective responses to climate change when both problem and potential solutions are framed as distant from normal, everyday human preoccupations. Making energy demand more visible, though, is directly related to daily practices, and the research evidence shows how visibility tends to increase interest in seeing the immediate or cumulative effect of change in these practices, along with changes in the physical fabric or equipment of the home.

Communicating energy demand more effectively to people who rely on electricity and natural gas, but understand little of how they are using it, is a relatively accessible project. It is one that could take us some distance from our default roles as consumers, towards a more engaged way of life as resource managers. There are hopes that a broader understanding of energy demand can catalyse transformations in the energy systems that we are most concerned about in industrial societies: those which supply electricity and natural gas. It is safe to assume that smart metering will bring about transformations in these systems: it has already started to happen. In order to reach its potential as a means of communication, it has to be configured in such a way as to give simple, graphic messages to users, and it has to be incorporated into systems that are designed and regulated for demand reduction, not only for the smooth operation of the supply business.

Acknowledgements

I gratefully acknowledge the support of the Economic and Social Research Council (ESRC), through a Research Councils' Energy Programme interdisciplinary research fellowship. The reviewers of this chapter gave constructive comments that were very helpful to me in completing the writing.

References

Abaravicius, J., Sernhed, K. and Pyrko, J. (2005) *Turn me on, turn me off! Techno-economic, environmental and social aspects of direct load management in residential houses*, Proceedings, ECEEE summer study, paper 7042

Abrahamse, W., Steg, L., Vlek, C. and Rothengatter, T. (2007) 'The effect of tailored information, goal setting, and tailored feedback on household energy use, energy-related behaviors and behavioral antecedents', *Journal of Environmental Psychology*, vol 27, pp265–276

Anderson, W. and White, V. (2009) *Exploring consumer preferences for home energy display functionality*. A report for the Energy Saving Trust, Centre for Sustainable Energy, Bristol, UK, http://www.cse.org.uk/downloads/file/CSE%20Report_%20 Consumer%20preferences%20for%20home%20energy%20display%20functional-ity%20FINAL.pdf

Aune, M. (2007) 'Energy comes home', *Energy Policy*, vol 35, pp5457–5465

Bertoldi, P., Rezessy, S., Lees, E., Baudry, P., Jeandal, A. and Labanca, N. (2010) 'Energy supplier obligations and white certificate schemes: Comparative analysis of experiences in the European Union', *Energy Policy*, vol 38, no 3, pp1455–1469

Darby, S. (2006) *The effectiveness of feedback on energy consumption*. A review for Defra of the literature on metering, billing and direct displays, Environmental Change Institute, University of Oxford, http://www.eci.ox.ac.uk/research/energy /electric-metering.php

Darby, S. (2009) *Implementing Article 13 of the Energy Services Directive and defining the purpose of new metering infrastructures*, Proceedings, European Council for an Energy-Efficient Economy summer study, paper 2262

DECC (2009) *Energy metering*. A consultation on smart metering for electricity and gas, May 2009, http://www.decc.gov.uk/en/content/cms/consultations/smart_ metering/smart_metering.aspx

Faruqui, A., Sergici, S. and Sharif, A. (2009) *The Impact of Informational Feedback on Energy Consumption – A Survey of the Experimental Evidence*, Brattle Group, San Francisco, http://www.smartgridnews.com/artman/uploads/1/The_Impact_of_ Informational_Feedback__05-20-09_.pdf

Fischer, C. (2008) 'Feedback on household electricity consumption: a tool for saving energy?', *Energy Efficiency*, vol 1, no 1, pp79–103

Gibson, J. J. (1977) 'The theory of affordances', in R. E. Shaw and J. Bransford (eds) *Perceiving, Acting, and Knowing: Toward an Ecological Psychology*, Lawrence Erlbaum Associates, Hillsdale, NJ, USA, pp67–82

Green, J. and Marvin, S. (1994) Energy Efficiency and home automation. Newcastle University Global Urban Research Unit Electronic Working Paper 3, http://www. ncl.ac.uk/guru/assets/documents/ewp3.pdf

Keirstead, J. (2005) *A double-dividend? Assessing the potential of photovoltaics in the UK domestic sector as a catalyst for energy conservation*, Proceedings, European Council for an Energy-Efficient Economy, Summer Study, Mandelieu, France, paper 6054

Kempton, W. and Montgomery, L. (1982) 'Folk quantification of energy', *Energy*, vol 7, pp817–827

Ostrom, E. (1990) *Governing the Commons: The Evolution of Institutions for Collective Action*, Cambridge University Press, Cambridge

Patterson, W. (2007) *Transforming energy within a generation*. Chatham House Briefing Paper, Energy Environment and Development Programme, EEDP CC BP 07/03, http://www.chathamhouse.org.uk/files/9253_bp0607climatewp.pdf

Shellenberger, M. and Nordhaus, T. (2004) *The death of environmentalism. Global warming politics in a post-environmental world*, http://www.thebreakthrough.org/images/Death_of_Environmentalism.pdf

Sternberg, R. J., Forsythe, G. B., Hedlund, J., Horvath, J. A., Wagner, R. K., Williams, W. M., Snook, S. A. and Grigorenko, E. L. (2000) *Practical Intelligence in Everyday Life*, Cambridge University Press, New York

UKERC (2009) *Eco-driving including in-car information systems.* United Kingdom Energy Research Centre, http://www.ukerc.ac.uk/Downloads/PDF/09/0904 TransEcoDriveTable.pdf

Wilhite, H. (2008) 'New thinking on the agentive relationship between end-use technologies and energy-using practices', *Journal of Energy Efficiency*, vol 1, pp121–130

13
The Role of New Media in Engaging the Public with Climate Change

Saffron O'Neill and Maxwell Boykoff

1. Introduction

'New media' are defined in this chapter as media which are integrated, inter-active and use digital code (as van Dijk, 2006). Defined as such, new media have been touted as 'one of the greatest tools in achieving a true democracy' (Dawson; cited in Head, 2009). Malone and Klein (2007, p26) go some way to showing a potential shape of this democracy, in their web-based forum thought experiment the 'Climate Collaboratorium', describing it as 'a kind of Wikipedia for controversial topics, a Sims game for the future of the planet, and an electronic democracy on steroids'. Yet others have called for a more critical reading of the use of new media in facilitating democracy (Sunstein, 2007), with Dietz and Stern (2008) stating that there is still some way to go in understanding the dynamics of new media engagement. With these con-flicting positions in mind, this chapter reviews and critically evaluates the current role, and potential future roles, new media could play in engaging the public with climate change. This chapter also contains a more detailed examination of two climate engagement approaches (one a community-based emissions-reduction programme, the other a climate contrarian engagement approach) that have successfully utilized new media to engage audiences with climate change.

2. Discovering new media

The innovations of new media come out of a rich history of mass media (see Starr, 2004; Briggs and Burke, 2006, for more). Most broadly, mass media range from entertainment to news media, spanning television, films, books, flyers, newspapers, magazines, radio and the internet. Together, these media are constituted by a diverse and dynamic set of institutions, processes and practices, that serve as mediators between communities, such as science, policy and public citizens. Members of the communications industry and profession – publishers, editors, journalists and others – produce, interpret and communicate images, information and imaginaries for varied forms of consumption.

In the past decade, there has been a significant expansion from consumption of traditional mass media – broadcast television, newspapers, radio – into consumption of new media, such as the internet and mobile phone communications. More recent developments in new media (described in more detail below) have signalled substantive changes in how people access and interact with information, who has access, and who are the authorized definers or claims makers. Essentially, in tandem with technological advances, these communications are seen to be a fundamental shift from one-to-many (often one-way) communications to many-to-many more interactive webs of communications. Flew (2006) recognizes the advantages of new media as being malleable and adaptable in creation, storage, delivery and use; networkable; and compressible, leading to large amounts of data existing in physically small spaces. There are three key characteristics of new media: the ability to deliver individualized messages simultaneously to those with access; the control of the content shared by each individual involved; and the dependence of new media on technology (Crosbie, 2002). Hence, new media agents include interactive television and digital radio (but not analogue television or radio), mobile telephones (but not landline phones), and all internet agents such as Internet Explorer or FireFox. The development of the internet, and particularly Web 2.0, are not discussed here; suffice to say, we follow Flew (2008) in recognizing that 'social networking media' is a commonly used alternative term to Web 2.0, incorporating such principles as being decentralized, user-focused and user-led.

New media agents

One of the simplest forms of new media, and one which perhaps is closest aligned to traditional media communication, is that of the written word. Examples of written new media agents include website text (this includes online versions of traditional news media such as newspapers), SMS messaging, blogs and microblogs, and RSS (really simple syndication) feeds. Much sound-based traditional media is migrating into the digital age, with switchovers to digital audio broadcasting (DAB) radio now occurring. Listeners may now access their preferred radio stations via the internet, rather than via a traditional receiver; opening up potential global audiences to even local radio stations. As well as radio, the internet has opened up opportunities for podcasting – the recording and posting of pre-recorded sound. New media agents that use imagery also have some crossover with traditional media. However, unlike the analogue technology inherent in traditional media, new media imagery is fully digitized and interactive. So, for example, users can upload photos or videos to an online gallery, where other viewers can comment on or rate the photos – or can use satellite mapping agents to explore new landscapes. The integrated agents of new media present opportunities that could not be replicated through traditional media. Individualized web spaces have fully integrated imagery, sound and text, with the opportunity to post real-time updates. These updates can include links to other websites, or photos and videos, linking in functionality from other social networking agents.

New media geographies

As noted above, a key feature of new media is its reliance on technology, whose availability, access and applications vary globally. Trends in mobile phone ownership and internet usage are thus briefly reviewed below.

Mobile phone access is commonplace in developed nations, with SMS ('short message service' or 'silent messaging service') text messaging used by the majority of mobile phone users; for example, of the nine in ten people using a mobile phone in Australia, 89 per cent of them will utilize SMS services (Mackay and Weidlich, 2008; Nielsen Media Research, 2008). Although there is lower mobile phone access in developing nations, the mobile phone market is growing fast, with 45 per cent of people in the developing world owning a mobile phone by 2007 (ITU, 2009). Mobile connectivity is not just important for access to SMS communications, however. Vinton Cerf, interviewed in Flew (2008), notes how 'there is no doubt that many people will first be introduced to the internet through appropriately equipped mobiles'.

It is estimated that around a quarter of the world's population, or over 1.5 billion people, are currently internet users – and this proportion is expanding rapidly (Internet World Stats, 2009; and Table 13.1 below). Growth in internet use is occurring most rapidly in Africa, the Middle East and Latin America; Asia has overtaken Europe and North America as the region with the highest percentage of internet users by region. Internet users as a percentage of population totals is currently still highest in North America, followed by Australia/Oceania and Europe. It is lowest in Asia and Africa, with under 7 per cent of the African population being internet users. It is noted that even in more developed regions, a significant proportion of the population are not internet users.

As well as between regions, there are significant socio-demographic variations in internet usage within countries. There is a general trend towards an

Table 13.1 *Internet users by region (Internet World Stats, 2009)*

Region	Population (million; est. 2009)	Internet users (million; June 2009)	Percentage population internet users	Growth in internet users 2000–9	Internet users as % of world total
Africa	991.0	65.9	6.7%	1360%	3.9%
Asia	3808.0	704.2	18.5%	516%	42.2%
Europe	803.9	402.4	50.1%	283%	24.2%
Middle East	202.7	48.0	23.7%	1360%	2.9%
North America	340.8	251.7	73.9%	133%	15.1%
Latin America/Caribbean	586.7	175.8	30.0%	873%	10.5%
Oceania/Australia	34.7	20.8	60.1%	173%	1.2%
Total	6767.8	1668.8			

urban–rural divide in internet accessibility; for example, major cities in Australia have a 66 per cent rate of household internet access, but this declines to 42 per cent in very remote areas (ABS, 2008). There is also evidence of a noteworthy trend in age-related access, and use, of the internet. In Australia, over 75 per cent of 15–24-year-olds have used the internet, compared to 28 per cent of 65–74-year-olds. Just 10 per cent of Australian over-75s use the internet (ABS, 2008). Recognition of the particular characteristics of different age-group cohorts is evident from terms used to describe them: from the 'Google-gen' (young people born after 1993 growing up in a world dominated by the internet; CIBER, 2008) to the 'silver surfers' (over-50s who spend much time using the internet; OED, 2009).

There is some evidence of a relationship between internet access, educational attainment and income. The Australian census found 88 per cent of individuals with a degree-level qualification or above had internet access, compared to 63 per cent of those without formal school qualifications. Income shows a greater influence; with almost nine out of ten individuals in the top income quintile having internet access, compared to slightly less than five in ten of the lowest quintile. Evidence from the USA indicates that internet use is becoming more polarized by income, with a slow diffusion of internet use in low-income groups; though this trend is not found in European countries (Martin and Robinson, 2007). Another trend – which may be echoed in indigenous communities elsewhere – is that just over one-third of Aboriginal Australians have internet access, compared to the two-thirds Australian population average (ABS, 2009).

3. New media in climate change engagement

In considering the role of new media in climate change engagement, three overlapping key themes are evident. The first is *information*. Clearly, new media present individuals with a wealth of previously inaccessible information on an endless variety of topics. But how is this information source used – and possibly abused? The second key theme is new media *interactivity*. Web 2.0 technologies give new opportunities to individuals to engage with many others, and create their own online content. Does this lead to new forms of community? Or do messages become more fragmented and increase the risk of polarization? The final theme is that of *inclusivity*. New media agents may act to enable and enhance contact and engagement between individuals, communities, organizations and others with climate change. But are individuals really interacting, and interacting more often, with more diverse audiences and information? The following sections reflect critically on each theme, as summarized in Table 13.2 below.

Information

New media present individuals with a wealth of information on an endless variety of topics. There are currently over 35 million websites containing the terms 'climate change', 'global warming' or 'greenhouse effect'.[1] Climate change information is available via new media through an array of professional

Table 13.2 *Opportunities and limitations (technological, technical and human) for climate change engagement using new media*

Theme	Opportunities	Limitations
Information	Amount of information available	Information overload
	Searchable information	Lack of search skills, ability to manipulate results from search queries
	Quality sites from key bodies	Many low-quality sites
	Personalizable information	Security risks of personalized or accessible information
	Breaking down of expert 'ivory towers'	Trust issues around information sources, role of climate contrarians[2] online
Interactivity	Many-to-many communication and content creation	Web 2.0 limited by speed to broadband users, difficulty of follow-up (e.g. behavioural impact)
	Building of new online communities, making global links	Increased fractionalization possible
Inclusivity	Potential for wide geographical and socio-economic participation	Lack of internet access and skills in poorer and older populations, and in less developed nations
	Equality of opinions and agenda setting	Many (often hidden) vested interests exist online
	Vehicle for grassroots activism	Online-led activism can hinder cause if not viewed as professional
	Fewer resources needed to engage audiences	To engage effectively often still requires significant buy-in and resources
	Anonymous nature allows participation from diverse audiences, as different 'characters' (business leader, citizen, mother)	Problems of anonymity on web forums and in blogs (e.g. lack of 'netiquette')
	Decrease distance between experts/ policy makers, science and the public	Can inadvertently increase distance through growth of contrarianism, lack of trust or 'cringe factor'[3]

bodies, such as government (see, for example, the UK's Department of Energy and Climate Change; DECC, 2009); businesses (see retailer Marks & Spencer, 2009); NGOs (see Friends of the Earth, 2009); and even scientists themselves (see the IPCC reports online; IPCC, 2009, and the Real Climate website; Real Climate, 2010). Gavin (forthcoming) suggests that individuals searching the web for information on climate change are often prompted to do so by an item in the conventional news media. However, it is precisely this availability of information that presents one of new media's biggest challenges – individuals can be inundated and overloaded with information. How does one find useful and high-quality information?

Individuals use search facilities through agents like Google and Yahoo to navigate through this sea of information, and gain access to the information they require. Yet searching new media requires particular skills. A 2008 CIBER report investigated the information-seeking behaviour of the researchers of the future. Although CIBER were particularly interested in the behaviour of younger new media users, their results are of interest more widely to a discussion around information searching in new media. Their report reveals that although there is an intuitive assumption that users are expert searchers, it is dangerous to assume that digital literacy and information literacy go hand in hand. CIBER also report that the speed of web searching means little time is spent in evaluating information for relevance, accuracy or authority. Although data do not exist regarding climate change search activities specifically, it may then follow that individuals searching for climate information are also not actively evaluating the source of the information they come across.

A range of professional bodies provide climate information and engagement tools online. This wide range of bodies can cater to different audiences with tailored, meaningful climate engagement information. The growth of new media has provided ways for established institutions, as well as grassroots organizations, to engage individuals in more personally meaningful ways. For example, the National Museum of Australia has a Flickr site (National Museum of Australia, 2009) inviting individuals to post their own interpretations of the cultural dimensions of climate change: 'Share with us your photos that record how climate change is changing your place. Tell us how you feel about the ecological changes that you are witnessing. Are these changes affecting how you think about people and our place in the world?' The Facebook application ('app') 'Global Warming's Six Americas' (Maibach, 2009) is a further example of how individuals can receive more personally relevant information. This app guides the user through a number of questions designed to determine which one of six climate attitude segments they fall into, and suggests behavioural changes based on their attitude type. Before the app can be accessed, users must allow it access information including their name, profile picture, gender, networks, user IDs, list of friends, and any other information they share with everyone. Whilst such approaches provide opportunities for engaging large audiences with tailored information, the use of tools which require access to personal information in order to work does represent a potential security risk (Flew, 2008).

There is a wealth of climate information and engagement approaches that utilize new media, including contrarian approaches. Lockwood (2008) maintains that new media are important players in the spread of what he calls 'sceptical climate discourses' (and what we call here 'contrarian discourses'; see also footnote 2). First, he finds that these discourses in new media have been used to support more mainstream reporting of climate contrarian viewpoints. Lockwood provides an example of the UK's mainstream television Channel Four using comments from a supportive online message to shore up against criticism directed at them for the screening of the contrarian documentary *Great Global Warming Swindle*. Second, Lockwood considers that new media contribute to the volume of contrarian climate discourses. He points to evidence including that of the growth in popularity of the contrarian blog, with four of the 20 most popular science blogs written by climate contrarians. Third, Lockwood finds new media have a significant impact on the climate discourse, citing, amongst other evidence, the impact of contrarian blogger Steve McIntyre in influencing the US Congressional Committee to examine the IPCC's hockey stick graph. Perhaps then, even more than with traditional media and communications vehicles, evaluating information (and knowing who and what to trust) is a key issue in climate engagement through new media. As Sunstein (2007, p143) comments: 'those who consult blogs will learn a great deal. But they will have a tough time separating falsehoods from facts,'

3.2. Interactivity

Much has been made of new media's many-to-many form of communication. Web 2.0 technologies, especially in individualized web spaces, create opportunities for people to receive, engage and create their own content. An example of this is the online encyclopaedia Wikipedia. The entry for 'global warming' has been edited by thousands of individuals, and has over 130 linked references.[4] New media utilize a web-like, rather than a linear, communication process. Consider, for example, the Facebook app 'Global Warming's Six Americas' (Maibach, 2009) again, which simultaneously engages multiple audiences. The app announces the individual's attitude type once they have completed a short survey, and encourages the viewer to take a number of pre-determined behavioural actions specific to the attitude group. Importantly then, the user is then encouraged to send a link to the app to up to 24 of their friends, reporting both which group they fall into and encouraging their friend also to take part. A limitation to these Web 2.0 technologies is that they are restricted to users with fast internet connections, which limits their accessibility amongst some users (see Table 13.2). A further problem with these engagement processes is the lack of follow-up, or lack of commitment to behavioural actions. Without a supportive community to remind, reiterate and reinforce lower emissions choices, new media mitigation engagement approaches may be unlikely to engage individuals more than superficially.

New media offer opportunities for people to get involved in building new communities and making global linkages. Grassroots organization Camp for Climate Action UK volunteers have effectively used new media to take direct action in central London, at power stations and at airports, to emphasize their messages of education, direct action, sustainable living and building a climate action movement of a self-stated 'pretty diverse bunch' of people (Camp for Climate Action, 2009). Their 2007 Heathrow Climate Camp attracted over 2000 campers within a few hundred metres of the airport. Climate Camp use their website to inform protestors of the general location of planned action. SMS and microblogging agent twitter are vital conduits of information to inform people of the specific location in a last-minute 'swoop' – used as a way to mitigate the group's concerns about policing.[5] The Camp has now attracted similar movements in 16 other countries.

Whilst new networks are being brought together and maintained by new media, some authors raise concerns that new media are in fact leading to increased fractionalization, and new forms of localism. Woolgar (2002) recognizes this in one of his five rules of virtuality. He finds that rather than overcoming identity as grounded in a sense of belief, location or experience, virtual communication is more likely to lead to an increase in their embeddedness. Hence, in climate change engagement, we should perhaps not be surprised to find that new media are generally not utilized to engage with communities situated in different cultural contexts, as they will retain attachment to their own identities (although see Chapter 9 for one example of cross-cultural online engagement); but, instead, used as an additional tool to keep individuals engaged who may already have some connection with each other (despite in some cases still having strong identities).

Sunstein (2007) discusses new media and the likelihood of increased fractionalization, and is scathing in his criticism of web 'echo chambers': virtual walls put up around web surfers to block themselves off from topics and opinions that they find unpleasant or uninteresting. He notes how mass media, through general media intermediaries, have to cater to a mass audience; and thus face the likelihood of both being exposed to new (albeit sometimes unsettling) opinions, but also to issues one might not have previously considered. With the growth of agents such as personalized news RSS feeds, blogs from favoured authors, and tools such as online retailer Amazon's 'today's recommendations for you', it is much easier to avoid general news items than with a general media intermediary such as a national newspaper. Sunstein (2007) suggests that this narrowing in online forums is unlikely to produce mixed opinion discussion of the kind that would lead to a desirable form of deliberation and learning, and is instead more likely to lead to the breeding of polarization and extremism.

Thus it is important to be aware of the potential limitations of new media through echo chambers. However, there is evidence that some approaches can help to minimize these limitations, or act within the echo chambers to increase visibility of certain types of information. For example, echo chambers can lead to some forms of information which, often originating from celebrities, assume greater visibility and appeal than they may have otherwise. Increasingly, researchers have placed a critical gaze upon how celebrities – seen as neo-millennial charismatic megafauna in climate debates – influence discourses on climate change via 'traditional' as well as 'new' media (see Boykoff et al, 2009).

Constituted by interacting and interactive media representations (Littler, 2008), celebrities have become 'intimate strangers' (Schickel, 2000), shaping our perceptions and actions on a range of issues, including climate change mitigation and adaptation. In efforts to understand and catalogue the growing role of celebrities in connection to climate change via media, Boykoff and Goodman (2009) have developed a 'taxonomy of climate celebrities'. An example of celebrity engagement through new media includes involvement by Sienna Miller with the organization Global Cool, to make green actions 'eco-chic not eco-geek'. Miller (and others such as Josh Harnett and Rosario Dawson) encourage people to do things such as recycle unwanted cell phones and send bi-monthly SMS messages to friends offering energy-saving tips. These calls for action are purported to 'help consumers in the fight against global warming' (Global Cool, 2009). Another illustration of these interactions can be found in the MTV 'switch off' campaign, begun in 2007 (MTV, 2009). This initiative has harnessed the 'star power' of celebrities like Enrique Iglesias, Cameron Diaz, Xzibit, Good Charlotte, Kelly Rowland, Rufus Wainwright and Shaggy, to offer public service announcements (PSAs) promoting 'environmentally friendly lifestyle choices amongst youth in order to reduce the carbon emissions that contribute to climate change' (MTV Switch, 2009). The website is the hub of multimedia messaging, containing videos, a user-generated weblog, news, downloads and a carbon footprint calculator. On the website is the pronouncement: 'Everyone, no matter what age or where they live, can take action to reduce their carbon footprint. The MTV Switch PSAs seek to entertain, intrigue and inspire viewers to take on simple climate conscience acts such as unplugging mobile chargers and turning the thermostat down one degree' (MTV, 2009).

Iyengar et al (2007) offer online Deliberative Polling as a way of minimizing the echo chamber effect. Deliberative Polling presents a fairly structured engagement approach, but one that can be carried out online at far lower cost than traditional face-to-face engagement approaches, and one that can be fitted in at a convenient time for the target audience. Iyengar et al discuss an experiment, where online polling is run against face-to-face polling. Online participants were randomly assigned to groups to ensure a diversity of opinions, and led in online deliberations by a trained moderator. Iyengar et al found similar levels of deep deliberation and information uptake in both the online and face-to-face experiments, concluding that whilst the online deliberations may not have had all the qualities of the face-to-face deliberations, they had enough to prove it as a viable engagement approach and one that may ultimately be more appropriate than face-to-face methods for global scale issues like climate change (Dietz and Stern, 2008).

Inclusivity

An earlier section describes how access to new media is widening to diverse geographical and socio-economic populations, which provides new opportunities for engaging individuals with climate change. However, access to, or acceptability of, new media technologies is still more limited in poorer, rural and older populations. Around three-quarters of the world's population do not have access to the internet. As Gavin (2009) has concluded for the use of new media in political engagement with climate change, it is likely that only a small fraction of the population is currently using new media to engage with the issue. Yet, if one of the aims of climate engagement online is to encourage decarbonized lifestyles which are currently heavily dependent on fossil fuels, those currently accessing new media sources are a key audience.

Contrast the inclusive nature of new media with the gate-keeping of traditional media. Should an individual want to engage with others about climate change through a newspaper, or a television show, he or she would have to approach the editor to gain access – and would likely not be successful. New media on the other hand offer individuals a platform where there is an equality of opinions and agenda setting. These shifts have altered the dynamics of what Carvalho (2007) has described as the 'authorized definers' of climate change (p232). If an individual wishes to create content, then there are many agents which can make that possible. There have been demonstrations of the power of new media agents to even bolster their traditional counterparts. In the UK in October 2009, an attempt was made to gag the *Guardian* newspaper through a court super-injunction, in order to prevent the newspaper from reporting a parliamentary question regarding alleged dumping of toxic waste in the Ivory Coast by mining company Trafigura. However, bloggers overran new media agent Twitter with posts on the theme, prompting the case to be dropped, and the *Guardian* and twitter bloggers to claim a victory for free speech.

Just as grassroots organizations, or committed individuals, can use new media to engage audiences with narratives that might not occur through traditional media sources, so can powerful organizations and vested interests also find forums to engage individuals. As discussed above, little time is spent in evaluating online information for relevance, accuracy or authority. Groups that have seized on these new media technologies in order to create the appearance of widespread grassroots organizing have been referred to as 'astroturf' organizations (Fifeld, 2009).

New media can be used to successfully support committed individuals and groups (e.g. grassroots activists), thus widening participation in climate engagement. In the USA, an open source, web-based organization called Step It Up (2009) organized days of action 'dedicated to stopping climate change'. New media enable Step It Up to cast a wide net and capture many interested, but widely dispersed, individuals. New media also facilitate the organization to empower local leaders and establish relationships with more mainstream media sources (Minion et al, 2008). Establishing these relationships is a key aim of some grassroots activist groups. Plane Stupid is a UK-based organization that uses high-profile stunts to gain media attention and raise the profile of aviation's role in climate change. Gavin (2009) warns though that although Plane Stupid have been relatively successful so far in gaining more mainstream media coverage from events such as storming Heathrow, there must be attempts to rein in 'hot heads' in the organization or diligent online campaigning can be undone. Gavin concludes that activist engagement with audiences through new media is not a sufficient condition for *effective* mobilization of audiences, which still depends on factors that have little to do with new media itself.

New media vehicles and agents are more inclusive, in that they allow engagement approaches to start up with few facilities and resources. The groups Climate Camp and Step It Up both emphasize how they started with low expectations, and were surprised how the campaigns grew with little or no knowledge of organizing nationwide campaigns. Both have well-maintained, professional looking websites that are easily found in online searches, however. This suggests at least some significant skills in content creation and management are required. And, again, contrarians are often well placed to provide considerable resources to engaging individuals with sceptical discourses through professional websites and increased search engine hits.

New media are inherently place-less, as their apparent forms, images, and texts are based in cyber-space rather than rooted in a geographical location. Referring to food consumption, Kloppenburg et al (1996) refer to 'a global everywhere yet nowhere ... in particular' (p34). The same holds true for new media consumption. Thus identities are only revealed if and when desired. In the case of virtual reality simulations (such as computer games or VR simulation 'Second Life'), participants can choose to act the part of a fictitious character. Both the identity-protection and role-playing aspects of new media's anonymity can make climate change engagement more inclusive, by allowing participants to engage more freely and openly. For example, events in Second Life have included a fictitious flood which prompted discussion of climate change (Green, 2007), as well as a virtual online conference on climate change run by the journal *Nature*, including live speakers from Imperial College, London and Stanford University, California (Nature Publishing Group, 2009).

This inherent anonymity does, however, also bring significant challenges, particularly in web comment forums and on blogs – although these challenges are by no means limited to climate change alone, but rather characterize wider participation within liberal democracies. Gavin (2009) reviews an article for the *Guardian* newspaper by climate writer George Monbiot, and its associated comment board. Gavin finds that the dialogue between participants on the discussion is fast-paced – indeed, sometimes Monbiot communicates directly with message posters, and then to general readers. But Gavin finds the postings generally disjointed, difficult to follow, often uninspiring, and in places descending to 'playground level' sniping – more 'rantosphere' (2009, p5) than blogosphere. With the anonymity of participants through new media, such 'netiquette'[6] problems are all too often encountered.

Whilst new media can increase the inclusivity of engagement at a grassroots level, they can also decrease the perceived distance between scientists and institutions and their audiences. New media have enabled a blurring of the traditional scientific peer-review process with the launch of *Nature* journal's online resources, including the online publication *Nature Reports Climate Change* and the associated *Climate Feedback* blog. Heffernan (2009) reports that bloggers can provide new angles on climate topics and can break news faster than traditional media. Heffernan also notes how Web 2.0 has allowed researchers to communicate their own results into the blogosphere outside the traditional peer-review system. Mooney and Kirschenbaum (2009) put a caveat on this engagement though, considering it likely that these science blogs will only reach a very small (and already engaged) proportion of the public.

New media can help provide a more personal face to large institutions. The previous UK Prime Minister Gordon Brown, for example, had a Twitter, Flickr, Youtube and Facebook profile. Brown's attempts to utilize new media through Number10.gov.uk were not wholly successful, and left some wondering who was actually posting under Brown's profile (Kiss, 2009). Unlike Gordon, his wife Sarah Brown has become one of the most popular celebrity tweeters on Twitter. This has been attributed to her genuine and personalized use of the new media agent (Beckett, 2009), utilizing it as a two-way engagement with her followers, rather than using it as a PR-managed one-way communications tool. Indeed, IBM's organizational change consultant Karen Tipping comments that governments are afraid of losing control of engagement processes using new media, as Web 2.0 technologies are so user driven (see Head, 2009). A further issue with more traditional institutions using new media is understanding how such engagement approaches might be perceived. As Gavin (2009) states, quoting Fiecschi (2007): 'social networking should also be seen in the context of the "cringe factor" ... attending the efforts of some politicians ... to engage with "the youth"' (p9).

The following case study boxes present two very different approaches, which have used new media as an opportunity to engage audiences with climate change. Each case study provides a more illustrative example of how the three interacting themes of information, interactivity and inclusivity in new media can act to engage audiences with climate change. Whilst Box 13.1 details a UK-based programme targeting emissions reductions in university residences, Box 13.2 demonstrates how climate contrarians have also successfully mobilized engagement through new media.

4. Conclusions

In thinking critically about the role of new media in climate change engagement, it is enlightening to consider the 2009 case of the illegal hacking of thousands of personal emails sent or received over the course of 13 years by

---

Box 13.1 *Case study: the Student Switch Off, UK*

The Student Switch Off (SSO, 2009) is a UK-based not-for-profit campaign, which aims to encourage students to consider energy-saving measures when they move into university halls of residence. The SSO is based around the principal of habit breaking during times of lifestyle change (see Chapter 1 of this volume, Verplanken, for a discussion on habits). There is generally no incentive, financial or otherwise, for students in university residences to use energy carefully (e.g. they typically pay a fixed amount for energy, which is often included in their total rent). Thus, there exist substantial opportunities to reduce energy consumption from heating, lighting, cooking and electrical appliances in university residences. The SSO is based on the assumption that becoming energy conscious at a key milestone in young peoples' lives, as they first move away from home, may set norms for energy conservation as students move into their own residences, but it is also based on the idea of spillover behaviour (see Whitmarsh and O'Neill, 2009): that taking the first steps to being energy conscious may promote decarbonization in the students' other lifestyle decisions and in the longer term.

The SSO uses new media as a source of information for students interested in the campaign. Each university hosting the SSO has a dedicated Facebook page, which students are encouraged to join to find out about energy-saving measures and how their hall of residence is doing in their attempts to reduce energy usage. The information provided is targeted to student residents living in university residences. Students are further encouraged to take part in the campaign and, given targeted information, through the posting of light-hearted videos on YouTube and photos on Facebook, featuring both SSO members of staff and the students themselves.

The SSO considers it important that the campaign reaches beyond the usual 'green suspects' (i.e. already committed to acting sustainably). To do this, they incentivize individuals with little prior interest or knowledge in energy and climate change to become involved by making the campaign appealing and fun; with activities designed to create a sense of community, and frequent competition prize incentives such as Ben & Jerry's ice cream vouchers, free tickets to Student Union activities and organization of communal parties in order to incentivize hall residents to save energy. Picture competitions on Facebook (where students post pictures of themselves performing energy-saving actions) and the use of YouTube videos act as viral marketing techniques for the spread of energy-saving messages. The viral nature of these communications also enables messages to be transferred from peer-to-peer rather than in a top-down manner – so the messages are more likely to be trusted and acted upon.

Eco Power Rangers are students recruited via face-to-face sign-up, e-mail and Facebook to provide leadership in each university, and encourage residents to take an active role in saving energy. To become an Eco Power Ranger, students must pledge to use energy carefully, and encourage others to do the same. The students are further incentivized to become Eco Power Rangers by specific targeted prize-giving, such as the monthly photo competition on Facebook, which awards the best photo taken by the student conveying a message about energy-saving. Building a committed community of Eco Power Rangers at each university fosters social norms around energy saving. In the academic year 2008–9, the campaign recruited over 15.3 per cent of the students living in halls (total hall population of over 33,000) as Eco-Power Rangers, so the campaign had, on average, an advocate in every flat in the residences.

A key part of the campaign is the creation of a sense of competition in energy-saving between different halls of residents. Information on energy saved is therefore available on Facebook, on the SSO website, and posters are also distributed around the halls to foster a sense of inter-hall competition. The website also allows individuals to view the results in aggregate by university, fostering inter-university competition.

The results of the campaign are measured through electricity meters in the halls of residence. The SSO provides feedback to each hall of residence of the CO_2 saved per month or quarter, and also to the owners of the hall of residence (usually the university) on the amount of money saved through reduced electricity bills. In the academic year 2008–9, the SSO reduced electricity usage in residences at 11 UK universities by an average of 9.3 per cent, saved over 1300 tonnes of CO_2 and over 217,000 GBP in electricity expenditure. The campaign has expanded from one university in the pilot academic year of 2006–7 to 33 universities in 2009–10. Thus new media have played a key role in aiding the SSO engagement approach.

Box 13.2 *Case study: Americans for Prosperity, USA*

The US-based group 'Americans for Prosperity' (AFP) provides an example of aforementioned amplified presence of climate contrarianism online and in the public arena. Through internet organizing – mass emails, web announcements, Tweets, Facebook communications, YouTube clips, blog posts – the group has assembled a number of influential anti-climate legislation campaigns (Fifeld, 2009). Among them has been the 'Hot Air' tour, initiated in the summer of 2008. To date, this tour has held events in approximately 40 US cities such as Houston, Texas, Wichita, Kansas, Washington, DC and Kansas City, Missouri, with the message that global warming rhetoric is alarmist, and sought to 'expose the ballooning costs of global warming hysteria' (Lean, 2009). In particular, the 'Hot Air' campaign propagated the message that cap-and-trade legislation needed to be blocked, as it would prove detrimental for personal freedoms (such as the constraints on choice of lightbulbs and ability to fill automobile tanks with petrol). As part of this tour, AFP spokespeople also made emphatic claims about how climate legislation would lead to significant job losses, as well as tax increases for US citizens. Other activities that garnered media attention in the summer of 2008 included an AFP action where they flew a large hot-air balloon over the Tennessee home of former US Vice President Al Gore, in order to draw connections between high costs and heavy taxation with climate solutions that Gore had proposed. The summer 2008 tour intersected with wider politically conservative movements in the USA, such as the 'Tea Party movement' that protested taxation measures on 'Tax Day' in April 2009, and the anti-healthcare reform organizations that have protested public funding for healthcare in 2009 in various rallies and town hall meetings across the country.

AFP organizers have repeatedly touted the organization to be a 'grassroots group' (Fifeld, 2009). While current manifestations of AFP activities can be argued as such, the 'roots' of the organization tell a much different story of 'astroturf campaigning', where carbon-based industry interests lurk behind the community-based facade (Fifeld, 2009). The group is registered as a non-profit organization, and a conservative think tank based in Washington, DC. Media Transparency (2009) has documented that AFP receives ongoing funding from conservative foundations such as the Koch Family Foundation. The Koch Family Foundation and its connected organizations have demonstrated a penchant for ideological conservatism, and have provided funding for the creation of a number of other conservative organizations, including the Cato Institute and Freedomworks. This Family Foundation has generated funds from the success of Koch Industries, which is the largest privately owned energy company in the USA. At present, Koch Industries generates energy from fossil fuels and has a large stake in oil refining processes (Fifeld, 2009).

Overall, these activities in recent years have represented new engagements and new means (through new media) to voice their concerns in a political milieu where the US President and Congress had moved from Republican to Democrat control. Many conservatives have expressed concern that the President and those controlling US Congress no longer espouse values and priorities such as small governments, free market economics, anti-climate legislation and anti-taxation. As one response to this perception of de-institutionalized voices, AFP encouraged citizens to challenge elected officials that support multi-scale climate legislation like the Waxman–Markey and Kerry–Boxer bills working their way through the US Congress in 2009 and 2010. In 2009, AFP also began a web-based campaign called 'No Climate Tax', where constituents can send emails to their elected officials to encourage them to send a 'No Climate Tax Pledge'. In addition, AFP hosts ongoing web-based campaigns called 'Stop the Power Grab', to contest US Environmental Protection Agency actions to regulate CO_2 emissions without the explicit support of US Congress.

Whilst the success of these activities and influences remains difficult to quantify, what is clear is that carbon-based industry interests have recognized the power of new media to communicate and propagate their views. By harnessing new media in these ways, particular interests have garnered the attention of policy actors and public citizens, as well as other journalists and bloggers who have covered their ongoing movements. Furthermore, US Congressional activity in the arena of climate mitigation remains highly contentious and far from resolved at present.

climate scientists at the Climatic Research Unit, University of East Anglia, UK. The emails were widely disseminated on the internet just before the UN Climate Change Conference at Copenhagen in December 2009, prompting widespread (both traditional and new) media coverage debating climate change science. Not only was the posting of the emails facilitated through new media, the affair gained traction through the posting of a searchable cache of emails online, and through the many blogs and new media news sources covering the story. Just a few weeks after the controversy broke, over four million websites made some mention of the 'CRU emails'.[7]

This exemplifies how actors and agents are increasingly turning to new media to contribute to the framings of climate change. Yet, it is important to consider the traction of new media in context. As Rosati (2007, p10) states: 'media do not produce society ... media are not just object or "things in themselves" but processes whose significance is composed dialectically within the dominant social relations that make them necessary'. Thus, only within particular contexts can new media discourses be 'read' and understood. At the time of writing, it remains to be seen what impact the publication of these emails might have on climate policy and on public engagement with climate change more generally. This episode exemplifies the struggles between actors and agents within the climate change discourse, within which media (especially, in this case new media) representations are part of the expanding circulating frameworks for understanding the world. The different discourses – which range from climate change as fraud to climate science as vilified (and many others besides) – represent struggles of social beliefs and meanings. It has led Hulme and Ravetz (2009) to conclude that the pervasiveness of new media in many people's social exchanges, and the inherent cultural lens through which we view climate change, demands changes in the very way science is conducted and citizens are engaged.

This chapter has highlighted that there is no one role for new media in climate change engagement. Instead, new media actors and agents play multiple roles – providing information, facilitating engagement, widening participation. Equally, new media actors can provide 'dis-information', increase fragmentation or not reach beyond already-engaged audiences. Approaches to engage audiences through new media are only just beginning to be explored. Important questions remain around new media and climate change engagement; such as exploring who is currently engaged (e.g. Allen (2008) suggests blogging on climate change is overwhelmingly an Anglo–Saxon dominated activity), and who may be engaged in the future. Indeed, do demographic or cultural dominances act to disengage some audiences? What is clear is that critical, and empirical, evaluations of new media in climate change engagement are needed – an appreciation of both the opportunities and limitations of new media in climate adaptation and mitigation.

Acknowledgements

Many thanks to Neil Jennings for his insights into the Student Switch Off scheme, and to Mike Hulme and Neil Gavin for providing thoughtful comments on a draft version of the chapter. This version remains the responsibility of the authors.

Notes

1 Calculated using a Google.com search, 8 December 2009.
2 This characterization of 'contrarians' does not include diverse 'sceptical' individuals or organizations – be they those, for example, who are still unconvinced by the science, suspicious of political manoeuvring on climate, or unconvinced by proposed solutions. Rather, we build on McCright's definition of 'contrarians', as those who 'publicly challenge what they perceive as the false consensus of "mainstream" climate science – the reality of anthropogenic climate change. They proclaim their strong and vocal dissent from this growing consensus by criticizing mainstream climate science in general and pre-eminent climate scientists more specifically, often with considerable financial support from American fossil fuels industry organizations and conservative think tanks' (2007, pp200–201). Our treatment here expands on McCright's connections between claims-making and funding, in that we also account for ideological motives behind criticizing and dismissing aspects of climate change science.
3 'Cringe factor' here refers to an involuntary inward shiver of embarrassment, awkwardness or disgust, and hence feeling extremely embarrassed or uncomfortable (OED online, 2009).
4 See www.en.wikipedia.org/w/index.php?title=Global_warming&action=history, accessed 16 December 2009.
5 These concerns are listed in an open letter to the London Metropolitan Police at, http://www.climatecamp.org.uk/blog/2009/08/20/open-letter-to-the-met, accessed 26 November 2009.

6   'Netiquette' refers to 'an informal code of practice regulating the behaviour of
     internet users when using e-mail, bulletin boards' (OED Online, 2009). Netiquette,
     when blogging, may include such actions as avoiding off-topic posting to facilitate
     comment reading and avoiding personal character attacks.
7   Performed using a Google.com search, 8 December 2009.

References

ABS (2008) Australian Bureau of Statistics: 4102.0 Australian social trends 2008:
     internet access at home, www.abs.gov.au/AUSSTATS/abs@.nsf/Lookup/4102.0
     Chapter10002008, accessed 20 October 2009
Allen, M. (2008) 'Minority report', *Nature Geoscience*, vol 1, p209
Beckett, A. (2009) 'Can Sarah Brown rescue Labour?', *The Guardian* (online), avail-
     able at www.guardian.co.uk/politics/2009/sep/25/women-gordon-brown, accessed
     25 September 2009
Boykoff, M. and Goodman, M. (2009) 'Conspicuous redemption: Promises and perils
     of celebrity involvement in climate change', *Geoforum*, vol 40, pp395–406
Boykoff, M., Goodman, M. and Curtis, I. (for 2009) 'The cultural politics of climate
     change: Interactions in the spaces of everyday', in Boykoff, M. (ed) *The Politics of
     Climate Change*, Routledge, London, pp136–154
Briggs, A. and Burke, P. (2006) *A Social History of the Media: From Gutenberg to the
     Internet*, Polity Press, Cambridge, MA
Camp for Climate Action (2009) *About Us: Camp for Climate Action*, www.climate-
     camp.org.uk/about, accessed 8 December 2009
Carvalho, A. (2007) 'Ideological cultures and media discourses on scientific knowledge:
     re – reading news on climate change', *Public Understanding of Science*, vol 16,
     pp223–243
CIBER (2008) Information behaviour of the researcher of the future: A CIBER brief-
     ing paper, 35pp, Centre for information behaviour and evaluation of research,
     University College London
Crosbie, V. (2002) What is new media?, www.sociology.org.uk/as4mm3a.doc,
     accessed 20 October 2009
DECC (2009) Home: Department of Energy and Climate Change, www.decc.gov.uk,
     accessed 16 December 2009
Dietz, T. and Stern, P. C. (2008) *Public Participation in Environmental Assessment and
     Decision Making*, National Academies Press, Washington
Fifeld, A. (2009) 'US rightwing activists curb efforts to cut CO_2 emissions', *Financial
     Times*, 3 November
Flew, T. (2008) *New Media: An Introduction*, Oxford University Press, USA
Friends of the Earth (2009) Friends of the Earth: Climate change, www.foe.co.uk/
     campaigns/climate/issues/climate_change_index.html, accessed 16 December 2009
Gavin, N. (2009) 'The web and climate change politics: lessons from Britain?', in T.
     Boyce and J. Lewis (eds) *Media and Climate Change*, Peter Lang, Oxford
Gavin, N. (2010) 'Pressure group direct action on climate change: the role of the media
     and the web in Britain – a case study', *British Journal of Politics and International
     Relations*, vol 12, pp459–475
Global Cool (2009) Global Cool home, www.globalcool.org/, accessed 7 December
     2009
Green, H. (2007) Cataclysmic climate change in Second Life, www.treehugger.com/
     files/2007/04/catacysmic_cli.php, accessed 7 December 2009
Head, B. (2009) The age of Government 2.0. Information Age: Aug–Sept, pp23–25

Hitwise Australia (2008) What are Australians doing online?, http://weblogs.hitwise.com/sandra-hanchard/2008/02/what_are_australians_doing_onl.html, accessed 20 October 2009

Hulme and Ravetz (2009) 'Show your working': What 'ClimateGate' means. BBC Online, news.bbc.co.uk/2/hi/8388485.stm, accessed 16 December 2009

Internet World Stats (2009) World Internet usage news and world population stats, www.Internetworldstats.com/stats.htm, accessed 20 October 2009

IPCC (2009) Intergovernmental Panel on Climate Change, www.ipcc.ch/, accessed 16 December 2009

ITU (2009) International Telecommunications Union: Global ICT developments, www.itu.int/ITU-D/ict/statistics/ict/index.html, accessed 20 October 2009

Iyengar, S., Luskin, R. C. and Fishkin, J. S. (2008) Facilitating informed public opinion: evidence from face-to-face and online deliberative polls, in Annual meeting of the American Political Science Association, Philadelphia, http://pcl.stanford.edu/common/docs/research/iyengar/2003/facilitating.pdf, accessed 20 October 2009

Kiss, J. (2009) 'Gordon Brown is twittering: Or is he?', *The Guardian: The Digital Content Blog*, www.guardian.co.uk/media/pda/2008/apr/18/gordonbrownistwitteringor, accessed 20 October 2009

Kloppenburg, J., Hendrickson, J. and Stevenson, G. W. (1996) 'Coming into the foodshed', *Agriculture and Human Values*, vol 1, no 3, pp33–42

Lean, G. (2009) 'American economists recognize the climate change threat', *The Telegraph*, 6 November

Lenhart, A. (2009) Adults and social network websites: a Pew Internet project data memo. Pew Internet & American life project, www.pewInternet.org/~/media//Files/Reports/2009/PIP_Adult_social_networking_data_memo_FINAL.pdf, accessed 20 October 2009

Lockwood, A. (2008) Seeding doubt: how sceptics use new media to delay action on climate change. Conference Paper: Association for Journalism Education 'New Media, New Democracy?', Sheffield, 12 September 2008

Malone, T. W. and Klein, M. (2007) 'Harnessing collective intelligence to address global climate change', *Innovations: Technology, Governance, Globalisation*, vol 2, pp15–26

Marks and Spencer (2009) Marks & Spencer Plan A, plana.marksandspencer.com/we-are-doing/climate-change, accessed 16 December 2009

Martin, S. P. and Robinson, J. P. (2007) 'The income digital divide: trends and predictions for levels of Internet use', *Social Problems*, vol 54, pp1–22

McCright, A. M. (2007) 'Dealing with climate change contrarians', in S. Moser and L. Dilling (eds) *Creating a Climate for Change*, Cambridge University Press, Cambridge, pp200–212

Media Transparency (2009) http://mediamattersaction.org/transparency/, accessed 26 November 2009

Milesi, K. and Civins, N. (2009) 'Why you should Twitter', *Information Age*, Aug–Sept, pp43–45

Minion, J., O'Neil, C., Kinsella, W. and Peterston, T. (2008) Taking steps for democracy: using new communication media to revitalise citizen participation in climate change activism. Paper presented at International Congress for Conservation Biology, Convention Centre, Chattanooga, TN, 23 May 2009

Mooney, C. and Kirschenbaum, S. (2009) *Unscientific America: How Scientific Illiteracy Threatens our Future*, Basic Books, NY

MTV (2009) MTV networks international launches first youth-focused, global, multiplatform climate change campaign – MTV switch, www.mtvnetworks.co.uk/mtvswitch, accessed 26 November 2009

National Museum of Australia (2009) Flickr: Changing Places, www.flickr.com/groups/changingplaces/, accessed 7 December 2009

Nature Publishing Group (2009) Home: Elucian Island, www.nature.com/secondnature/index.html, accessed 7 December 2009

OED (2009) *Oxford English Dictionary Online*, Oxford University Press, UK

Real Climate (2010) Climate science from climate scientists, www.realclimate.org/, accessed 3 February 2010

Rosati, C. (2007) 'Media geographies; Uncovering the spatial politics of images', *Geography Compass*, vol 1, no 5, pp995–1014

SSO (2009) The Student Switch Off, www.studentswitchoff.org/, accessed 16 December 2009

Starr, P. (2004) *The Creation of the Media: Political Origins of Modern Communications*, Basic Books, New York

Step It Up (2009) Step It Up: Index, www.stepitup2007.org, accessed 16 December 2009

Sunstein, C. R. (2007) Republic.com 2.0, Princeton University Press

Van Dijk, J. (2006) *The Network Society*, 2nd edn, Sage, London

Whitmarsh, L. and O'Neill, S. J. (2009) 'Green identity, green living? The role of pro-environmental self-identity in determining consistency across diverse pro-environmental behaviours', *Journal of Environmental Psychology*, in press

Woolgar, S. (2002) Five rules of virtuality, in S. Woolgar (ed) *Virtual society?: Technology, Cyberbole, Reality*, Oxford University Press, UK

14

Low-carbon Communities: A Grassroots Perspective on Public Engagement

Tracey Todhunter

1. Introduction

Repeated polls demonstrate that citizens of the UK and most countries of the world understand that climate change is an urgent threat (e.g. Upham et al, 2009), and most governments, policy makers and environmentalists agree we need to respond rapidly and collectively if we are to deal with the social and environmental impacts effectively (e.g. King, 2004). UK citizens do not respond well to climate change campaigns, which attempt to use fear to motivate behavioural changes (e.g. O'Neill and Nicholson-Cole, 2009), yet the UK Government must develop and maintain a long-term campaign to provide more accessible information around low-carbon consumer choices and behaviours. How is this to be achieved? In this chapter, I argue we need to begin a dialogue about how society reaches the ambitious carbon reduction targets the public wants, and this dialogue must allow for active participation by citizens in exciting and meaningful ways if it is to influence both local and national government policy.

In the New Politics of Climate Change (Hale, 2008), Stephen Hale wrote:

> *The emergence of a far larger and more committed movement of people, living low carbon lifestyles is critical to securing the political action we need. Millions of people, demonstrating through personal choices that a low carbon lifestyle is more fulfilling and rewarding, would exert tremendous influence on other members of the public, the private sector, and thus on the political process.*

This movement, still in its infancy, is beginning to mobilize, and a number of recent events have demonstrated that Hale is right in his assertion.

The international World Wide Views project[1] set out to show that it is possible to engage the public in complex debates about climate change. What makes this event different from most of the previous focus group studies on climate change is that on 26 September 2009 residents from across the world (China, India, Malawi, Japan, the USA and many others) joined 100 members of the public who sat down in Kettering, UK, to discuss climate change. In total, 4400 people from 38 countries participated in the first attempt to engage citizens around the world in deep deliberation on the issues of climate change mitigation and adaptation (World Wide Views, 2009). In order to allow for comparison, all events used the same format, provided the participants with the same information and asked the same questions.

The UK citizens represented a variety of backgrounds, skills and experiences, according to Involve who coordinated the UK consultation, and many arrived with a relatively limited understanding of climate change science (Involve, 2009). The main findings related to consultation about the Copenhagen climate change talks in December 2009, but are interesting in a broader sense as they demonstrate that participants' attitudes had changed as a result of learning more about climate change; in particular, there was heightened awareness of their connectedness to others around the world and the need for equity in carbon reduction strategies. The results of the UK World Wide Views process show what the most successful low-carbon communities have already discovered for themselves – that, when members of the public are given access to the most up-to-date information, they are able to make reasoned and effective contributions to the climate change debate.

There is a growing demand at the individual level for policy makers to take action on climate change and to impose a framework which will move us towards a lower carbon future. This was illustrated by the Liberal Democrat Opposition paper tabled by Simon Hughes MP in the UK Parliament on 21 October 2009 (Hansard, 2009), which called for government and all public sector bodies to achieve a 10 per cent reduction in greenhouse gas emissions by the end of 2010, and further called on the Government to bring a delivery plan before Parliament by the end of 2009 on how these objectives will be achieved.

An appetite for action was demonstrated by an online campaign coordinated by the organization 38 Degrees[2] requesting that MPs support a 10 per cent cut in emissions across Parliament, the Government Estate and the Public Sector during 2010. In a campaign which lasted less than a week, over 10,000 individuals in the UK had engaged online or by phone with their elected representatives. Although the motion failed to succeed in getting cross-party agreement on a commitment to a 10 per cent cut in emissions in 2010, as an exercise in participatory democracy it was a resounding success. Inspired by the 10:10 campaign,[3] which had launched just six weeks earlier and was supported by the British public and across all political parties, public response to the debate illustrated that when individuals are given a platform to make their opinions heard, the demand for clear leadership on climate change is audible and visible. Daniel Vockins, Campaign Manager at 10:10, remarks: 'It's staggering that almost ten thousand people emailed their MPs in just 48 hours to tell the politicians we need a step change in their response to the climate challenge. The British public is doing its bit, and now politicians of all stripes have started putting aside party politics to follow' (personal communication). The 10:10 campaign captured the imagination of UK citizens. Starting as an online campaign, the team quickly moved their focus into communities, workplaces and the media, organizing events and producing resources aimed at communicating a positive message that individuals, businesses and government can act fast and act together to reduce our carbon emissions, and live more rewarding lives in the process.

Finding ways to talk and listen to, not just instruct, communities is vital if we are to adapt to and mitigate the social, economic and environmental threats we face in a warming world. Fundamental changes in lifestyles and behaviour are needed. Although this is accepted by most policy makers and regularly makes the headlines, people on the whole have carried on living their lives as usual. If the information they read about the scale of the climate 'problem' concerns them, they rarely show it (Randall, 2005; Platt and Retallack, 2007). As outlined in the Introduction to this book, there is a disconnect between levels of public understanding about the impacts of climate change and levels of individual action to reduce it. Families continue to book foreign flights, leave their homes uninsulated, buy the latest gadgets, regardless of how or where they come from, and when reminded of the uncomfortable truths behind these actions, appear to react with irritation or complaint (Platt and Retallack, 2009). The UK Government's approach to this has been to deliver communications on behaviour change geared towards advice on 'easy wins', such as replacing incandescent lightbulbs with compact fluorescent alternatives or switching off electric devices when not in use. DECC (Department for Energy and Climate Change) and Defra (Department for Environment, Food and Rural Affairs) have both come to realize that a bolder strategy is required, that providing information is not enough and that they need to attempt new ways to 'engage' the public in the issue of climate change (Defra, 2008). The Greener Living Fund, which Defra launched as part of their Third Sector Strategy in November 2008 to promote more sustainable living across England, aims to influence behavioural change at a grassroots level to individuals and communities. Regular project updates are made available on a dedicated website.[4] The aim is to provide communities with advice on low-carbon transport, food and lifestyles through trusted third sector organizations such as the National Trust. For most government campaigns, engagement is measured by what people know and then do as a result of being informed about climate change. For communities, engagement may be seen as synonymous with active participation or support for an initiative, and there is a general acceptance that different (though complementary) methods and messages are needed to enthuse and motivate people to get involved. DECC's Low Carbon Communities Fund, launched in September 2009 as a two-year programme to provide financial and advisory support to 20 'test-bed' communities in England, Wales and Northern Ireland, came about as a result of the recognition that communities can motivate each other, and the finalists selected will be used to demonstrate that successful grassroots carbon reduction projects can inspire other communities who want to reduce their carbon emissions.

The case studies described in this chapter explore how community initiatives have led people from being passive consumers of products and services, to active citizens taking meaningful and appropriate decisions about lifestyle choices which directly affect their carbon emissions. I hope to demonstrate by providing examples of active community-led projects in England that an individual's actions can be altered as a result of their interaction with others, and to show that many UK citizens want to be part of the decision-making process which will lead us towards the Government's ambition of a low-carbon economy.

The UK is not unique: similar examples of community-led engagement are to be found in other parts of the world, and have been well documented in case studies such as those which can be accessed via the Changing Behaviour Project website and newsletters.[5] The communities described here are offered as examples of current best practice, chosen because their initiatives have rarely received the media spotlight or been the subject of academic research.

In this chapter, I present the views of members of voluntary groups. Many of these individuals recounted stories of how the people they meet feel anxious and ill-equipped to deal with the scientific arguments around which climate change is framed. Many citizens describe feeling overwhelmed and unsure how their individual actions contribute to a significant reduction in our impacts on the climate. They exhibit a sense of discontent in modern industrialized society, which has led to desire being interpreted as 'need', and conspicuous accumulation of wealth and possessions has become the norm (Randall, 2005; Ereaut and Segnit, 2006; see also Chapter 5). This makes it difficult for citizens to imagine a life with 'less' of anything which can indicate success or social acceptance. The mainstream media have also been complicit, to some degree, in messaging that an ecologically sustainable life will be difficult and worthy, lacking enjoyment, indulgence and everyday pleasures (Ereaut and Segnit, 2006). Maybe the media needs to relearn how to present the stories of low-carbon lifestyles? Rather than presenting case studies or poking mild fun at people who give up, go without or downshift, the media needs to present a compelling narrative of what the journey to a low-carbon future might look and feel like.

The Transition Towns Network, which defines itself as a movement 'To support community-led responses to peak oil and climate change, building resilience and happiness', has, like the Low Carbon Communities Network, sometimes been represented in the media as evangelical, spreading messages on what communities 'must do' rather than what they 'can do'. In reality, the most successful community-led projects learnt a long time ago that the best way to gather support and enthusiasm for their projects is to provide easy routes to participation, building self esteem and rewarding those who make the shift to a low-carbon lifestyle by celebrating their achievements. In its support of the 10:10 Campaign, the *Guardian* sought out examples of ordinary people, celebrities and organizations choosing to adopt low-carbon lifestyles to inspire and inform readers of choices which could be made mainstream (*Guardian*, 2009). But this is not true of every newspaper. Often we are presented with extremes – the multi-millionaire celebrity who spends thousands 'greening' their lifestyle – is presented as a contrast to the family who choose to live off-grid, without a car, or deny themselves the luxuries of modern life. Neither extreme presents a practical choice for most UK households, yet if we are to create a society which consumes lower levels of fossil fuels, we need to present options which are both achievable and aspirational for the majority of our citizens.

2. Characterizing community-led responses to climate change

This chapter is an attempt to characterize the nature of community-led responses to climate change in order to learn more about what they need to flourish, and how the stories of people who are living, working or learning together (or in some way define themselves as a 'low-carbon community') can help us begin to imagine what the low-carbon future we want citizens to aspire to might be like. In the process of researching this chapter, I interviewed 25 practitioners and academics working in the field of sustainability communications, about how we might make this aspiration tangible and desirable. Among this group there was a frustration that the stories or narratives around which we frame low-carbon lifestyles needs to be revisited, or as Solitaire Townsend, Co-founder of Futerra Sustainability Communications,[6] stated: 'No-one has given me a compelling vision of what a low carbon life might look or feel like; in order to sell the desire to move to a low carbon lifestyle we need those stories.' She goes on to argue that practitioners and educators need to present the future as positive, hopeful and maybe even playful; to put the joy back into communicating how our lives could be if we put ourselves in control of the choices we make around energy consumption and re-examine the behaviours we currently accept as normal (see also Moser and Dilling, 2007).

If we accept that new approaches to climate change communications are required and that we need compelling stories to help us envision how the abstract concept of a low-carbon society might operate, where are they to be found? Until recently, there has been little attempt to characterize the nature of community-led responses to climate change and even less understanding of their potential to communicate successful approaches to carbon emissions reduction to a wider public. There has been some progress in encouraging peer-to-peer support between community groups, some of which has been facilitated by the Low Carbon Communities Network.[7] But, on the whole, little attention has been paid to how the communities discussed here might be able to influence citizens who have so far chosen not to adopt low-carbon behaviours. The argument I present here, shared by the Sustainable Development Commission (SDC, 2009), is that not only is there potential for people-led responses to climate change to begin to offer the political space for governments to take more radical action, but that community activists can tell stories which might captivate their friends, neighbours and work colleagues. Typical of the interviews conducted with community activists (i.e. those who take an active part in a voluntary-led, local initiative) is this comment: 'There's nothing special about what we did, we saw that people needed to feel brave enough to say that they didn't understand what reducing their carbon footprint meant and we set out to learn together.'

On the whole, government programmes designed to engage the public in climate friendly behaviours have focused on the individual. Yet we accept that individuals often feel their efforts are useless unless others participate. Energy consumption behaviours are based on socially shared conventions and assumptions about what is normal or acceptable (e.g. Nye et al, 2009). It could be argued that the most effective low-carbon community projects are setting new cultural norms, where communities can face social dilemmas together, where the helplessness felt by the individual can be acknowledged, and a solution found in new, shared values and actions. This is one of the principles which underpins the Carbon Conversations course developed and run by Cambridge Carbon Footprint.[8]

The Carbon Conversations course was developed by psychotherapist Rosemary Randall and her colleagues at Cambridge Carbon Footprint, a registered charity which was established in 2005. The underlying principle of the course is that when people have the space to explore their personal relationship to a high-carbon, consumption-driven lifestyle, their vulnerability around identity issues can be supported. Participants develop the confidence and resilience to make significant lifestyle choices which lead directly to a reduction in energy demand and fuel consumption. As a result, the social and economic pay-offs for members of these groups can be significant. People find the capacity to make measurable reductions in carbon emissions and a lasting commitment to new, more energy-efficient behaviours in an environment where they feel safe. In small groups they are able to explore openly their fears and discomfort about being regarded as 'green' or eco friendly, and learn to see themselves as smart householders instead.

Rosemary Randall's introduction to the course is reproduced below in Box 14.1. Here she explains in her own words the goal and rationale of the programme she developed.

Over the year 2008–9, Cambridge Carbon Footprint calculated almost 500 carbon footprints for local households, bringing the total to over 2500 homes since their project started. 'This means we have held a focused, individual conversation about climate change with around 5 per cent of Cambridge households,' Randall claims. There has been significant interest in the course from London, Norwich, South Cambridgeshire, Shropshire and Cheshire. At the time of writing, plans were being developed to roll out the scheme nationally.

The groups run as a cascade system. Members of the groups who are interested are encouraged to become facilitators, recruiting friends, colleagues or acquaintances to join their groups. The success of these groups can be measured directly in terms of carbon savings and the group report that the carbon reductions from these groups have been significant. 'We estimate from the evaluations that a conservative estimate is an average ½ tonne CO_2, per person, per year, with some people making much larger reductions,' Randall claims. Participation in the Carbon Conversations course enables individuals to access a range of other support services, including a network which

---

Box 14.1 *Goal and rational for the Cambridge Carbon Footprint programme (adapted from Randall, 2005)*

Our goal is to promote public engagement with the problem and facilitate substantial, permanent reductions in carbon dioxide emissions. We approach the problem from a psycho-socio-cultural standpoint. We are interested in why people find the problem hard to engage with, how they conceal its implications from themselves, and what the psychological and social mechanisms are that will allow engagement, release creativity, change behaviour and move us collectively towards a low-carbon society. Our emphasis is on providing tangible, practical help to individuals and communities within a framework of focused, effective, communication, culturally appropriate social support and transformational optimism. We express our approach as a list of five principles:

1 *The importance of the personal.* Climate change touches every aspect of our carbon-dependent lives: it is a personal as well as a political and environmental issue. We believe it is essential to understand the psychological barriers to attitude and behaviour change, and use personal contact to engage and motivate people.
2 *The necessity of connection.* We believe that relationships with others, a sense of common purpose and a shared project are essential: only when people feel supported and connected to others can they act.
3 *The power of creativity.* Humankind is an innovative and problem-solving species. When there is space for creativity, people take ownership of problems and develop solutions that work.
4 *The richness of diversity.* We believe that our work is enriched by embracing the distinctive views of our diverse communities.
5 *The translation of the technical.* We believe that the complex ideas surrounding climate change – about science, technology, culture and politics – must be communicated clearly, accessibly and in culturally appropriate ways.

---

provides continuing face-to-face and online support to Conversations group members through meetings and newsletters, and acts as a contact point for people interested in getting involved or in joining a Conversations group.

Cambridge Carbon Footprint do much more than run the Carbon Conversations courses, which were described by Ian Katz, Deputy Editor of the *Guardian*, as 'quietly inspiring' in his review of the Manchester Report, a two-day event held in Manchester to explore 'Ideas that might just save the planet' (Katz, 2009). Over the last two years, the focus of the group's activities has shifted significantly from simple awareness-raising events, through measuring carbon footprints, to creating strategies and activities that will engage people more deeply with the seriousness of the problem and then to support them in making changes in their own lives.

In order to enthuse the community, activities have been designed to make contact with a wider variety of local groups and organizations, and create more closely targeted presentations and workshops. On a more practical level, the group works with local architects to offer 'House Doctor' and DIY or home improvement services, in order to provide local people with relevant advice about how to make homes more energy efficient or plan a system of eco-refurbishment. The Carbon Conversations model allows individuals to work through their feelings and aspirations, to explore the practical barriers to adopting a lower carbon lifestyle. Its inclusion in the Manchester Report has raised the profile and brought the scheme under public scrutiny. As Cambridge Carbon Footprint have discovered, issues such as lack of funding and capacity within a small voluntary organization can lead to feelings of frustration when volunteers simply cannot meet the demand from other community groups who, now inspired by Cambridge Carbon Footprint's story, would like to follow their example. The Carbon Conversations model has been proven to work, is popular with participants, and leads directly to significant carbon savings. If properly resourced, the scheme would suit large-scale replication and provide local authorities with data on household energy use, which is needed for them to report on per capita carbon dioxide emissions.

Over the years there has been much research in the field of community development, which illustrates that improving the skills and knowledge of volunteers involved in a project builds 'social capital', which is usually defined as the attitude, spirit and willingness of people to engage in collective civic

Figure 14.1 *Residents at a typical Carbon Conversations meeting*

activities (Church, 2008). People report that participation gives them a sense of belonging, of being a part of the community and of being valued for their contribution. The diversity and creative responses to climate change which lead to these feelings of 'belonging', within and between communities, are their key strength. (Cambridge Carbon Footprint are not the only community-led project offering structured support designed to reduce household carbon emissions. Others worth noting here include Little Wenlock Carbon Reduction Action Group near Shrewsbury and Stretton Climate Care, in Shropshire, both of which I will discuss in more detail shortly.)

Bollington Carbon Revolution, based near Macclesfield in Cheshire, and established about the same time as Cambridge Carbon Footprint, has taken a different approach which encompasses local electricity generation, in addition to carbon reduction activities. Originally set up as a sub-group of the local Civic Society, the group's original plan was to research the feasibility of using hydro power, a feature of the town's Victorian past to produce electricity for the town. The group soon realized that a project which would give local residents practical, down-to-earth information about how to use less electricity would be a valuable exercise in gathering support and enthusiasm for the scheme. Their activities now include running Global Action Plan EcoTeams in the town, as described in Box 14.2.

Box 14.2 *Description of Global Action Plan's EcoTeams scheme, as implemented by Bollington Carbon Revolution*

An EcoTeam is a group of people who get together to learn how to reduce their environmental impact and save money. EcoTeams of six to eight people meet once a month for four months. At each meeting, EcoTeam members share experiences, ideas and achievements on the environmental actions that they have taken. Over the course of the four months, they measure the reduction in their environmental impact, and as an extra incentive, the household who makes the biggest reduction in waste, water or energy wins a prize. An EcoTeam is not just another meeting – it's a place to translate ideas into action. It's something for all ages, and groups with children and their parents can be arranged.

Past EcoTeams have made great environmental savings, such as one Bollington resident who reduced her waste by 55 per cent and electricity by 18 per cent by being part of an EcoTeam. 'I thought that there wasn't much else that I could do to easily change my lifestyle and reduce my CO_2 impact. I felt I had already hit the easy, big issues. However, I did learn that I was becoming complacent and that actually there are many, many small actions that I can take in my life choices. This I absorbed from our fun, convivial meetings and I made new local friends as an added bonus.' In 2008, four households completed the Global Action Plan EcoTeam pilot programme in Bollington, achieving a 42 per cent reduction in electricity, an 11 per cent reduction in waste and a 9 per cent reduction in gas (see also Chapter 10).

In response to local requests for advice and information, Bollington Carbon Revolution also organize an annual Eco Refurbishment course, in conjunction with the Centre for Alternative Technology.[9] Most recently, the group have taken over the lease of a Victorian toilet block situated in the town centre and plan to convert it into an advice centre, where local residents can be given practical and honest advice from others in the town who have been through the experience of reducing their carbon footprints. Sonia Mysko, one of the volunteers, explains:

> The toilet block will be retrofitted as a flagship demonstration project, with high levels of insulation, use of renewable energy systems, and materials with a low environmental impact such as timber sourced from sustainable forests and organic paints. We are currently in the process of researching what the new Centre might look like and sourcing funding for the retrofit.

Like Cambridge Carbon Footprint, the residents of Bollington have managed to tell the story of local people's journeys to a low-carbon lifestyle in ways that are honest and appealing. Their practical and down-to-earth approach has been communicated through videos, a Facebook group, newspaper articles and their attendance at community events across the North West. The group have found it difficult to attract funding for their project and remain hopeful that the valuable work they do will be recognized. As the UK Government begins a search to find communities showing leadership in telling compelling stories about low-carbon communities, they may be hard pressed to find a more professional and well-planned project than this.

Run by volunteers with full-time jobs and caring responsibilities, community groups such as Bollington Carbon Revolution often lack access to PR and communications support, or business planning necessary, to move the project on to a more sustainable footing. Their success is often down to a 'gut feeling' for an approach which will work in their neighbourhoods. This can only come out of the day-to-day interactions within the community. My own experience of working with the voluntary groups who make up the Low Carbon Communities Network is that small, close-knit teams of people who live or work together will continue to provide appropriate, relevant and appealing projects that local people will choose to participate in, and which make low-carbon living tangible. But we must find ways to support them. Groups which fail at this stage will often cite a lack of advice, support or funding as the reason why a group of volunteers, no matter how dedicated or successful, will describe themselves as 'burnt out', 'exhausted' or frustrated at a lack of opportunity to expand and live out their ambitions.

Of course, this hasn't stopped hundreds of groups across the UK initiating community-led projects. Low Carbon West Oxford[10] was set up by local residents in November 2007, prompted by concerns about local flooding, as well as about the impact of climate change around the world. Their most ambitious project to date is West Oxford Community Renewables, which was established for the specific purpose of building community-owned renewable energy schemes in West Oxford and thus to generate funds for the group.

They aim to spend all the monies received from issuing shares in the company to commission a renewable energy scheme, including solar panels on the roofs of local buildings, installing a micro-hydro plant and erecting small wind turbines on a nearby hill. The electricity generated will be sold to the building and land owners (with any excess sold to the grid), and the earnings will be donated to Low Carbon West Oxford to reinvest in community projects to make further cuts in carbon emissions. Speaking at a NESTA Big Green challenge event, Ed Miliband, then UK Secretary of State for Energy and Climate Change, said:

> Local solutions to the global problem of climate change are vital if we are to make the shift to a cleaner, greener future. Low Carbon West Oxford is a great example: they've come to grips with the issue, developed local action plans, and then simply got stuck in and made things happen. (LCWO, 2009)

The potential of this 'can do' approach has been recognized in Scotland. Here, the Climate Challenge Fund started to make funds directly available to Scottish grassroots projects working on carbon reduction in 2008. One of the most visible examples of the success of this approach has been Going Carbon Neutral Stirling,[11] which after three years of full-time volunteer effort, coordinated by local resident Rachel Nunn, finally received funding to enable them to develop a plan to reach every resident of Stirling. The Going Carbon Neutral Stirling example proves that a small, grassroots, volunteer-led initiative can work in an urban situation and on a large scale, providing it is funded and resourced to do so effectively.

This approach, which might be described as a response to local knowledge and perceived needs, is also to be found in the smaller community projects of Little Wenlock[12] and Stretton Climate Care.[13]

Little Wenlock Carbon Reduction Action Group (see Figure 14.2) was formed in 2005, following a carbon footprint survey of the parish conducted by staff from the local Energy Efficiency Advice (cf. Chapter 8). Hilary Betts, one of the coordinators of the project, explains:

> We found out that our average household carbon emissions were above the national average and set ourselves a target of 20 per cent reduction by the end of 2007. Of the small sample of 21 homes (10 per cent of households) that have had both an initial visit and reported back their results a year later, five have saved between 30 and 40 per cent, and average savings of 18 per cent were achieved. We are not claiming that these results are being achieved across the whole parish, but they do demonstrate what can be done, and will not be the only savings that have or will be made as the project continues.

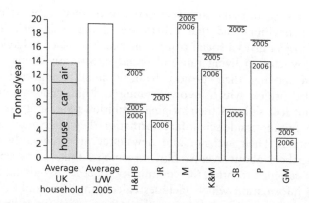

Figure 14.2 *Results of the 2008 Carbon Footprint Survey conducted by Little Wenlock Carbon Reduction Action Group*

The group have held public meetings, shown films such as 'An Inconvenient Truth', invited speakers, and put up stands about renewable technologies and energy efficiency advice at community events. 'We have taken practical local actions and produce a regular monthly newsletter informing every one of possible savings and celebrating the successful savings of individuals,' Betts states. As a result of the project, local people report they are more aware of climate change and of the impacts their own behaviours have. By working closely with the Parish Council and other community groups, Little Wenlock has succeeded in gaining the trust and respect of the community. This has led directly to the adoption of lower carbon behaviours and consumer choices, which are regularly acknowledged in the parish newsletter and website. Communities such as Little Wenlock have reached through practical experience, the same conclusions drawn by research bodies such as the Institute for Public Policy Research (IPPR), who reported recently: 'Our observations of 10 Now People receiving a home energy assessment highlighted the value of providing professional, independent, face-to-face information relating to energy use that is individually tailored, using engaging graphics and thermal imagery, and assessors who make people feel comfortable.' 'Now People' are often the target of marketing campaigns because they tend to have a high level of motivation to consume, and their prominent position within social circles makes them a driver of fashions and trends, meaning that they are a particularly powerful subsection of the population when it comes to determining consumption-related behaviours (Platt and Retallack, 2009, p45).

Often interviewees will say they find that climate change, or the solutions presented to them, is boring or uninspiring. Stretton Climate Care set out to show that low-carbon living can be playful too. They hold regular quiz nights in the local pub and chose to launch their electric bike scheme at Christmas rather than the height of the tourist season. Photographs in the local paper of Father Christmas arriving in Church Stretton on an electric bicycle captured local imagination, and imbued a sense of fun into what might otherwise have been reported in the media as dull or idiosyncratic.

There is a need to make sure everyone can be seen to be participating in low-carbon behaviours and that others are 'doing their bit'. Joining in a community project gives a social context in which to place behaviour change. By making low-carbon living fun and sociable, Stretton Climate Care have succeeded in moving their project from a small committed team to a community-led project which involves young and old, residents and tourists. They have not lost sight of their original ambition to raise awareness of climate change, but alongside scientific information they offer practical solutions and information. Their website and newsletter are frequently updated to inform subscribers about events, film screenings, talks from scientists and social events designed to bring the community together. By giving face-to-face support and information which includes calculating household carbon footprints, they are able to directly measure the carbon emissions reductions which have come about as a direct result of their initiative.

The Sustainable Development Commission (SDC) is the Government's watchdog on sustainable development, reporting to the Prime Minister and the First Ministers of Scotland and Wales. It aims to put sustainable development at the core of government policy through advocacy, advice and appraisal. The Breakthroughs event organized by the SDC in July 2009 attempted to show that communities do have well-developed ideas around how to influence behaviour change. A total of 285 community projects were submitted to the SDC, from which 40 were shortlisted. The final 19 included technological innovations, grassroots action and policy change. Not all the ideas were new, but in order to meet the Breakthrough criteria they had to demonstrate the potential to be scaled up and mainstreamed. SDC describe the projects they chose thus:

> the tip of a rather impressive iceberg ... For us a 'breakthrough' is something that moves us decisively away from the status quo or the usual incremental change. It provides some kind of step change, if not a quantum leap, towards a significant outcome ... Breakthroughs can be new ways of thinking or working. They may be new technological solutions. They can also be something that has been suggested before but for some reason hasn't happened yet; or something that is already happening that could be scaled up or applied across the UK. Sometimes the breakthrough can be how you get an idea to happen, rather than the idea itself. (SDC, 2009)

The Breakthroughs report (SDC, 2009) highlighted several areas which are of interest to the debate about engagement. The writers of the report estimated between 2000 and 4000 active community groups and web-based networks were already linking environmental projects at local level, to create more critical mass in the UK. The report confirms the findings from the interviews presented here that to secure real breakthroughs people have to be involved in the transformation – they have to be active participants, enabled to take action at the local level – with a big stake in the outcomes of the project. This is confirmed by the experiences of the community groups already mentioned here, all of whom are run by people who live and work locally.

Amongst the project's highlights in the Breakthroughs report, Project Dirt[14] is slightly different since it operates as an online network in London. Initiated by Mark Shearer and Nick Gardner, who recognized the need to link the plethora of community-led projects working on environmental improvement and so developed an Internet network to connect individuals with similar sustainability interests, helping to create a critical mass. They recognized very little was being done to consistently share best practice across and between these projects, and through Project Dirt they aim to make information readily accessible to everyone who wants to know what's happening close to where they live or work. The project is based on the assumption that information is best provided by people involved in current and planned projects. Visitors to the website are able to quickly find out what is or has been going on in their particular field of interest, and find others with similar or complimentary skills or experience. However, the real value in Project Dirt is the ability to facilitate interested people visiting their website who go on to become committed and active participants in their geographic area by creating opportunities for community-based action (see Figure 14.3).

3. Conclusion

The examples described here represent only a small fraction of the community groups which make up membership of the Low Carbon Communities

Figure 14.3 *Project Dirt members getting active in the community*

Network (LCCN). There are hundreds more, all working towards community-led carbon emissions reduction in some form or another. Until recently, communities were seen as a route to disseminating information to individuals, and there has been little emphasis on or support for communities who wish to take the lead in identifying their own approaches to carbon reduction, although DECC's Low Carbon Communities Fund (DECC, 2009) does seek to change this and has been welcomed by the LCCN. The results of NESTA's Big Green Challenge research clearly show the extent of innovation and imagination that exists in community groups, which can utilize leadership, ingenuity and creativity to build specific approaches to local needs and aspirations (NESTA, 2009). These approaches can offer tangible solutions to mitigate climate change and include balanced and well considered approaches to changing behaviour, as we saw with Cambridge Carbon Footprint.

We need to create a spotlight which makes people aware of the impact of community-led action and its potential to underpin social changes. The research presented here also indicates that while governments may shy away from telling people how to live their lives, communities are confident in taking a lead. By their distinctive approach of taking action together, communities become part of the solution rather than waiting for individuals to act alone. These projects develop collaboratively and ensure that proposed activities meet local needs, creating a system of structured support where neighbours share experiences and build cohesion and trust.

In a world of marketing, word of mouth is considered to be one of the most effective ways to 'sell' products and services. For LCCN members, the product they sell is ambition, and they do this by captivating the imagination and creating tangible representations of how low-carbon living can be accomplished. They effectively communicate how learning to live with 'different' is more rewarding than learning to live with 'less'. By encouraging people to take back control of how they use energy in the home, making them aware of the economic and environmental costs of their current behaviours, the most successful low-carbon projects are creating a compelling narrative that friends, neighbours and colleagues are all involved in the same activities. The stigma associated with not owning a car is removed if a community has access to a car club, walking to school becomes safer and more sociable if there are fewer cars on the school run, and having a solar panel on the roof of a community building or family home makes the choice more mainstream and aspirational. These are all examples taken from community projects operating in the UK today. Attempts to scale up, or replicate the projects described here, could be successful, so long as each community is able to choose their approach, based on the social context and local structures which already exist.

At the same time, funding, support and advice on a large scale needs to be available to enable communities to collaborate and learn from each other. Academics relying on desk-based research have often overlooked these stories, although there is an acknowledgement that up-scaling grassroots social innovations such as these is challenging, and requires identifying common interests and sharing skills in order to build critical mass; although this may, in turn, pose the risk that the core values which characterize these groups become diluted as the groups become more mainstream (Seyfang and Smith, 2007). All too often, the groups themselves are too busy keeping their projects going to seek out media coverage or raise their profile outside their local area. The LCCN was established to link and network these groups, to give them a voice, and to make politicians, academics and the media aware of community-led responses to climate change. There is still much work to be done in raising the profile of these communities (e.g. through partnering with policy and media organizations; see also Chapter 11).

As academics and practitioners working in this field, we have an obligation to find those communities who have, as Ed Miliband said, 'got stuck in', and responded to the stories of fear and threat presented by the Government and the media by creating opportunities for all of us to make a choice. This conclusion is borne out by research by Reg Platt and Simon Retallack (2009):

> *Our research suggests that success will lie in our collective ability to persuade consumers that, in adopting lower carbon lifestyles, they can save money and have fun ... they can do the right thing and look good without being an environmentalist, and they can be themselves. If we can achieve that, while putting the policies in place to ensure that lower-carbon options are affordable, attractive and visible, we will have gone a long way towards mobilising the power of consumers in the battle against climate change.*

The community stories told here show that it is possible to persuade people to adopt low-carbon behaviours at the local level, by accepting climate change as a given, moving on from messages of fear and threat, and providing examples of how individual actions can lead to positive social and environmental impacts. Taking action implies power: communities like Cambridge Carbon Footprint, Bollington Carbon Revolution and Project Dirt have the potential to make participants feel empowered and raise self esteem. By supporting community-led opportunities for householders to take back control of how they use energy, making low-carbon choices attractive and visible, and through creating networks like the Low Carbon Communities Network and 10:10 campaign, which allow people to access information and inspiration, we can create a collective desire for a low-carbon future.

Notes

1 www.wwviews.org
2 www.38Degrees.org.uk
3 www.1010uk.org
4 www.greenerlivingfund.org.uk
5 www.energychange.info
6 www.futerra.co.uk. Amongst other projects, Futerra has worked with Defra to develop their climate change communications campaigns.
7 www.lowcarboncommunities.net
8 www.cambridgecarbonfootprint.org

9   www.cat.org.uk
10 www.lowcarbonwestoxford.org.uk
11 www.goingcarbonneutralstirling.org.uk
12 www.littlewenlock.org
13 www.strettonclimatecare.org.uk
14 www.projectdirt.com

References

Church, C. (2008) *Better Places, Better Planet*, Community Development Foundation, London, available at http://www.cdf.org.uk/web/guest/publication?id=18693

DECC (2009) *Low Carbon Communities Challenge*, http://www.decc.gov.uk/en/content/cms/what_we_do/consumers/lc_communities/lc_communities.aspx, accessed 25 October 2009

Defra (2008) 'Framework for Pro Environmental Behaviours, London: Defra, available at http://www.defra.gov.uk/evidence/social/behaviour/documents/behaviours-jan08-report.pdf

Ereaut, G. and Segnit, N. (2006) *Warm Words How are we telling the climate story and can we tell it better?*, IPPR, London, available at www.ippr.org.uk/publication-sandreports/publication.asp?id=485

Guardian (2009) *G2 Supplement to mark the launch of the 10:10 campaign*, Tuesday 1 September 2009

Hale, S. (2008) *The New Politics of Climate Change, how we are failing and how we will succeed*, Green Alliance, available at http://www.green-alliance.org.uk/grea_p.aspx?id=3400

Hansard, 21 October 2009, Column 976, London, available at http://www.publications.parliament.uk/pa/cm200809/cmhansrd/cm091021/debtext/91021-0014.htm#09102134000003

Involve (2009) *The Road to Copenhagen: Citizens Shaping Global Debate*, available at http://www.involve.org.uk/world-wide-views-report/, accessed 25 October 2009

Katz, I. (2009) 'Twenty ideas that could save the world', *Guardian*, 13 July, available at http://www.guardian.co.uk/environment/2009/jul/13/manchester-report-climate-change

King, D. (2004) 'Climate change science: Adapt, mitigate, or ignore?', *Science*, vol 303, pp176–177

Low Carbon West Oxford (2009) Report of group's meeting with Ed Miliband, http://www.lowcarbonwestoxford.org.uk/index.php?option=com_contentandview=articleandid=48:lcwo-meet-ed-milibandandcatid=48:news-lcwoandItemid=40, accessed 25 October 2009

Moser, S. C. and Dilling, L. (2007) *Creating a Climate for Change: Communicating Climate Change and Facilitating Social Change*, New York, Cambridge University Press

NESTA (2009) *Research Summary: People Powered Responses to Climate Change*, available at www.nesta.org.uk, accessed 25 October 2009

Nye, M., Whitmarsh, L. and Foxon, T. (2009) 'Socio-psychological perspectives on the active roles of domestic actors in transition to a lower carbon electricity economy', *Environment and Planning A*, in press

O'Neill, S. and Nicholson-Cole, S. (2009) '"Fear won't do it": Promoting positive engagement with climate change through visual and iconic representations', *Science Communication*, vol 30, no 3, pp355–379

Platt, G. and Retallack, S. (2009) *Consumer Power: How the Public thinks Lower-*

Carbon Behaviour Could be Made Mainstream, IPPR, London, available at http://www.ippr.org/members/download.asp?f=%2Fecomm%2Ffiles%2Fconsumer_power.pdf

Randall, R. (2005) *Psychotherapy and Politics International*, Issue 3:3, September 2005, Copyright John Wiley and Sons Ltd. Also available online at http://www.identitycampaigning.org/wp-content/uploads/climate_ psychotherapy.pdf

Retallack, S. and Lawrence, T. (2007) *Positive Energy: Harnessing People Power to Prevent Climate Change*, IPPR, London, available at www.ippr.org.uk/publicationsandreports/publication.asp?id=541

SDC (Sustainable Development Commission) (2009) *Breakthroughs for the 21st Century*, available at http://www.sd-commission.org.uk/publications/downloads/SDC_Breakthroughs.pdf

Seyfang, G. and Smith, A. (2007) 'Grassroots innovations for sustainable development: Towards a new research and policy agenda', *Environmental Politics*, vol 16, no 4, pp584–603

Townsend, S. (2009) *Interview*, BBC Newsnight, 15 October, http://news.bbc.co.uk/1/hi/programmes/newsnight/8308989.stm

Upham, P., Whitmarsh, L., Poortinga, W., Purdam, K., Darnton, A., McLachlan, C. and Devine-Wright, P. (2009) *Public Attitudes to Environmental Change: A Selective Review of Theory and Practice. A Research Synthesis for the Living with Environmental Change Programme*, Research Councils UK, http://www.lwec.org.uk/sites/default/files/Public%20attitudes%20to%20environmental%20change_final%20report_301009.pdf

World Wide Views on Global Warming (2009) Consultation Analysis, www.wwviews.org

Conclusion: What Have We Learnt and Where Do We Go from Here?

Lorraine Whitmarsh, Saffron O'Neill
and Irene Lorenzoni

1. Introduction

Climate change is an issue with fundamental implications for societies and individuals. These implications range from everyday choices about energy use through living with an unprecedented rate of environmental change, to individuals' role in the accompanying social change. The role for individuals and communities in responding to climate change has been emphasized in this book, and we have seen through the preceding chapters the various ways in which the public may be engaged in efforts to mitigate and adapt to climate change.

This book directly responds to the interest in public engagement with climate change expressed by various societal stakeholders, including policy makers, businesses, NGOs and community groups, and individuals themselves. Thus we have considered the public (or, more precisely, 'publics') as citizens, consumers, members of social and geographically bounded communities, and expressors of values and identities. This volume is a timely, interdisciplinary analysis of how to engage these diverse publics. It has applied lessons from across different issue contexts, such as health and finance, to inform understanding and practice on communicating and stimulating behavioural and social change in relation to climate change. Finally, the book has brought together learning from a range of geographical contexts, including Europe, North America and Australia, providing an international perspective on public engagement. In this concluding chapter, we synthesize lessons about public engagement which span both theoretical (Part 1) and practical (Part 2), and themes and lessons of this volume, and conclude by outlining priorities for future research, policy and practice.

2. Diverse forms of engagement

One of the messages emphasized by several authors has been that 'public engagement' can (and should) be manifested in multiple forms. The traditional role for individuals, advocated by government and business, has been primarily as 'consumers' acting within various contexts (home, travel, leisure and so on) to make informed choices about buying and using low-carbon products and services. This is an important role, which some sections of the public have embraced, albeit to different degrees. As and when this role moves from the primarily *voluntary* (low-carbon living as a 'lifestyle choice') to the increasingly *required* (by government policy), individuals may be faced with making difficult decisions and considering trade-offs between different high-carbon choices – and under certain arrangements, such as Personal Carbon Trading proposals, may need to have the economic skills to manage carbon budgets. Or under less flexible policy arrangements, such as legislation and taxes, the public may simply see the relative attractiveness of high-carbon options diminish and be unconsciously steered in the direction of more sustainable choices.

On the other hand, there may be a more creative and proactive role for the public through 'public sphere' (e.g. political) engagement. We have seen in this volume that, beyond consumer and economic (i.e. 'private sphere') engagement, civic and community forms of engagement offer an *expanded* role for individuals in respect of defining climate change responses and shaping social change, and also conferring potential benefits in terms of fostering self-efficacy, democracy, community cohesion and social inclusion. Furthermore, though we have not covered this in the previous chapters, the public (in their professional capacities) also constitute the decision makers within government, schools, businesses and other workplaces. Considering these different contexts for public action, the need for public engagement with climate change becomes yet more evident, and the lessons about engagement from this book may be applied across a range of settings.

3. Multiple motivations for and barriers to individual engagement

With this understanding of the expanded role for the public in responding to climate change, the preceding chapters have highlighted the multiple motivations for individuals' engagement with mitigative or adaptive action. While certain sections of the public, particularly those with strong pro-environmental values, choose to reduce their carbon emissions explicitly because they are concerned about climate change, far more who act to reduce their emissions do so for proximal, personal or social reasons, such as convenience, saving money or improving health. Most often, the motivations for action are many such considerations, and even the most environmentally conscious individuals need to have other reasons to act before changing their lifestyle. Similarly, involvement with community groups may be as much about meeting like-minded people and improving the local environment as about addressing global climate change. Yet, we have also seen that behaviour is often not consciously motivated at all; rather, much of our behaviour is habitual (i.e. automatic and frequent responses to contextual cues). The habitual nature of behaviour perhaps poses one of the most fundamental challenges to fostering more sustainable lifestyles.

Similarly, we have seen that there are multiple barriers which individuals may perceive to making low-carbon, sustainable choices. At the individual level, these include lack of knowledge of the most effective action, and psychological biases in decision making or lack of appropriate (e.g. economic) skills. At the social, institutional and structural levels, barriers include lack of prior experience of civic and community engagement, lack of political efficacy, prevailing social norms to consume, and structural impediments (e.g. distance from workplace). Accordingly, a single approach to engagement will be insufficient to addressing the range of drivers and barriers to action.

4. Diverse methods, facilitators and scales of engagement

In this volume, we have described a range of approaches to engaging the public with climate change. These include informational, social, technological, institutional and infrastructural approaches, such as mass media campaigns, product marketing, new media communication, advice centres, 'open' (demonstration) eco-homes, community action and social processes (e.g. 'foot-in-the-door' technique), technology and infrastructure (e.g. smart meters), economic and regulation (e.g. Personal Carbon Trading). All are important in their own way to help address the diverse motivations for and barriers to engagement. Indeed, the need for multiple methods for promoting behaviour change has been noted previously (e.g. Gardner and Stern, 2002).

At the same time, effective public engagement requires collaboration and partnering of various social actors. This was a message emphasized by several chapter authors. Such partnering includes leveraging resources from the private sector and government to support (and up-scale) grassroots organizations that offer innovative approaches and context-specific knowledge, whilst also changing structures and production and supply systems to provide low-carbon, sustainable alternatives.

This multi-method, multi-stakeholder model enables engagement to take place across different temporal and spatial scales, something which is particularly important for climate change as a long-term global issue, which also demands short-term and local action. Different organizations offer distinct capabilities for engaging with people at these different levels; for example, a long-term and pan-societal mass media information campaign can generate widespread and sustained awareness, while new media deliberative methods can involve large proportions of the public in national or even international decision making. These large-scale approaches can reinforce more locally specific, intensive and focused approaches, which target particular motivations and barriers, and link to local concerns, issues and decision contexts.

Crucially, though, the challenge remains of ensuring this collaboration is coordinated and essentially consistent, rather than piecemeal or (as is often experienced) undermined by conflicting political, economic, or social messages and influences (e.g. airport expansion, low-cost flights and growing popularity – and normalization – of air travel). Here, though, there is a (thus far) unresolved tension between recognizing and incorporating the plurality of views and values, and the need to provide clear, credible and usable information which can support individual decision making about how to tackle and live with climate change. As we discuss later in the chapter, in identifying areas for future work, this tension may partly be resolved by public participation in defining the direction of societal development – and thus what constitutes 'valid' advice about how to respond to climate change. At the same time, so that this information may reflect an agreed goal (e.g. to cut carbon emissions), its effective delivery should reflect the plurality of publics, and of their particular contexts and interests.

5. Messages for engagement

This diversity of forms and modes of communication should be underpinned by a broadly consistent, common understanding of the importance of public responses to climate change, and the valuable roles that individuals and communities can play in mitigation and adaptation. Furthermore, while particular audiences will need their own, tailored messages (and methods of communication) which reflect their values and concerns (e.g. environmental, social, health, financial), identities and roles (consumer, citizen, community member, etc.), and are sensitive to local contexts (e.g. opportunities, barriers, norms), there are general lessons for communication which we can draw out from the wealth of experience and knowledge presented in this volume.

While there may be a role in climate change communication campaigns for fear messaging, many of the chapters argue for the importance of positive, motivational messaging. This is reinforced by findings from the wider literature, which stresses the need for caution in using fear to communicate risk without a clear action strategy to reduce risk (e.g. O'Neill and Nicholson-Cole, 2009). Instead, contributors here have highlighted the various non-climate benefits of responding to climate change and adopting more sustainable lifestyles; and the case studies discussed throughout the book highlight the very real, positive and inspirational effects that sustainable innovations can have.

Similarly, there is a need to use trusted sources of information – for many these may include local and known sources (e.g. friends and neighbours), but (independent) experts continue to be important, credible sources for communicating the findings from climate change research. We have also seen that with new media, there is potential for more selective information acquisition than compared to mass media methods; this innovation may act to restrict learning potential and polarize opinions, while also potentially democratizing climate change knowledge production and decision making.

6. Measuring success in engagement

A characterizing element of several chapters in this book is the call for evaluation of engagement activities, the rationale being that evaluation is key to a fuller understanding of the success, or otherwise, of such activities (see Chapters 8–13).

Although a commonly agreed protocol or set of criteria does not exist for evaluations of engagement, the contributions to this book point to some common principles of such evaluations, which can be summarized as follows:

- Clear working definition of what is to be measured: throughout this book 'engagement' denotes what people know, feel and do in relation to both mitigation and adaptation to climate change (see Introduction). Different engagement strategies may emphasize different aspects (e.g. knowledge raising versus behaviour change). Behavioural responses may not necessarily include attitude change about climate change (e.g. focusing on economic benefits of saving energy, or health benefits of alternative transportation methods).
- Identification of the purpose(s), aims and objectives of engagement activities: these can vary greatly (e.g. are these to achieve in-depth, sustained engagement of individuals and communities with climate change mitigation, adaptation and energy issues? Or is engagement understood to be more superficial, in terms of access to information?). As activities should, at a minimum, be evaluated on the basis of their defined aims, it is essential that these be clearly identifiable at the outset. In addition, activities may consequently be assessed in terms of other criteria.
- Acknowledgement of the limitations of the evaluation: any method used to assess an activity will invariably be constrained by its design. Thus, for instance, relying on memory implies recall bias, which needs to be taken into account when assessing the direct impacts of an activity; self-reported behaviour change may not necessarily correspond to actual change in behaviour; assessment of impact in the short term does not assess the effect over longer timescales.
- Undertaking of independent evaluation: this is necessary for the assessment to be carried out objectively, so that trust may be reposed in the findings of the evaluation by both the initiators of the engagement activities as well as the recipient individuals or communities.

In evaluating engagement with climate change, therefore, we argue that there is much scope to learn from the detailed research undertaken to date on evaluations of participatory public engagement exercises. These are 'forums for exchange that are organized for the purposes of facilitating communication between government, citizens, stakeholder and interest groups, and businesses regarding a specific decision or problem' (Renn et al, 1995, p2). Although the definition of engagement with climate change as used in this book is much broader than that used in participatory public engagement exercises, assessments of the latter can nonetheless provide fertile ground for systematically considering how evaluations of engagement with climate change may be undertaken. These literatures underline the importance of evaluating the engagement process, the outcomes and the context (see Burgess and Chilvers, 2006; Rowe et al, 2008; all of whom reflect upon large-scale public engagement exercises on national policy issues, including GM foods and nuclear waste). This evidence points to considering evaluation as an essential component of any activity, enabling deeper and longer-term learning in both the promoters as well as the participants of these events, as emphasized also from a different theoretical perspective by Pawson and Tilley (1997). Drawing upon these literatures, we propose that the following typology of climate change engagement activities (see Table C.1) might be a useful starting point in 'measuring' the success or otherwise of these activities.

7. Towards a conceptual framework for engagement

O'Neill et al (2010) argue that carrying out more physical science – and framing climate change as an awaited future catastrophe – will not enable large-scale, transformative social change. Instead, we need to recognize the essential, and diverse, roles other disciplines, knowledges and framings, besides those offered by the physical sciences, can play in engaging the public with climate change. Consistent with this position, the flavour of this volume is truly interdisciplinary in nature. The contributors to this book draw upon a range of disciplines and pertinent theories, including insights from sociology, psychology, media and communication studies, political science, neuroscience, and science and technology studies. Most of the chapters are influenced by a combination of disciplines to enhance understanding.

In the Introduction chapter, we specified that engagement is a state, comprising three dimensions of knowledge, emotion and behaviour. This definition has been useful and is applied throughout this volume. The various authors, based on their own experiences and knowledge, have focused upon these dimensions. The chapters emphasize the need for both promoting engagement (based upon research stemming from relevant theories and applying appropriate tools and methods) and measuring engagement (some provide examples of existing indicators and evaluations). Importantly, various contributions to this volume point out the existing limitations of the current engagement activities which are based on simple rational choice models, thus ignoring the persistent influence on behaviours of habits (e.g. Chapter 1), of social context in terms of norms and expectations (Chapters 9 and 10), of the political and institutional settings which can help facilitate or constrain individual action (Chapters 2 and 3), and methods or tools that can enhance engagement (Chapters 12 and 13).

A crucial contribution of this volume to public engagement at the individual and community levels with climate change is the more in-depth understanding of the variety of influences on engagement. We have summarized these in Figure C.1 below.

Table C.1 Typology of climate change engagement activities

Aim of activity*	Format**	Strategy	Description	(Possible) Evaluation***
Awareness raising at the public level, focusing on individuals	(a) Top-down (b) Bottom-up (e.g. 10:10)	Information provision and education	At-a-distance approaches (communication through mass media, online and press; e.g. leaflets, advertisements, web promotion)	Post hoc measurement or (ideally) assessment of change over time with respect to pre-intervention baseline. Interviews with individuals; surveys
Behaviour change at individual and/or at community level(s), plus awareness raising	(a) Top-down (e.g. ACT ON CO_2) (b) Hybrid (e.g. EcoTeams; M&S Plan A; Personal Carbon Trading) (c) Bottom-up (e.g. community energy projects; Transition Towns)	Information provision, education, interactive involvement, data collection, monitoring, measurement and feedback	(a) At-a-distance approaches (communication through mass media, online and press; e.g. leaflets, advertisements, web promotion) (b) and (c) involvement with groups enabling their empowerment and fostering long-term change	Assessment of change over time with respect to pre-intervention baseline. Interviews with individuals; surveys; focus groups; 'objective' behaviour measures (e.g. reading meters; weighing waste). May include assessment of process/participation
Increased public involvement in climate change policy and decision making	Mainly top-down participatory exercises; some grassroots initiatives such as networks (e.g. LCCN)	Support for individuals and community groups; consultation; dialogue; deliberation	Targeting and engaging citizens and stakeholders through a variety of methods, including, for instance, citizen panels and juries, deliberative mapping (see Burgess and Chilvers, 2006, for more details)	Systematic, based on assessment of process and outcome (short and long term) according to predefined agreed criteria (see Rowe and Frewer, 2000; also Burgess and Chilvers, 2006)

* Most of the aims of engagement activities can be combined (e.g. usually behaviour change activities imply awareness raising); in other words, they are not mutually exclusive.

** We use the broad terms 'top-down' and 'bottom-up' to refer to governmental and non-governmental (particularly community-led) initiatives.

*** Most evaluations are carried out during or shortly after the formal conclusion of an activity or strategy. However, it is often recognized informally that the impacts can be much longer lasting. Thus, an evaluation beyond the direct duration of the campaign in the form of a longitudinal study might capture the longer-term effects. Resource constraints often limit evaluations to immediate or short time-scales.

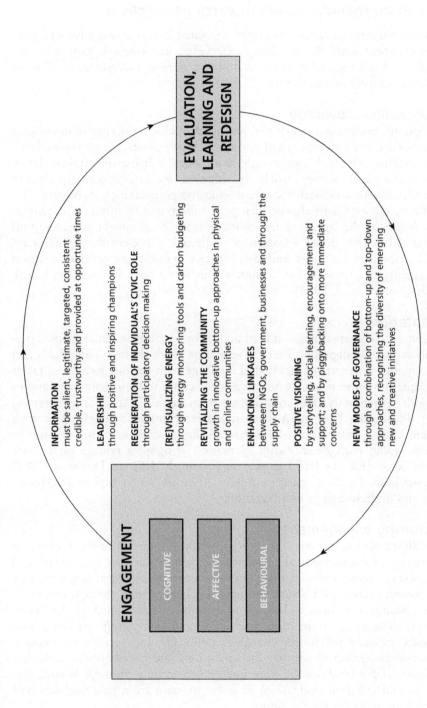

ENGAGEMENT

COGNITIVE

AFFECTIVE

BEHAVIOURAL

INFORMATION
must be salient, legitimate, targeted, consistent credible, trustworthy and provided at opportune times

LEADERSHIP
through positive and inspiring champions

REGENERATION OF INDIVIDUAL'S CIVIC ROLE
through participatory decision making

[RE]VISUALIZING ENERGY
through energy monitoring tools and carbon budgeting

REVITALIZING THE COMMUNITY
growth in innovative bottom-up approaches in physical and online communities

ENHANCING LINKAGES
between NGOs, government, businesses and through the supply chain

POSITIVE VISIONING
by storytelling, social learning, encouragement and support; and by piggybacking onto more immediate concerns

NEW MODES OF GOVERNANCE
through a combination of bottom-up and top-down approaches, recognizing the diversity of emerging new and creative initiatives

EVALUATION, LEARNING AND REDESIGN

Figure C.1 *Positive influences on (dimensions) of engagement*

8. Food for thought: future research perspectives

This volume aims to speak to readers interested in promoting sustained public engagement with climate change. However, key research gaps still exist which need addressing in order to foster a deeper understanding of some aspects of climate engagement.

Geographical coverage

Perceptions, understandings of and responses to climate change in developing countries are less well researched, for a variety of reasons, than those in developed nations. Although increasingly more work is being undertaken (large-scale quantitative survey work, in addition to smaller-scale qualitative research), due to historical, socio-economic and political legacies of particular locations, mitigation of climate change is subservient to interests in adaptation. Much of the legacy of this work is from development considerations (rather than citizen-based engagement), although it is clear that community-based adaptation initiatives, and their capacity to foster long-term engagement and significant prospects for change, are in some cases limited (Coulthard, 2009; Goulden et al, 2009).

Adaptation

Responses to climate change (at least in developed countries) have focused predominantly on mitigation. There is very little work on how individuals and communities interpret, understand and engage with various forms and facets of adaptation, in terms of its meaning, significance to their daily lives, and to the wider community. The contribution from Leith (Chapter 6) is a starting point, illustrating how an Australian grazier community is engaging with climate change adaptation. Broader-scale approaches are also missing in understanding engagement with adaptation – opinion polling on climate change issues (e.g. the Defra tracker surveys in the UK; see Thornton, 2009) examine individual-level mitigation issues, but are yet to explore interpretations and understandings of adaptation.

Measuring engagement

As outlined above, initiatives incorporating measurements of the success (or otherwise) of engagement are increasingly being valued by individuals and promoters of those activities alike, given the importance of learning from past and present events, with a view to improving engagement, through more efficient resource use, new techniques and tools (as mentioned in the above section). The need to increase individual and community resilience and response capacity to climate change is politically and socially paramount. Thus it is important to identify the limitations and pitfalls of the activities, processes and procedures we have undertaken to date, through honest, systematic and coherent evaluation, in order to learn from past mistakes and improve perspectives for the future.

The role of participation

Proponents of public participation in science and policy making argue that involving the public in knowledge production and decision making can lead to better quality and more acceptable decisions, improve relationships, and build trust (e.g. Dietz and Stern, 2008). Critics point out that the manipulation of participation may be used in the unjust and illegitimate exercise of power (Cooke and Kothari, 2001), or that involving groups of non-experts in complex, technical decisions is inappropriate, inefficient or produces less environmentally sustainable outcomes (e.g. Hajer and Kesselring, 1999). This volume has presented differing – though broadly positive – perspectives on the role of publics in knowledge production and decision making. Leith's chapter highlights that adaptation knowledge and action can be usefully informed by lay (public) input; and Höppner and Whitmarsh (Chapter 3), and Wolf (Chapter 7), also highlight an important role for citizens in decision making about climate change mitigation. Yet, there remains an oft-unspoken tension between these democratic ideals, and the pragmatic and pressing need to address the risks posed to society by climate change (and related sustainability challenges) which may be at odds with individuals' self-interest. Developing an equitable and flexible yet effective (target-driven) framework for societal action is a major political challenge, but we have in this volume indicated options (such as personal carbon trading; Chapter 2) that may move us in this direction. Yet we have not fully resolved this tension here, and hope it will be more explicitly reflected on in future research and policy.

9. Conclusion

The 15th meeting of the Conference of the Parties to the UNFCCC, which convened in Copenhagen in December 2009, illustrates well the complex relationships between science, individual behaviour, collective behaviour, communication channels and policy. Working towards consensus for ongoing international climate policy was hampered by nations' political, cultural and economic differences. On the eve of negotiations, over a thousand emails, sent from and to climate scientists at the Climatic Research Unit (CRU) at the University of East Anglia, were released online (see Chapter 13). The Copenhagen Conference produced a hitherto unprecedented peak in media coverage of climate change (Boykoff and Mansfield, 2009), though many discourses were focused on disaster-oriented rhetoric around climate stabilization (e.g. Gray, 2009). As many contributors to this volume have noted, the limits of such rhetoric and dialogue to meaningfully engage individuals with climate change – with the fear and guilt associated with such appeals – are perhaps likely to promote an active disengagement rather than meaningful engagement.[1] The release and subsequent forensic examination by the media of the CRU emails may well contribute to existing public uncertainty about climate change (e.g. Upham et al, 2009), and even damage public confidence in the science of climate change (BBC, 2010).

So where to go with climate engagement henceforth? The authors find in their personal and mediated interactions that a frequent question regarding climate change and public engagement is the 'doom' question, as in: 'are we doomed'? Indeed, it is easy to feel despondent. International climate policy is a huge challenge for international diplomacy involving a myriad of actors, and local actions can feel insignificant in scale for this global phenomenon. However, this is not to say we shouldn't engage with climate change mitigation and adaptation, but instead to ask: 'how can we refocus the debate in climate engagement?'

Refocusing the debate in public engagement and climate change

The authors conclude that perhaps international climate negotiations are just too large, messy and complex a challenge. In considering mitigation, Patt (2009) has written of how regional energy policy could be a solution to what we see as international deadlock on climate mitigation. He writes memorably of the difference between regulating ozone (an oft-compared 'environmental' policy problem), and regulating energy production and use: 'unlike air conditioning and ice cold Fanta, a country's energy security is central to its economic growth, employment, and quality of life, and national governments are extremely risk averse when signing away accountability'. He instead outlines how regional energy governance may be far more successful in promoting mitigation, with energy security being just one of the reasons why regions may want to consolidate their energy supplies.

There are other reasons why individuals might engage with climate change beyond the discourse of reducing carbon emissions – the many authors in this volume have comprehensively demonstrated that improving community connectedness, considering health issues, or becoming involved in the regeneration of individuals' civic role, for example, offer ample chances to 'piggyback' climate change onto other more approachable issues. Several authors have illustrated how positive leadership and visioning of the future can lead to enhanced climate engagement: so, for example, rather than seeing the global financial crisis as a challenge to engagement with climate, it is instead an opportunity to re-envisage how communities could be shaped in the future. Already mayors, cities, communities, religious leaders and others around the world are engaging with climate change in new and meaningful ways (see also Hulme, 2010).

Engaging with climate adaptation means engaging with case-based studies: whilst international agreements flounder, nations, states, local governments and individuals find many reasons to adapt to living in a changing climate. Whilst adaptation has been seen as a technical problem, requiring a technical solution, we echo the emerging climate resilience literature (e.g. Adger, 2006; Nelson et al, 2007; Adger et al, 2009; Marshall, 2010) in viewing climate change as just one aspect of individuals' vulnerability. Instead of working from the top-down to quantify climate vulnerabilities, a bottom-up approach focusing on broader and more tangible goals – for example, fulfilling such Millennium Development Goals as ending poverty and hunger, and promoting gender equality – would provide a potent start. Such an approach could enable learning and increase resilience to the challenges communities and individuals already face (though emerging paradoxes deserve attention, see Armitage et al, 2008) and will face increasingly in the future.

This volume joins with other voices in starting the conversation to refocus the climate change engagement debate. Taking forward the lessons from the approaches contained in this volume can play a role in steering the discussion towards a more meaningful public engagement with climate change.

Note

1   See O'Neill and Hulme (2009), who note the conceptual difference between a *lack* of engagement and *dis*engagement. An approach might not engage the individual, and therefore would have no impact on that individual's level of engagement. However, approaches might also engage negatively if they cause an active disengagement with the issue. Importantly, approaches which cause active disengagement may put in place future barriers to engagement.

References

Adger, N. (2006) 'Vulnerability', *Global Environmental Change*, vol 16, pp268–281

Adger, W. N., Lorenzoni, I. and O'Brien, K. (eds) (2009) *Adapting to climate change*, Cambridge University Press, UK

Armitage, D., Marschke, M. and Plummer, R. (2008) 'Adaptive co-management and the paradox of learning', *Global Environmental Change*, vol 18, no 1, pp86–98

BBC Poll (2010) BBC Climate Change Poll – February 2010, www.news.bbc.co.uk/nol/shared/bsp/hi/pdfs/05_02_10climatechange.pdf, accessed 9 February 2010

Boykoff, M. and Mansfield, M. (2009) 2004–2009 World newspaper coverage of climate change or global warming, www.sciencepolicy.colorado.edu/media_coverage/, accessed 9 February 2010

Burgess, J. and Chilvers, J. (2006) 'Upping the ante: a conceptual framework for designing and evaluating participatory technology assessments', *Science and Public Policy*, vol 33, no 10, pp713–728

Cooke, B. and Kothari, U. (eds) (2001) *Participation: The New Tyranny?*, Zed Books, London

Coultard, S. (2009) 'Adaptation and conflict within fisheries: insights for living with climate change', in W. N. Adger, I. Lorenzoni and K. O'Brien (eds) *Adapting to Climate Change*, Cambridge University Press, UK, pp255–268

Dietz, T. and Stern, P. C. (eds) (2008) *Public Participation in Environmental Assessment and Decision Making*, National Academies Press, Washington, DC

Gardner, G. and Stern, P. (2002) *Environmental Problems and Human Behavior*, 2nd edn, Pearson Custom Publishing, Boston

Goulden, M., Naess, L. O., Vincent, K. and Adger, W. N. (2009) 'Accessing diversifications, networks and traditional resource management as adaptations to climate extremes', in W. N. Adger, I. Lorenzoni and K. O'Brien(eds) *Adapting to Climate Change*, Cambridge University Press, UK, pp448–464

Gray, L. (2009) Copenhagen summit is last chance to save the planet, Lord Stern, *The Telegraph* (online), www.telegraph.co.uk/earth/copenhagen-climate-change-confe/6701307/Copenhagen-summit-is-last-chance-to-save-the-planet-Lord-Stern.html, accessed 9 February 2010

Hajer, M. and Kesselring, S. (1999) 'Democracy in the risk society? Learning from the new politics of mobility in Munich', *Environmental Politics*, vol 8, pp1–23

Hulme, M. (2010) 'Moving beyond climate change', *Environment: Science and Policy for Sustainable Development*, vol 52, no 3, pp15–19

Marshall, N. A. (2010) 'Understanding social resilience to climate variability in primary enterprises and industries', *Global Environmental Change*, vol 20, no 1, pp36–43

Nelson, D., Adger, W. and Brown, K. (2007) 'Adaptation to environmental change: contribution of a resilience framework', *Annual Review of Environment and Resources*, vol 32, pp395–419

O'Neill, S. J. and Nicholson-Cole, S. (2009) '"Fear won't do it": Promoting positive engagement with climate change through visual and iconic representations', *Science Communication*, vol 30, no 3, pp355–379

O'Neill, S. J. and Hulme, M. (2009) 'An iconic approach for representing climate change', *Global Environmental Change*, vol 19, pp402–410

O'Neill, S. J., Hulme, M., Turnpenny, J. and Screen, J. (2010) 'Disciplines, geography and gender in the framing of climate change', *Bulletin of the American Meteorological Society*, vol 91, pp997–1002

Patt, A. G. (2009) 'Effective regional energy governance – not global environmental governance – is what we need right now for climate change', *Global Environmental Change*, vol 20, pp33–35

Pawson, R. and Tilley, N. (1997) 'Realistic evaluation', Sage Publications Ltd, London

Renn, O., Webler, T. and Wiedemann, P. (eds) (1995) *Fairness and Competence in Citizen Participation: Evaluation Models for Environmental Discourse*, Kluwer, Dordrecht

Rowe, G. and Frewer, L. (2000) 'Public participation methods: a framework for evaluation', *Science Technology and Human Values*, vol 25, no 1, pp3–29

Rowe, G., Horlick-Jones, T., Walls, J., Poortinga, W. and Pidgeon, N. F. (2008) 'Analysis of a normative framework for evaluating public engagement exercises: reliability, validity and limitations', *Public Understanding of Science*, vol 17, pp419–441

Thornton, A. (2009) *Public Attitudes and Behaviours Towards the Environment-Tracker Survey: A Report to the Department for Environment, Food and Rural Affairs*, TNS, Defra, London

Upham, P., Whitmarsh, L., Poortinga, W., Purdam, K., Darnton, A., McLachlan, C. and Devine-Wright, P. (2009) *Public Attitudes to Environmental Change: a selective review of theory and practice. A research synthesis for the Living with Environmental Change Programme*, Research Councils UK, www.lwec.org.uk/sites/default/files/Public%20attitudes%20to%20environmental%20change_final%20report_301009.pdf, accessed 1 December 2009

Index